Beasts of Abigaile

vol.2

Spica Aoki

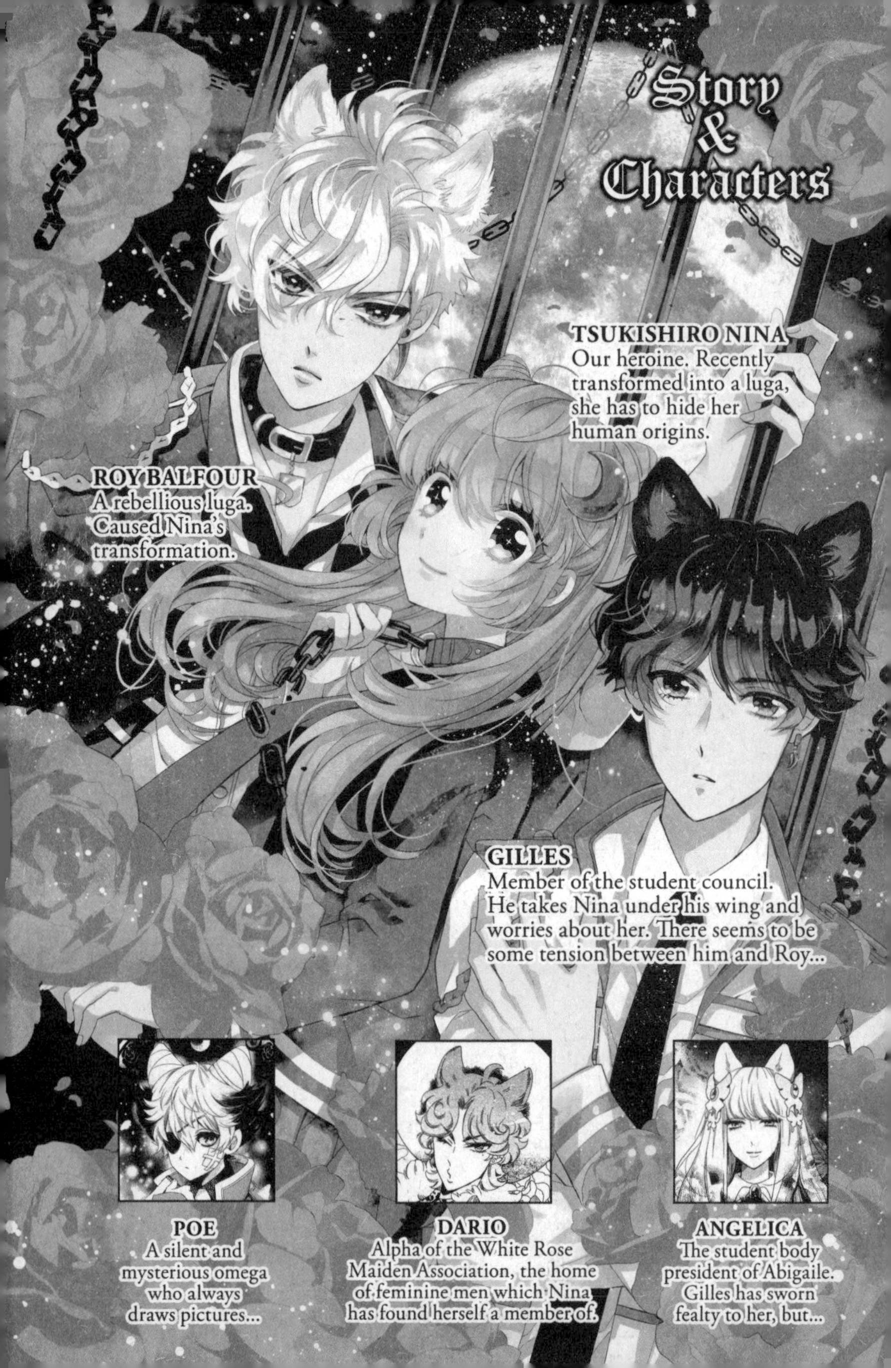
Story & Characters
TSUKISHIRO NINA
Our heroine. Recently transformed into a luga, she has to hide her human origins.
ROY BALFOUR
A rebellious luga. Caused Nina's transformation.
GILLES
Member of the student council. He takes Nina under his wing and worries about her. There seems to be some tension between him and Roy...
POE
A silent and mysterious omega who always draws pictures...
DARIO
Alpha of the White Rose Maiden Association, the home of feminine men which Nina has found herself a member of.
ANGELICA
The student body president of Abigaile. Gilles has sworn fealty to her, but...

† After moving to Ruberia, the land of sea and roses, Japanese high school student Tsukishiro Nina goes on a walk, where she encounters a creature out of legend-- a wolfman. He bites her on the neck, and she loses consciousness. Upon awakening, Nina discovers that she has become a wolfgirl.

† Along with a bunch of wolfchildren who call themselves luga, she is taken to the 'academy' prison, Abigaile Island. This is a penitentiary where the luga are trained to be loyal slaves for the humans of Ruberia.

† Nina begins to panic. Then, who should appear but Roy Balfour--the very wolfman who turned her into a luga and kicked off the events that brought her to this prison!

† When they meet again inside the prison, Roy threatens Nina for being a former human. He steals her first kiss, informing her that he is 'marking' her. Stunned from all these shocking developments, Nina is taken to the reflection room. There she meets Dario, who shows her to her first class, but Roy appears again and ruins the lecture.

† As punishment for disrupting class, Nina and Roy must serve as waitstaff at one of the secret parties that the human instructors hold every week.

※**Terminology:**
Home – a luga group equivalent to a wolf pack.
Alpha, Gamma, Omega – the luga hierarchy.

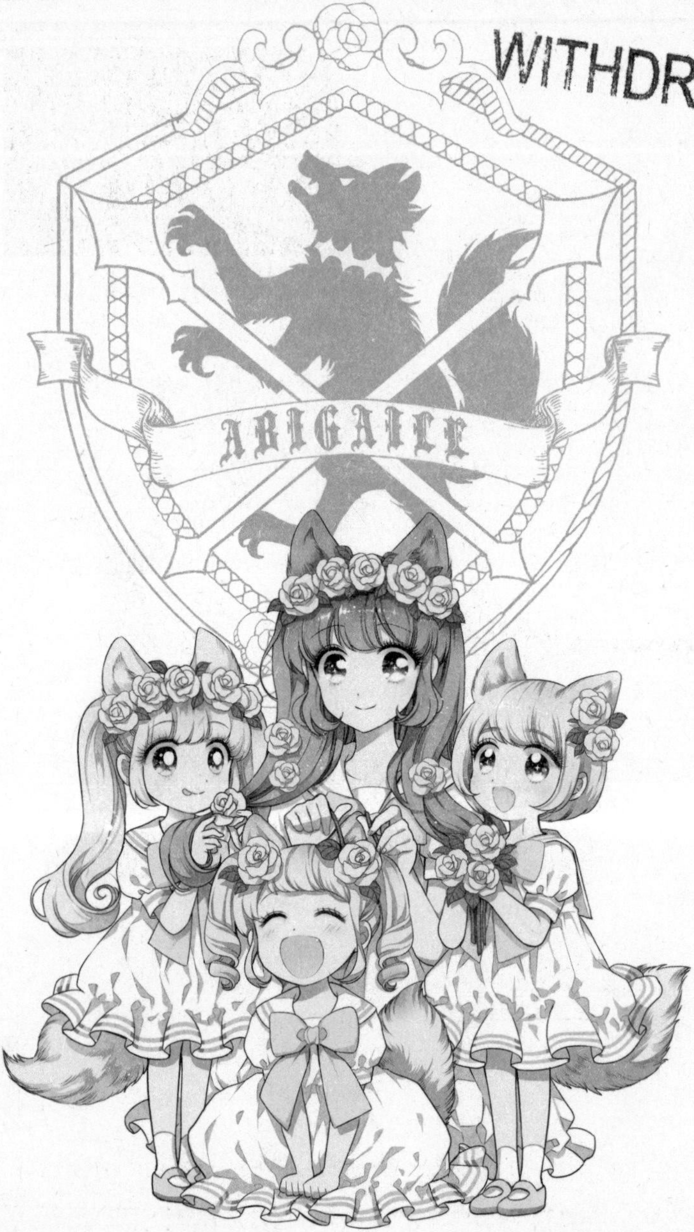
ABIGAILE

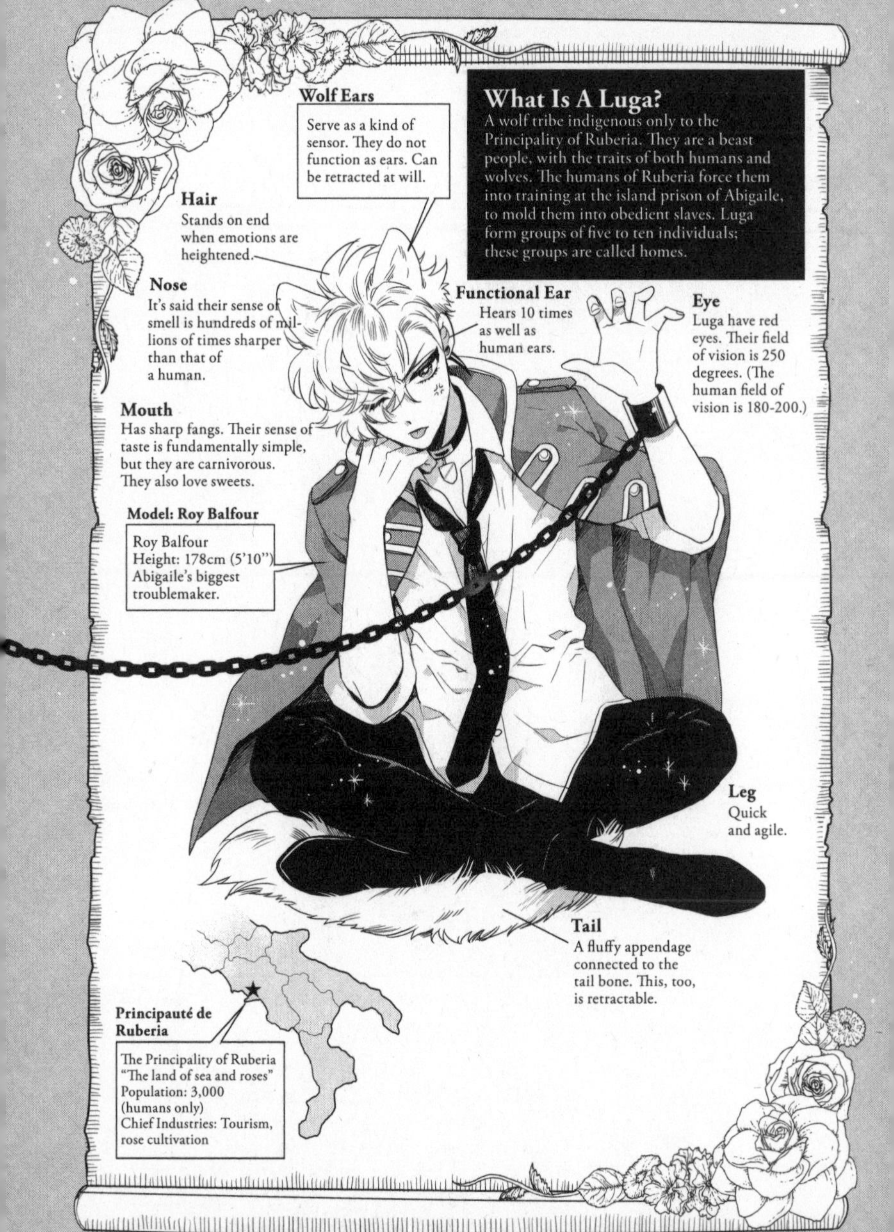
What Is A Luga?
A wolf tribe indigenous only to the Principality of Ruberia. They are a beast people, with the traits of both humans and wolves. The humans of Ruberia force them into training at the island prison of Abigaile, to mold them into obedient slaves. Luga form groups of five to ten individuals; these groups are called homes.
Wolf Ears
Serve as a kind of sensor. They do not function as ears. Can be retracted at will.
Hair
Stands on end when emotions are heightened.
Nose
It's said their sense of smell is hundreds of millions of times sharper than that of a human.
Functional Ear
Hears 10 times as well as human ears.
Eye
Luga have red eyes. Their field of vision is 250 degrees. (The human field of vision is 180-200.)
Mouth
Has sharp fangs. Their sense of taste is fundamentally simple, but they are carnivorous. They also love sweets.
Model: Roy Balfour
Roy Balfour
Height: 178cm (5'10")
Abigaile's biggest troublemaker.
Leg
Quick and agile.
Tail
A fluffy appendage connected to the tail bone. This, too, is retractable.
Principauté de Ruberia
The Principality of Ruberia
"The land of sea and roses"
Population: 3,000
(humans only)
Chief Industries: Tourism, rose cultivation

6th Break

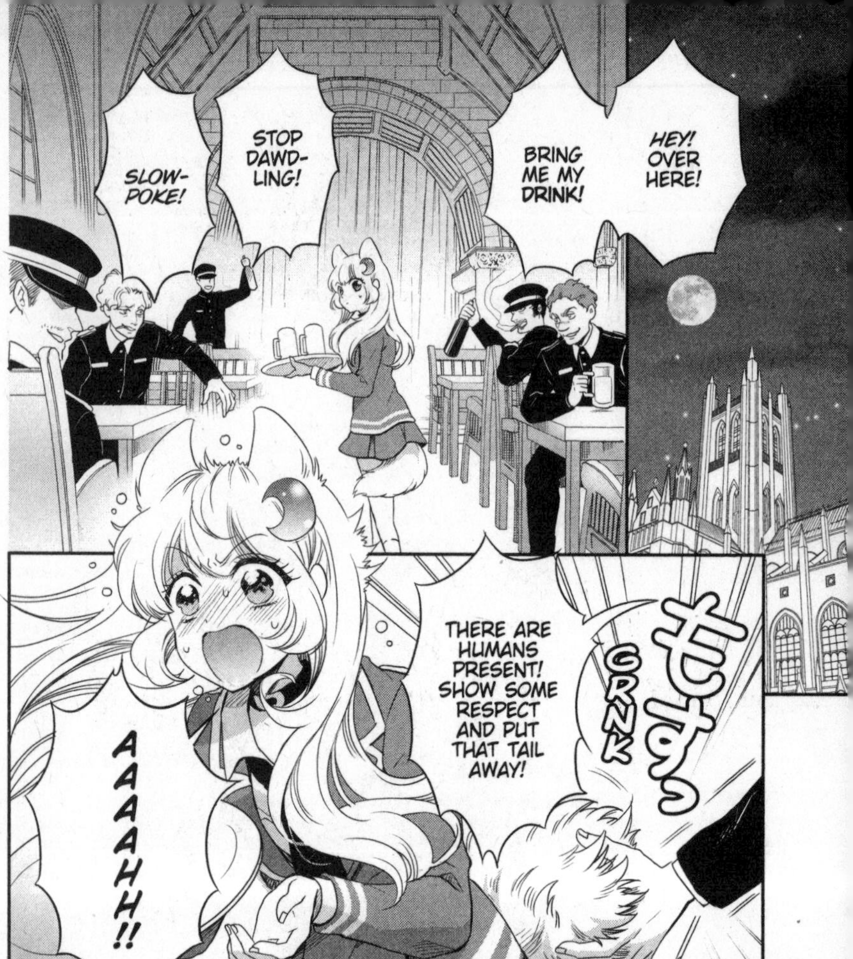
HEY! OVER HERE!
BRING ME MY DRINK!
STOP DAWD-LING!
SLOW-POKE!
もすっ
GRNK
THERE ARE HUMANS PRESENT! SHOW SOME RESPECT AND PUT THAT TAIL AWAY!
AAAAAHH!!

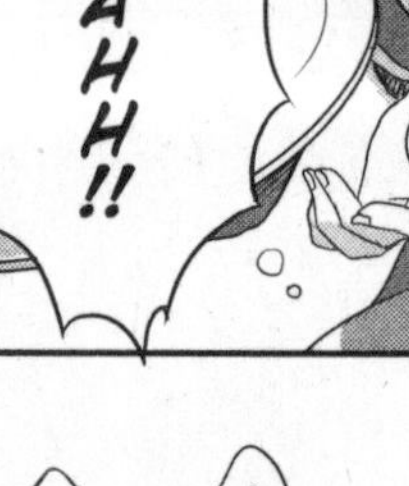

Hello, Spica Aoki here! *BoA* is at Volume Two! Sorry there's nothing interesting in the bonus spaces!! Maybe it's because once I get started on something, I have to keep going until it's done, and I've spent all of my time making corrections yet again... But the story!! Please enjoy the story!!

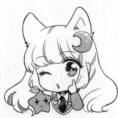

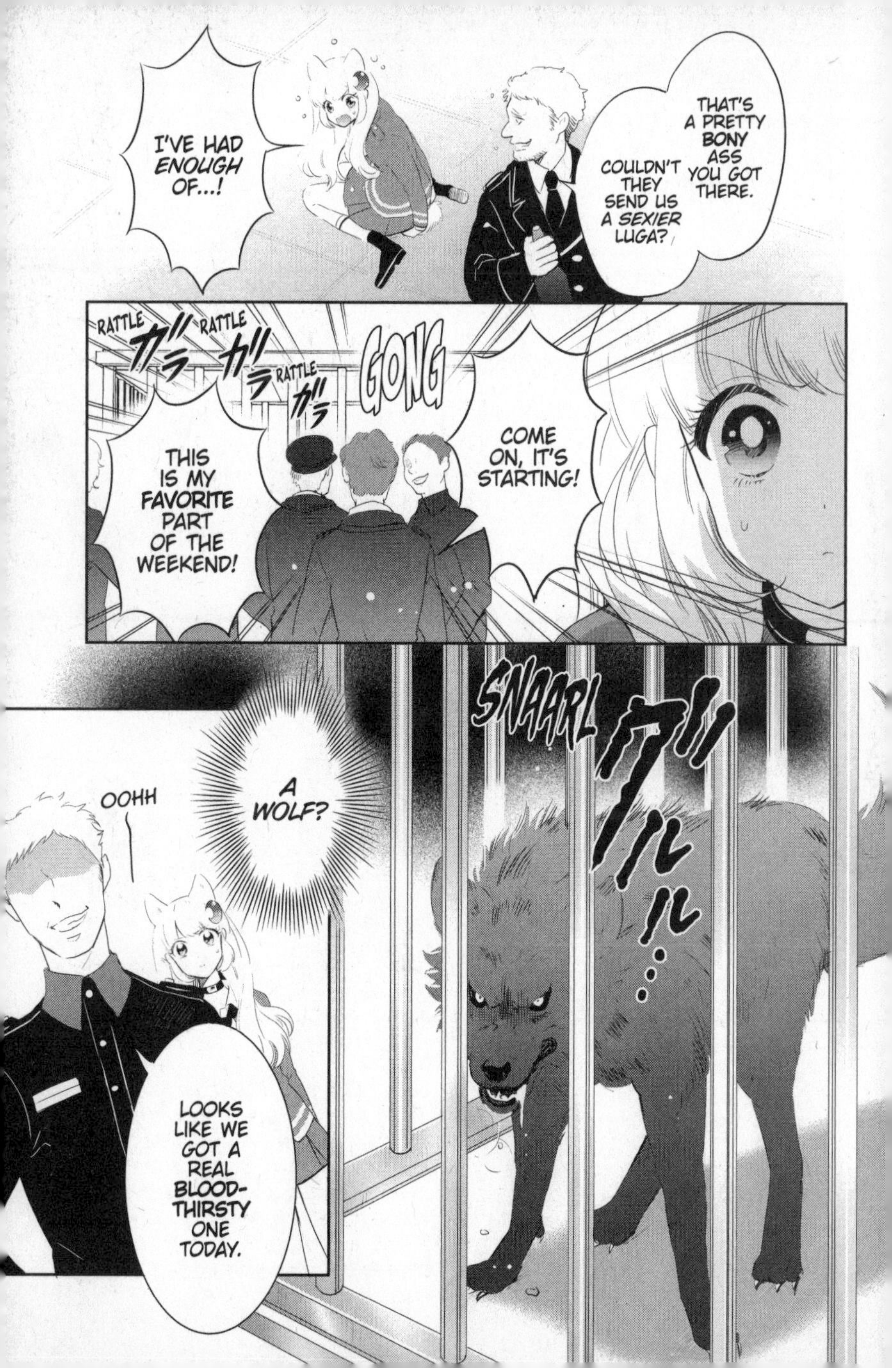
THAT'S A PRETTY BONY ASS YOU GOT THERE.
COULDN'T THEY SEND US A SEXIER LUGA?
I'VE HAD ENOUGH OF...!
GONG
COME ON, IT'S STARTING!
RATTLE ガラ RATTLE ガラ RATTLE ガラ
THIS IS MY FAVORITE PART OF THE WEEKEND!
SNAARL グルルル...
A WOLF?
OOHH
LOOKS LIKE WE GOT A REAL BLOOD-THIRSTY ONE TODAY.

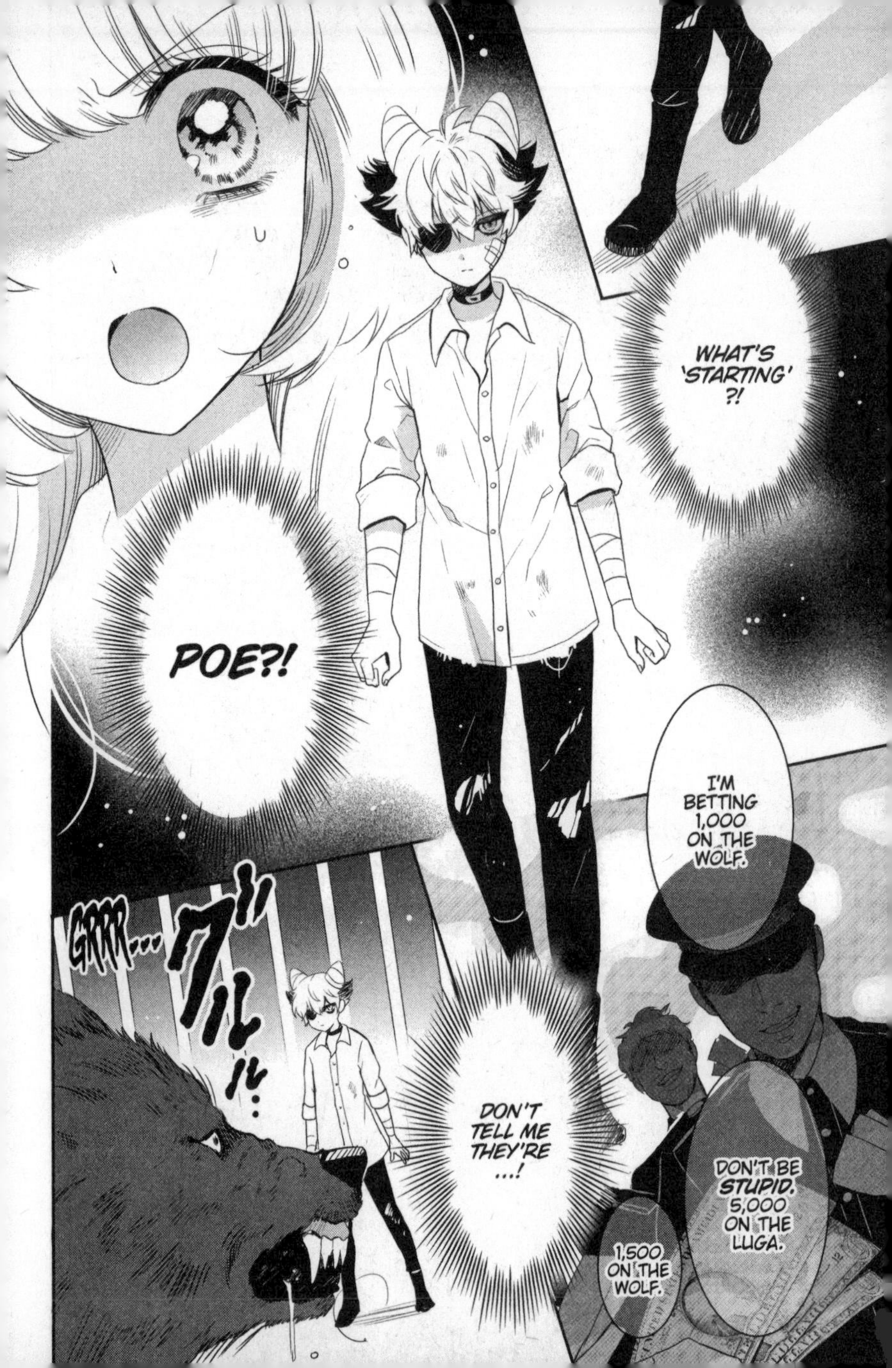
WHAT'S 'STARTING' ?!
POE?!
I'M BETTING 1,000 ON THE WOLF.
DON'T BE STUPID. 5,000 ON THE LUGA.
1,500 ON THE WOLF.
DON'T TELL ME THEY'RE ...!
GRRR... グルル!!

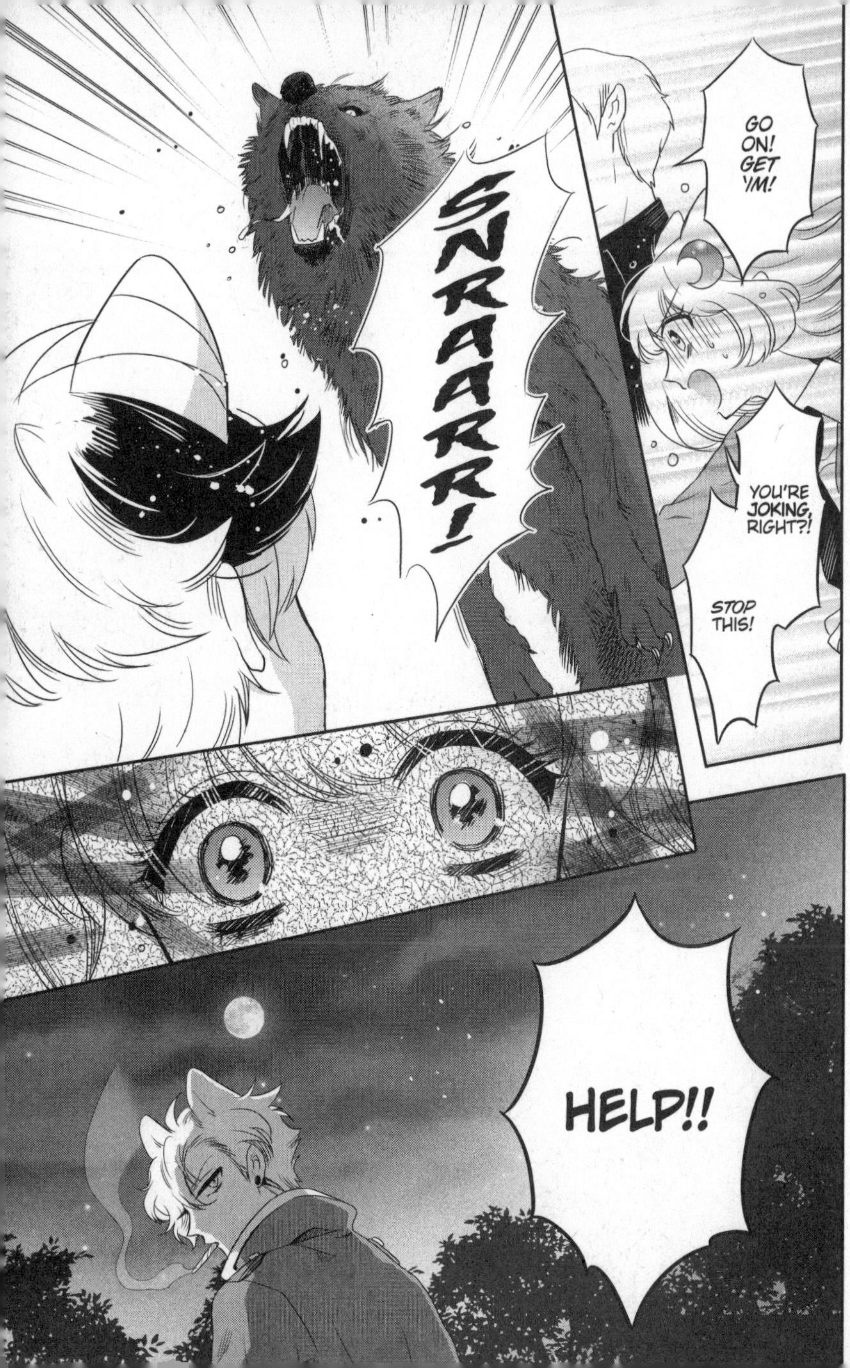
GO ON! GET 'IM!
YOU'RE JOKING, RIGHT?!
STOP THIS!
SNRAARR!
HELP!!

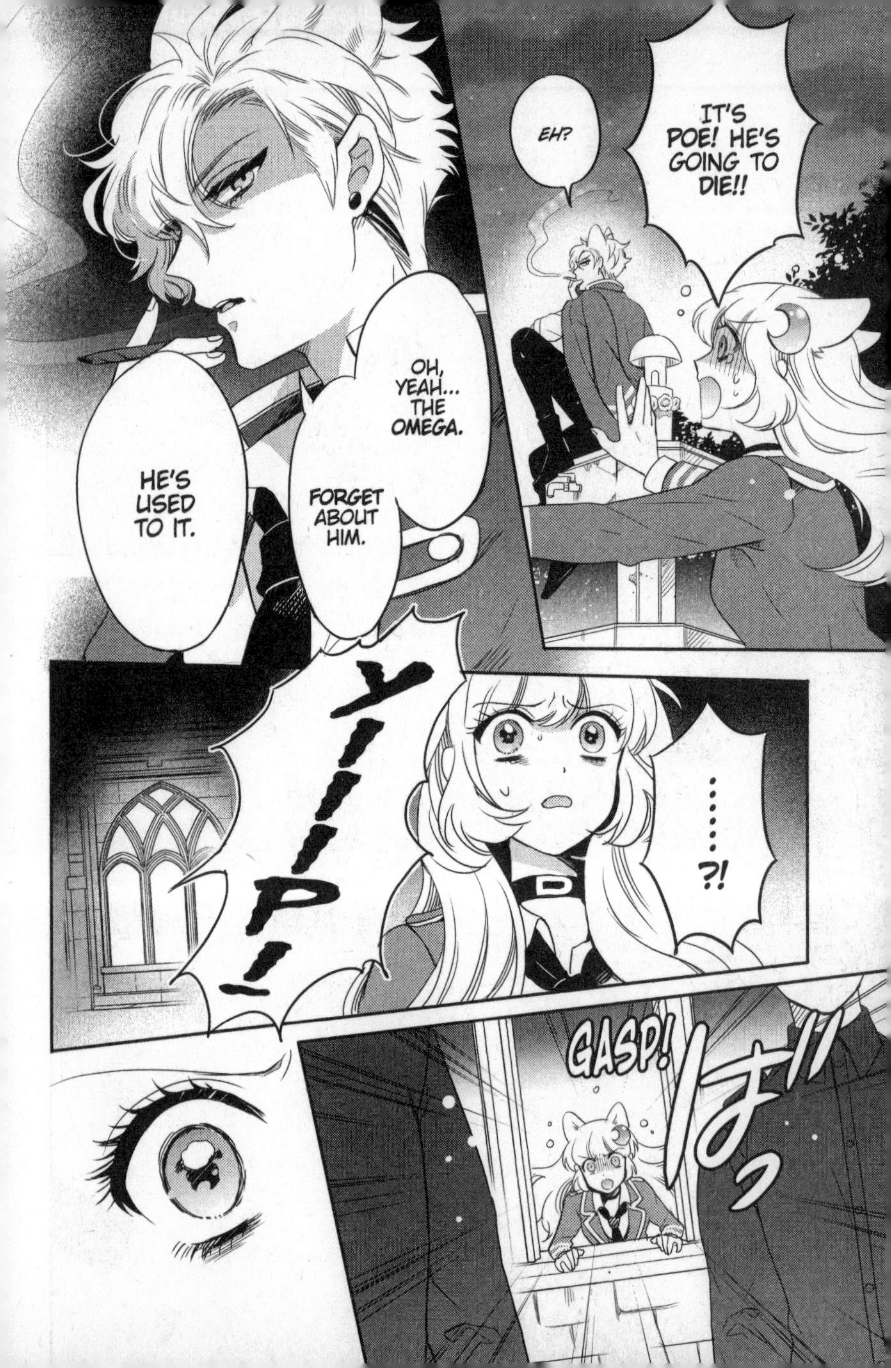
IT'S POE! HE'S GOING TO DIE!!
EH?
OH, YEAH... THE OMEGA.
FORGET ABOUT HIM.
HE'S USED TO IT.
......?!
YIIIP!
GASP!
はっ

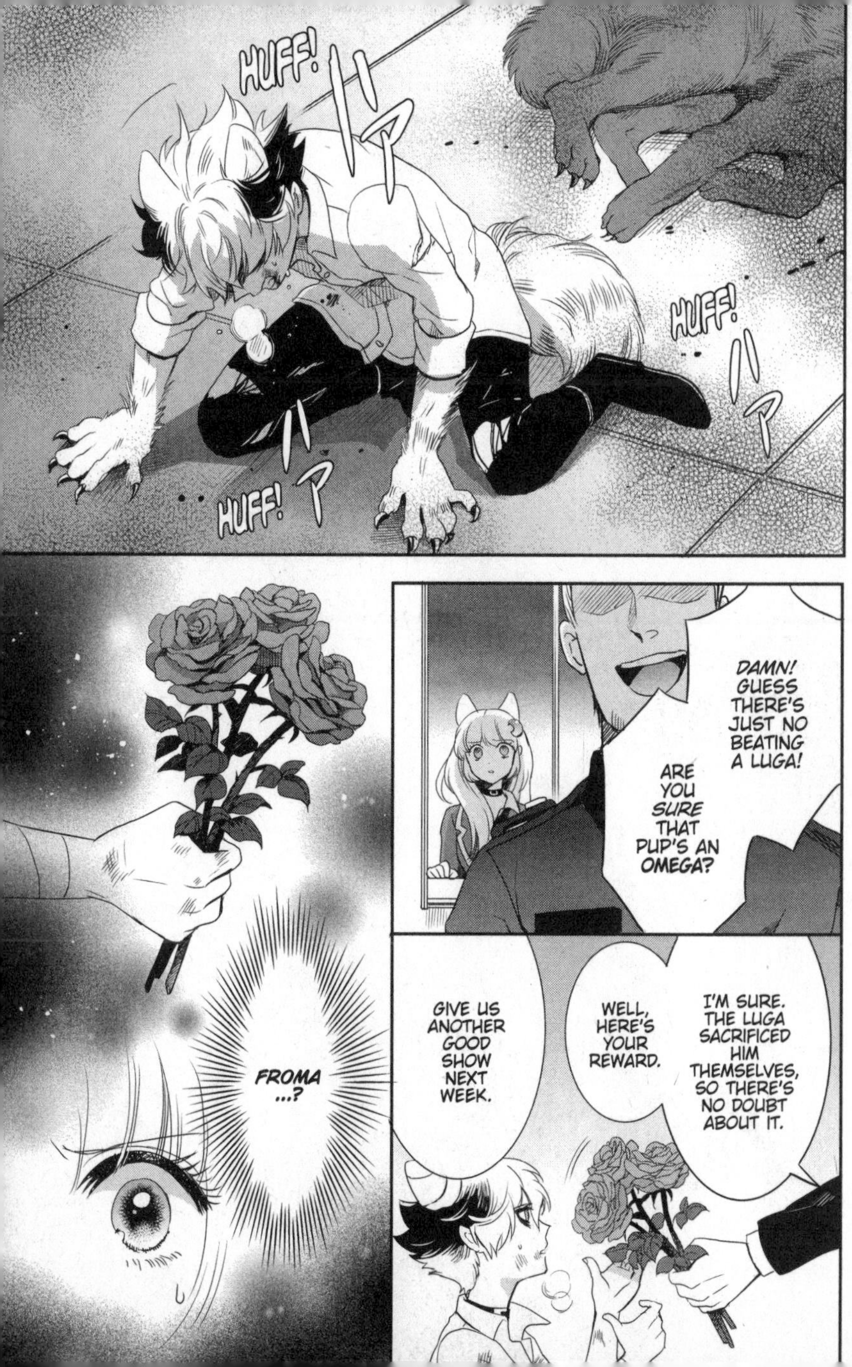
HUFF!
ハア
HUFF!
ハア
HUFF!
ハア
DAMN! GUESS THERE'S JUST NO BEATING A LUGA!
ARE YOU *SURE* THAT PUP'S AN OMEGA?
I'M SURE. THE LUGA SACRIFICED HIM THEMSELVES, SO THERE'S NO DOUBT ABOUT IT.
WELL, HERE'S YOUR REWARD.
GIVE US ANOTHER GOOD SHOW NEXT WEEK.
FROMA ...?

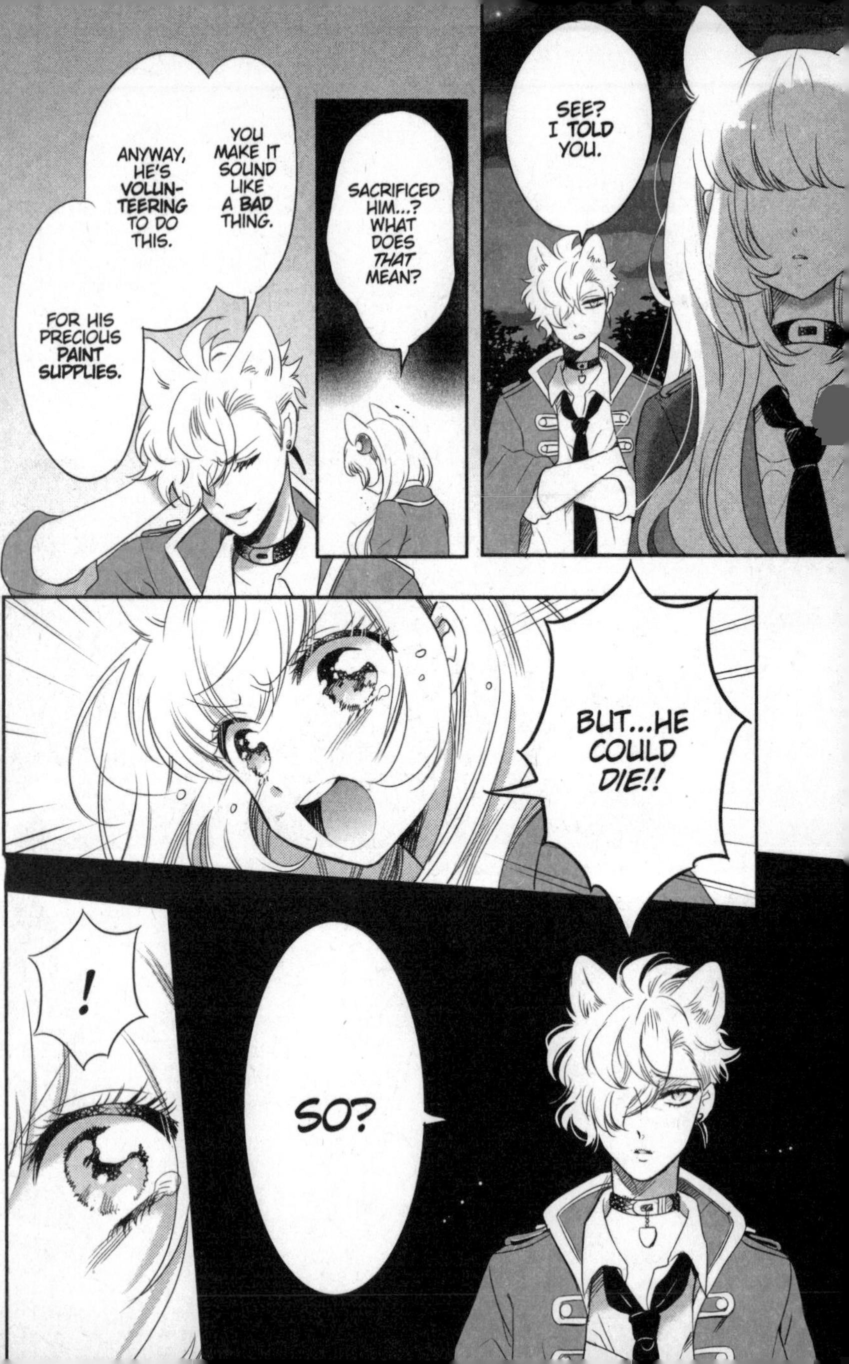
SEE? I TOLD YOU.
SACRIFICED HIM...? WHAT DOES THAT MEAN?
YOU MAKE IT SOUND LIKE A BAD THING.
ANYWAY, HE'S VOLUN-TEERING TO DO THIS.
FOR HIS PRECIOUS PAINT SUPPLIES.
BUT...HE COULD DIE!!
SO?
!

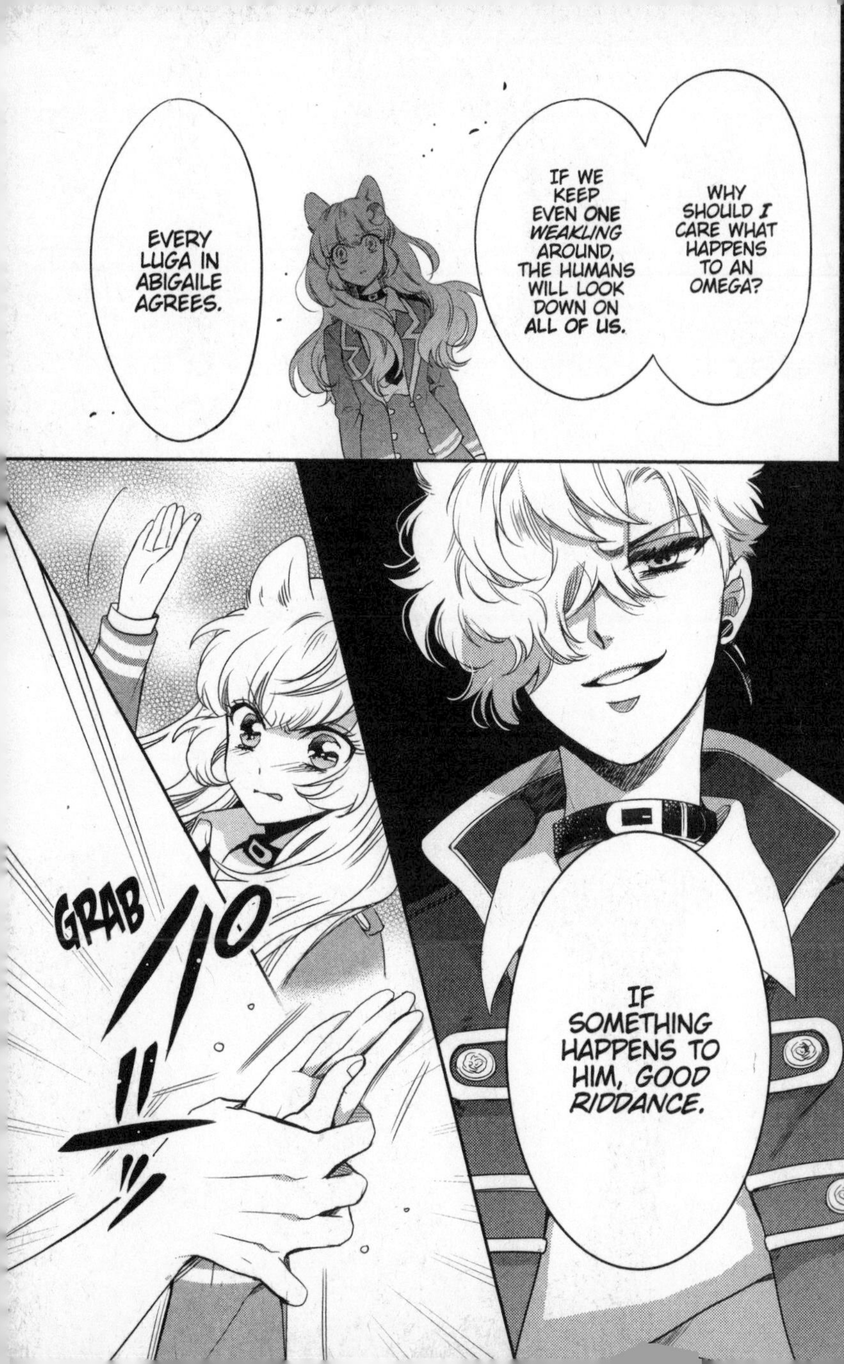
WHY SHOULD *I* CARE WHAT HAPPENS TO AN OMEGA?
IF WE KEEP EVEN ONE *WEAKLING* AROUND, THE HUMANS WILL LOOK DOWN ON ALL OF US.
EVERY LUGA IN ABIGAILE AGREES.
IF SOMETHING HAPPENS TO HIM, *GOOD RIDDANCE.*
GRAB

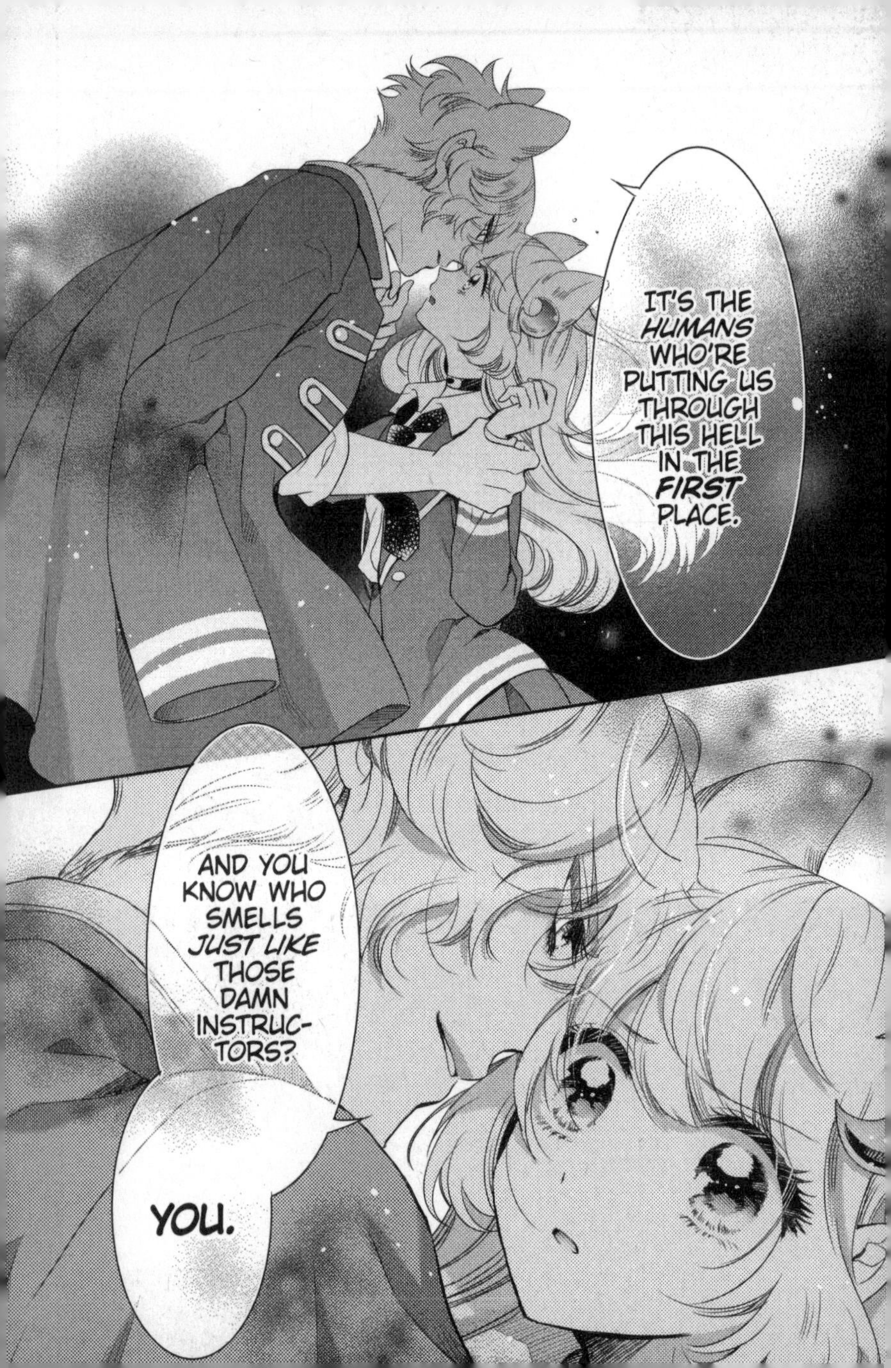
IT'S THE *HUMANS* WHO'RE PUTTING US THROUGH THIS HELL IN THE *FIRST* PLACE.
AND YOU KNOW WHO SMELLS *JUST LIKE* THOSE DAMN INSTRUC-TORS?
YOU.

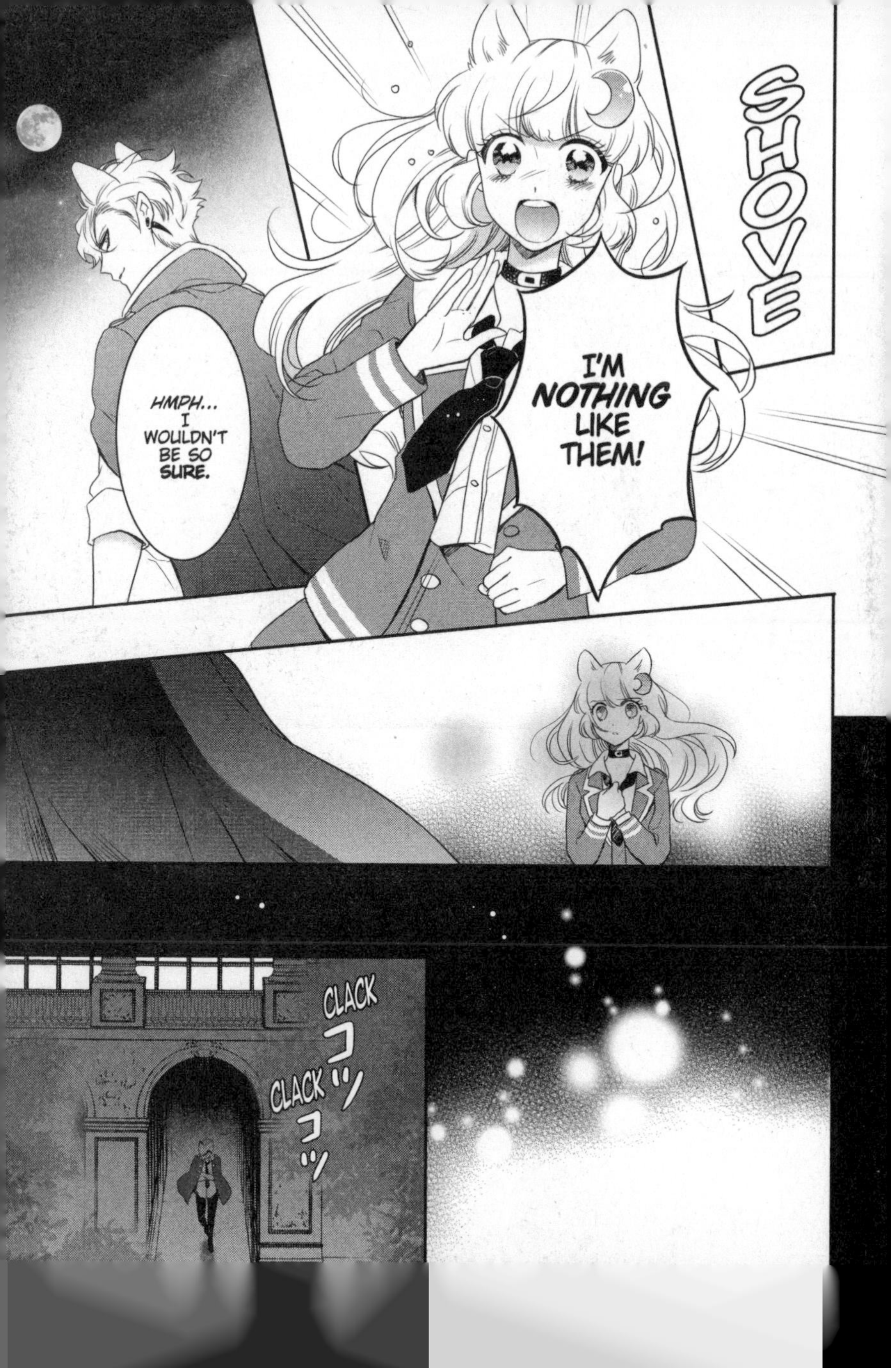
SHOVE
I'M NOTHING LIKE THEM!
HMPH... I WOULDN'T BE SO SURE.
CLACK コッ
CLACK コッ

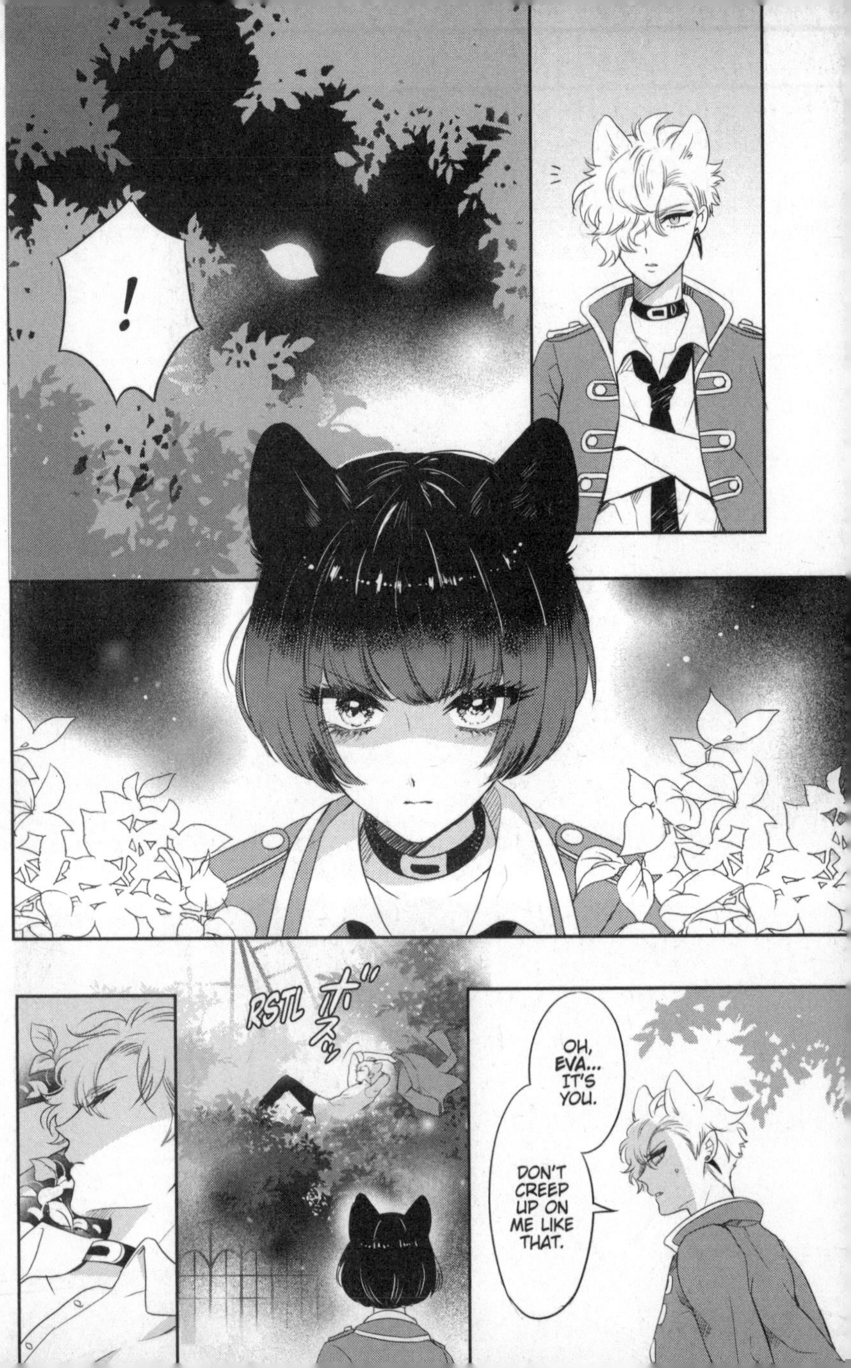
!
RSTL
ボスッ
OH, EVA... IT'S YOU.
DON'T CREEP UP ON ME LIKE THAT.

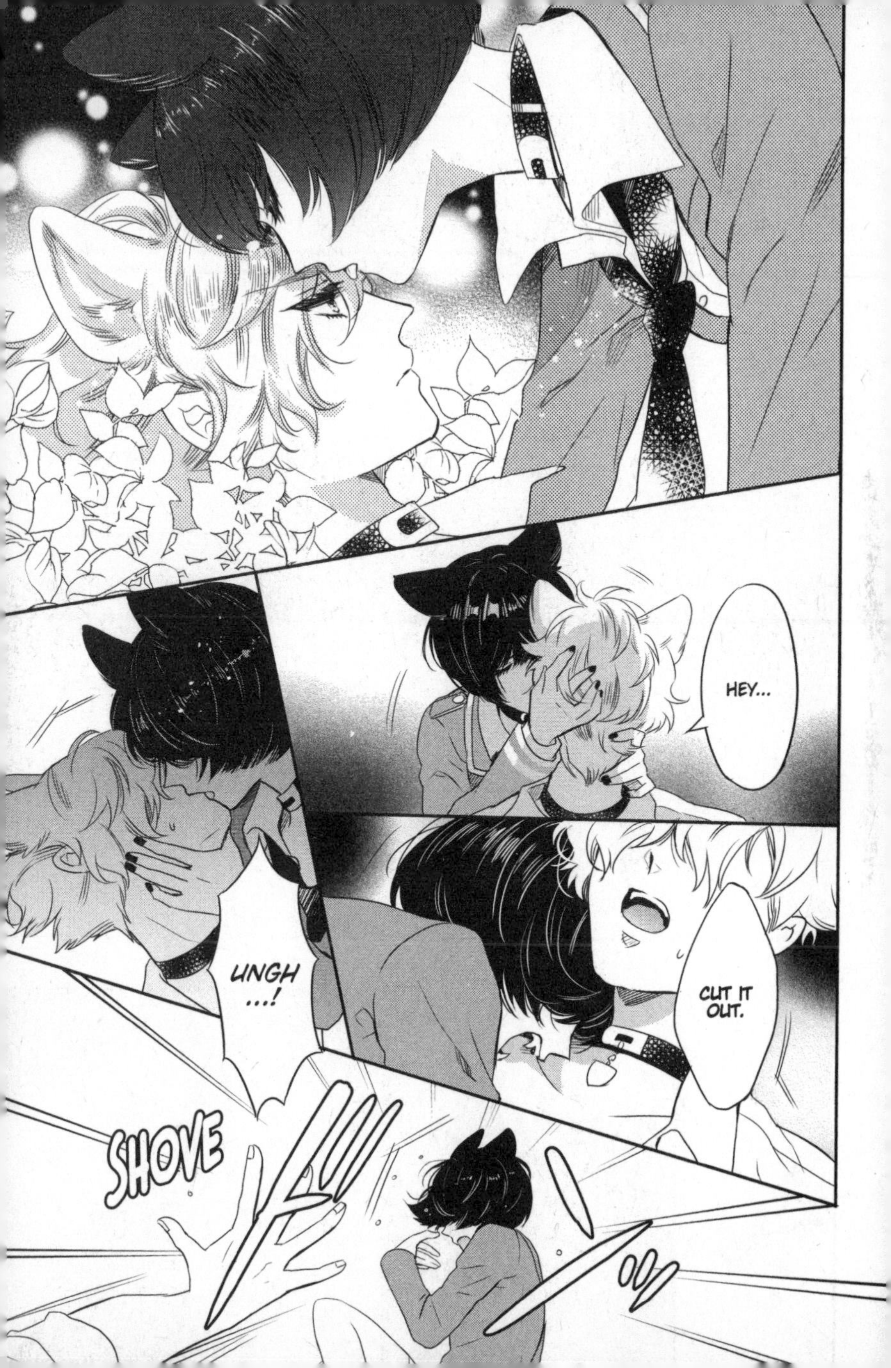
HEY...
CUT IT OUT.
UNGH ...!
SHOVE

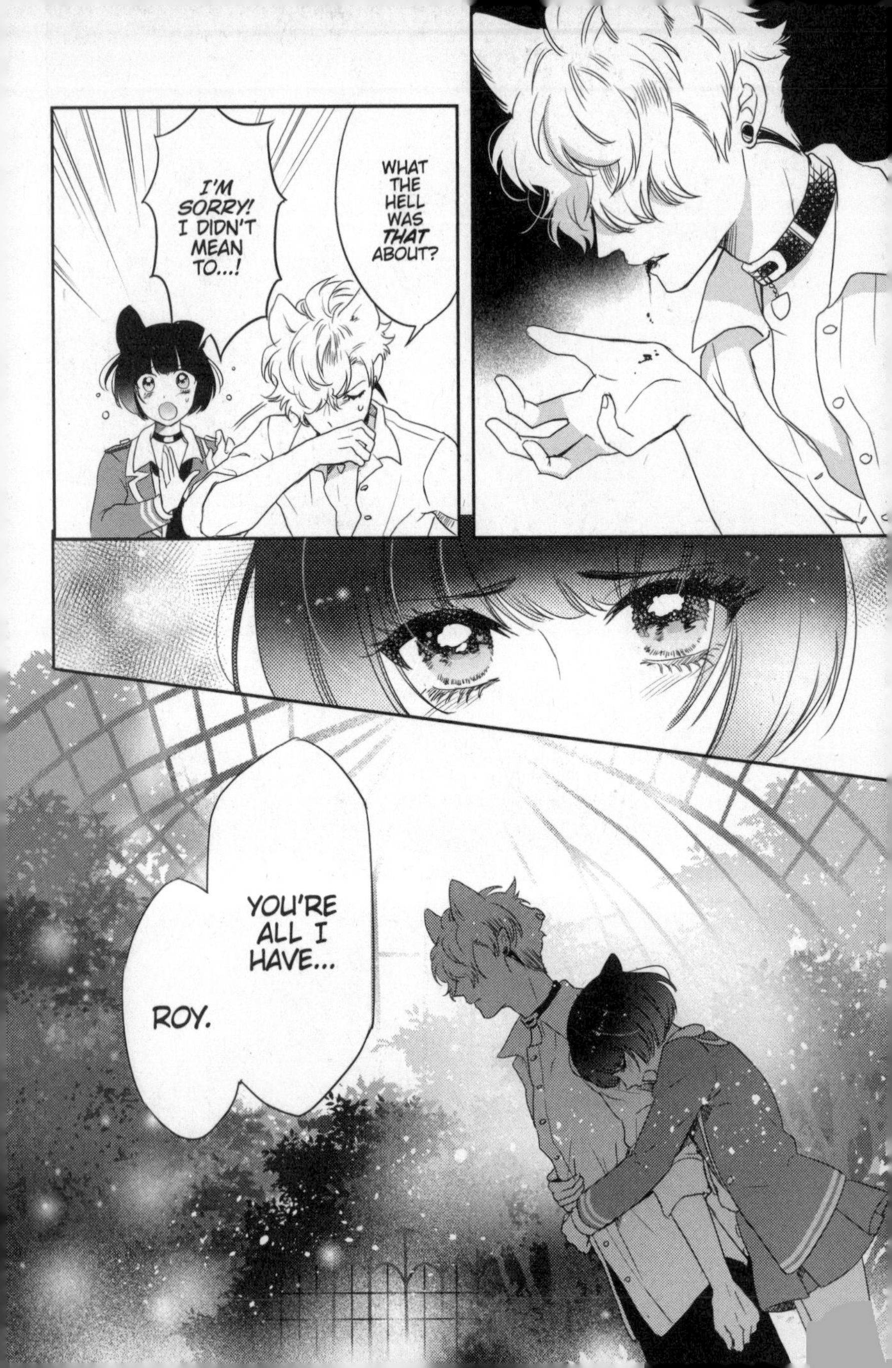
WHAT THE HELL WAS *THAT* ABOUT?
I'M SORRY! I DIDN'T MEAN TO...!
YOU'RE ALL I HAVE...
ROY.

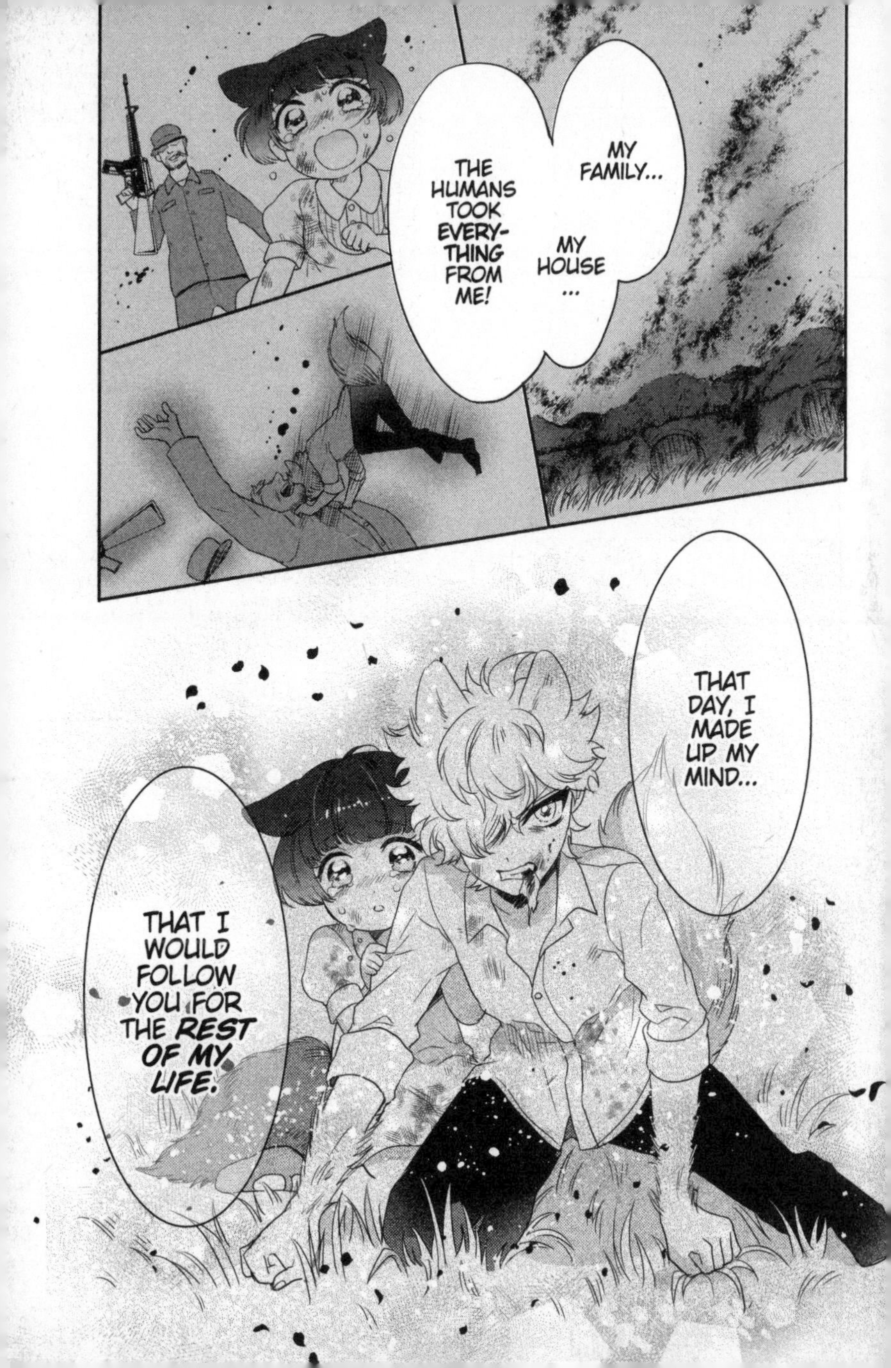
MY FAMILY...
MY HOUSE...
THE HUMANS TOOK EVERYTHING FROM ME!
THAT DAY, I MADE UP MY MIND...
THAT I WOULD FOLLOW YOU FOR THE *REST OF MY LIFE.*

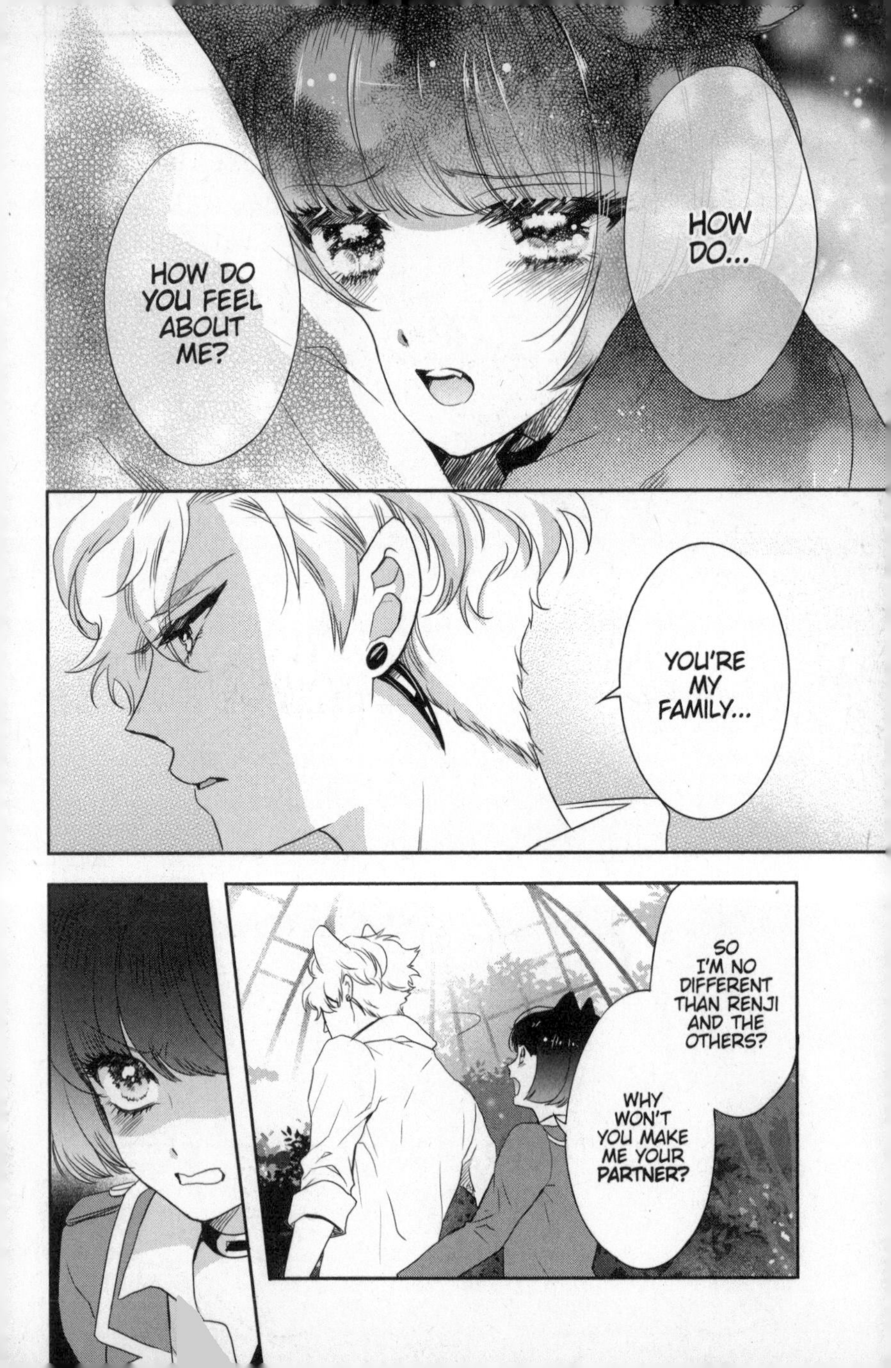
HOW DO...
HOW DO YOU FEEL ABOUT ME?
YOU'RE MY FAMILY...
SO I'M NO DIFFERENT THAN RENJI AND THE OTHERS?
WHY WON'T YOU MAKE ME YOUR PARTNER?

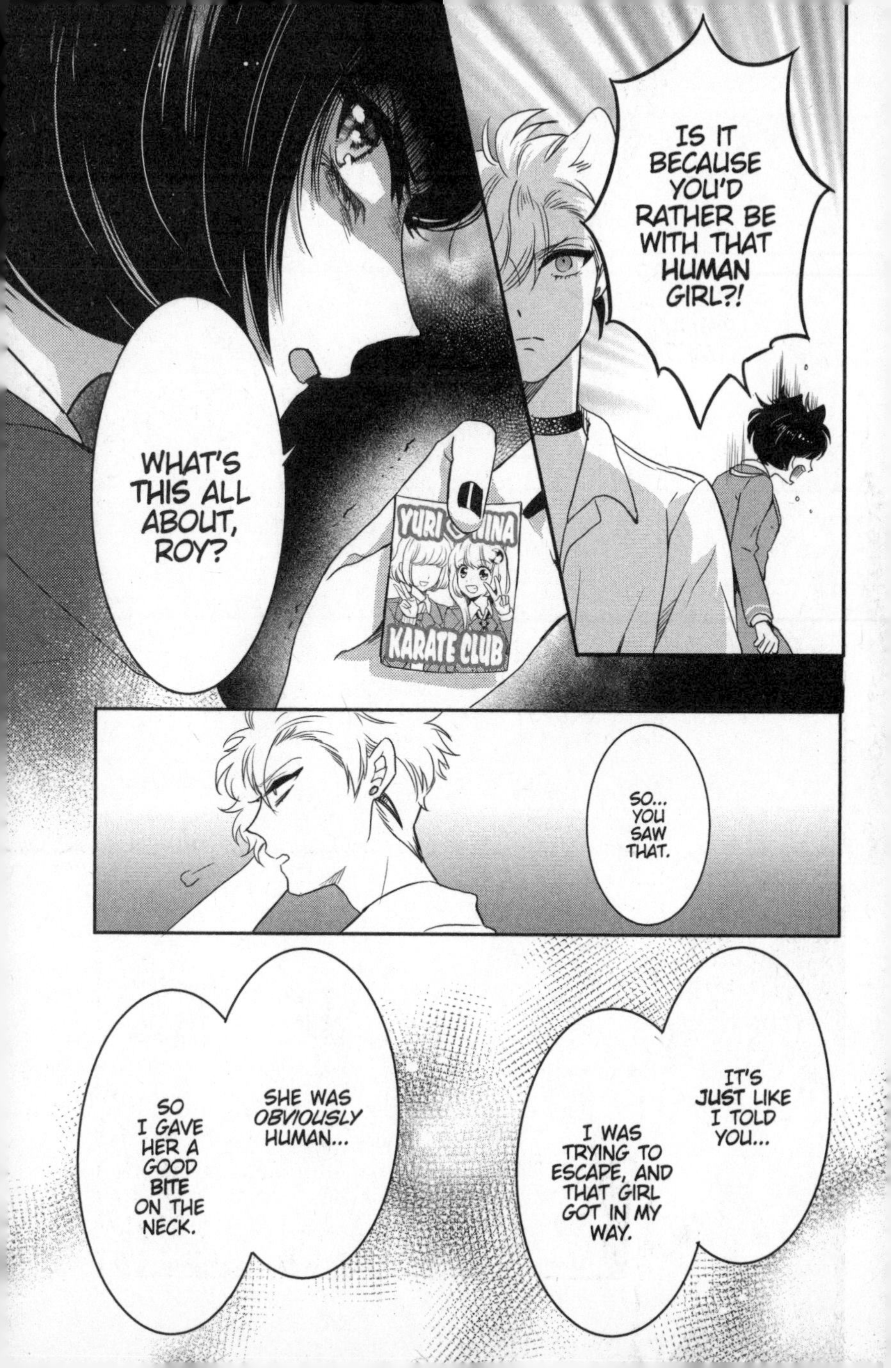
IS IT BECAUSE YOU'D RATHER BE WITH THAT HUMAN GIRL?!
WHAT'S THIS ALL ABOUT, ROY?
KARATE CLUB
SO... YOU SAW THAT.
IT'S JUST LIKE I TOLD YOU...
I WAS TRYING TO ESCAPE, AND THAT GIRL GOT IN MY WAY.
SHE WAS *OBVIOUSLY* HUMAN...
SO I GAVE HER A GOOD BITE ON THE NECK.

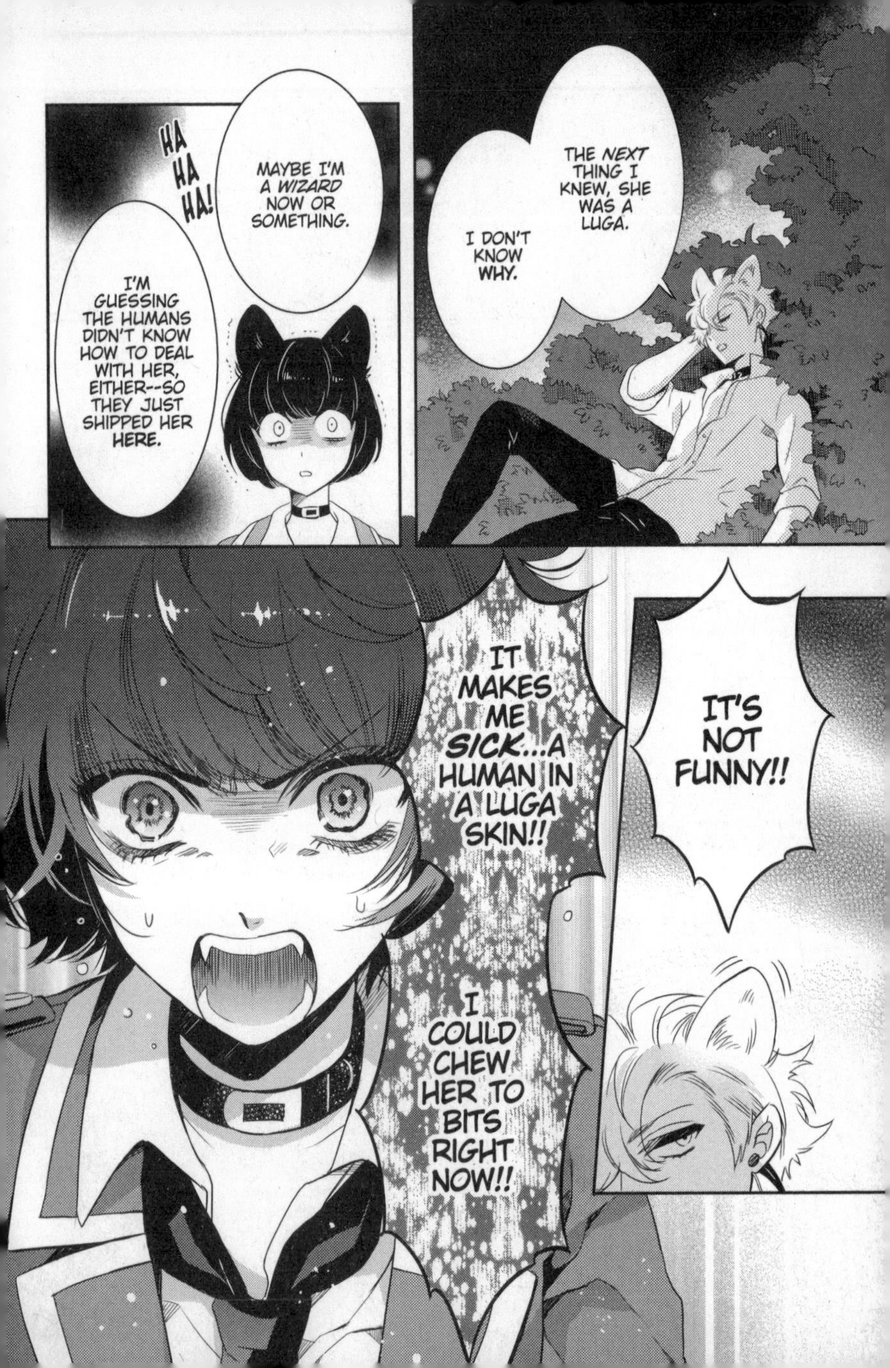
THE *NEXT* THING I KNEW, SHE WAS A LUGA.
I DON'T KNOW WHY.
MAYBE I'M A *WIZARD* NOW OR SOMETHING.
HA HA HA!
I'M GUESSING THE HUMANS DIDN'T KNOW HOW TO DEAL WITH HER, EITHER--SO THEY JUST SHIPPED HER HERE.
IT'S NOT FUNNY!!
IT MAKES ME *SICK*...A HUMAN IN A LUGA SKIN!!
I COULD CHEW HER TO BITS RIGHT NOW!!

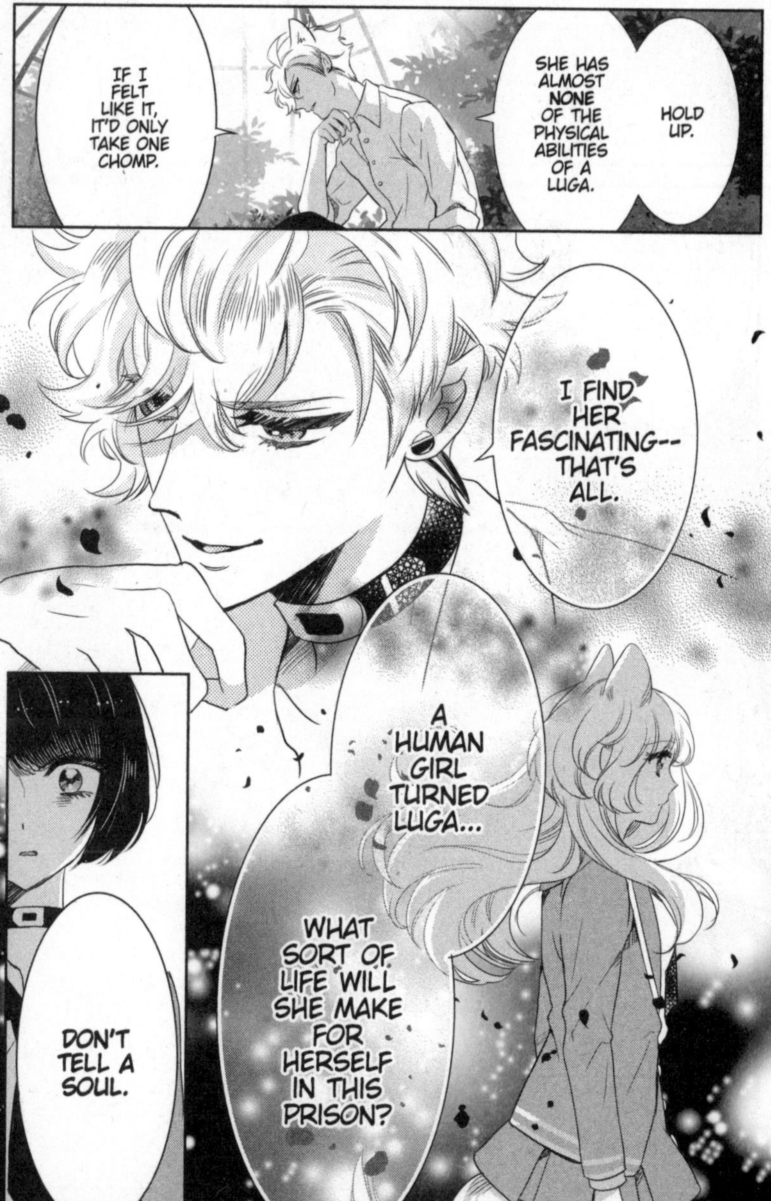
HOLD UP.
SHE HAS ALMOST NONE OF THE PHYSICAL ABILITIES OF A LUGA.
IF I FELT LIKE IT, IT'D ONLY TAKE ONE CHOMP.
I FIND HER FASCINATING--THAT'S ALL.
A HUMAN GIRL TURNED LUGA...
WHAT SORT OF LIFE WILL SHE MAKE FOR HERSELF IN THIS PRISON?
DON'T TELL A SOUL.

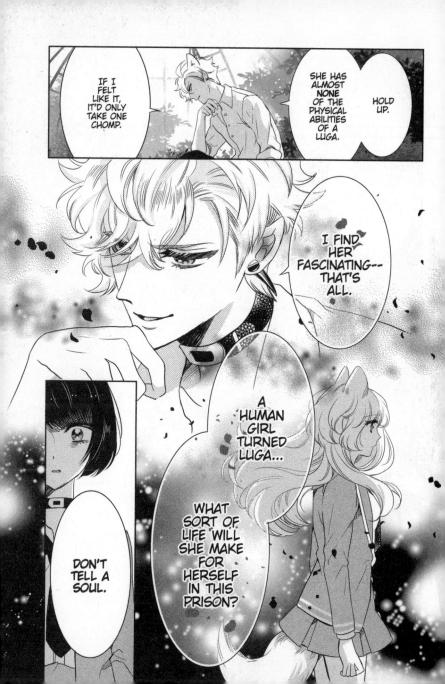

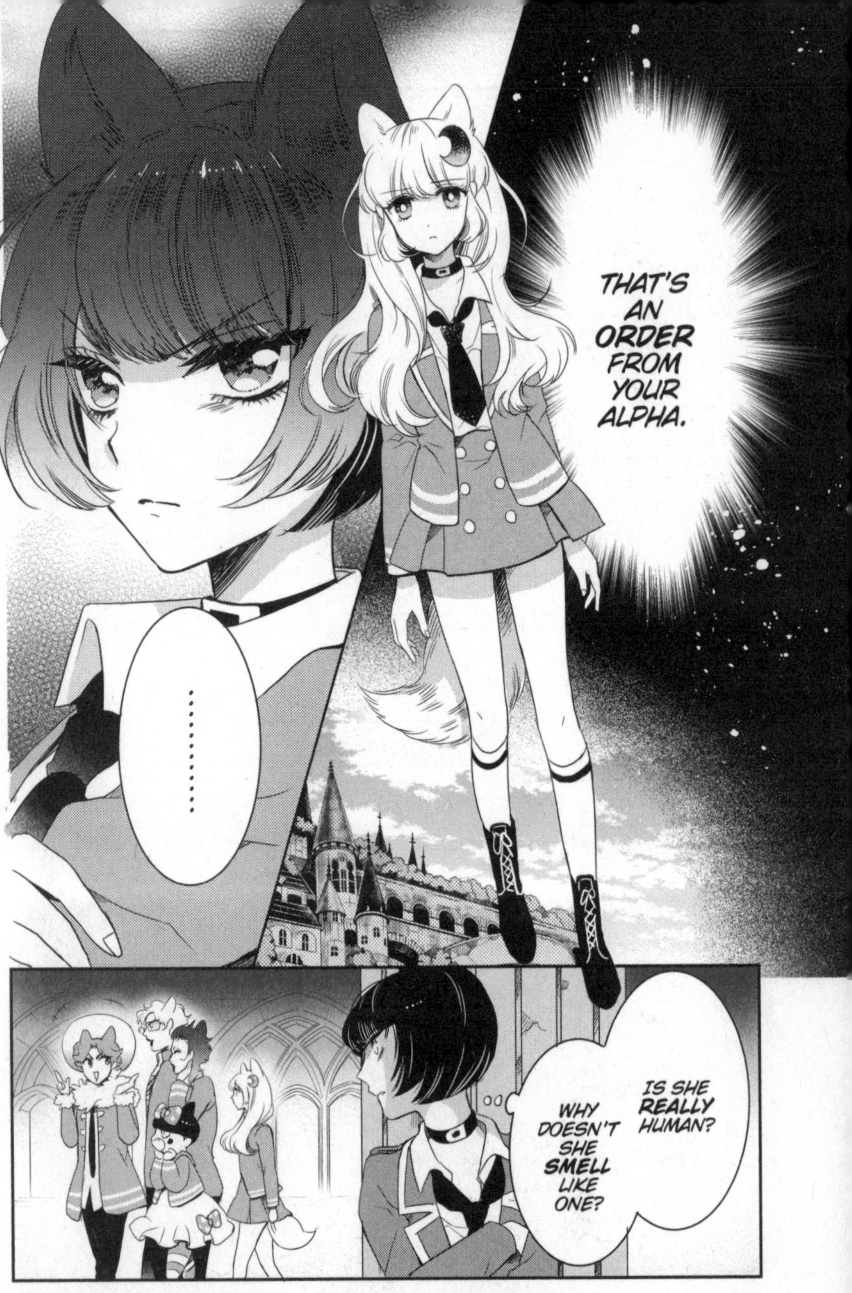
THAT'S AN ORDER FROM YOUR ALPHA.
......
IS SHE REALLY HUMAN?
WHY DOESN'T SHE SMELL LIKE ONE?

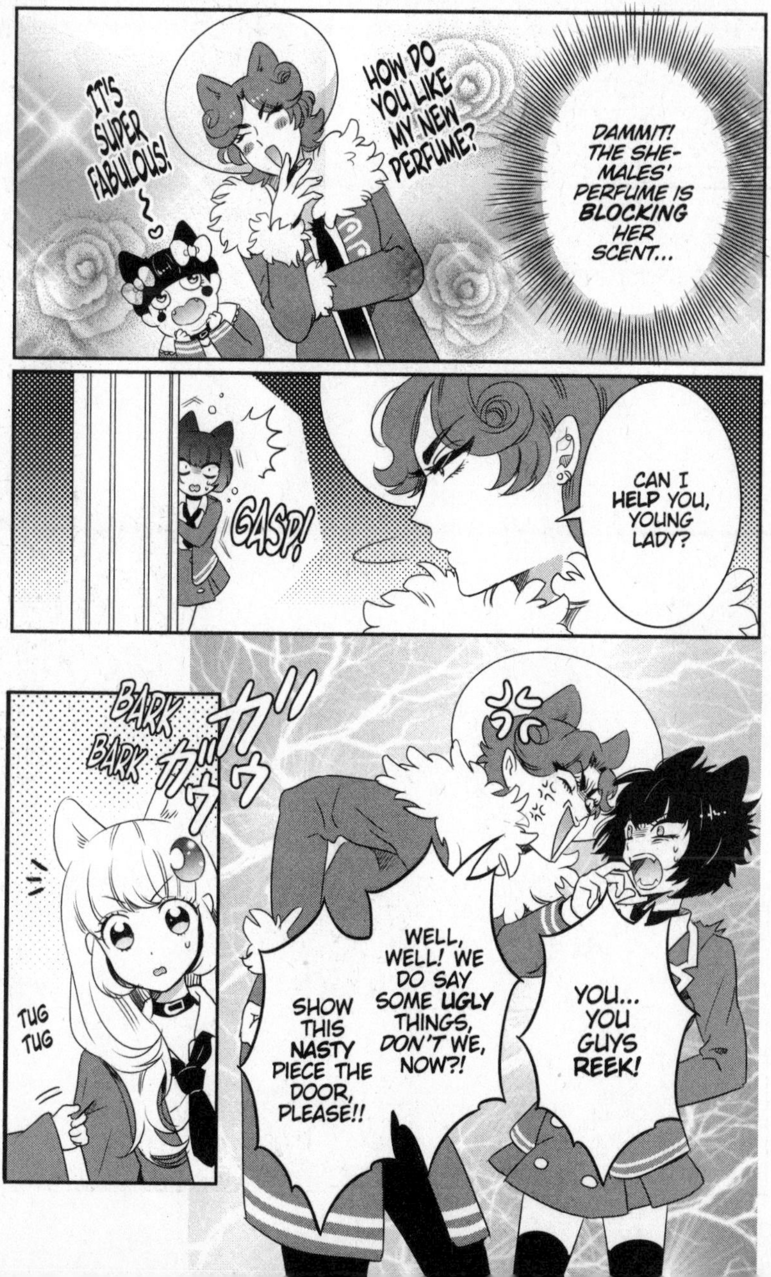
DAMMIT! THE SHE-MALES' PERFUME IS BLOCKING HER SCENT...
HOW DO YOU LIKE MY NEW PERFUME?
IT'S SUPER FABULOUS!
CAN I HELP YOU, YOUNG LADY?
GASP!
YOU... YOU GUYS REEK!
WELL, WELL! WE DO SAY SOME UGLY THINGS, DON'T WE, NOW?!
SHOW THIS NASTY PIECE THE DOOR, PLEASE!!
BARK BARK
ガウガウ
TUG TUG

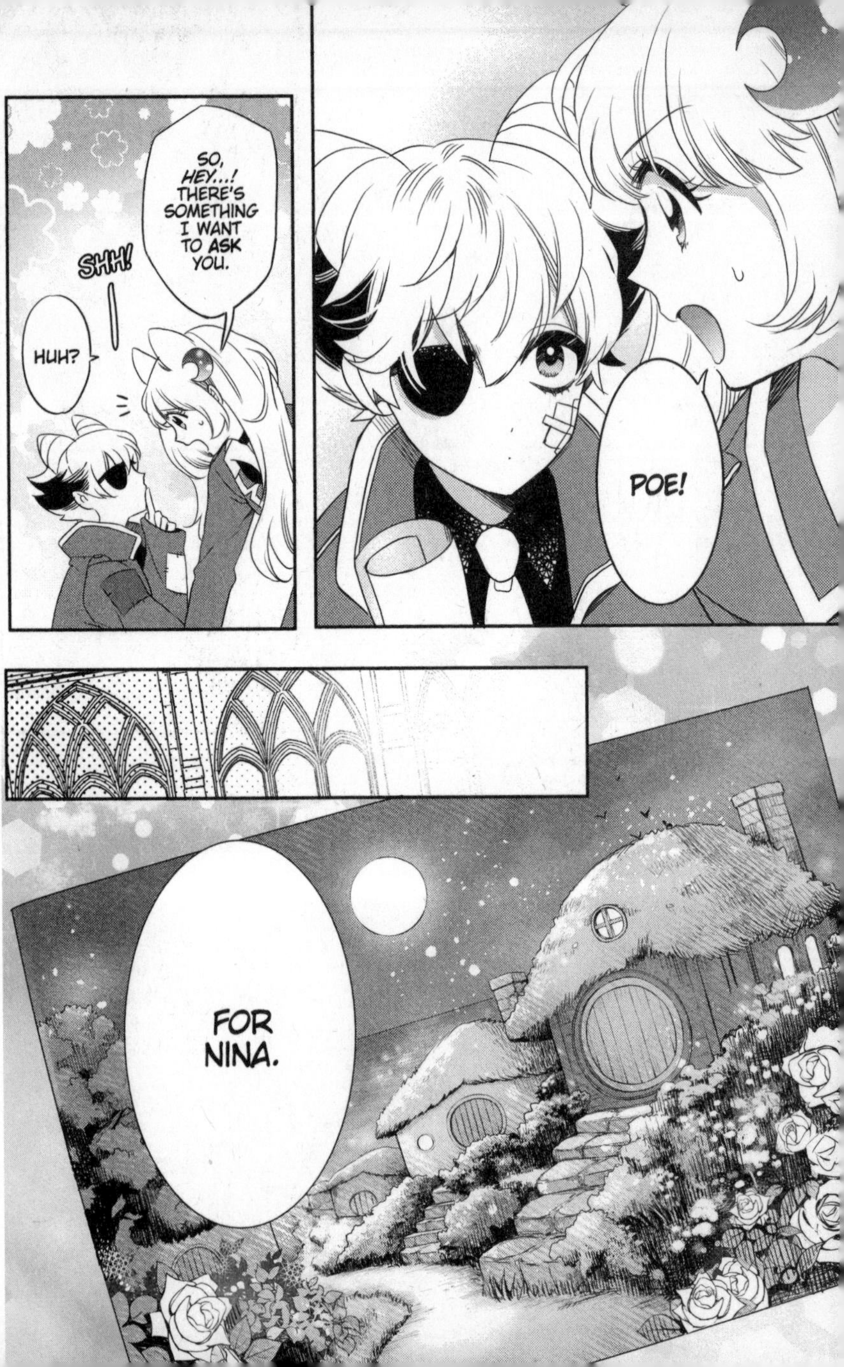
POE!
SO, HEY...! THERE'S SOMETHING I WANT TO ASK YOU.
SHH!
HUH?
FOR NINA.

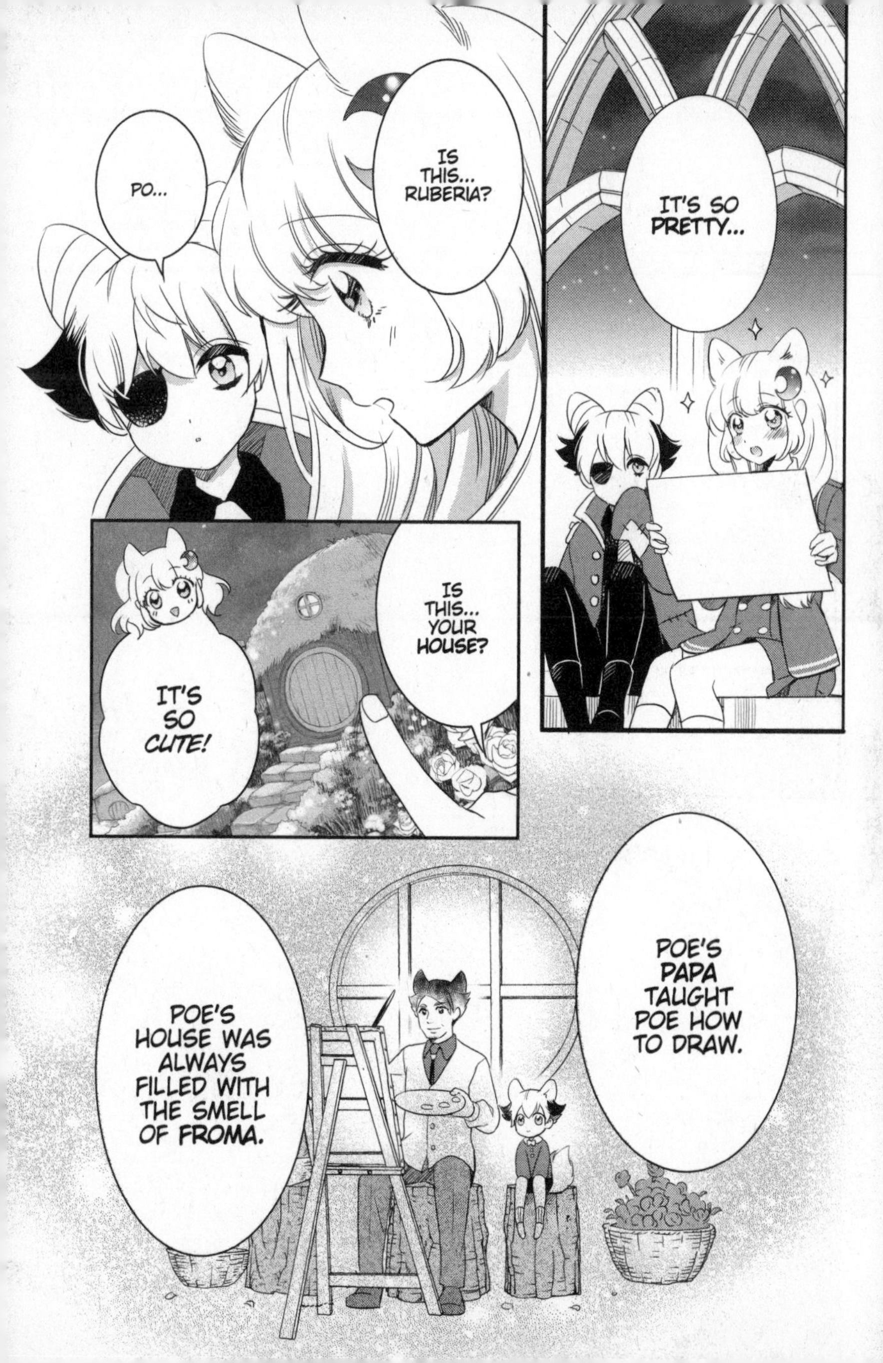
IT'S SO PRETTY...
IS THIS... RUBERIA?
PO...
IS THIS... YOUR HOUSE?
IT'S SO CUTE!
POE'S PAPA TAUGHT POE HOW TO DRAW.
POE'S HOUSE WAS ALWAYS FILLED WITH THE SMELL OF FROMA.

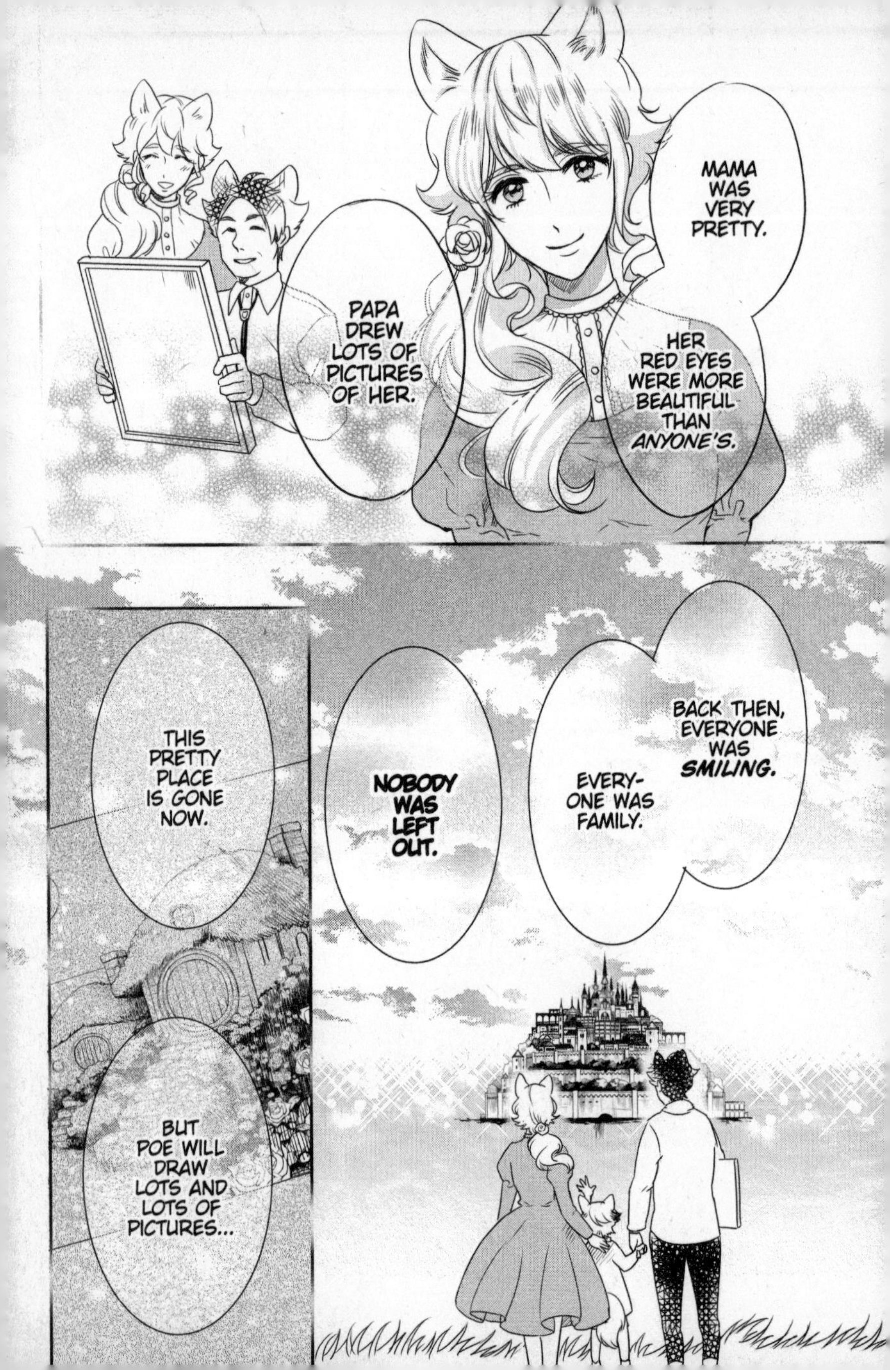
MAMA WAS VERY PRETTY.
HER RED EYES WERE MORE BEAUTIFUL THAN ANYONE'S.
PAPA DREW LOTS OF PICTURES OF HER.
BACK THEN, EVERYONE WAS SMILING.
EVERY-ONE WAS FAMILY.
NOBODY WAS LEFT OUT.
THIS PRETTY PLACE IS GONE NOW.
BUT POE WILL DRAW LOTS AND LOTS OF PICTURES...

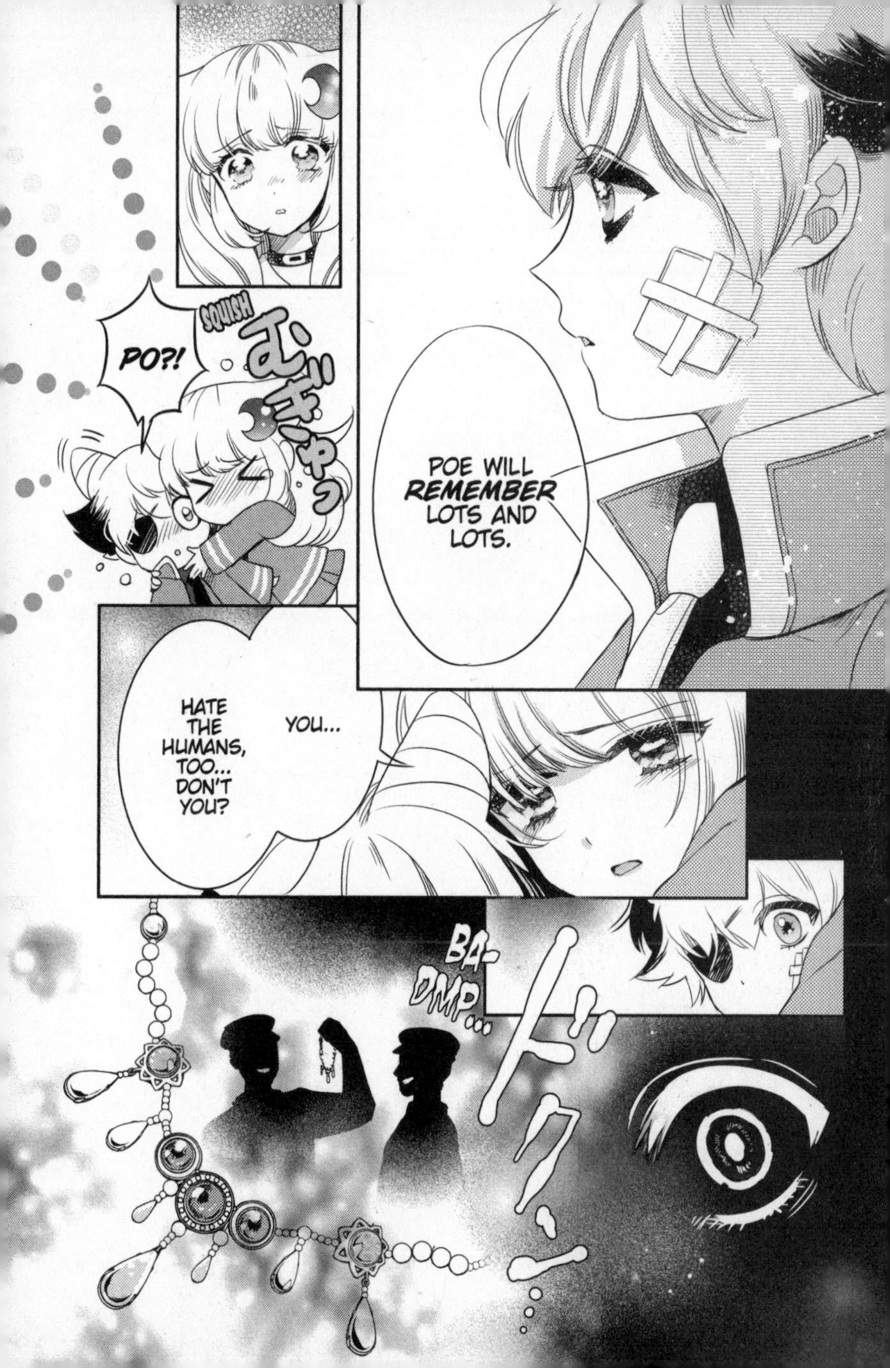
POE WILL REMEMBER LOTS AND LOTS.
SQUISH
PO?!
YOU...
HATE THE HUMANS, TOO... DON'T YOU?
BA-DMP...

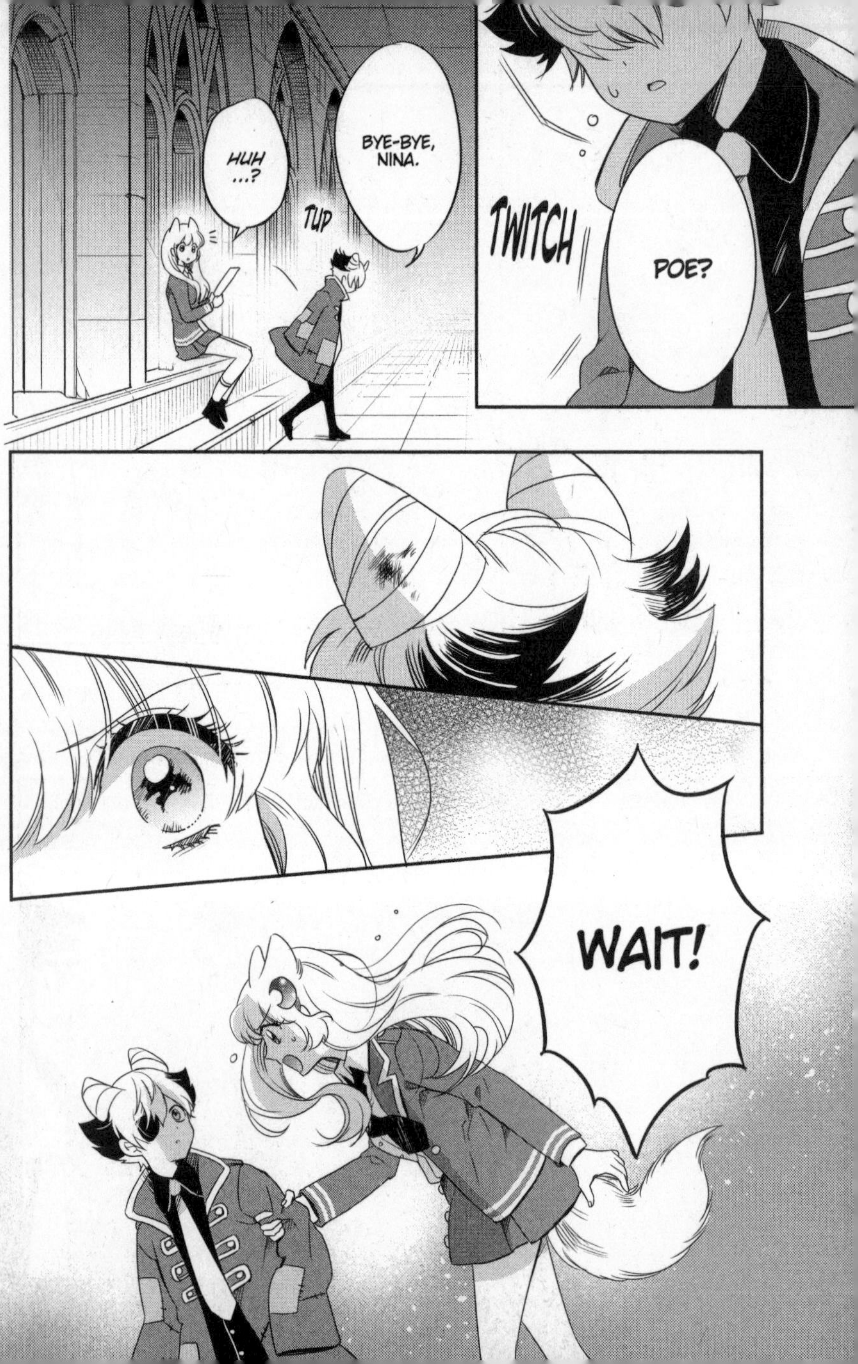
TWITCH
POE?
BYE-BYE, NINA.
HUH ...?
TUP
WAIT!

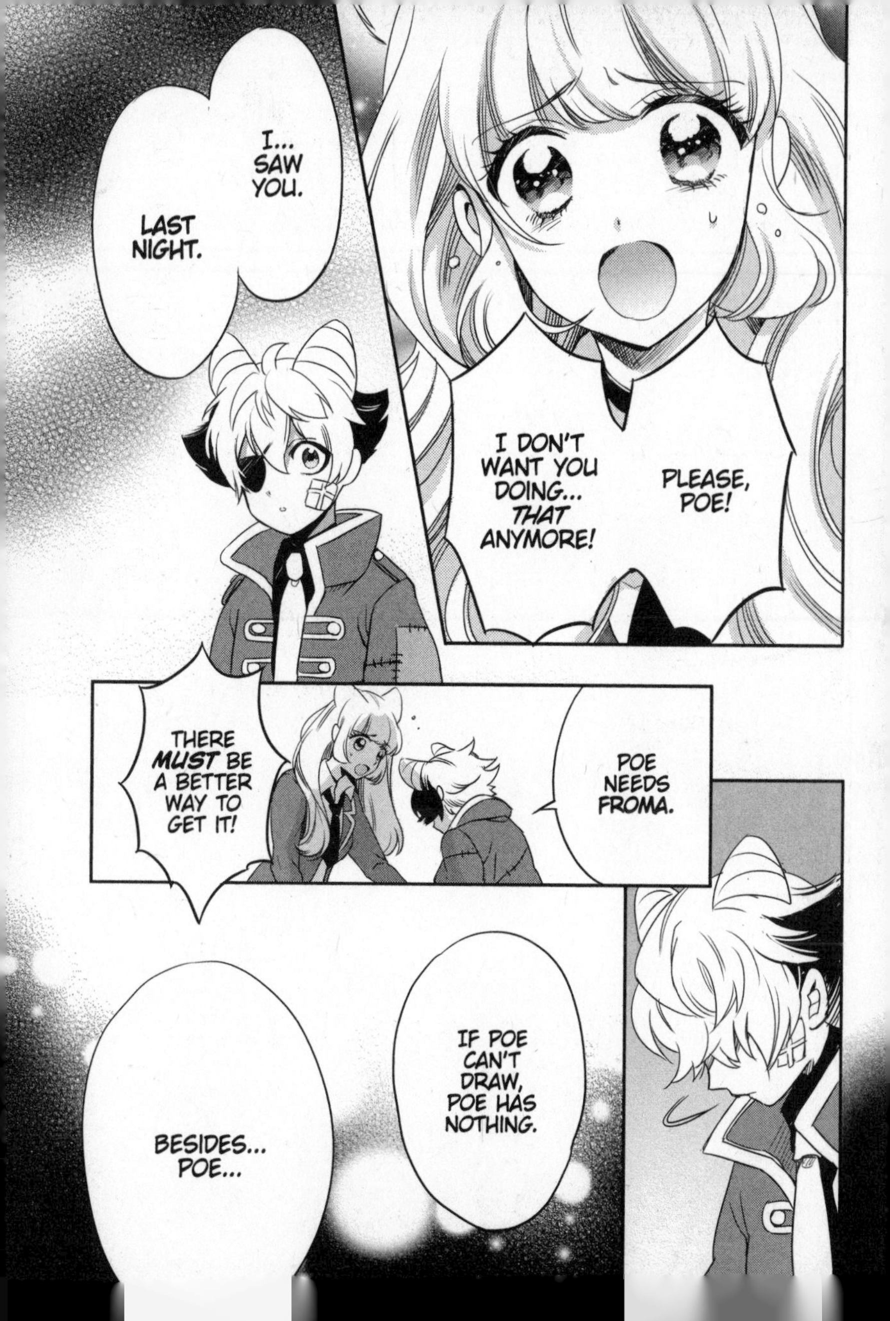
PLEASE, POE!
I DON'T WANT YOU DOING... *THAT* ANYMORE!
I... SAW YOU.
LAST NIGHT.
POE NEEDS FROMA.
THERE **MUST** BE A BETTER WAY TO GET IT!
IF POE CAN'T DRAW, POE HAS NOTHING.
BESIDES... POE...

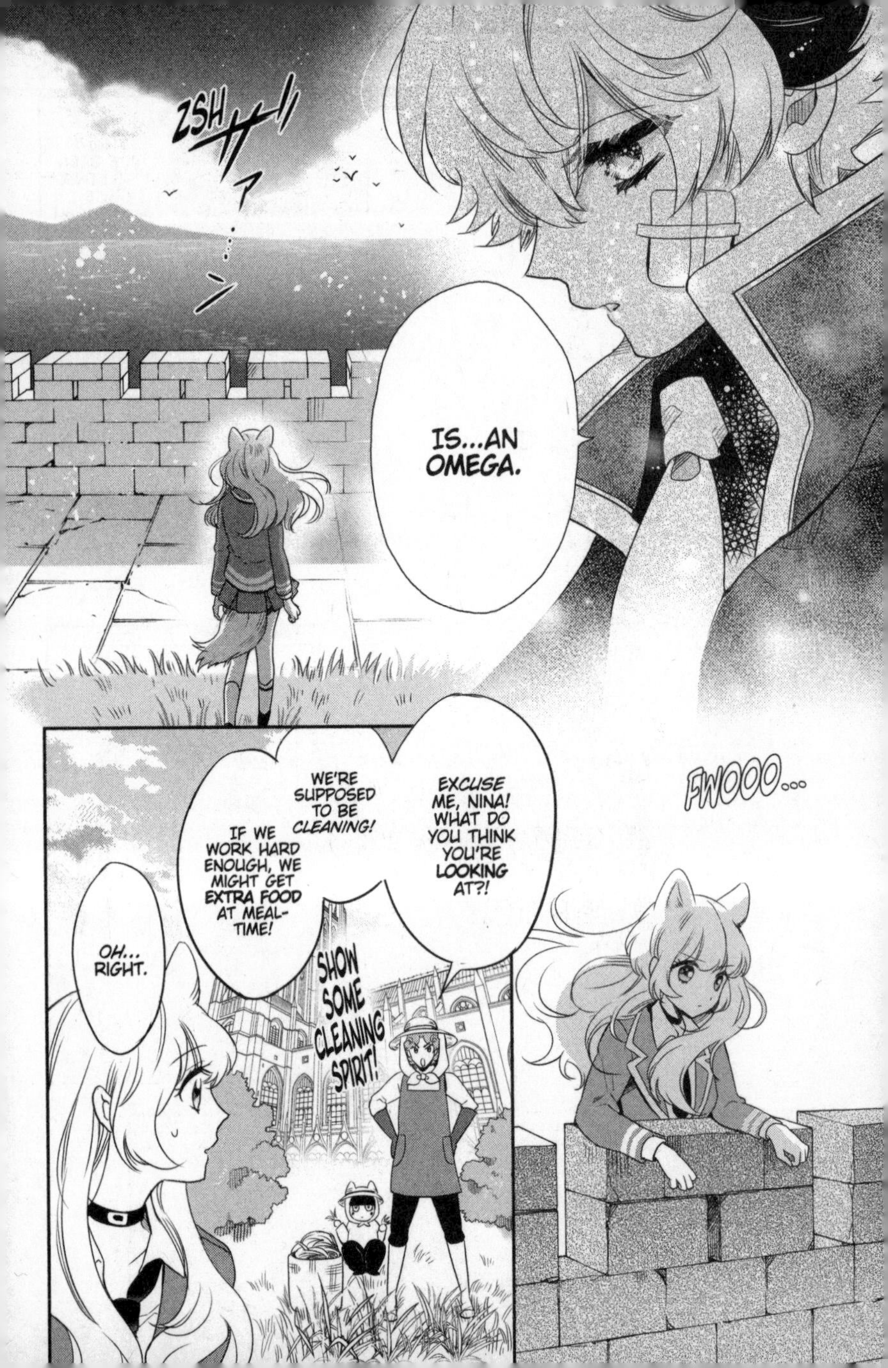
IS...AN OMEGA.
ZSH
FWOOO...
EXCUSE ME, NINA! WHAT DO YOU THINK YOU'RE LOOKING AT?!
WE'RE SUPPOSED TO BE CLEANING!
IF WE WORK HARD ENOUGH, WE MIGHT GET EXTRA FOOD AT MEAL-TIME!
SHOW SOME CLEANING SPIRIT!
OH... RIGHT.

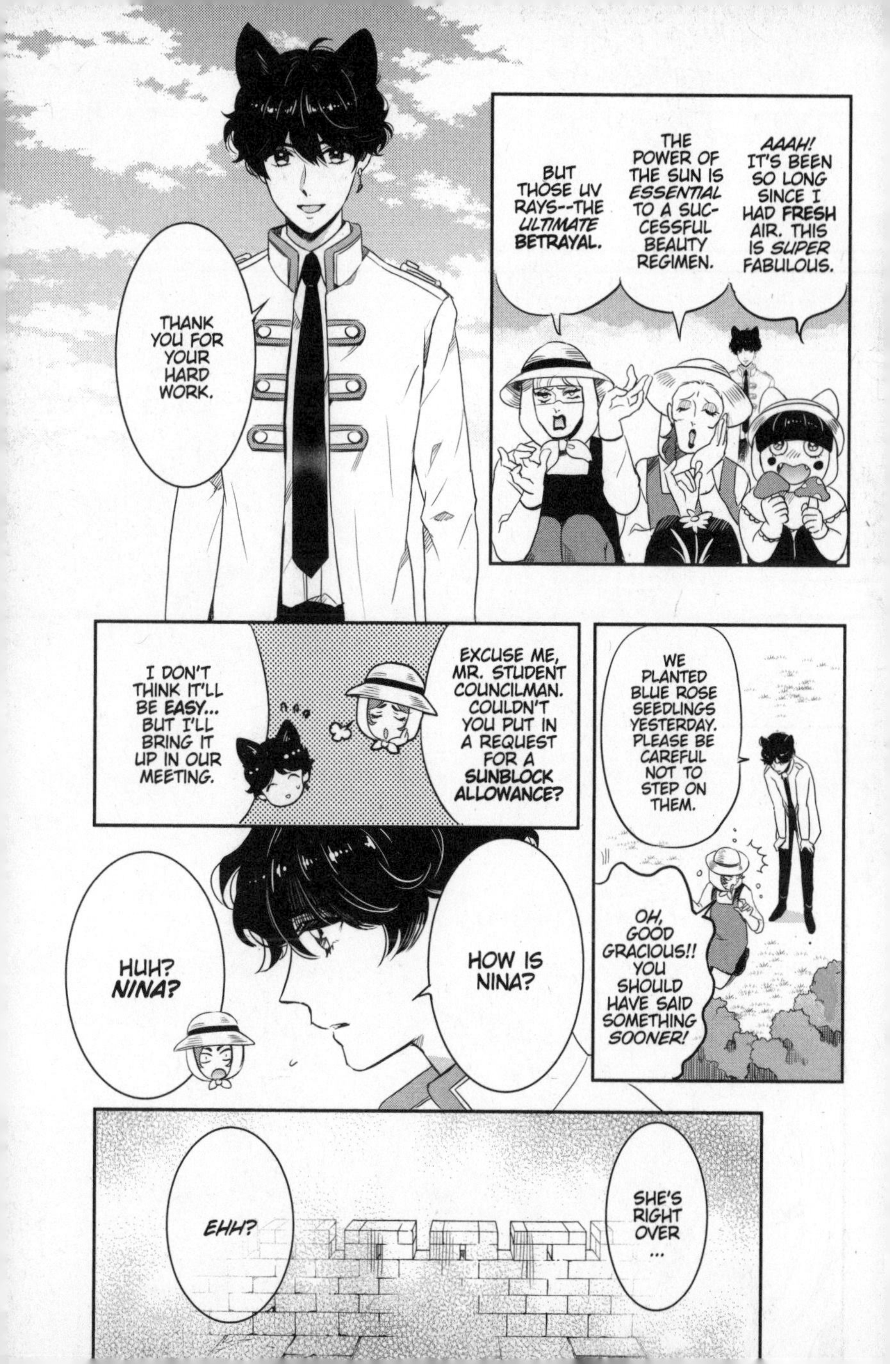
AAAH! IT'S BEEN SO LONG SINCE I HAD FRESH AIR. THIS IS SUPER FABULOUS.
THE POWER OF THE SUN IS ESSENTIAL TO A SUC-CESSFUL BEAUTY REGIMEN.
BUT THOSE UV RAYS--THE ULTIMATE BETRAYAL.
THANK YOU FOR YOUR HARD WORK.
WE PLANTED BLUE ROSE SEEDLINGS YESTERDAY. PLEASE BE CAREFUL NOT TO STEP ON THEM.
OH, GOOD GRACIOUS!! YOU SHOULD HAVE SAID SOMETHING SOONER!
EXCUSE ME, MR. STUDENT COUNCILMAN. COULDN'T YOU PUT IN A REQUEST FOR A SUNBLOCK ALLOWANCE?
I DON'T THINK IT'LL BE EASY... BUT I'LL BRING IT UP IN OUR MEETING.
HOW IS NINA?
HUH? NINA?
SHE'S RIGHT OVER ...
EHH?

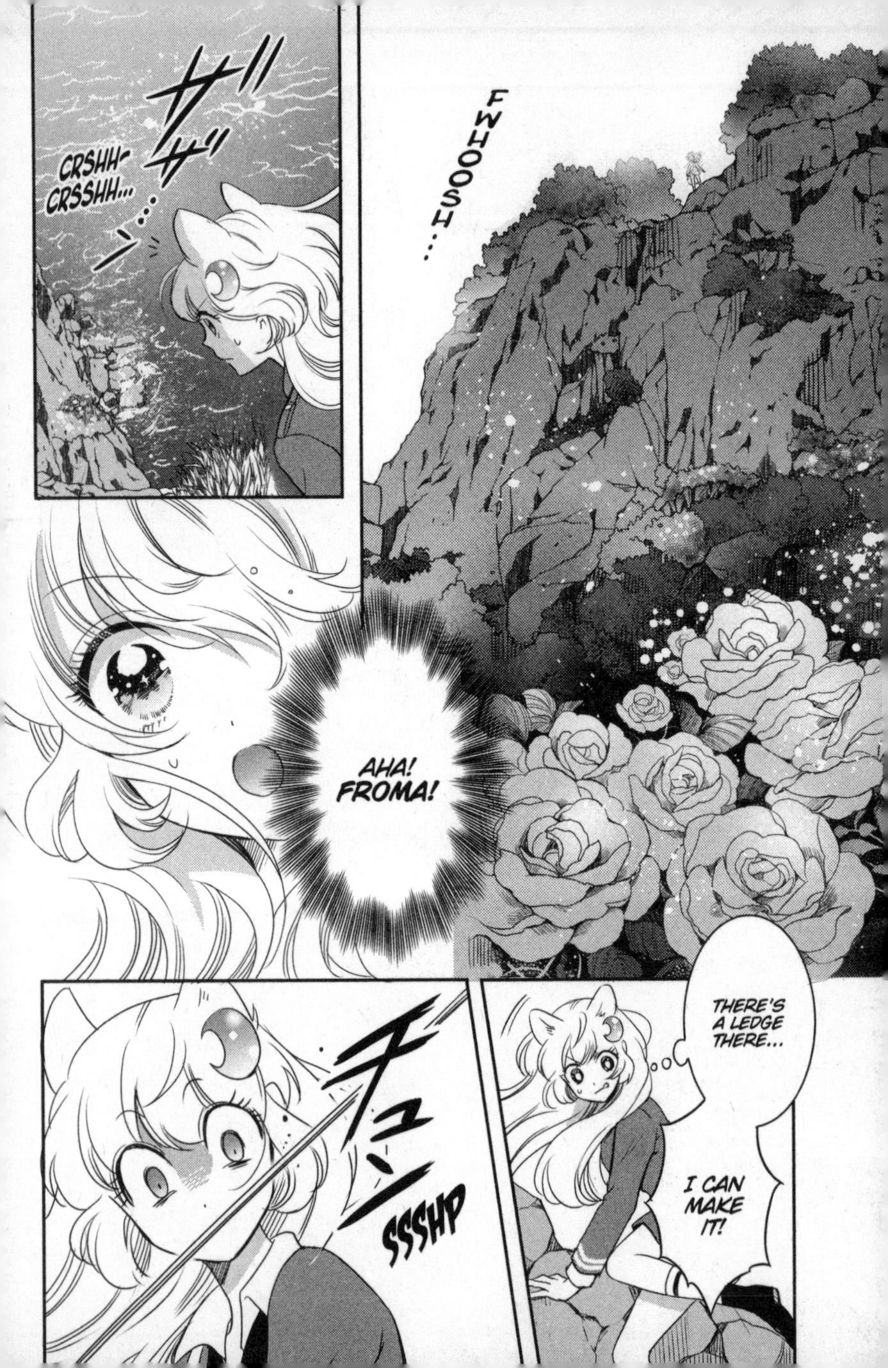
FWHOOSH...
CRSHH-CRSSHH...
AHA! FROMA!
THERE'S A LEDGE THERE...
I CAN MAKE IT!
SSSHP

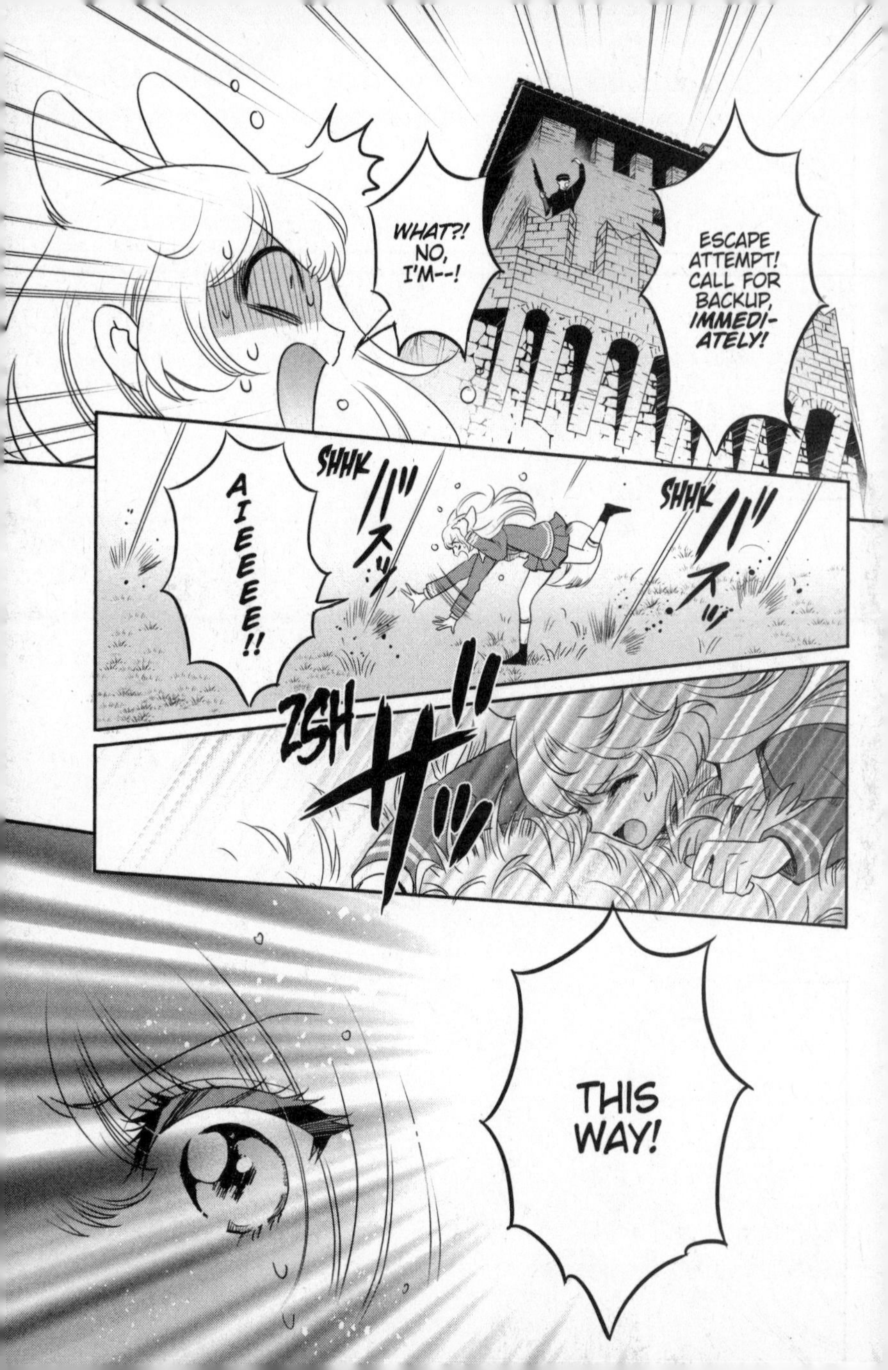
ESCAPE ATTEMPT! CALL FOR BACKUP, IMMEDI-ATELY!
WHAT?! NO, I'M--!
SHHK
SHHK
AIEEEEE!!
ZSH
THIS WAY!

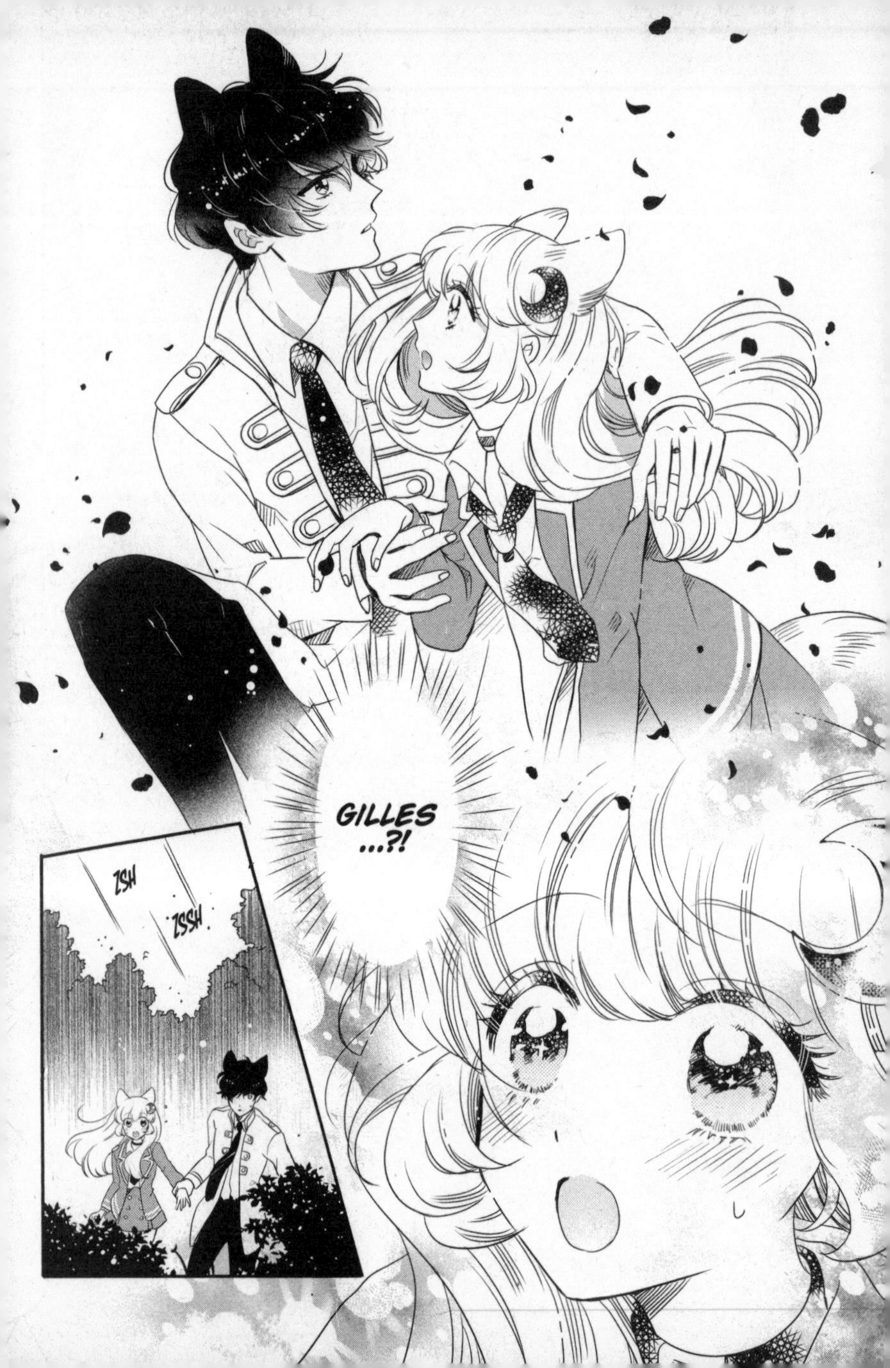
GILLES ...?!
ZSH
ZSSH

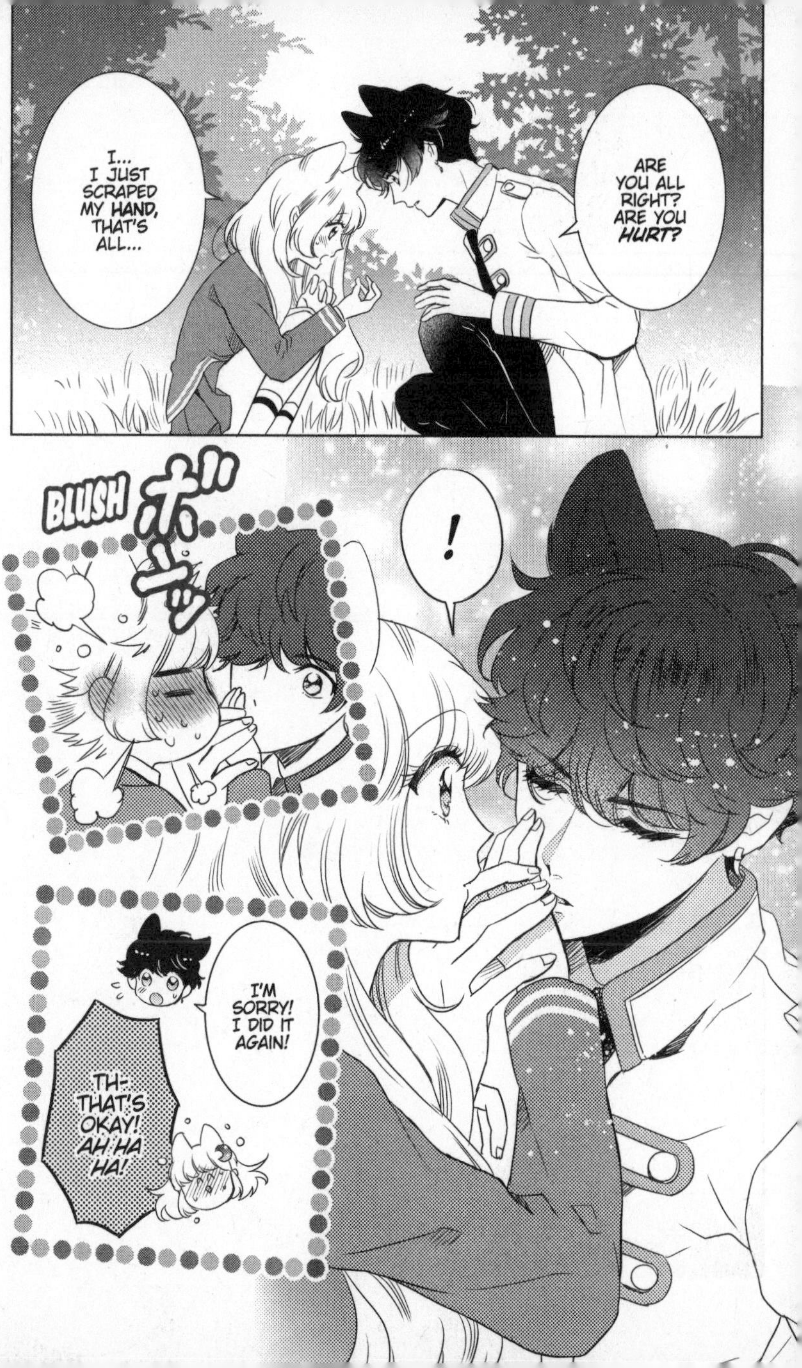
ARE YOU ALL RIGHT? ARE YOU HURT?
I... I JUST SCRAPED MY HAND, THAT'S ALL...
!
BLUSH
I'M SORRY! I DID IT AGAIN!
TH-THAT'S OKAY! AH HA HA!

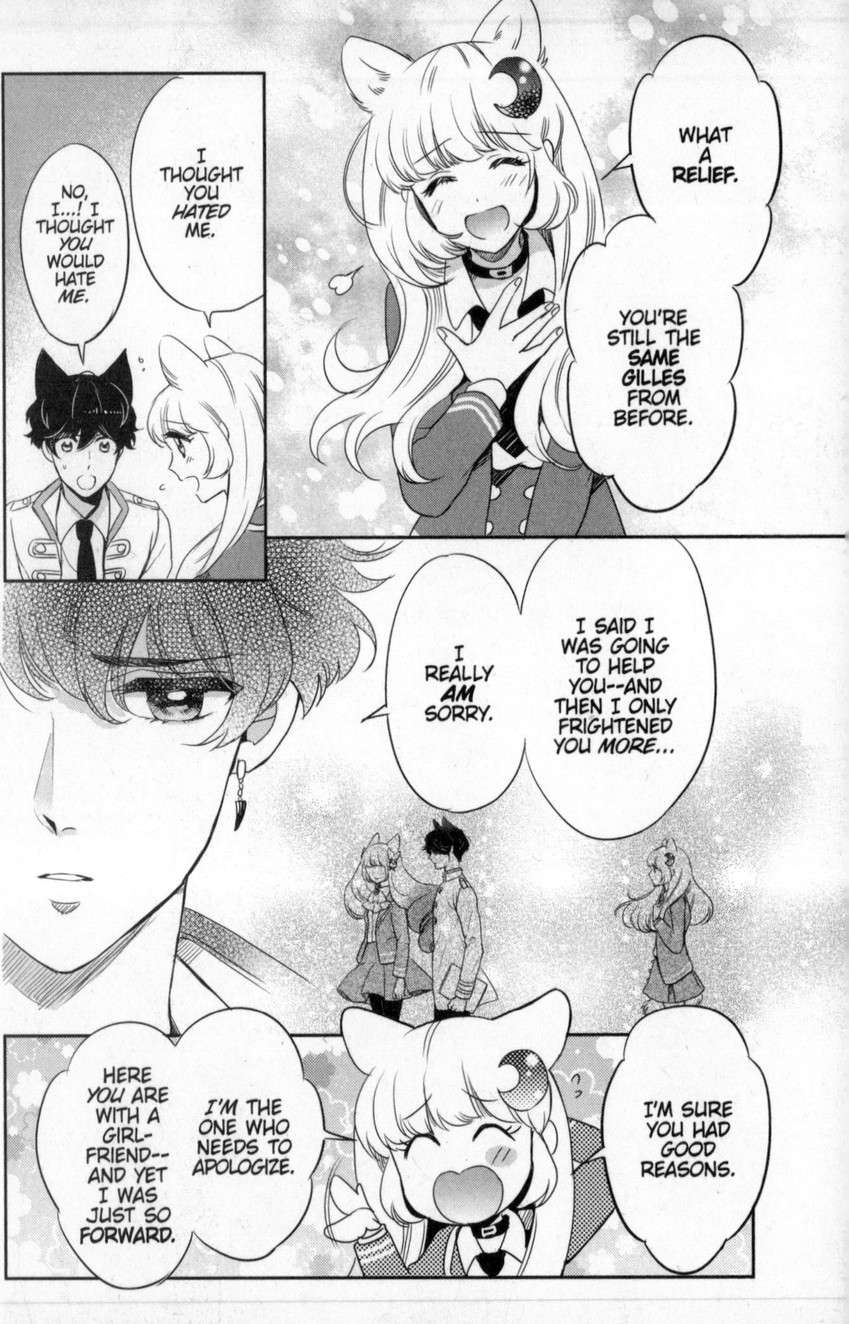
WHAT A RELIEF.
YOU'RE STILL THE SAME GILLES FROM BEFORE.
I THOUGHT YOU HATED ME.
NO, I...! I THOUGHT YOU WOULD HATE ME.
I SAID I WAS GOING TO HELP YOU--AND THEN I ONLY FRIGHTENED YOU MORE...
I REALLY AM SORRY.
I'M SURE YOU HAD GOOD REASONS.
I'M THE ONE WHO NEEDS TO APOLOGIZE.
HERE YOU ARE WITH A GIRL-FRIEND--AND YET I WAS JUST SO FORWARD.

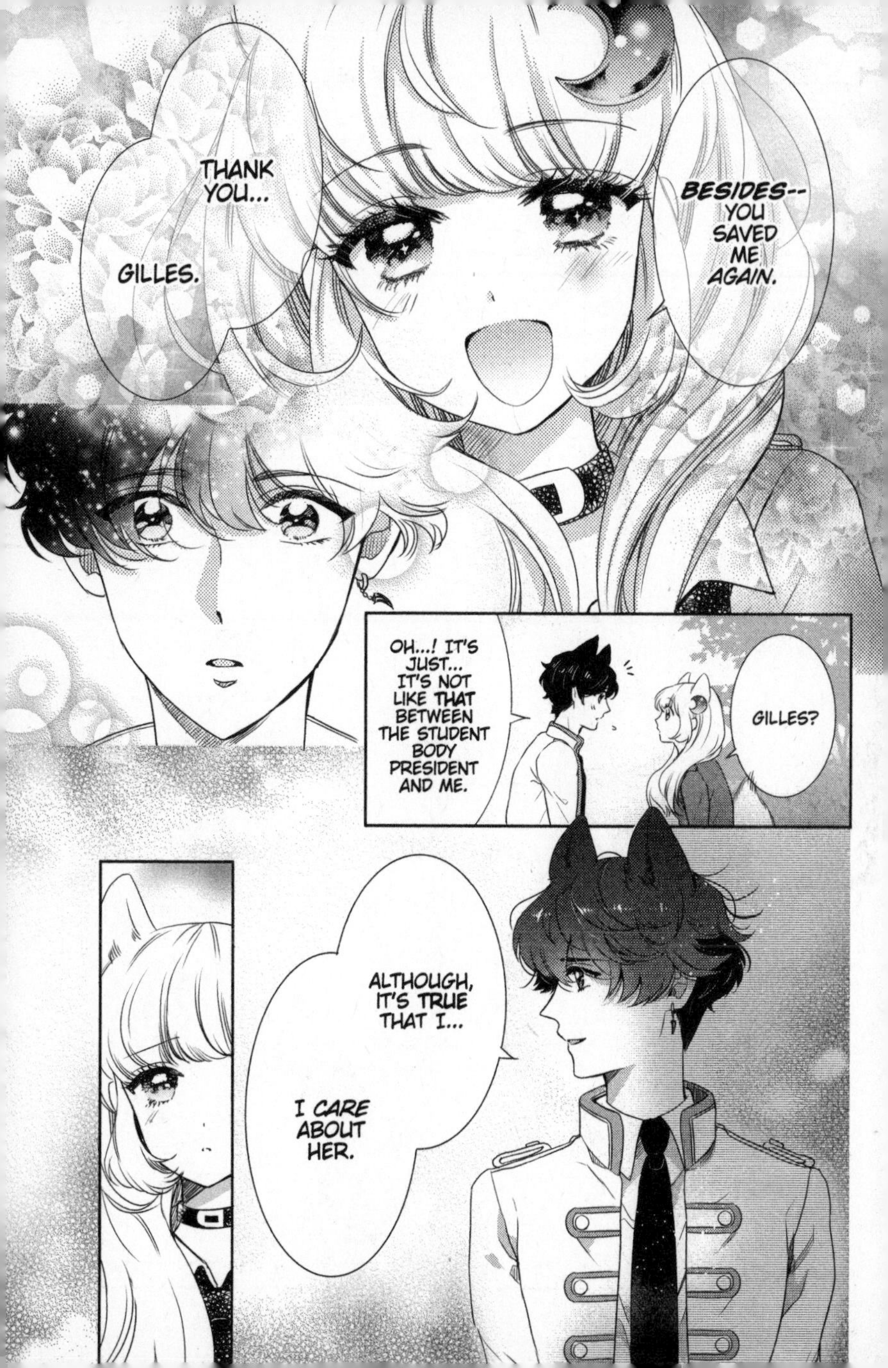
THANK YOU... GILLES.
BESIDES-- YOU SAVED ME AGAIN.
GILLES?
OH...! IT'S JUST... IT'S NOT LIKE THAT BETWEEN THE STUDENT BODY PRESIDENT AND ME.
ALTHOUGH, IT'S TRUE THAT I...
I CARE ABOUT HER.

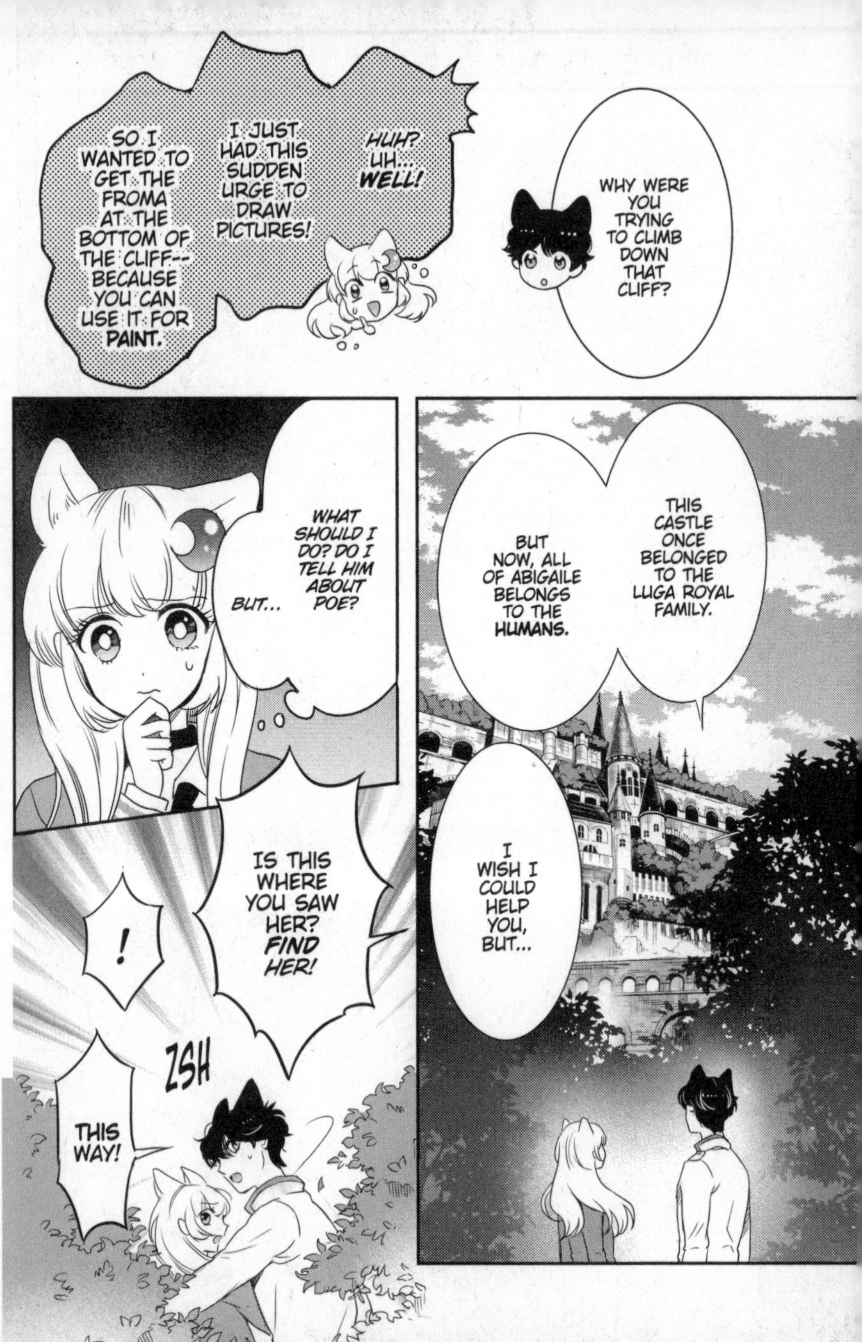

WHY WERE YOU TRYING TO CLIMB DOWN THAT CLIFF?
HUH? UH... WELL!
I JUST HAD THIS SUDDEN URGE TO DRAW PICTURES!
SO I WANTED TO GET THE FROMA AT THE BOTTOM OF THE CLIFF-- BECAUSE YOU CAN USE IT FOR PAINT.
THIS CASTLE ONCE BELONGED TO THE LUGA ROYAL FAMILY.
BUT NOW, ALL OF ABIGAILE BELONGS TO THE HUMANS.
I WISH I COULD HELP YOU, BUT...
WHAT SHOULD I DO? DO I TELL HIM ABOUT POE?
BUT...
IS THIS WHERE YOU SAW HER? FIND HER!
!
ZSH
THIS WAY!

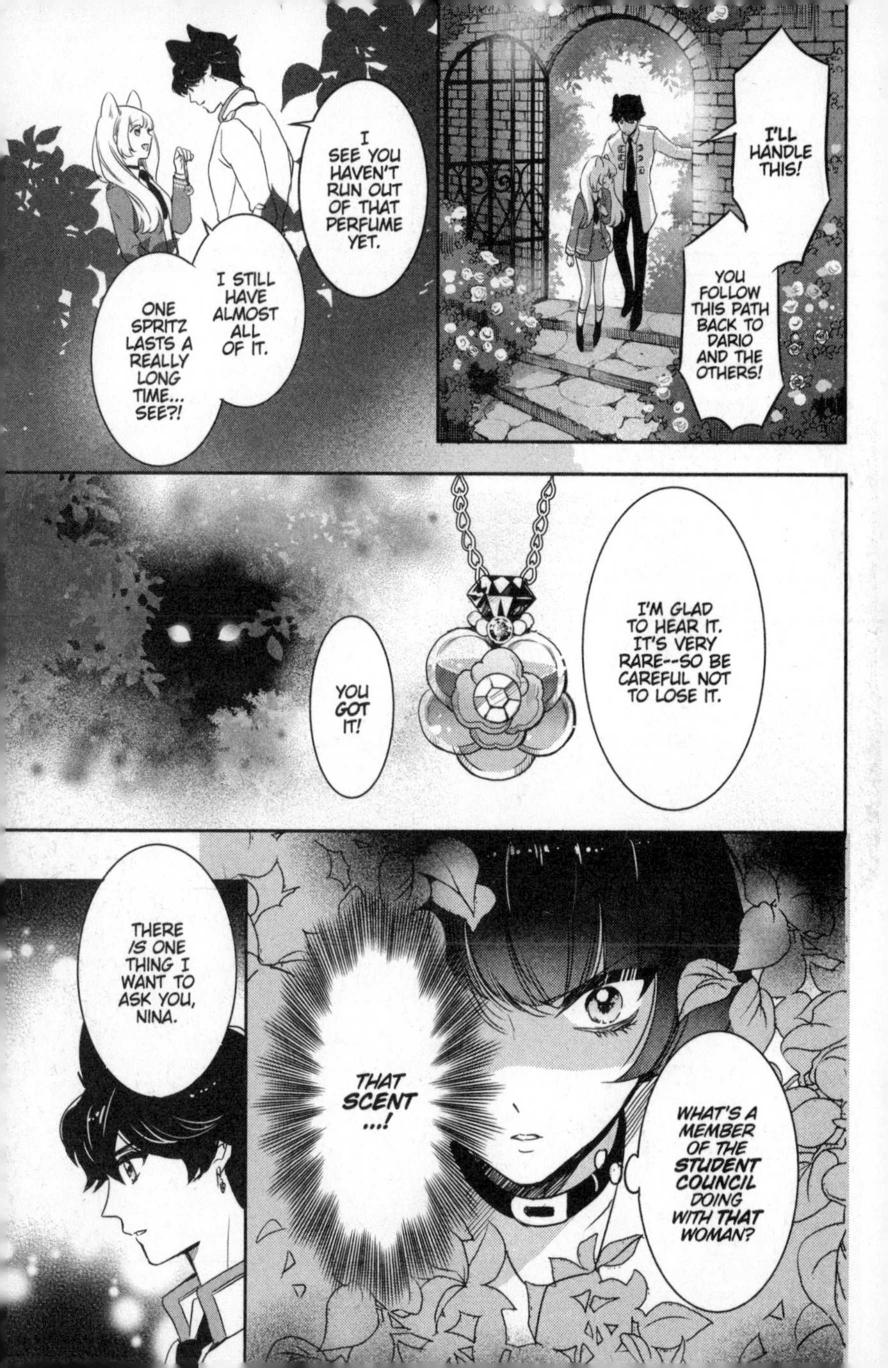
I'LL HANDLE THIS!
YOU FOLLOW THIS PATH BACK TO DARIO AND THE OTHERS!
I SEE YOU HAVEN'T RUN OUT OF THAT PERFUME YET.
I STILL HAVE ALMOST ALL OF IT.
ONE SPRITZ LASTS A REALLY LONG TIME... SEE?!
I'M GLAD TO HEAR IT. IT'S VERY RARE--SO BE CAREFUL NOT TO LOSE IT.
YOU GOT IT!
WHAT'S A MEMBER OF THE STUDENT COUNCIL DOING WITH THAT WOMAN?
THAT SCENT ...!
THERE IS ONE THING I WANT TO ASK YOU, NINA.

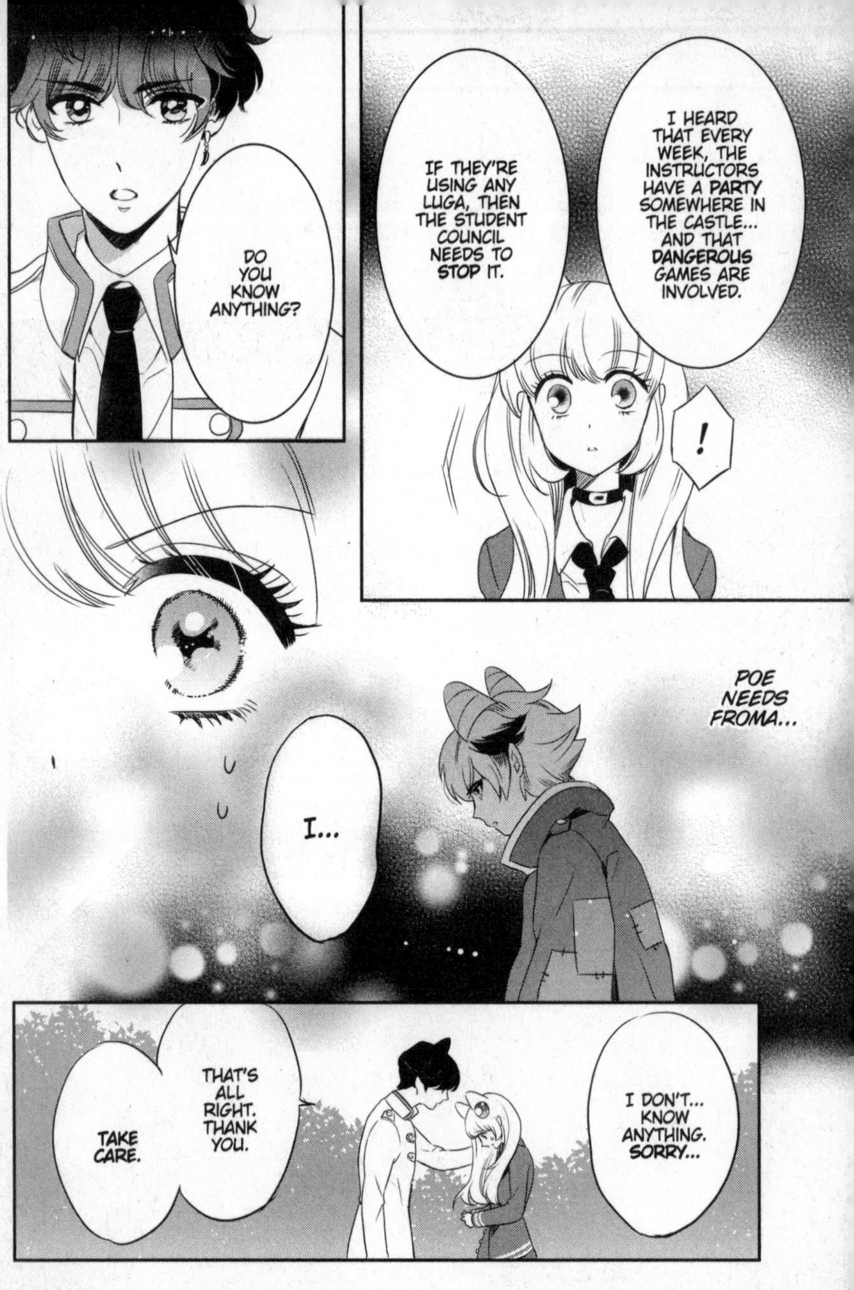

I HEARD THAT EVERY WEEK, THE INSTRUCTORS HAVE A PARTY SOMEWHERE IN THE CASTLE... AND THAT DANGEROUS GAMES ARE INVOLVED.
IF THEY'RE USING ANY LUGA, THEN THE STUDENT COUNCIL NEEDS TO STOP IT.
!
DO YOU KNOW ANYTHING?
POE NEEDS FROMA...
I...
I DON'T... KNOW ANYTHING. SORRY...
THAT'S ALL RIGHT. THANK YOU.
TAKE CARE.

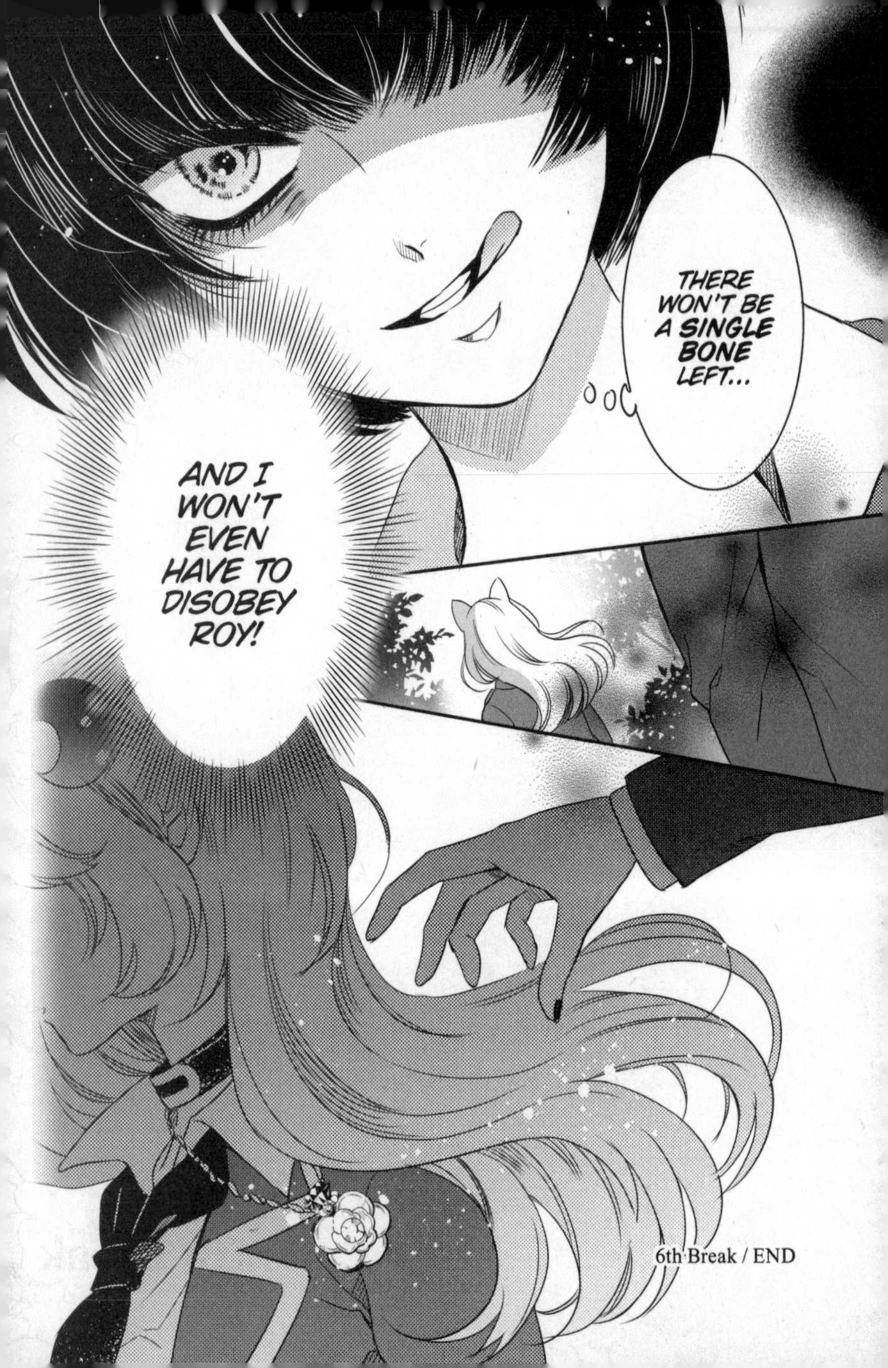
THERE WON'T BE A SINGLE BONE LEFT...
AND I WON'T EVEN HAVE TO DISOBEY ROY!
6th Break / END

7th Break

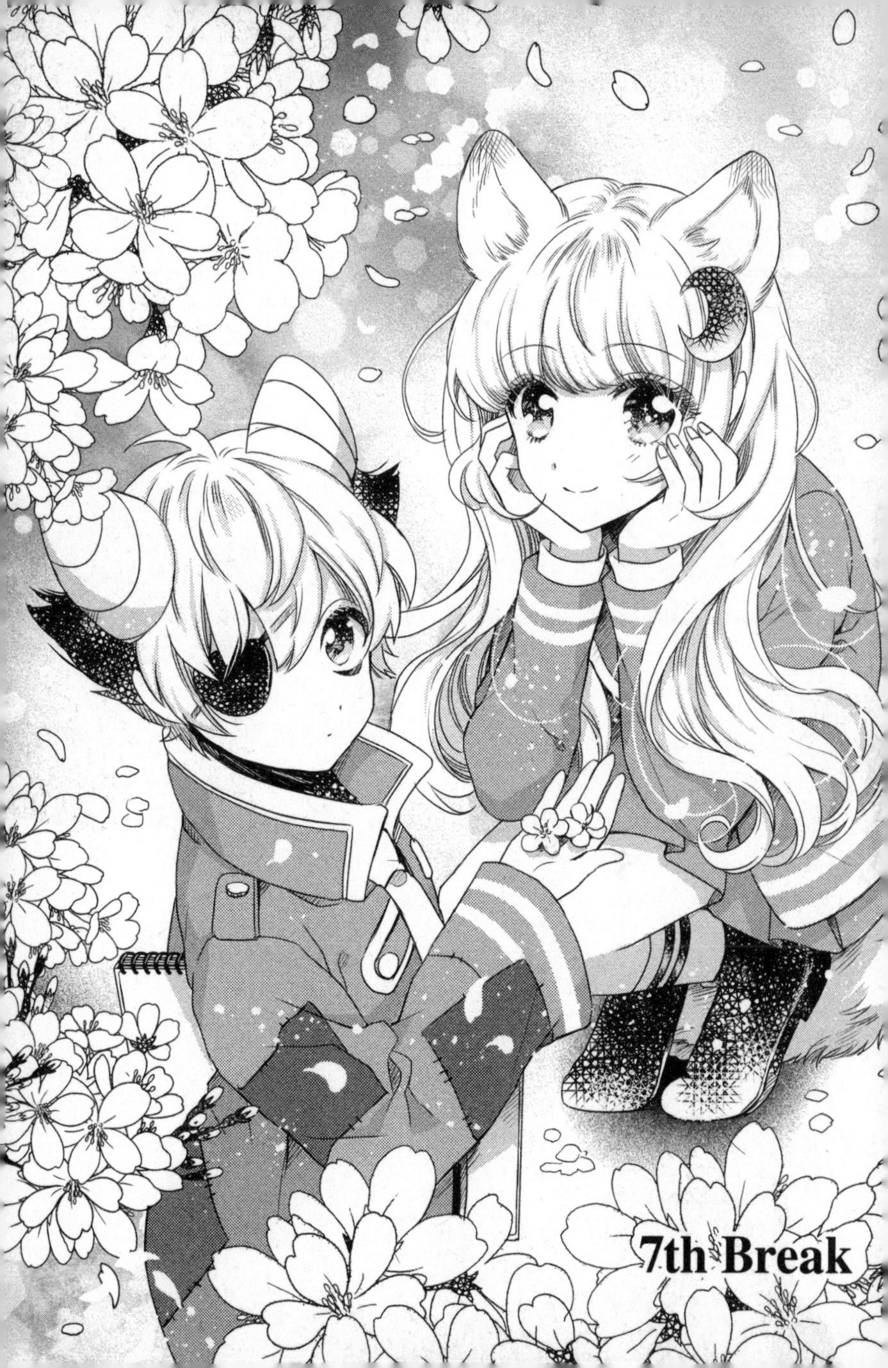

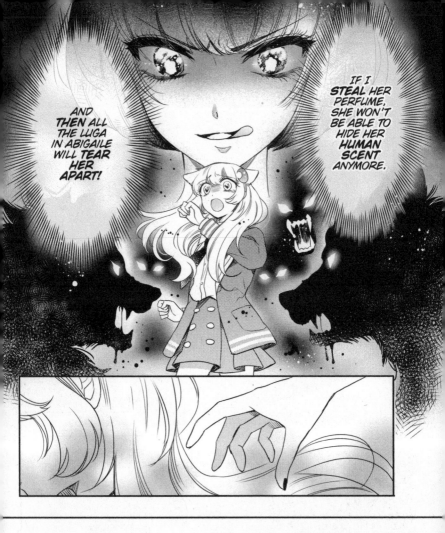

IF I STEAL HER PERFUME, SHE WON'T BE ABLE TO HIDE HER HUMAN SCENT ANYMORE.
AND THEN ALL THE LUGA IN ABIGAILE WILL TEAR HER APART!

The collar that all students are required to wear. It cannot be removed by the wearer and comes equipped with a homing device, so that any luga who escapes the castle can be located immediately.

If the wearer does anything to cause trouble, this flashes red.
There's heavy-duty iron under the leather.
Beeps alert the wearer of events such as mealtime.
Each class is assigned a different collar color.

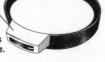

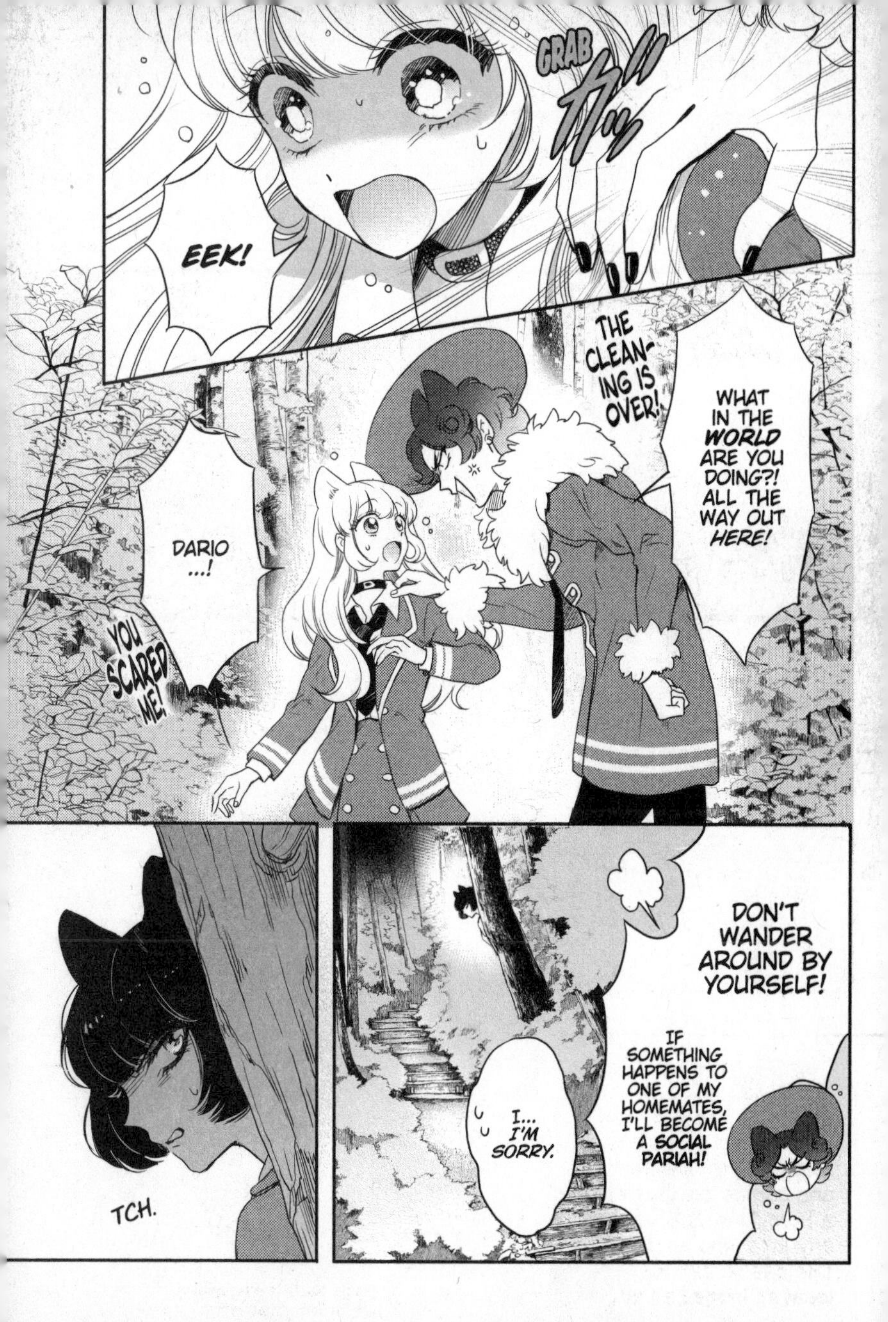
GRAB
EEK!
THE CLEANING IS OVER!
WHAT IN THE WORLD ARE YOU DOING?! ALL THE WAY OUT HERE!
DARIO ...!
YOU SCARED ME!
DON'T WANDER AROUND BY YOURSELF!
IF SOMETHING HAPPENS TO ONE OF MY HOMEMATES, I'LL BECOME A SOCIAL PARIAH!
I... I'M SORRY.
TCH.

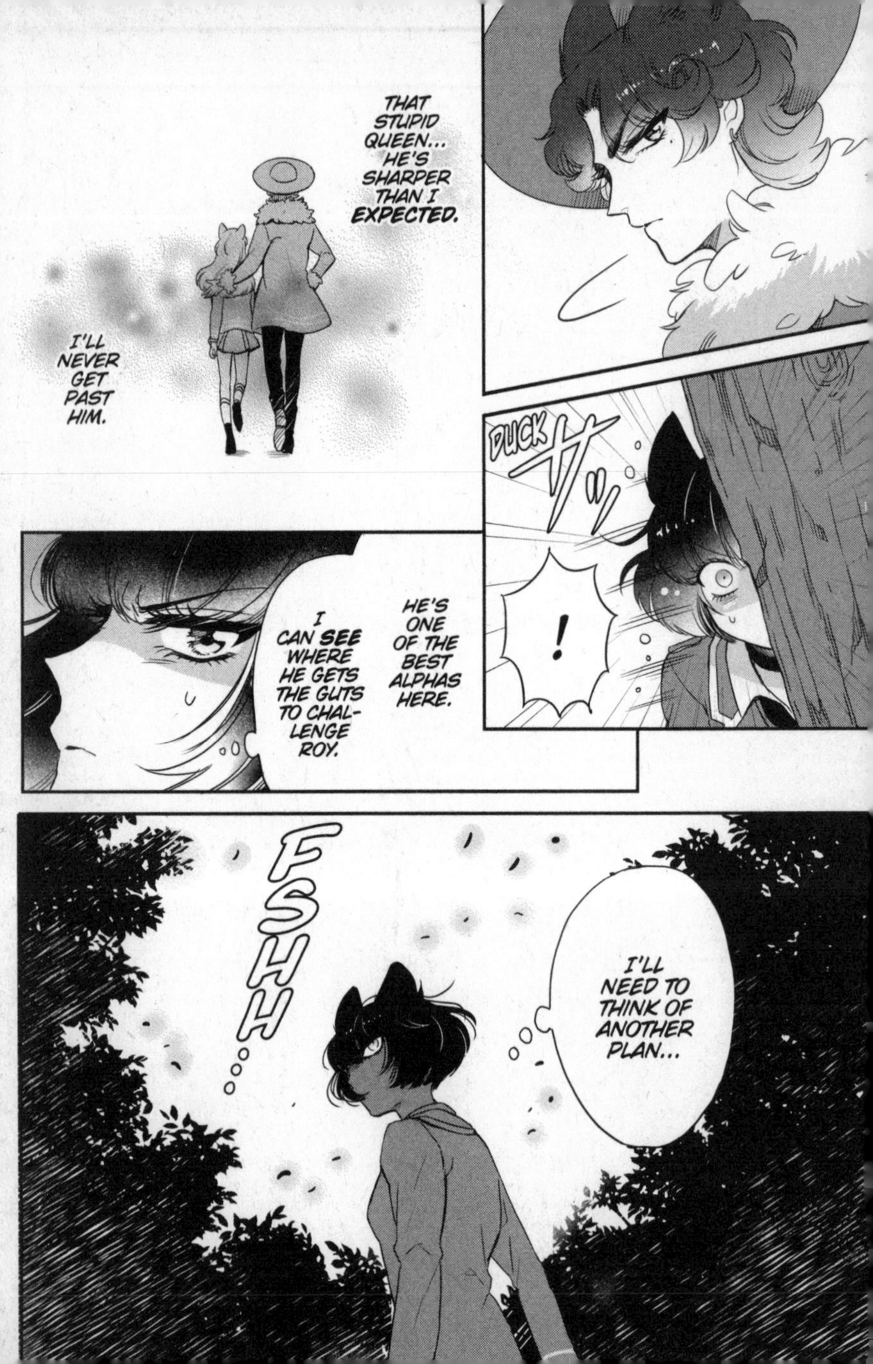
THAT STUPID QUEEN... HE'S SHARPER THAN I EXPECTED.
I'LL NEVER GET PAST HIM.
DUCK
!
HE'S ONE OF THE BEST ALPHAS HERE.
I CAN SEE WHERE HE GETS THE GUTS TO CHAL-LENGE ROY.
I'LL NEED TO THINK OF ANOTHER PLAN...
FSHH

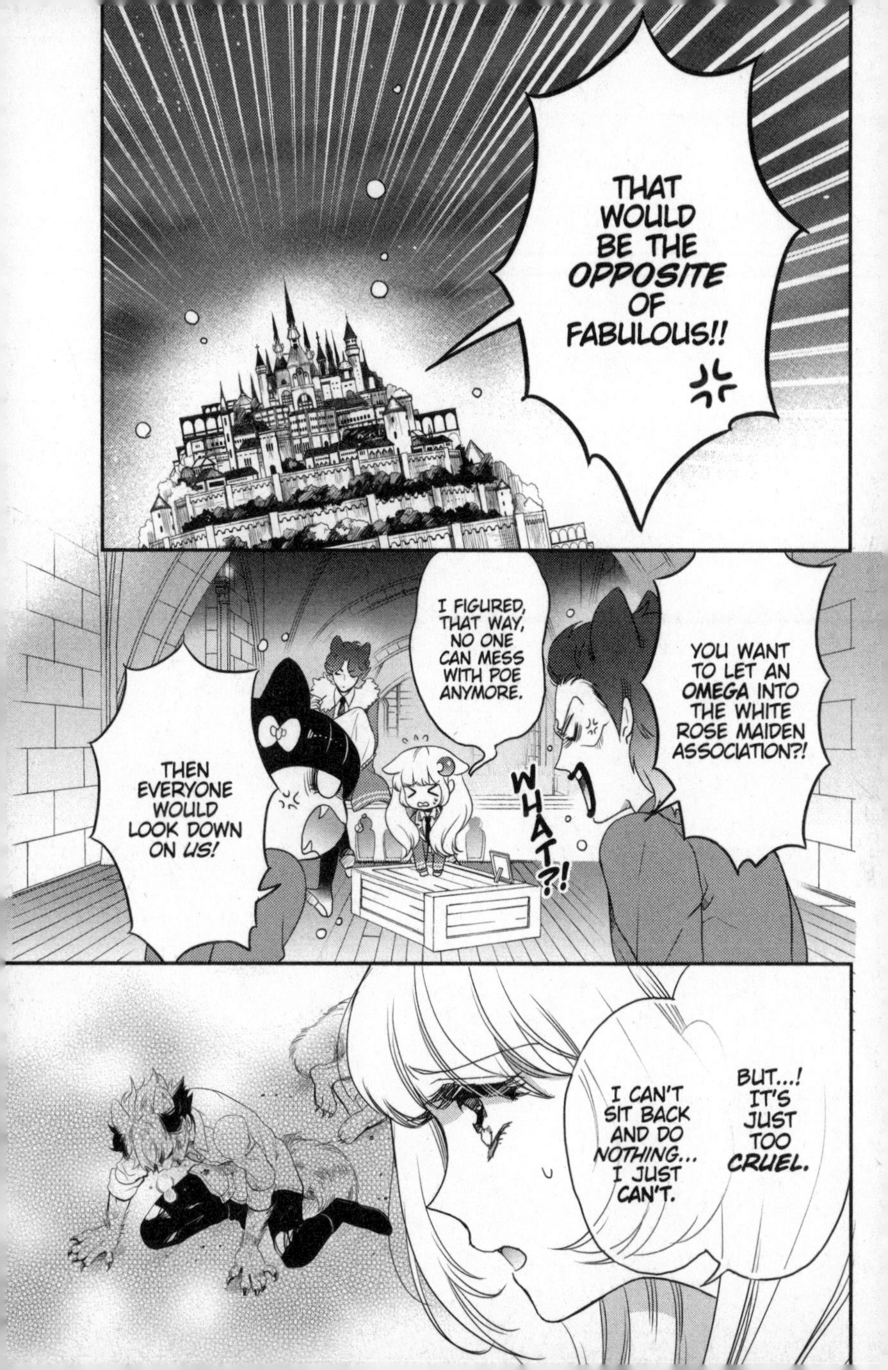
THAT WOULD BE THE OPPOSITE OF FABULOUS!!
YOU WANT TO LET AN OMEGA INTO THE WHITE ROSE MAIDEN ASSOCIATION?!
WHAT?!
I FIGURED, THAT WAY, NO ONE CAN MESS WITH POE ANYMORE.
THEN EVERYONE WOULD LOOK DOWN ON US!
BUT...! IT'S JUST TOO CRUEL.
I CAN'T SIT BACK AND DO NOTHING... I JUST CAN'T.

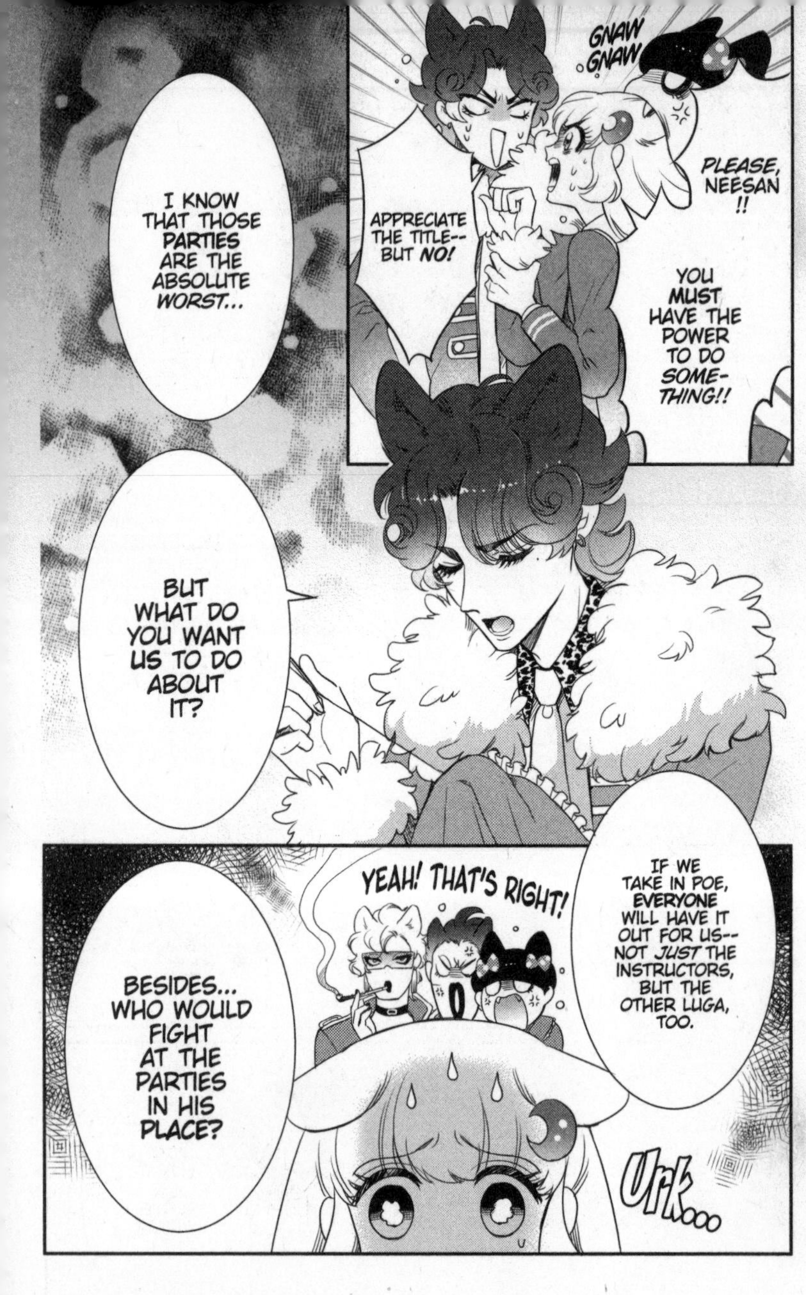
GNAW GNAW
PLEASE, NEESAN!!
YOU MUST HAVE THE POWER TO DO SOMETHING!!
APPRECIATE THE TITLE-- BUT NO!
I KNOW THAT THOSE PARTIES ARE THE ABSOLUTE WORST...
BUT WHAT DO YOU WANT US TO DO ABOUT IT?
IF WE TAKE IN POE, EVERYONE WILL HAVE IT OUT FOR US-- NOT JUST THE INSTRUCTORS, BUT THE OTHER LUGA, TOO.
YEAH! THAT'S RIGHT!
BESIDES... WHO WOULD FIGHT AT THE PARTIES IN HIS PLACE?
Urk...

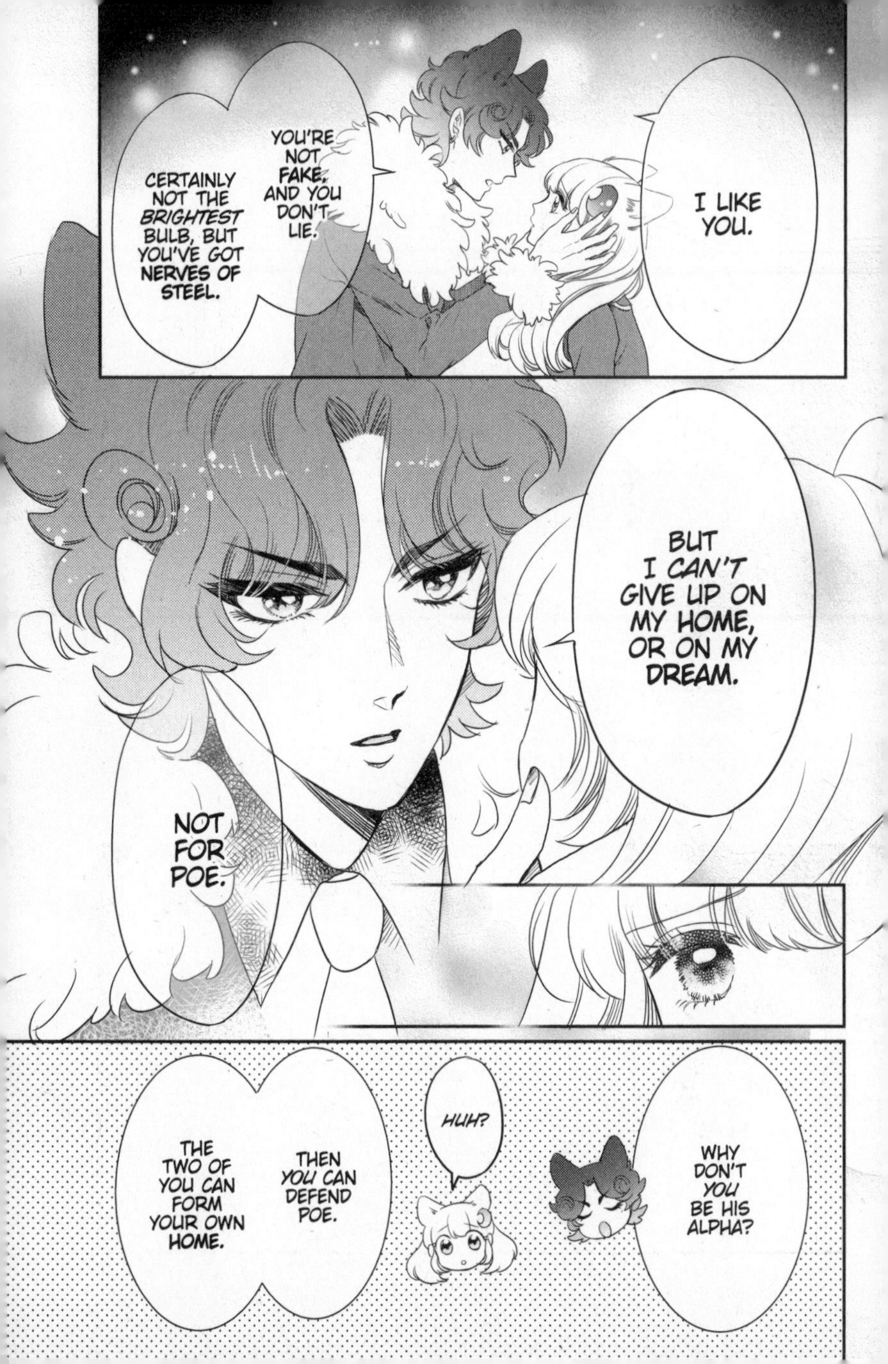
I LIKE YOU.
YOU'RE NOT FAKE, AND YOU DON'T LIE.
CERTAINLY NOT THE *BRIGHTEST* BULB, BUT YOU'VE GOT NERVES OF STEEL.
BUT I *CAN'T* GIVE UP ON MY HOME, OR ON MY DREAM.
NOT FOR POE.
WHY DON'T *YOU* BE HIS ALPHA?
HUH?
THEN *YOU* CAN DEFEND POE.
THE TWO OF YOU CAN FORM YOUR OWN HOME.

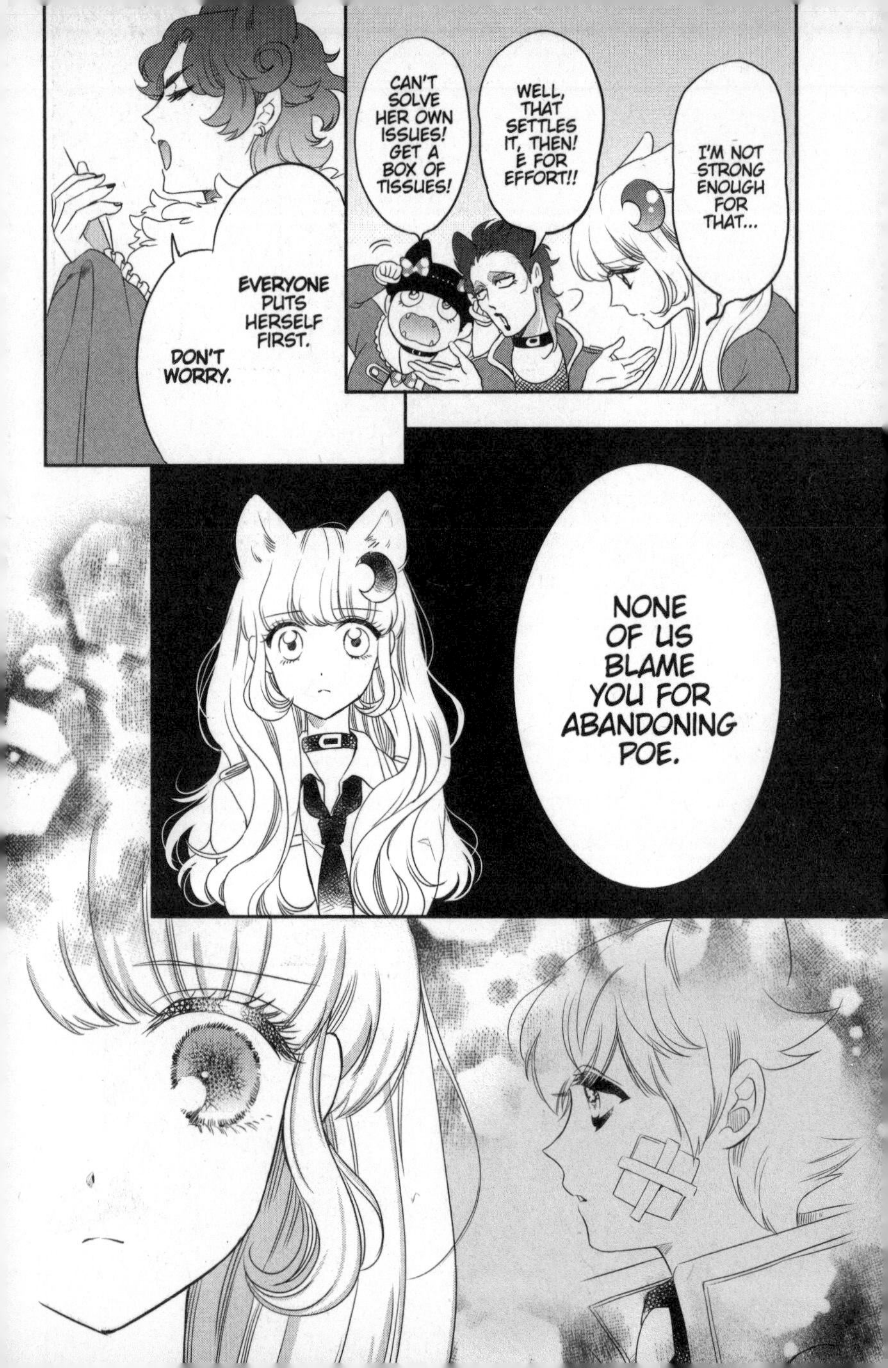
I'M NOT STRONG ENOUGH FOR THAT...
WELL, THAT SETTLES IT, THEN! E FOR EFFORT!!
CAN'T SOLVE HER OWN ISSUES! GET A BOX OF TISSUES!
EVERYONE PUTS HERSELF FIRST.
DON'T WORRY.
NONE OF US BLAME YOU FOR ABANDONING POE.

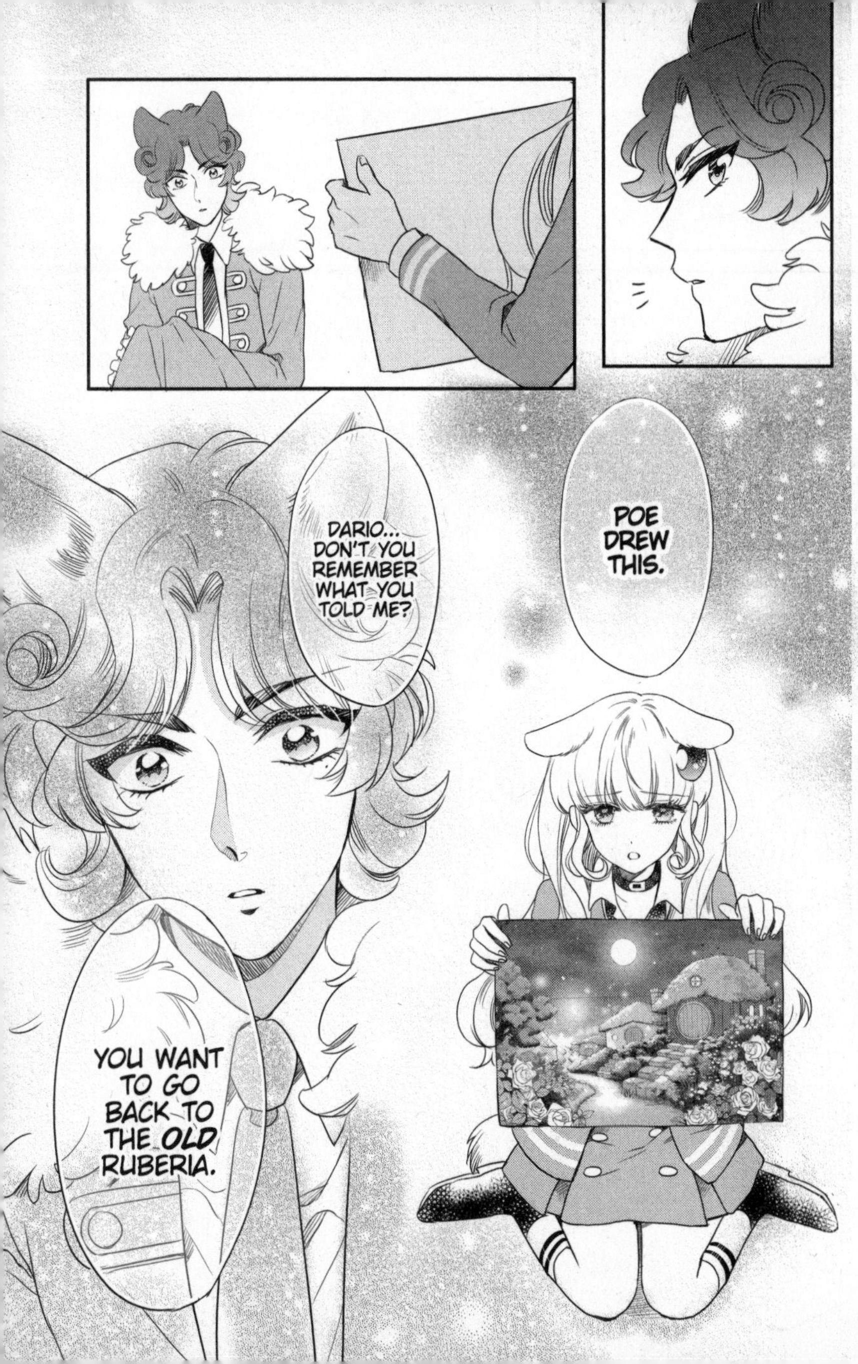
POE DREW THIS.
DARIO... DON'T YOU REMEMBER WHAT YOU TOLD ME?
YOU WANT TO GO BACK TO THE *OLD* RUBERIA.

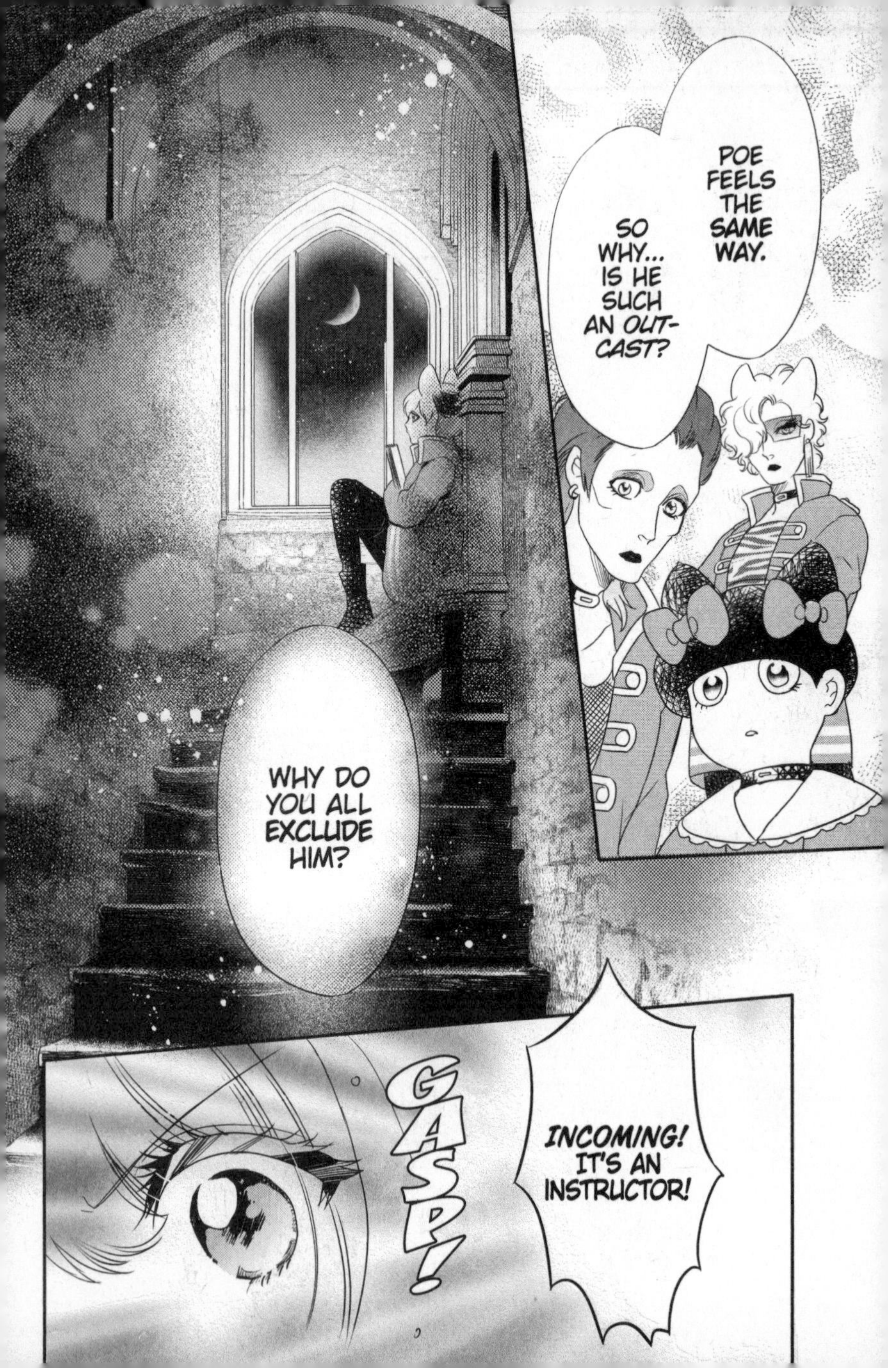
POE FEELS THE SAME WAY.
SO WHY... IS HE SUCH AN *OUT-CAST?*
WHY DO YOU ALL EXCLUDE HIM?
INCOMING! IT'S AN INSTRUCTOR!
GASP!

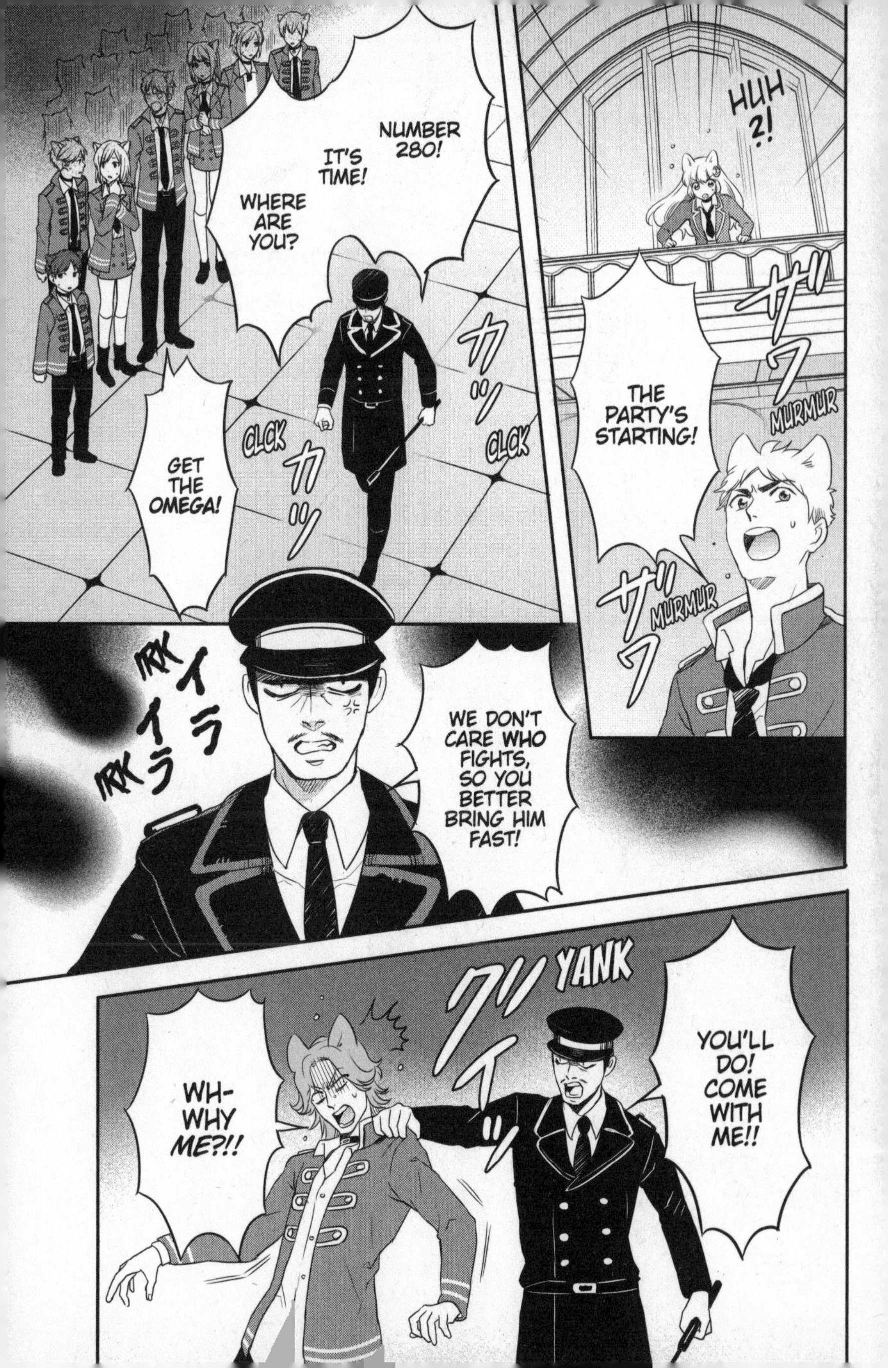
HUH ?!
ザワ
MURMUR
THE PARTY'S STARTING!
ザワ
MURMUR
NUMBER 280!
IT'S TIME!
WHERE ARE YOU?
カッ
CLCK
カッ
CLCK
GET THE OMEGA!
イラ
IRK
イラ
IRK
WE DON'T CARE WHO FIGHTS, SO YOU BETTER BRING HIM FAST!
グイ
YANK
YOU'LL DO! COME WITH ME!!
WH- WHY ME?!!

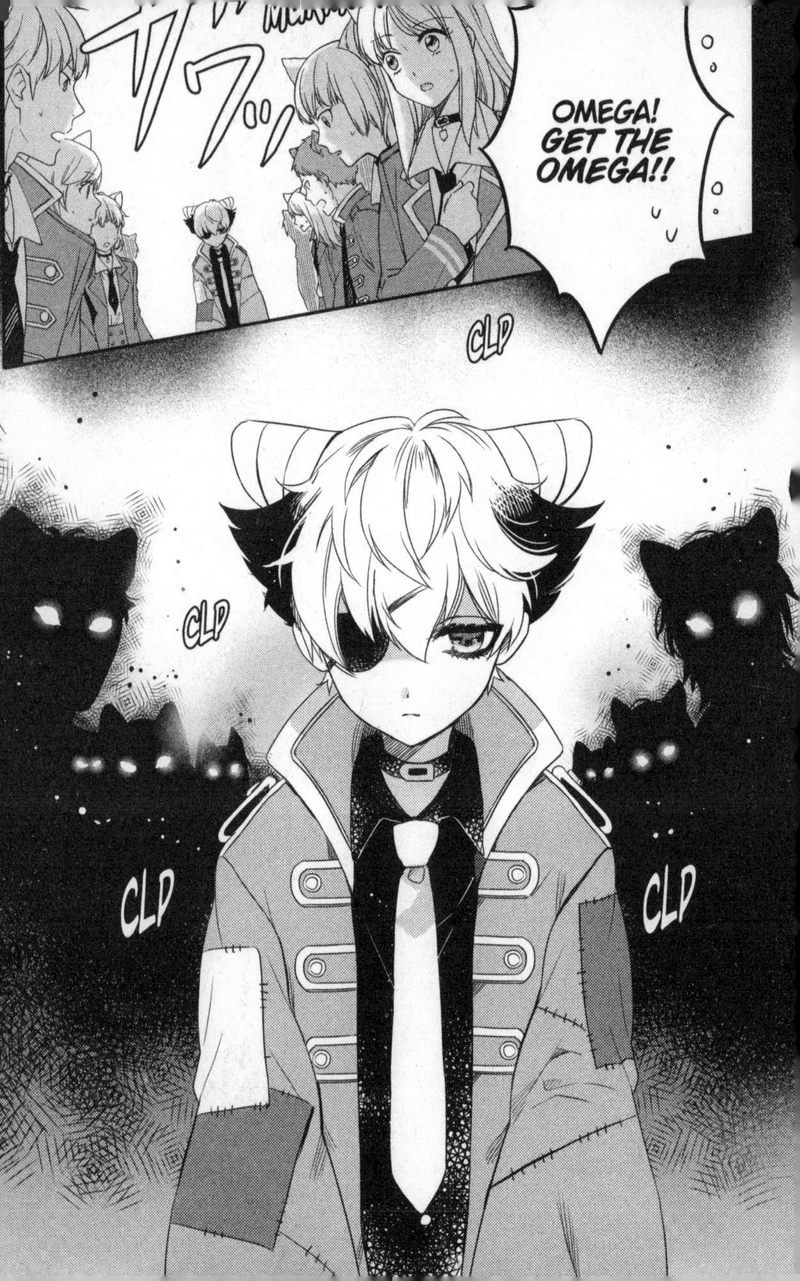
OMEGA! GET THE OMEGA!!
CLP
CLP
CLP
CLP

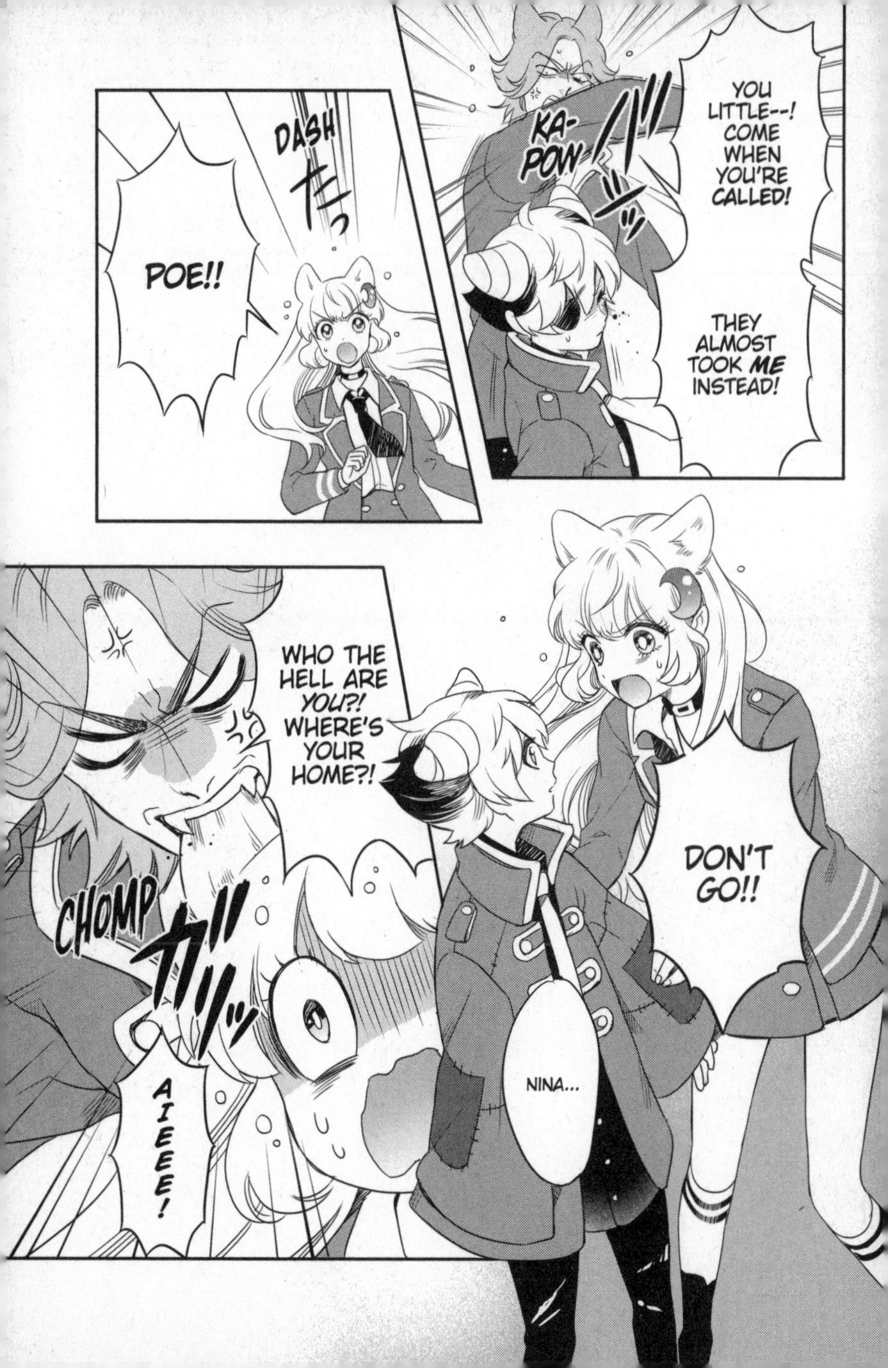
YOU LITTLE--! COME WHEN YOU'RE CALLED!
KA-POW
THEY ALMOST TOOK *ME* INSTEAD!
DASH
POE!!
DON'T GO!!
WHO THE HELL ARE *YOU*?! WHERE'S YOUR HOME?!
NINA...
CHOMP
AIEEE!

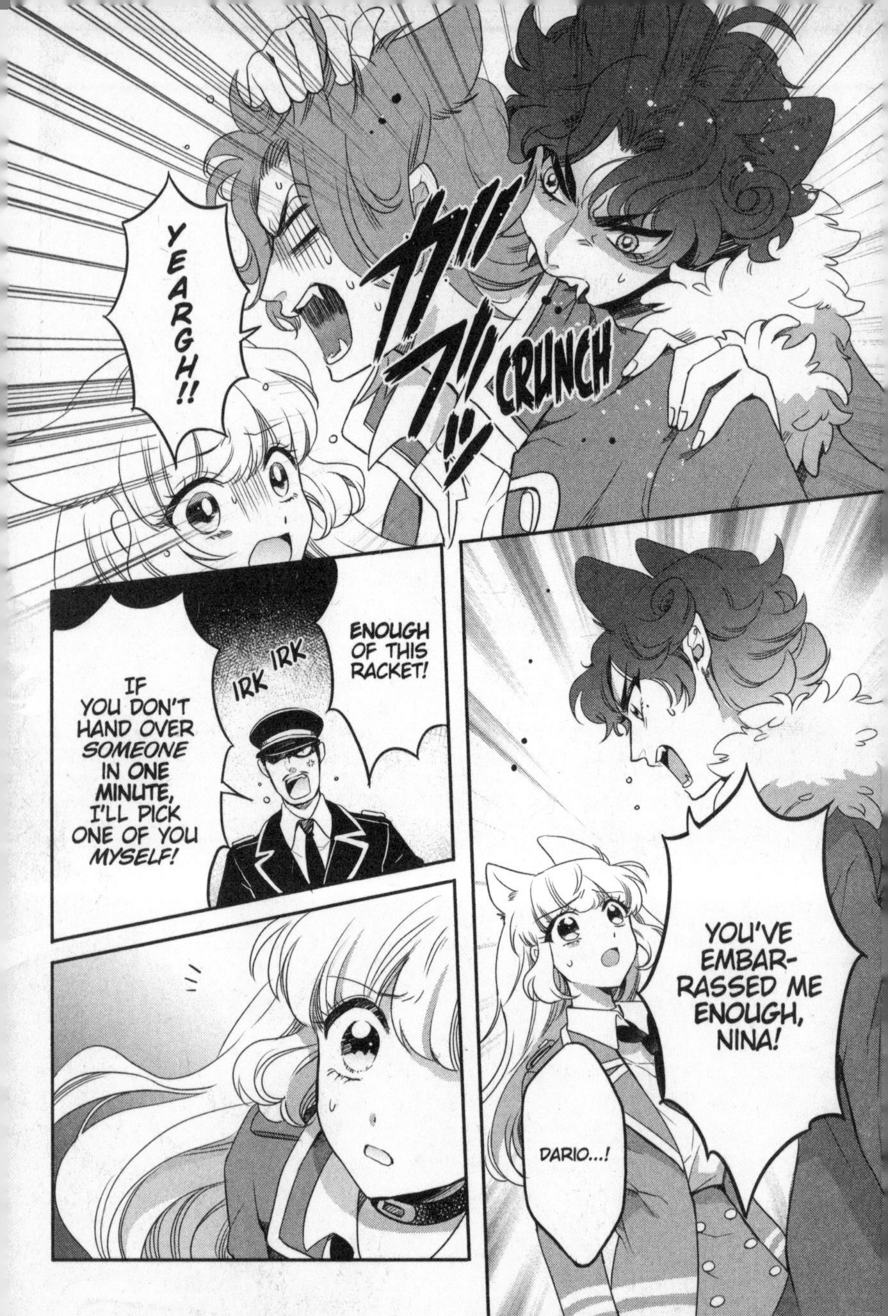
YEARGH!!
CRUNCH
YOU'VE EMBAR-RASSED ME ENOUGH, NINA!
DARIO...!
ENOUGH OF THIS RACKET!
IRK IRK
IF YOU DON'T HAND OVER SOMEONE IN ONE MINUTE, I'LL PICK ONE OF YOU MYSELF!

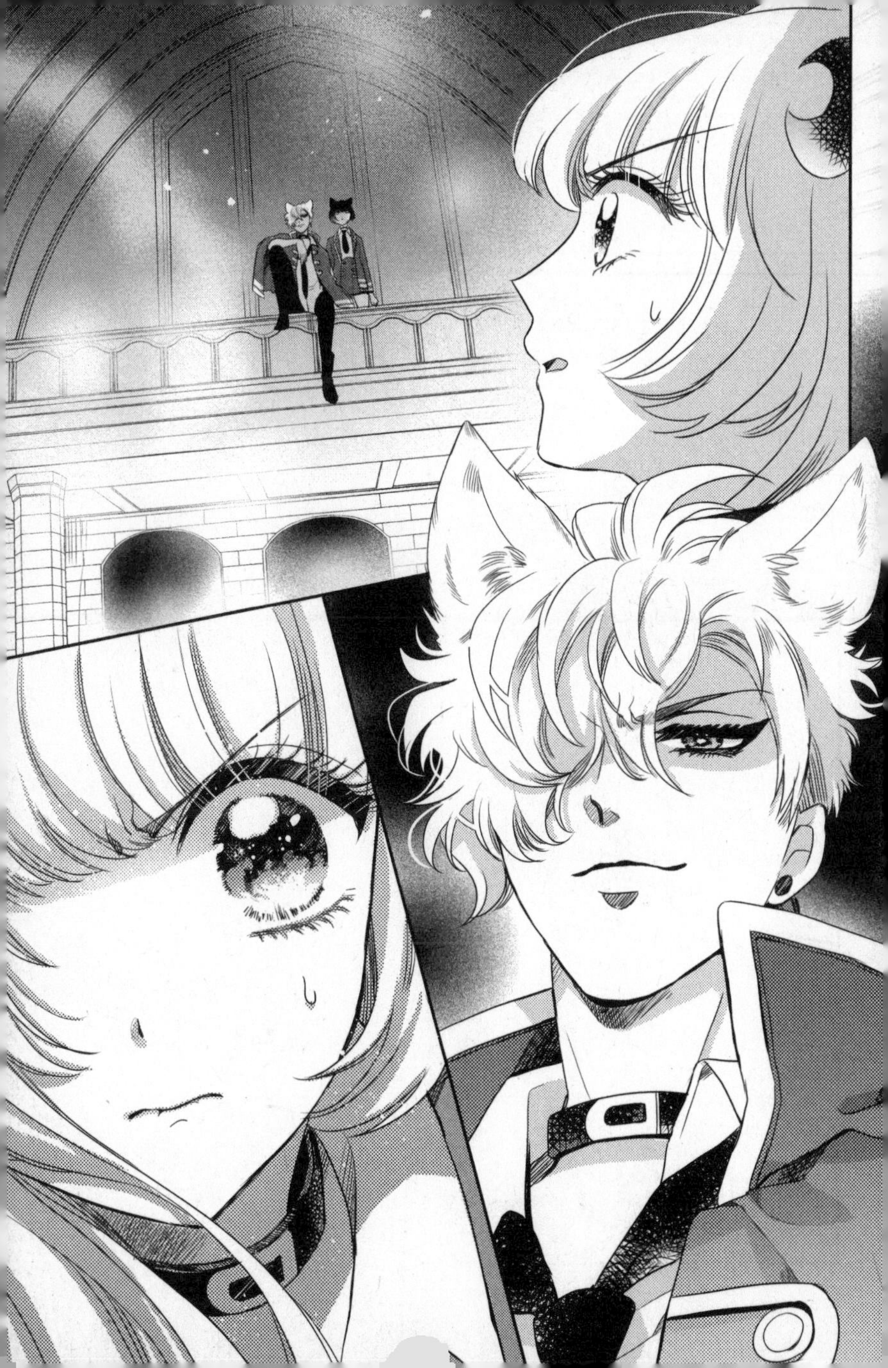

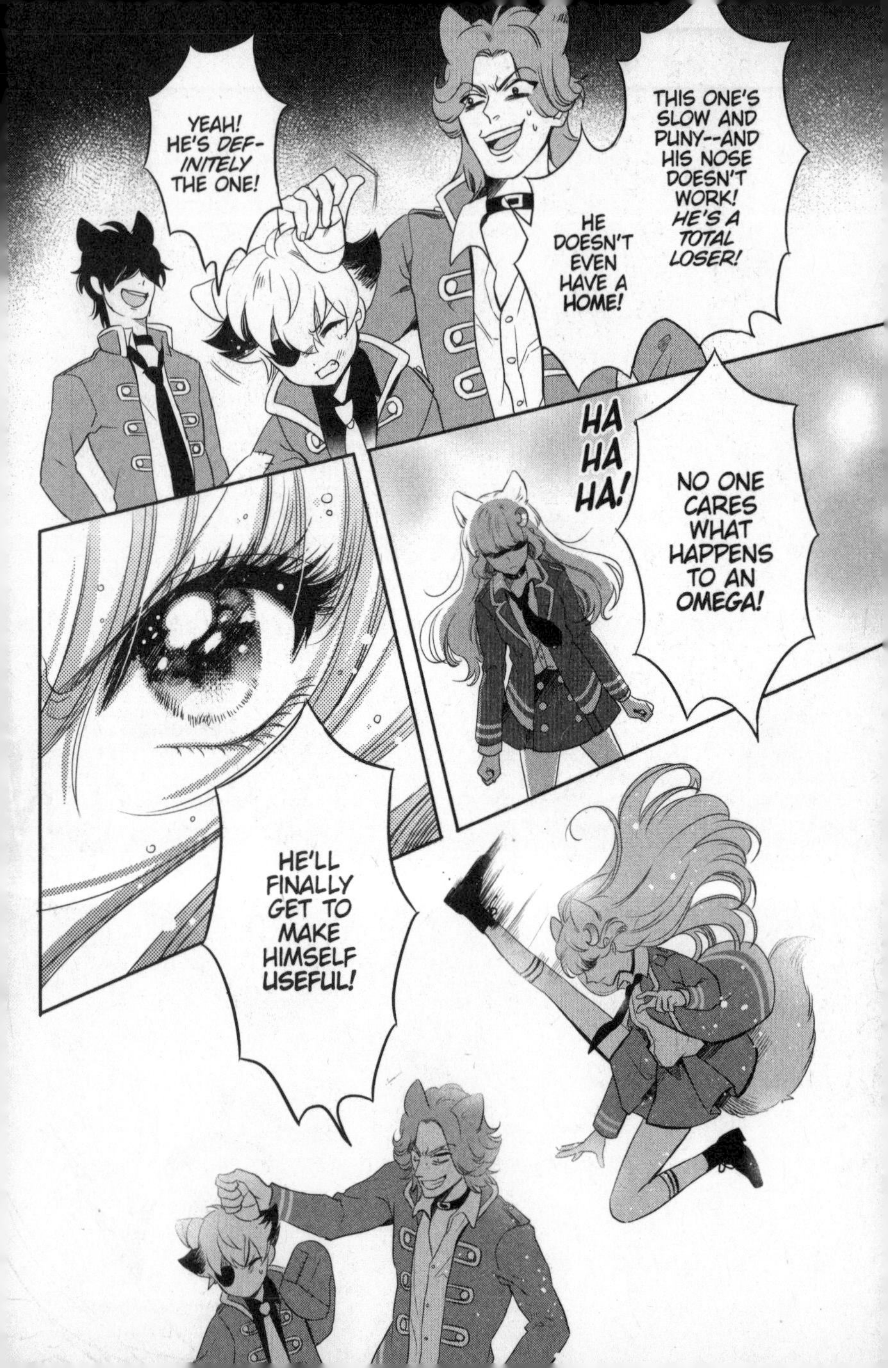
THIS ONE'S SLOW AND PUNY--AND HIS NOSE DOESN'T WORK! HE'S A TOTAL LOSER!
HE DOESN'T EVEN HAVE A HOME!
YEAH! HE'S DEF-INITELY THE ONE!
NO ONE CARES WHAT HAPPENS TO AN OMEGA!
HA HA HA!
HE'LL FINALLY GET TO MAKE HIMSELF USEFUL!

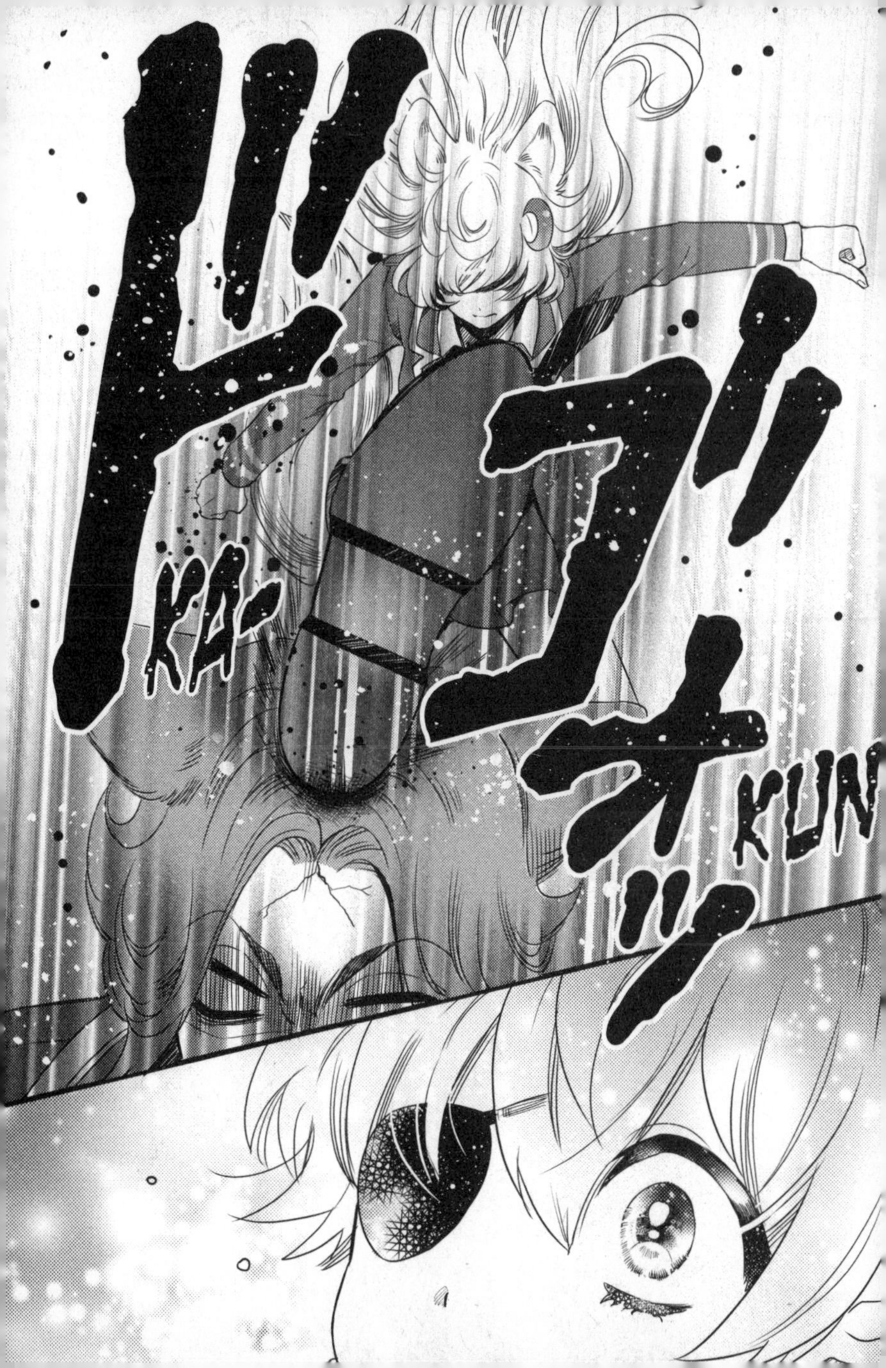
ドゴォッ
KA-
KUN

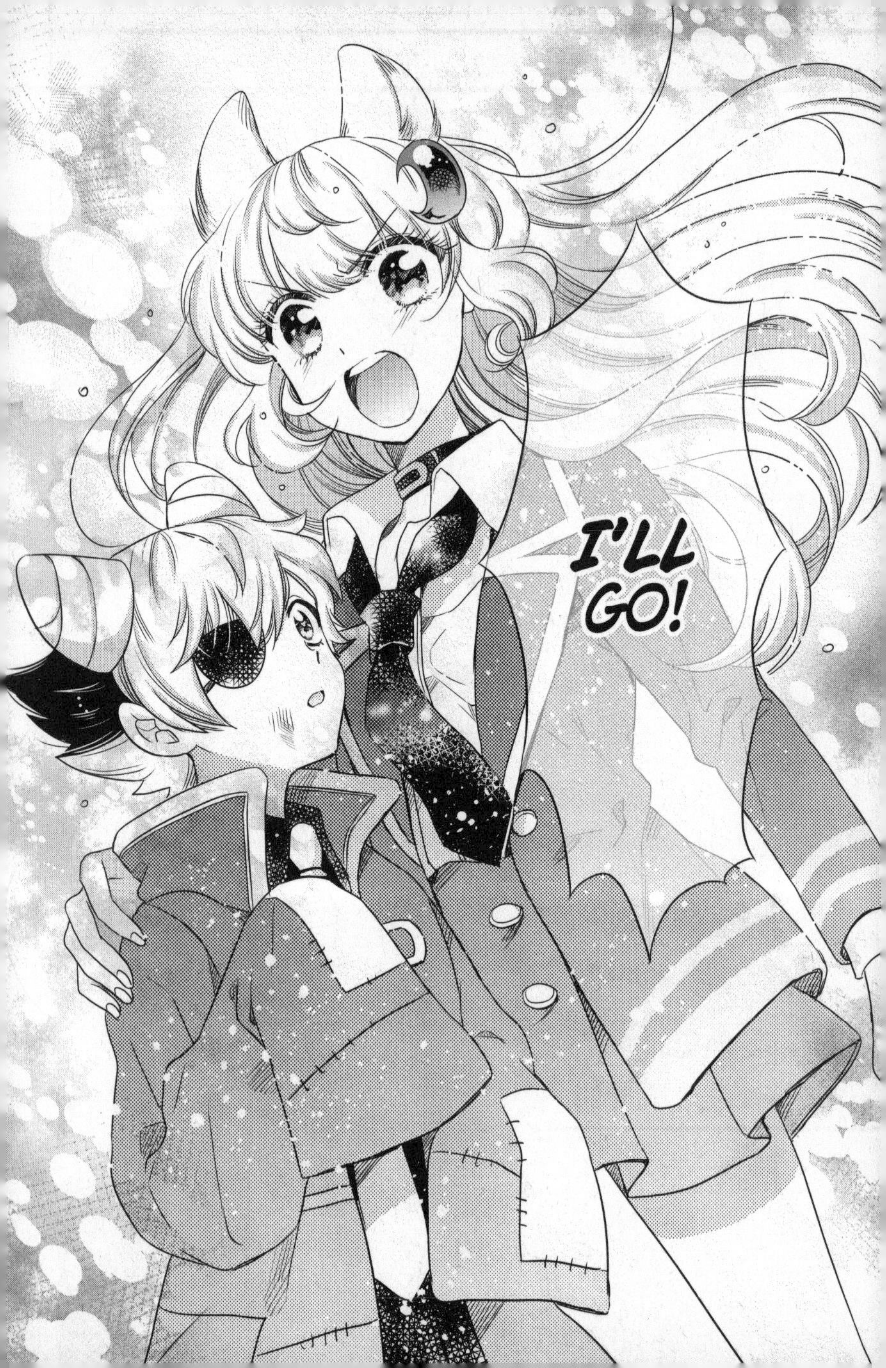
I'LL GO!

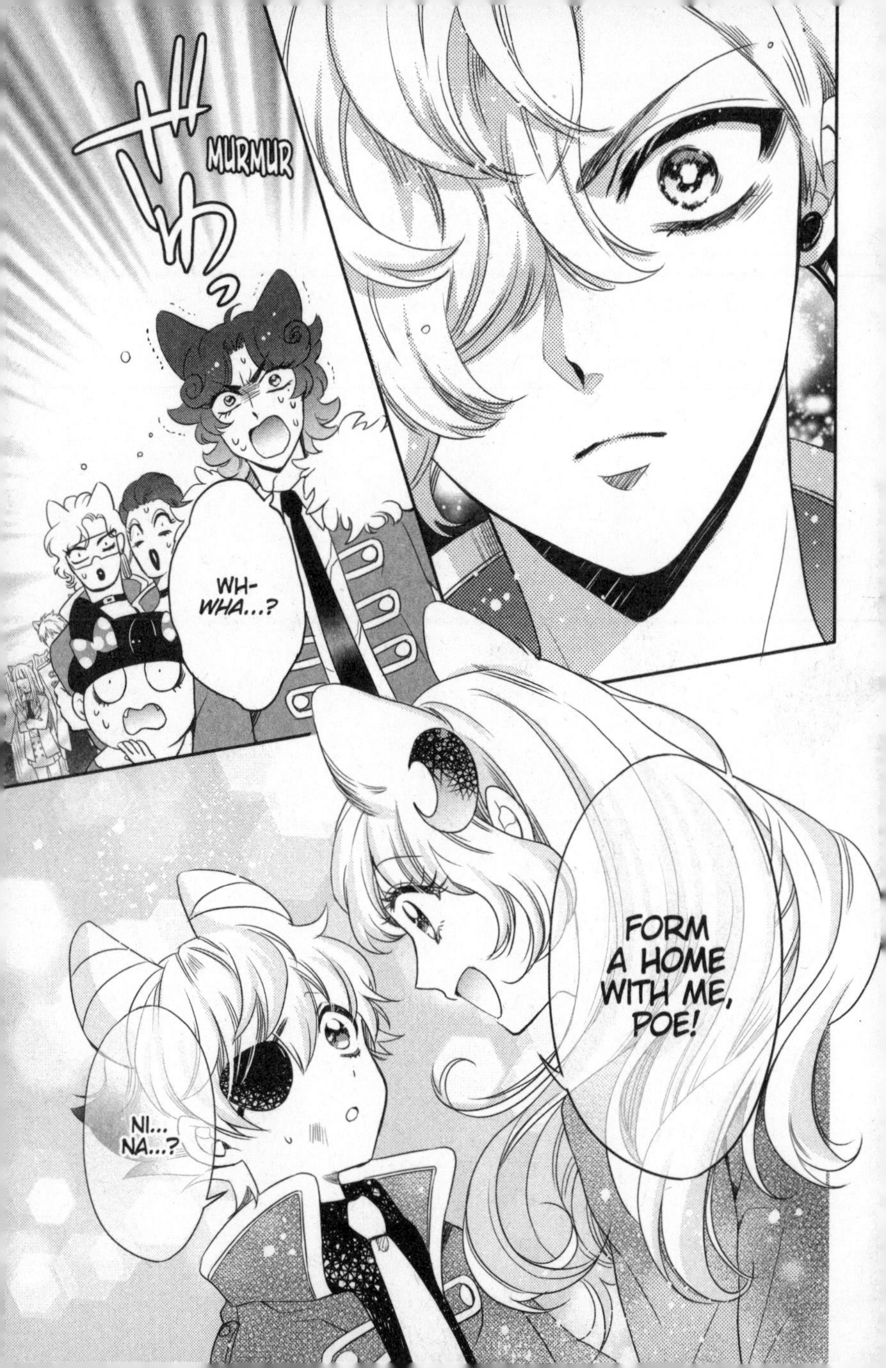
MURMUR
WH- WHA...?
FORM A HOME WITH ME, POE!
NI... NA...?

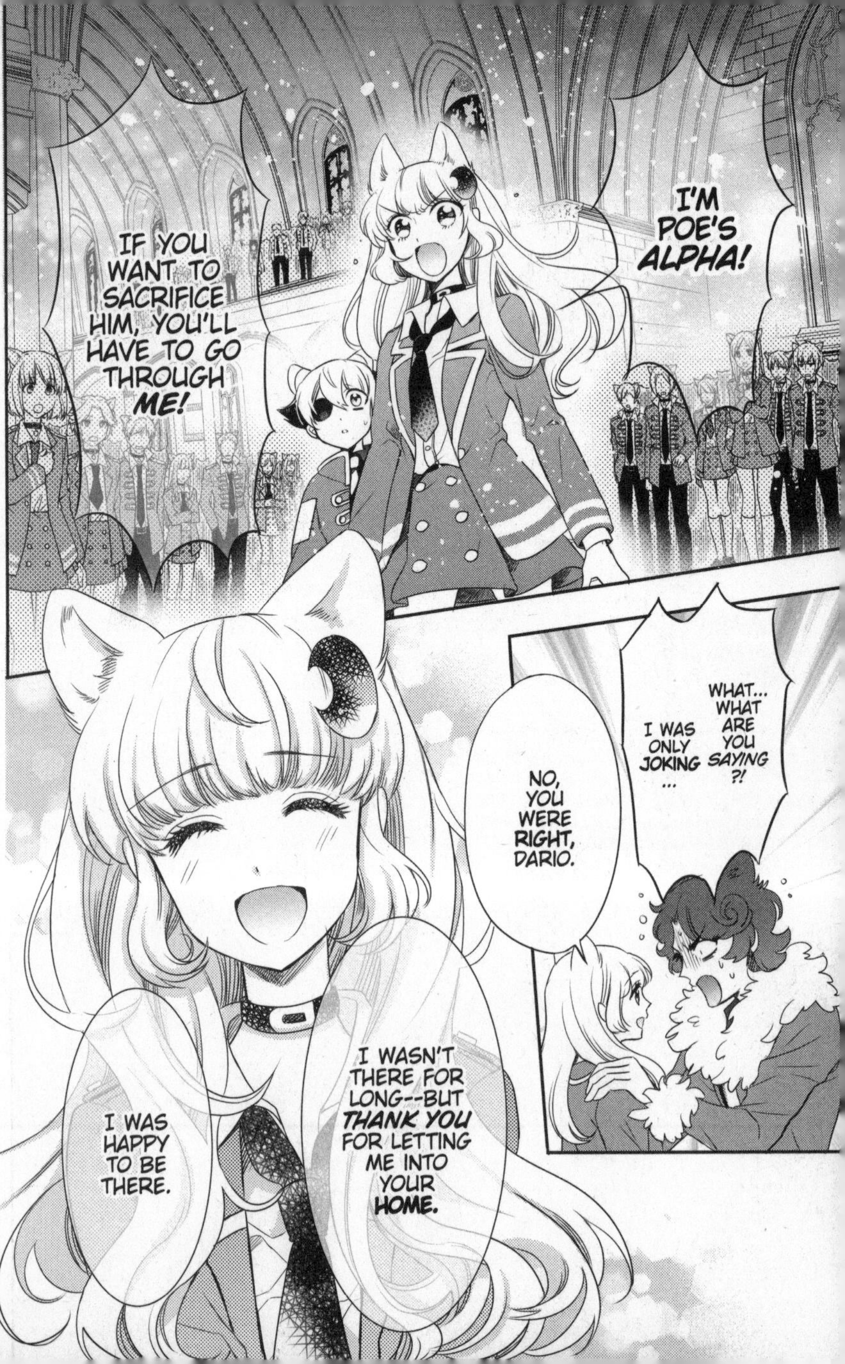
I'M POE'S ALPHA!
IF YOU WANT TO SACRIFICE HIM, YOU'LL HAVE TO GO THROUGH ME!
WHAT... WHAT ARE YOU SAYING?!
I WAS ONLY JOKING...
NO, YOU WERE RIGHT, DARIO.
I WASN'T THERE FOR LONG--BUT THANK YOU FOR LETTING ME INTO YOUR HOME.
I WAS HAPPY TO BE THERE.

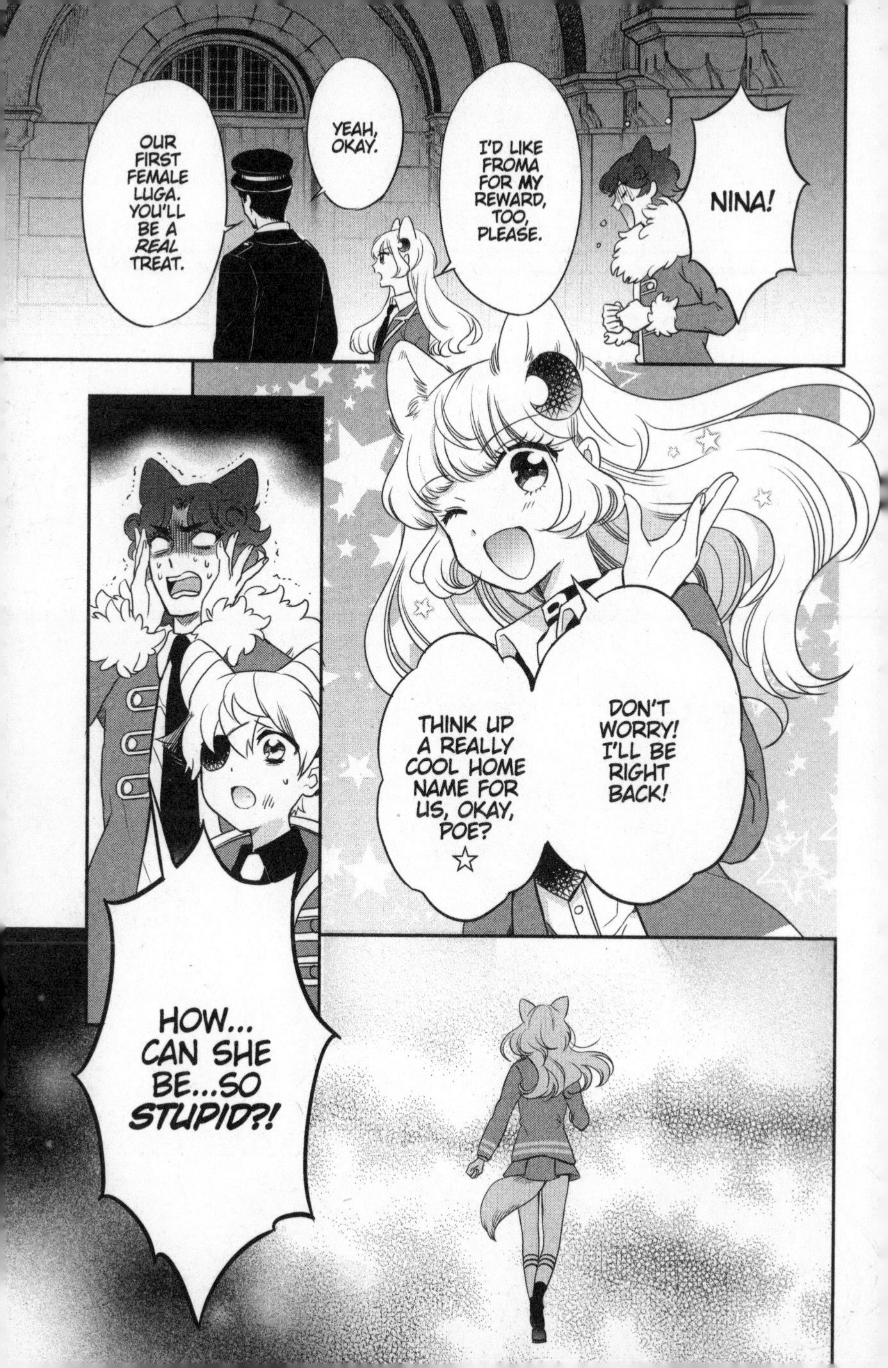
NINA!
I'D LIKE FROMA FOR MY REWARD, TOO, PLEASE.
YEAH, OKAY.
OUR FIRST FEMALE LUGA. YOU'LL BE A *REAL* TREAT.
DON'T WORRY! I'LL BE RIGHT BACK!
THINK UP A REALLY COOL HOME NAME FOR US, OKAY, POE? ☆
HOW... CAN SHE BE...SO *STUPID?!*

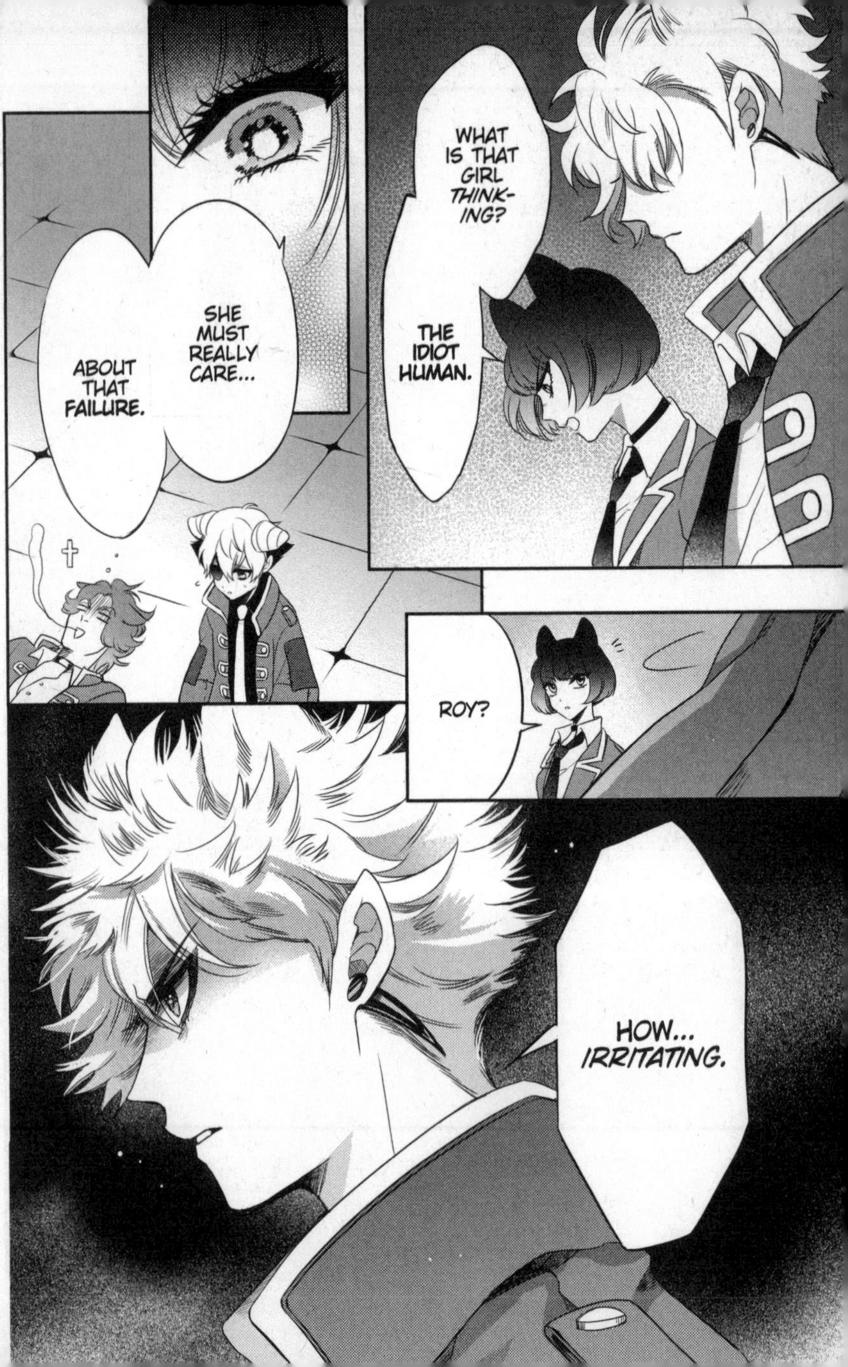
WHAT IS THAT GIRL THINKING?
THE IDIOT HUMAN.
SHE MUST REALLY CARE...
ABOUT THAT FAILURE.
ROY?
HOW... IRRITATING.

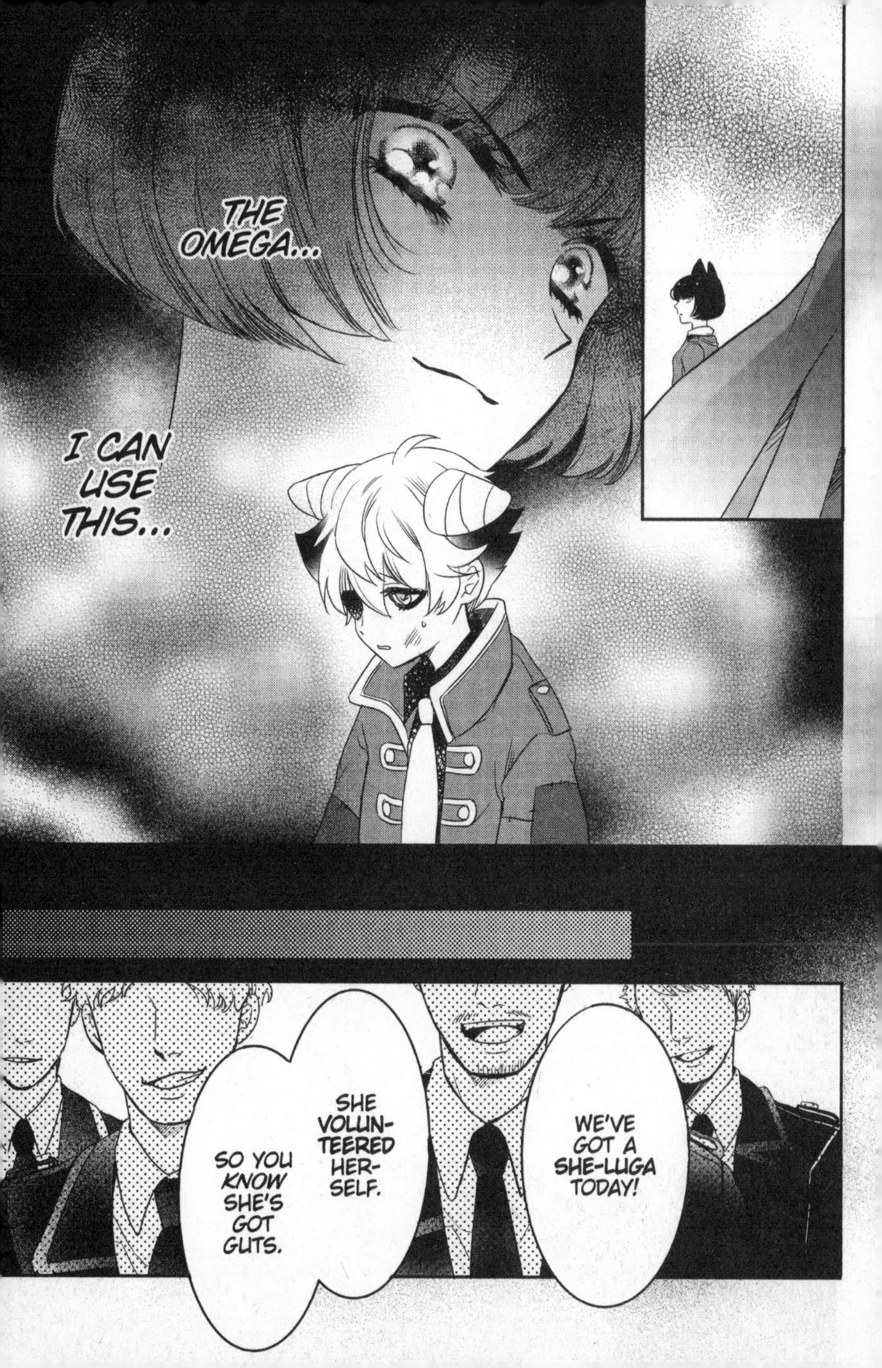
THE OMEGA...
I CAN USE THIS...
WE'VE GOT A SHE-LUGA TODAY!
SHE VOLUNTEERED HERSELF.
SO YOU KNOW SHE'S GOT GUTS.

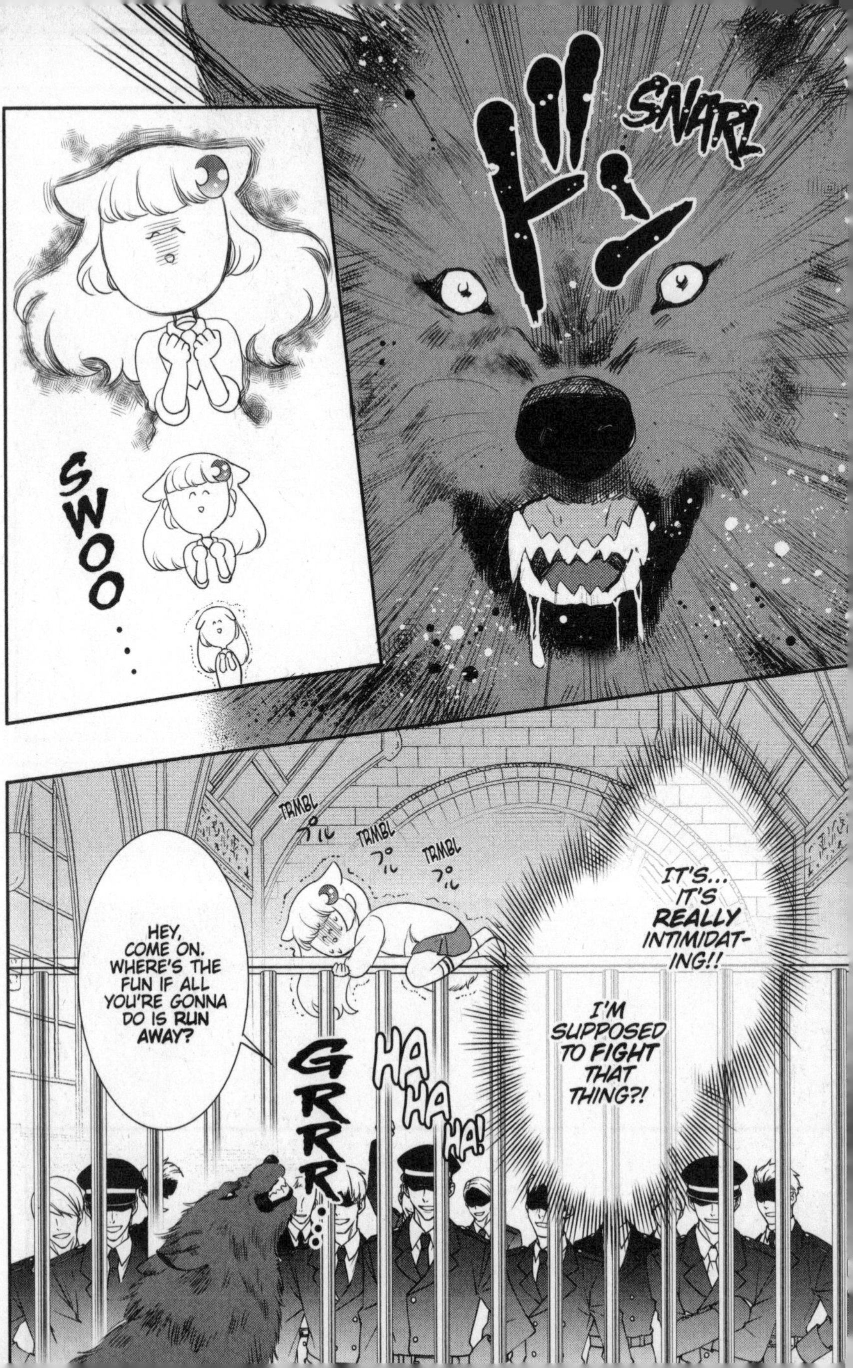
ドン
SNARL
SWOO...
IT'S... IT'S REALLY INTIMIDAT-ING!!
I'M SUPPOSED TO FIGHT THAT THING?!
TRMBL プル
TRMBL プル
TRMBL プル
HA HA HA!
GRRR...
HEY, COME ON. WHERE'S THE FUN IF ALL YOU'RE GONNA DO IS RUN AWAY?

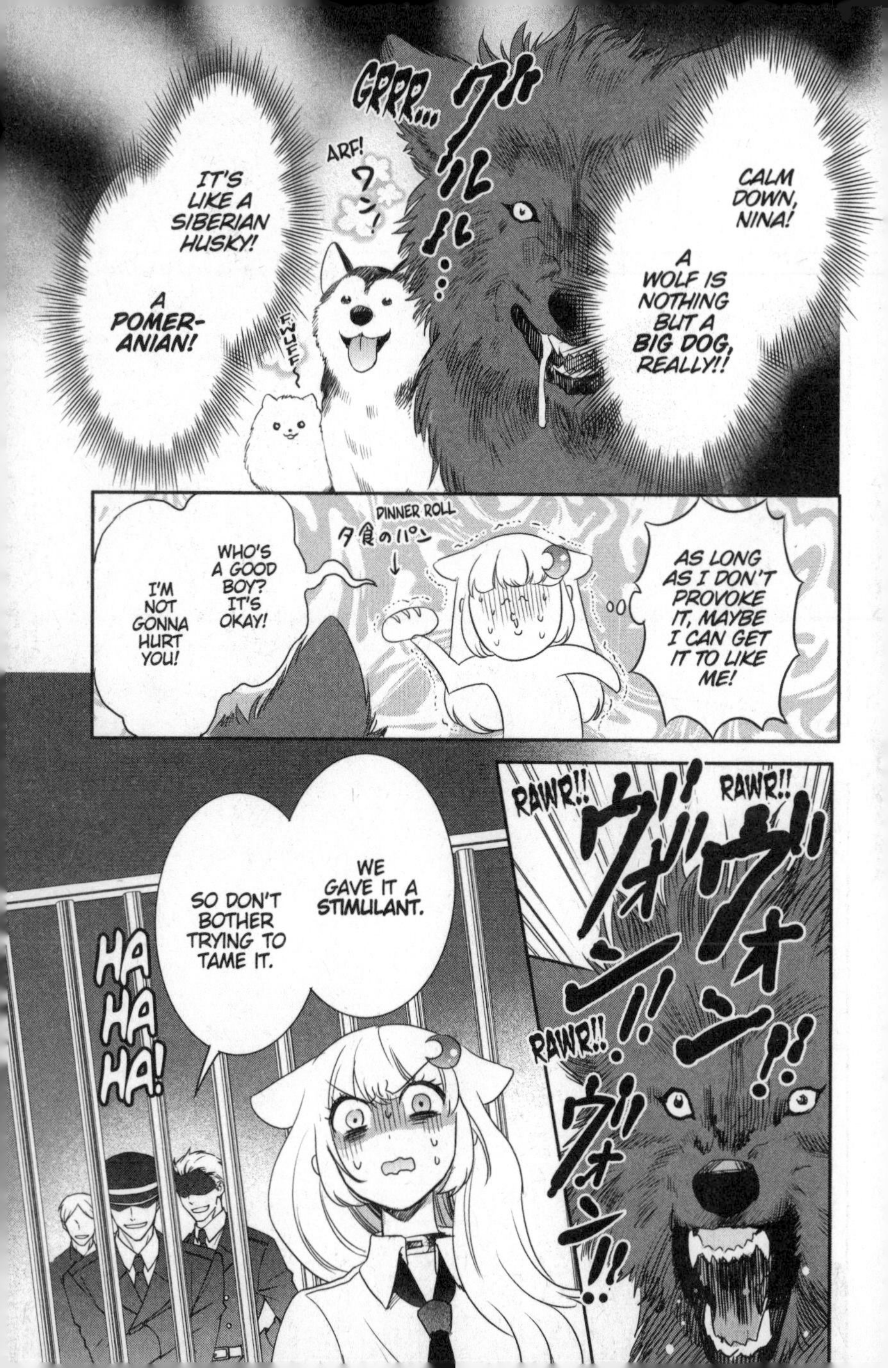
CALM DOWN, NINA!
A WOLF IS NOTHING BUT A BIG DOG, REALLY!!
GRRR... グルル…
ARF! ワン!
FWUFF
IT'S LIKE A SIBERIAN HUSKY!
A POMERANIAN!
AS LONG AS I DON'T PROVOKE IT, MAYBE I CAN GET IT TO LIKE ME!
DINNER ROLL 夕食のパン
WHO'S A GOOD BOY? IT'S OKAY!
I'M NOT GONNA HURT YOU!
RAWR!! RAWR!! RAWR!!
ヴォン!! ヴォン!! ヴォン!!
WE GAVE IT A STIMULANT.
SO DON'T BOTHER TRYING TO TAME IT.
HA HA HA!

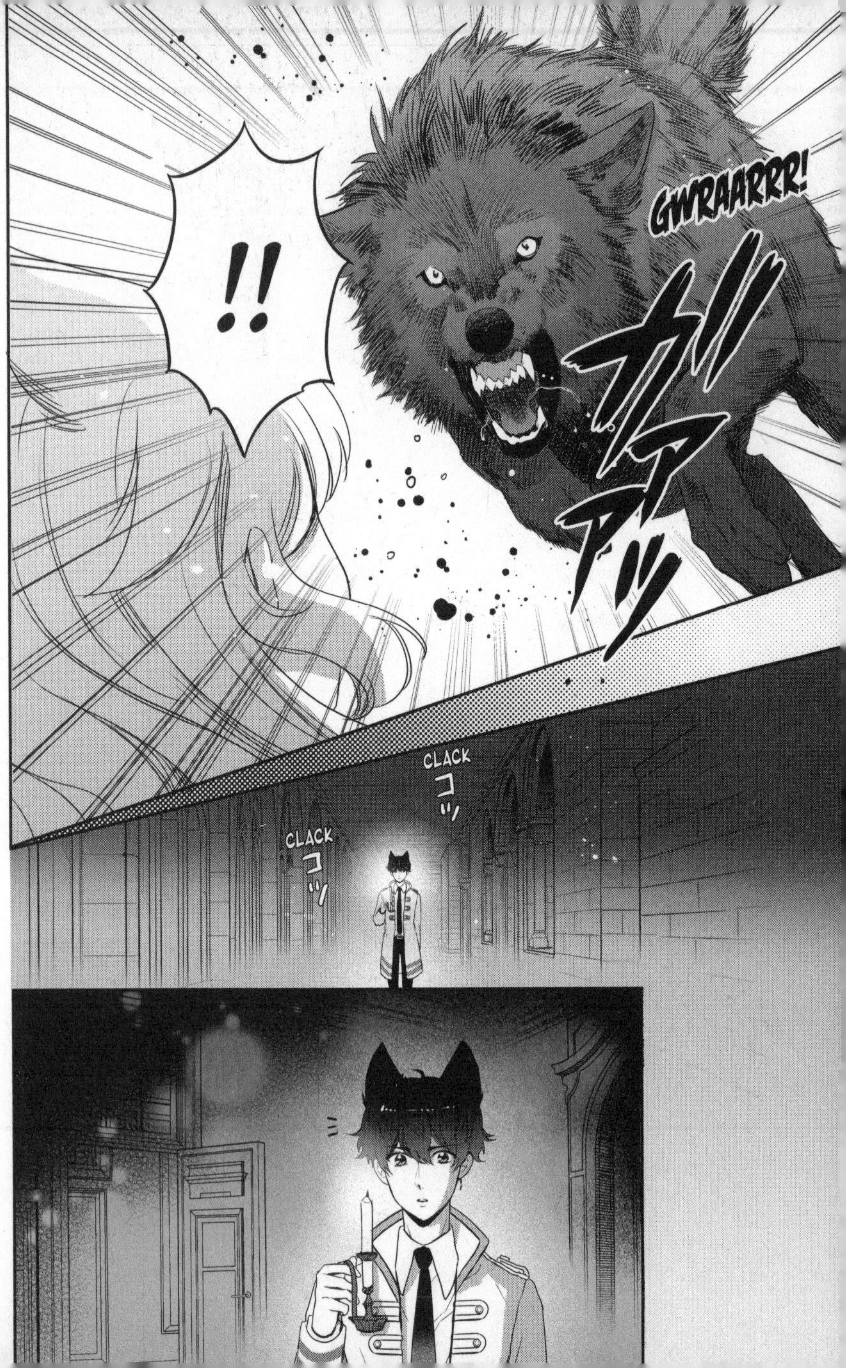

!!
GWRAARRR!
ガァアアッ
CLACK
コッ
CLACK
コッ

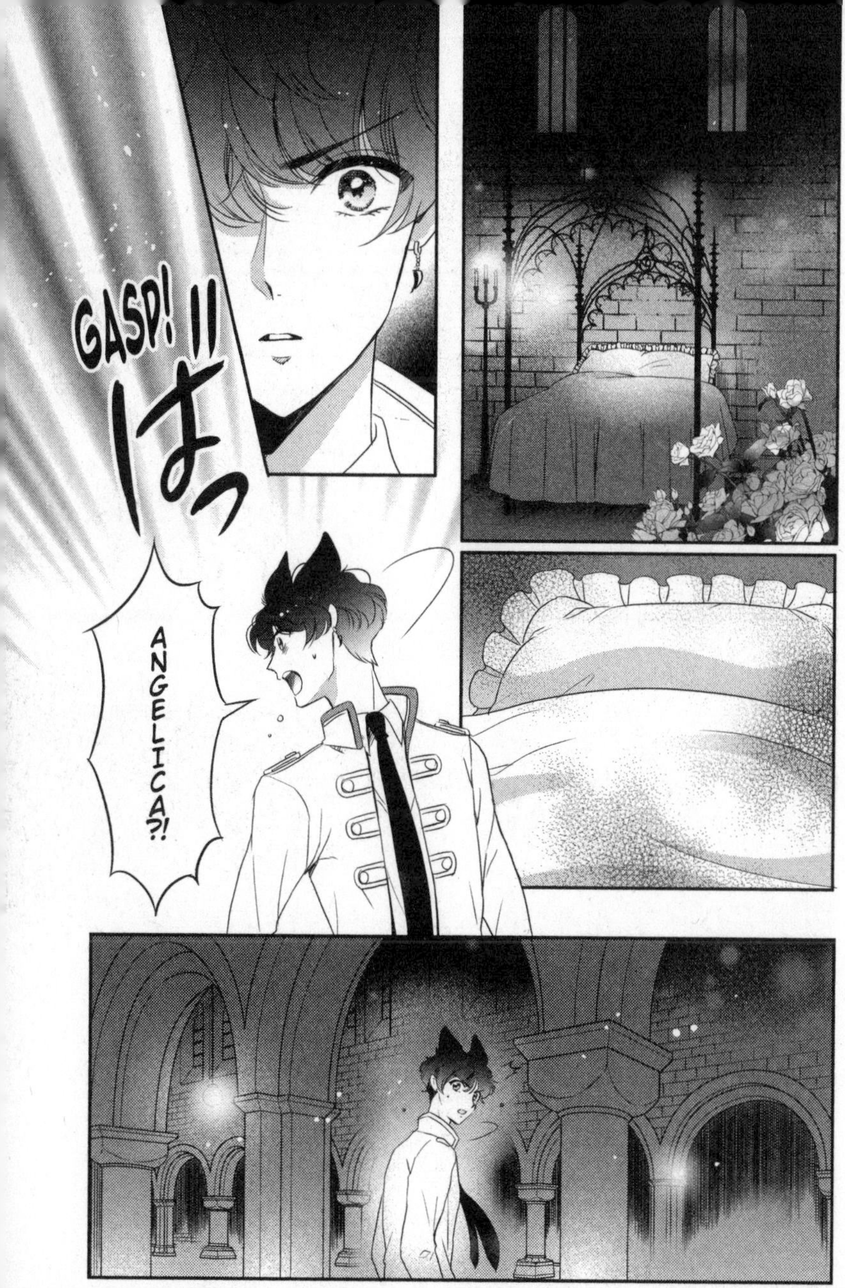
GASP!!
はっ
ANGELICA?!

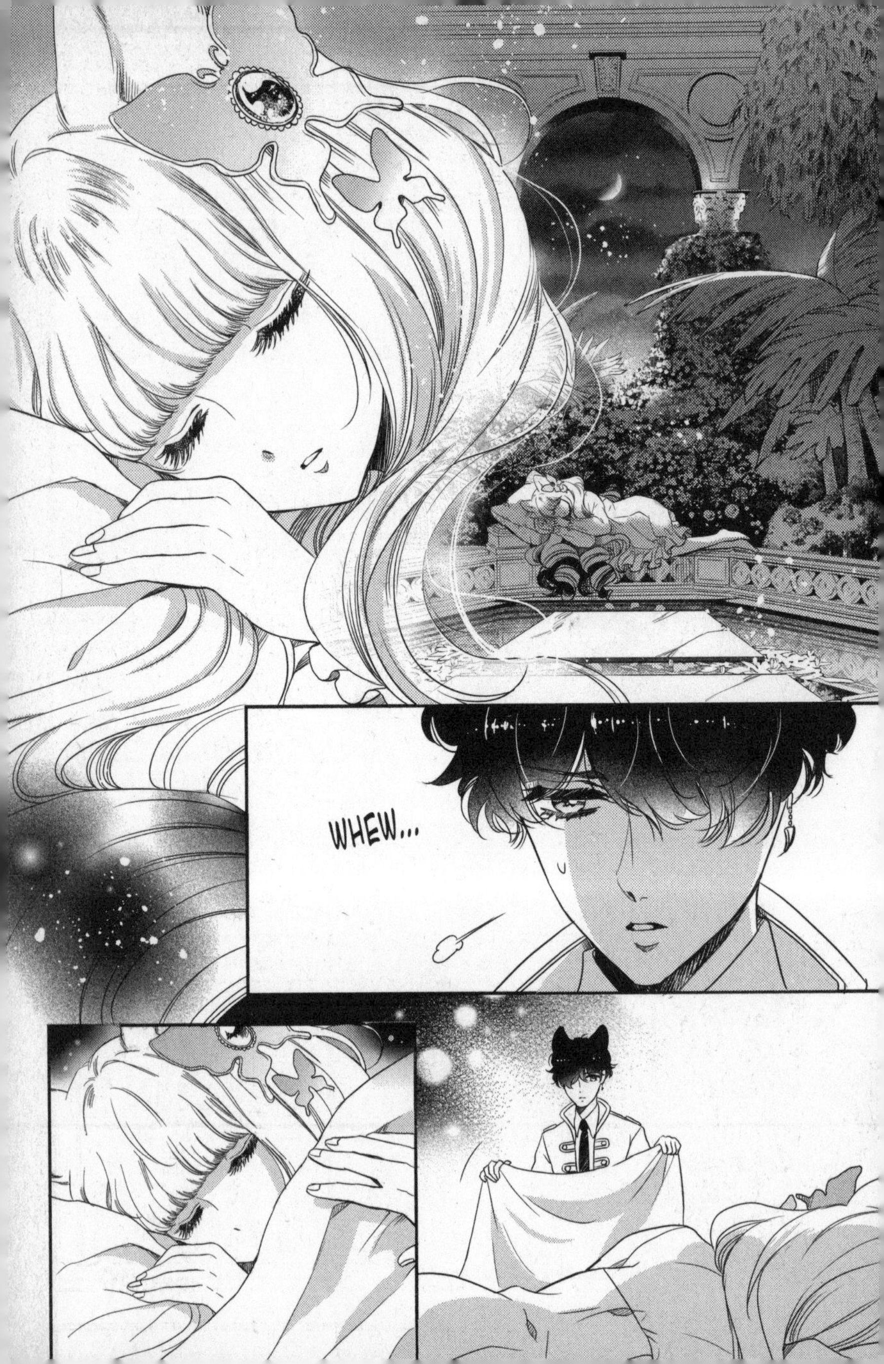
WHEW...

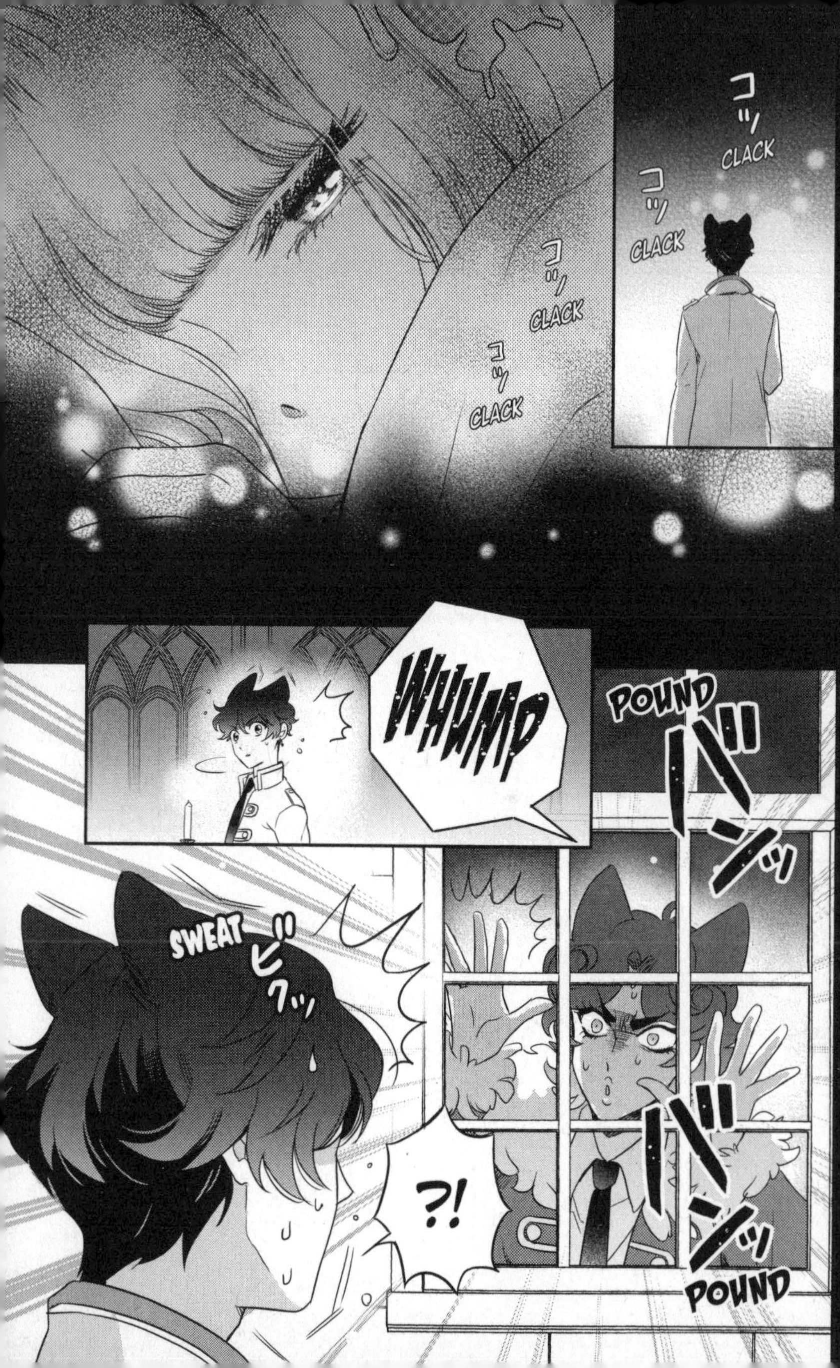

コツ
CLACK
コツ
CLACK
コツ
CLACK
コツ
CLACK
POUND
バンッ
バンッ
POUND
WHUMP
SWEAT
ビクッ
?!

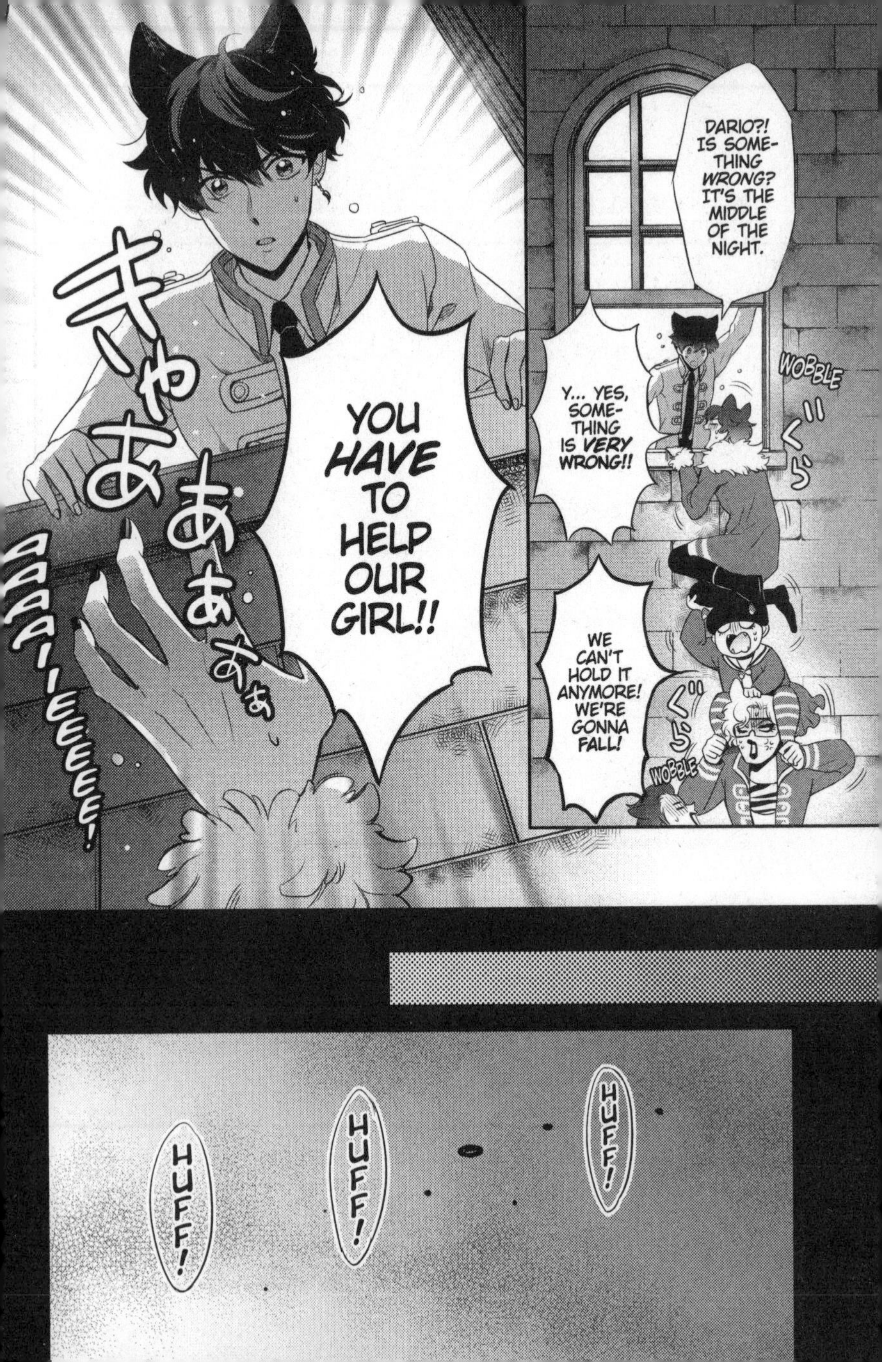
DARIO?! IS SOMETHING WRONG? IT'S THE MIDDLE OF THE NIGHT.
Y... YES, SOMETHING IS VERY WRONG!!
WOBBLE
ぐら
WE CAN'T HOLD IT ANYMORE! WE'RE GONNA FALL!
ぐら
WOBBLE
YOU HAVE TO HELP OUR GIRL!!
きゃあああぁぁ
AAAAIIEEEEEE!
HUFF!
HUFF!
HUFF!

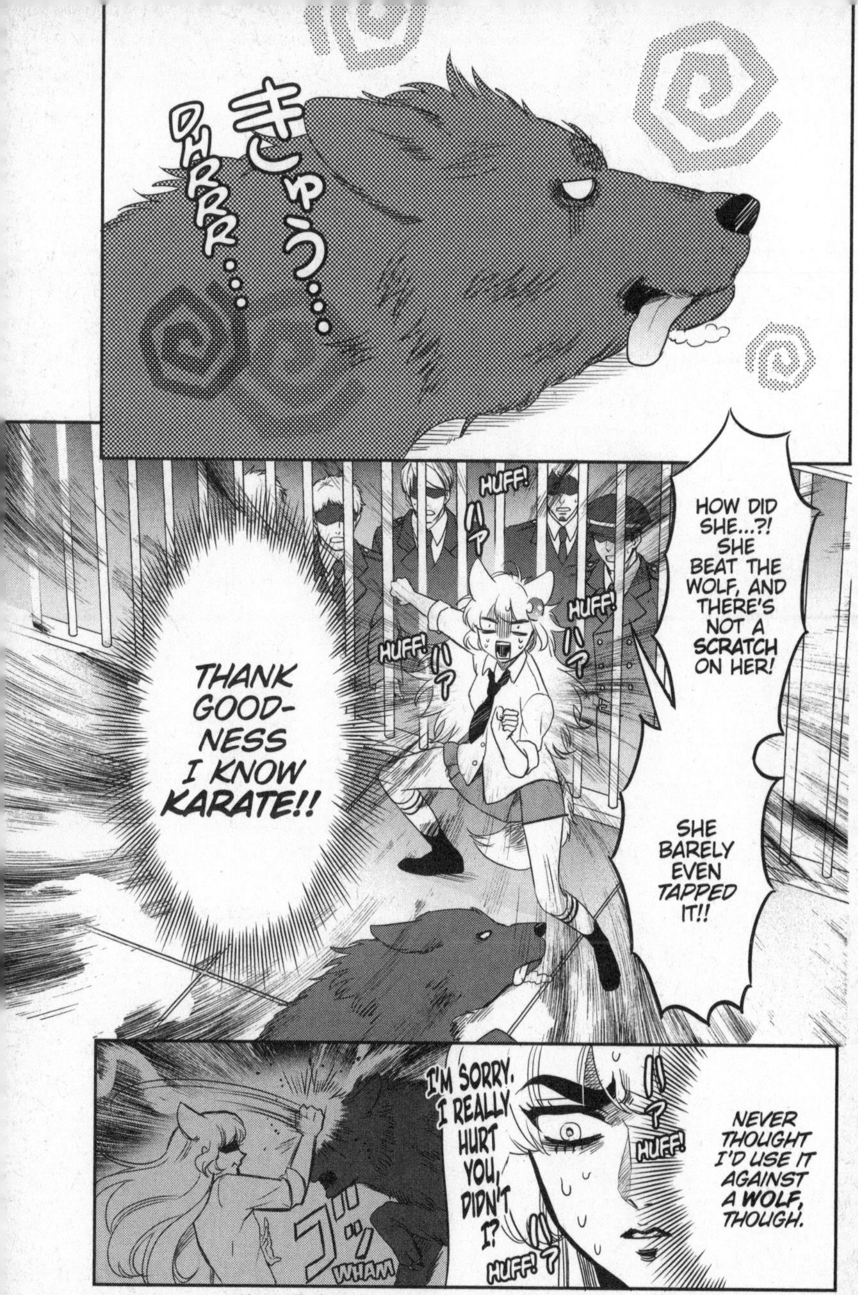
きゅう…
DHRRR…
HOW DID SHE…?! SHE BEAT THE WOLF, AND THERE'S NOT A SCRATCH ON HER!
SHE BARELY EVEN TAPPED IT!!
HUFF! ハァ
HUFF! ハァ
HUFF! ハァ
THANK GOODNESS I KNOW KARATE!!
NEVER THOUGHT I'D USE IT AGAINST A WOLF, THOUGH.
ハァ HUFF!
I'M SORRY. I REALLY HURT YOU, DIDN'T I?
ハァ HUFF!
ゴッ WHAM

HAMMER FIST.

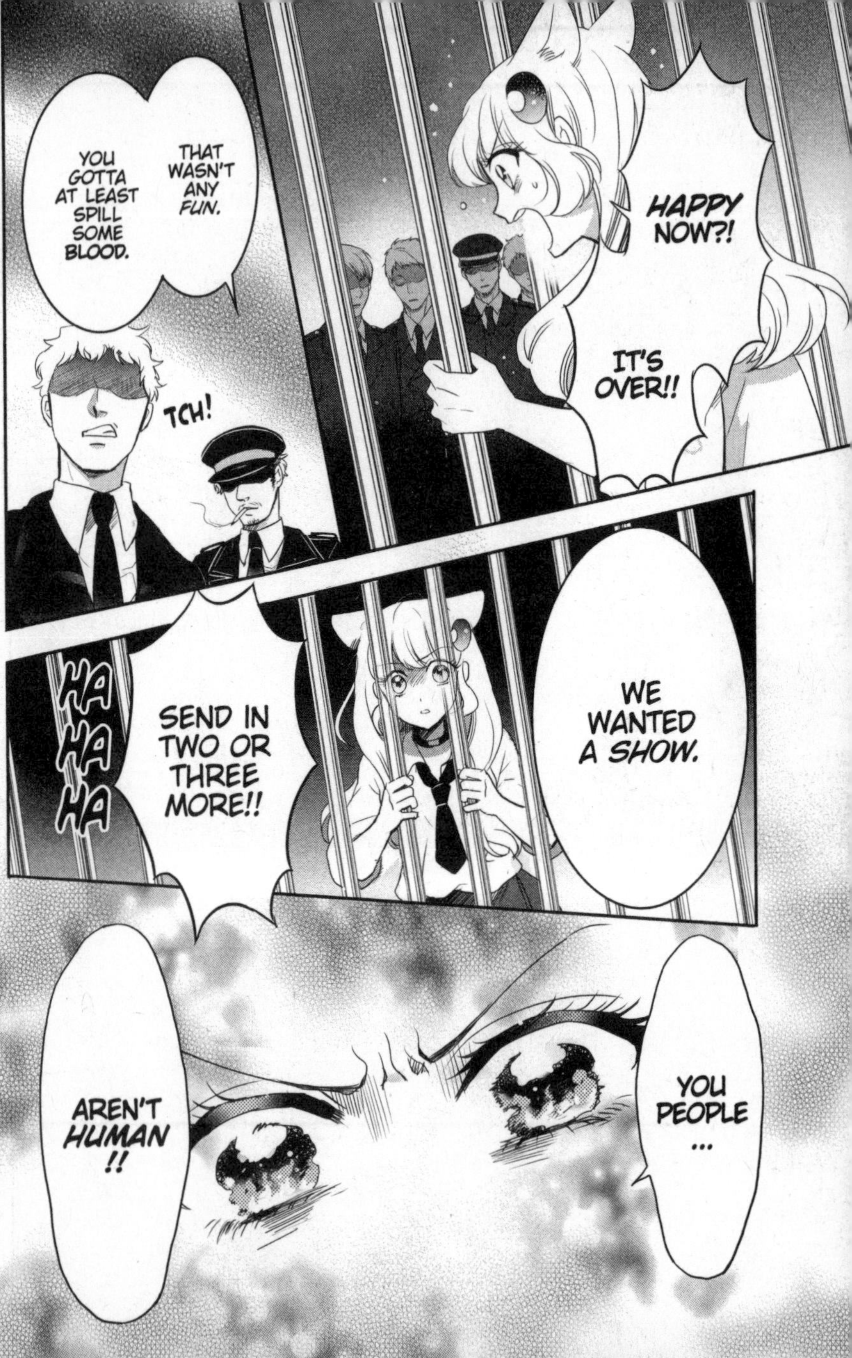
HAPPY NOW?!
IT'S OVER!!
THAT WASN'T ANY FUN.
YOU GOTTA AT LEAST SPILL SOME BLOOD.
TCH!
WE WANTED A SHOW.
SEND IN TWO OR THREE MORE!!
HA HA HA HA
YOU PEOPLE ...
AREN'T HUMAN !!

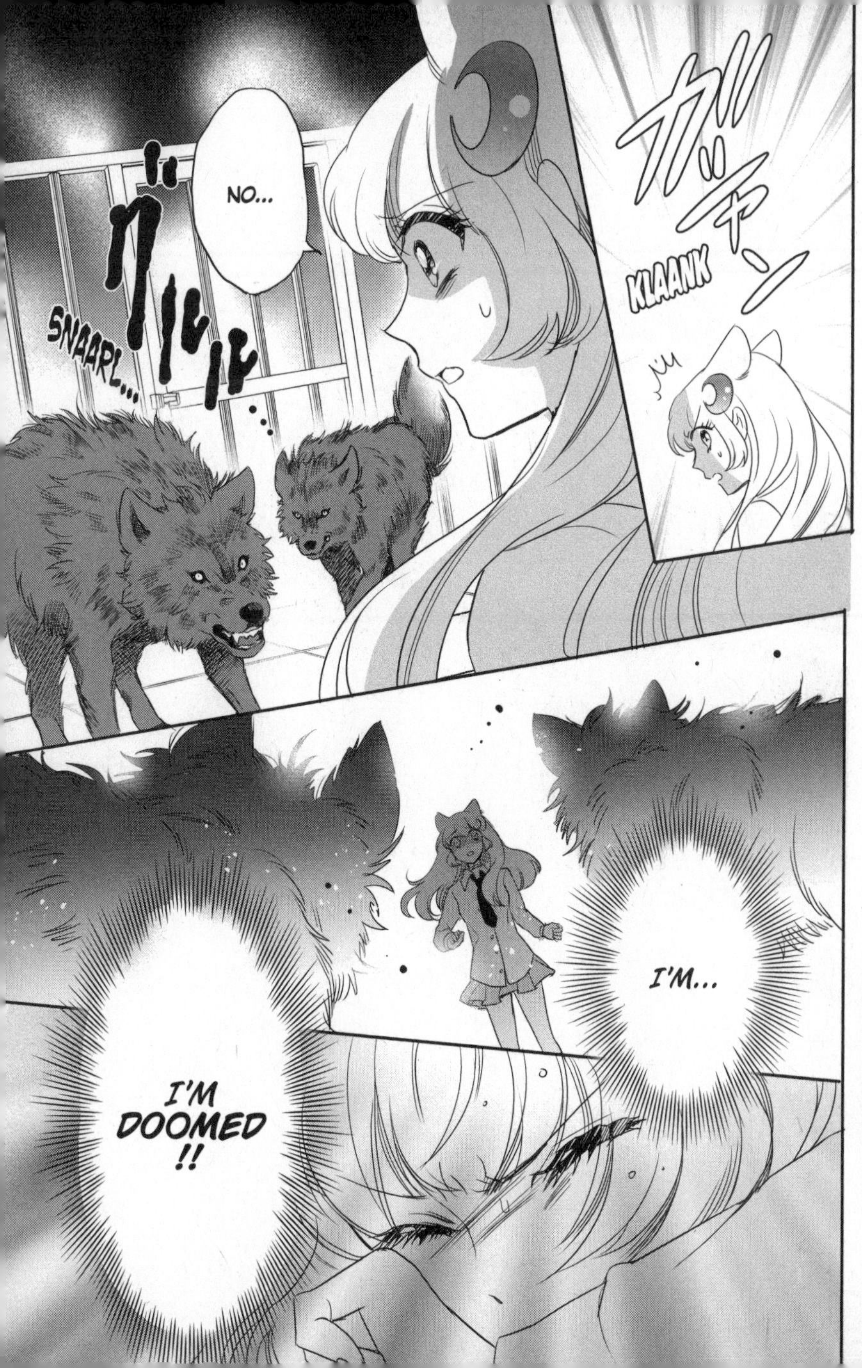
KLAANK
NO...
SNAARL...
I'M...
I'M DOOMED!!

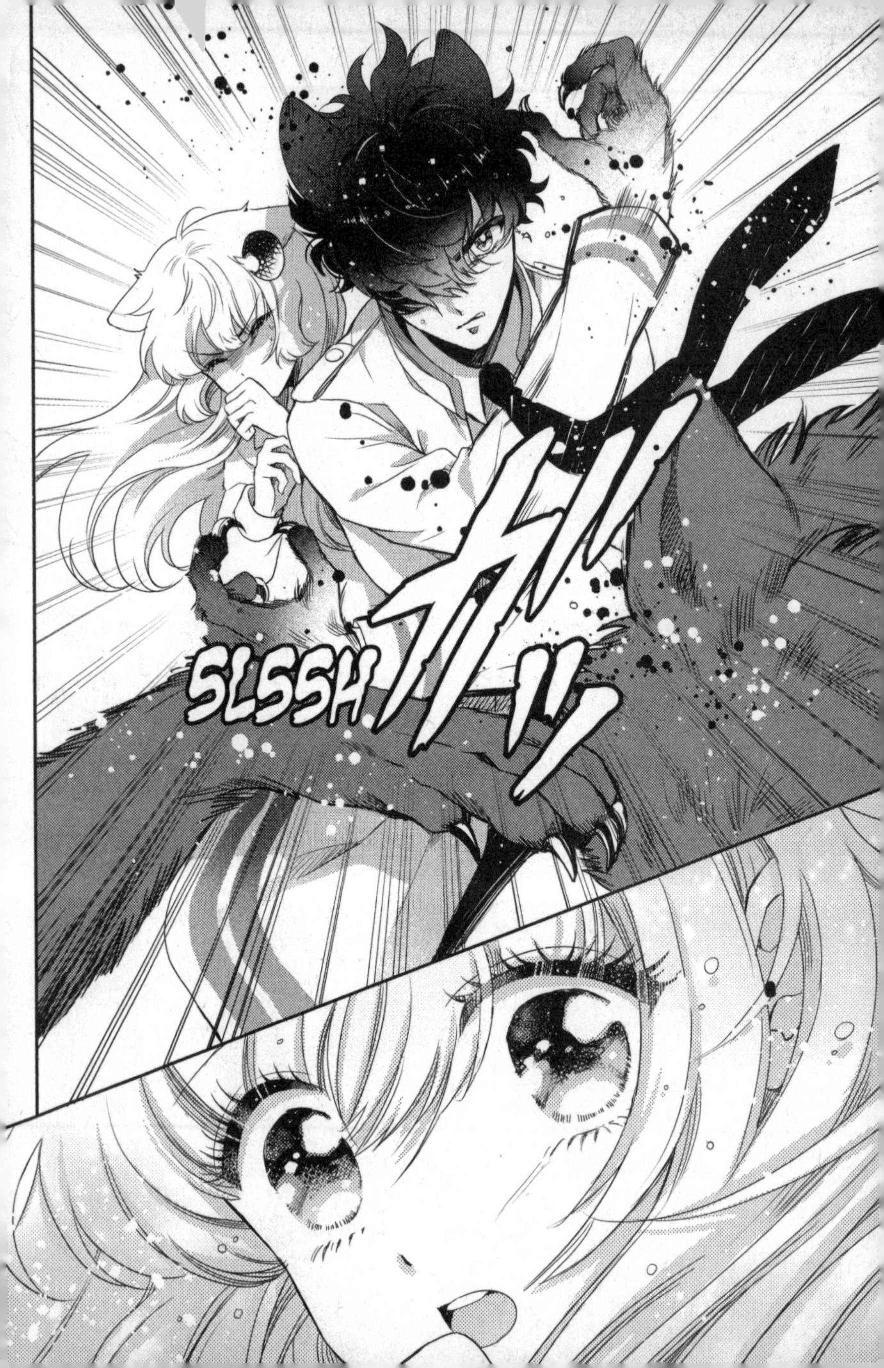
SLSSH

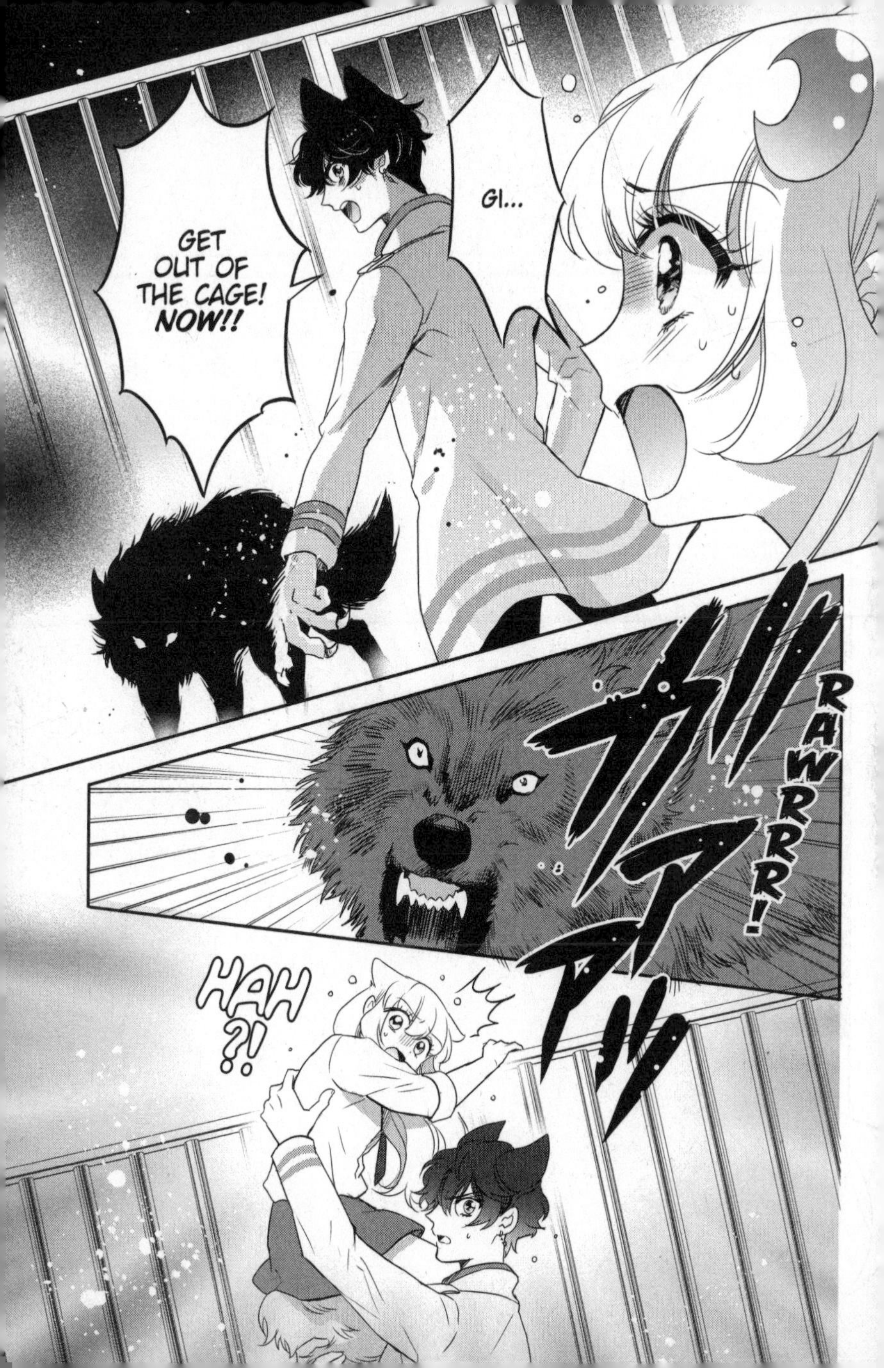
GI...
GET OUT OF THE CAGE! NOW!!
RAWRRR!
HAH ?!

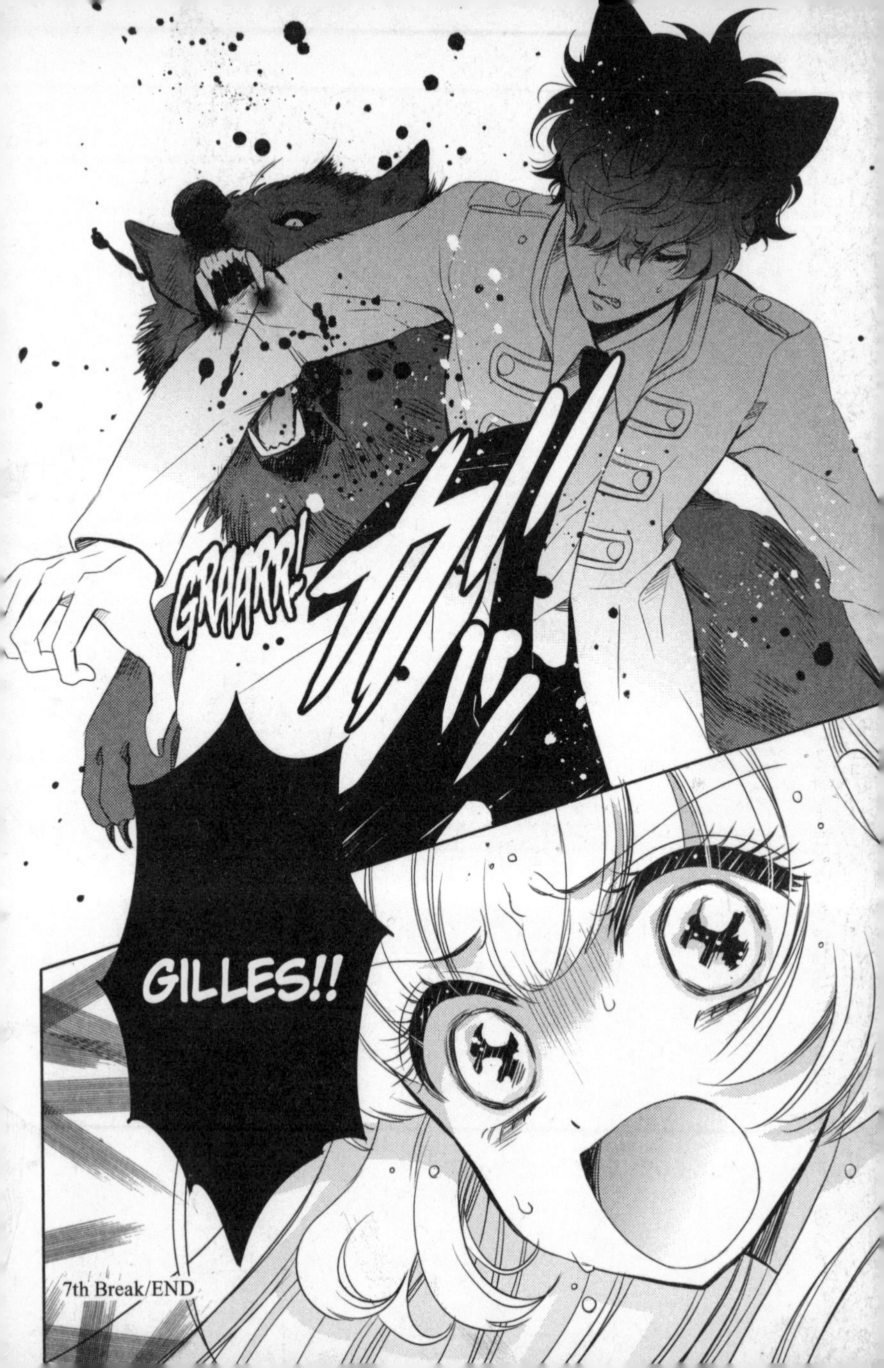
GRAAARR!
GILLES!!
7th Break/END

8th Break

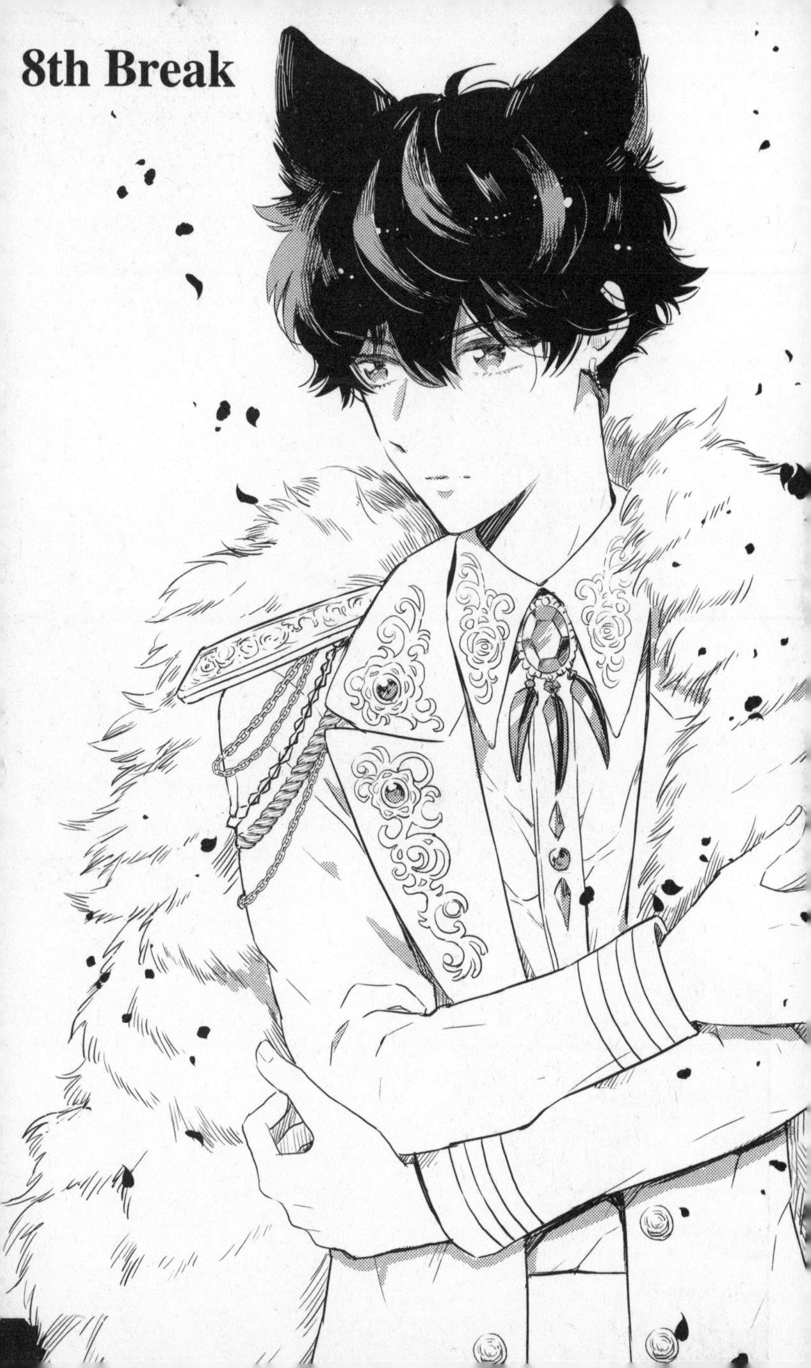

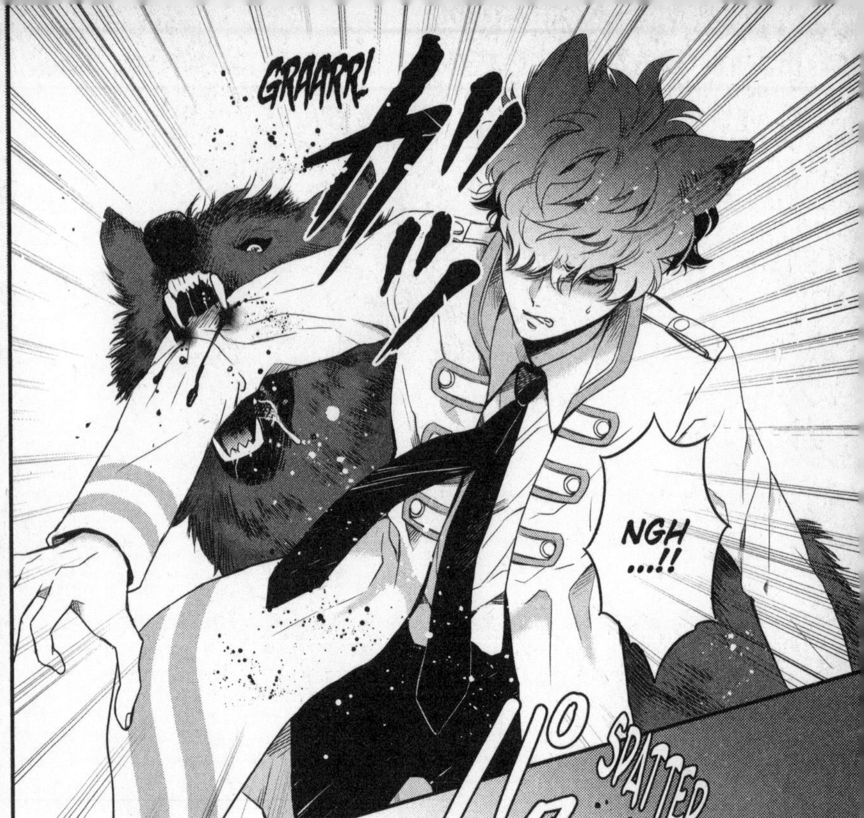
GRAAARR!
NGH ...!!
SPATTER

White Swan Perfume

Perfume extracted from a very rare breed of pale, aurora-white rose. The liquid itself is light pink in hue. It can instantly transform even the most pungent of aromas into a sweet, elegant fragrance. One spritz will reportedly last five to seven days.

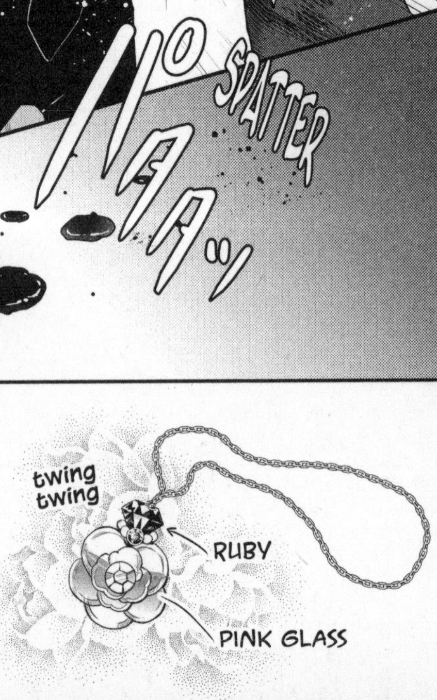
twing
twing
RUBY
PINK GLASS

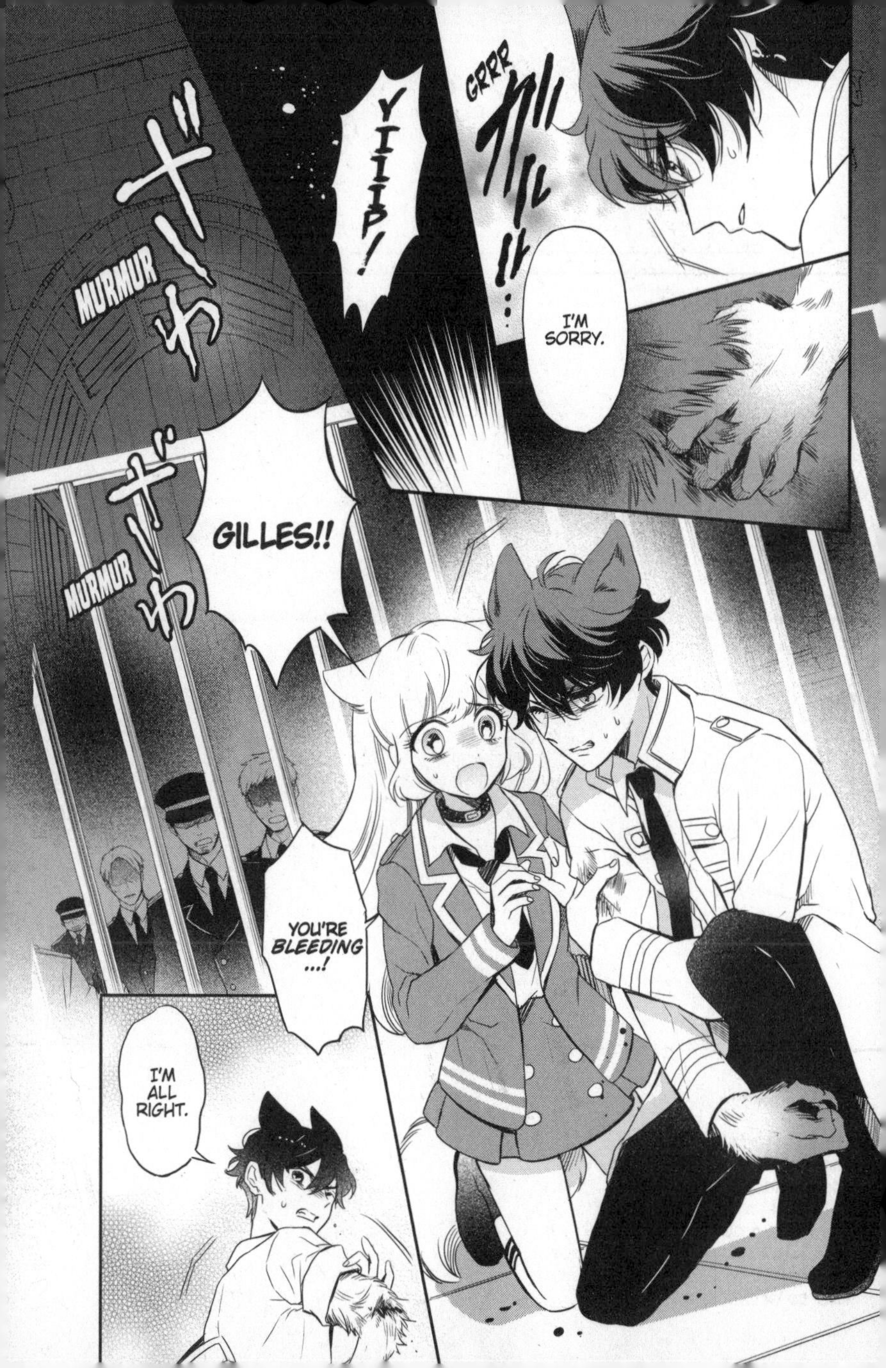
GRRR
I'M SORRY.
YIIIP!
MURMUR
MURMUR
GILLES!!
YOU'RE BLEEDING ...!
I'M ALL RIGHT.

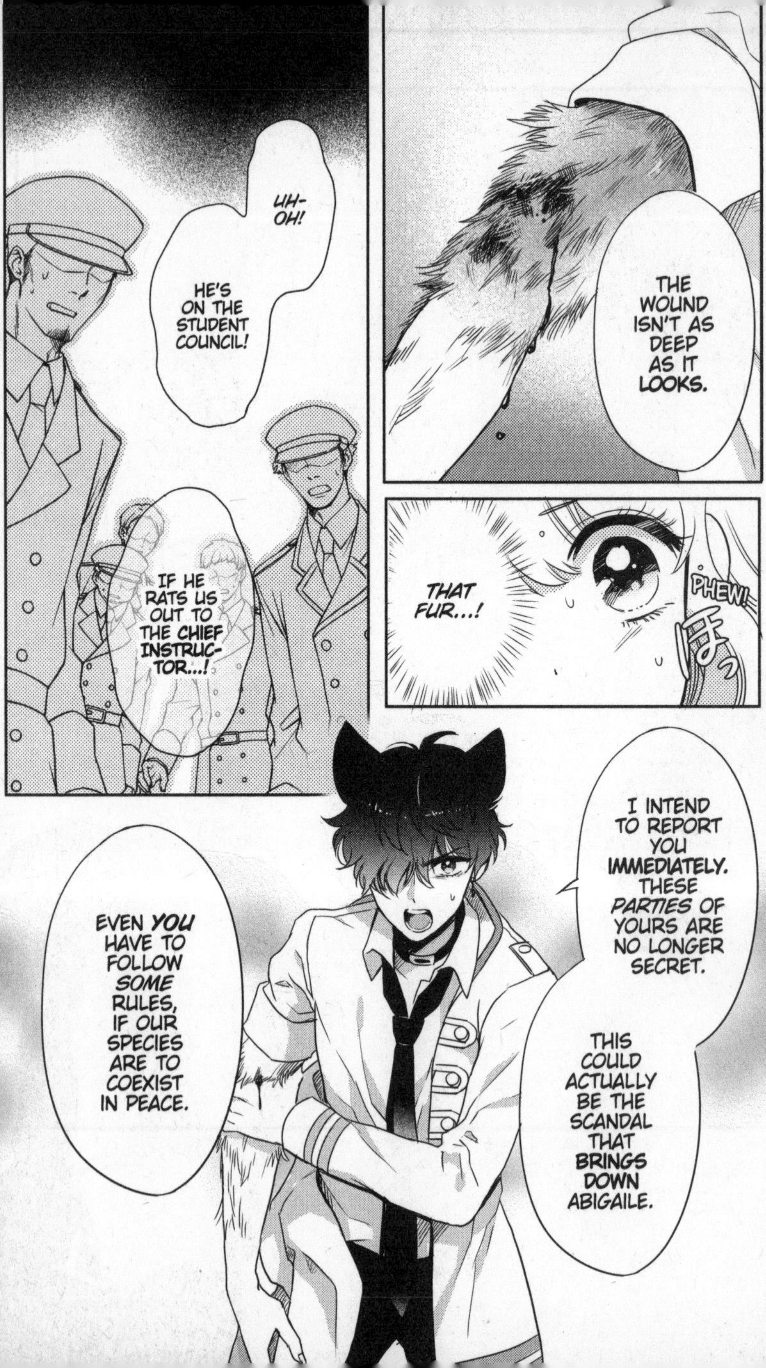
THE WOUND ISN'T AS DEEP AS IT LOOKS.
THAT FUR...!
PHEW!
ほっ
UH-OH!
HE'S ON THE STUDENT COUNCIL!
IF HE RATS US OUT TO THE CHIEF INSTRUC-TOR...!
I INTEND TO REPORT YOU IMMEDIATELY. THESE *PARTIES* OF YOURS ARE NO LONGER SECRET.
THIS COULD ACTUALLY BE THE SCANDAL THAT BRINGS DOWN ABIGAILE.
EVEN *YOU* HAVE TO FOLLOW *SOME* RULES, IF OUR SPECIES ARE TO COEXIST IN PEACE.

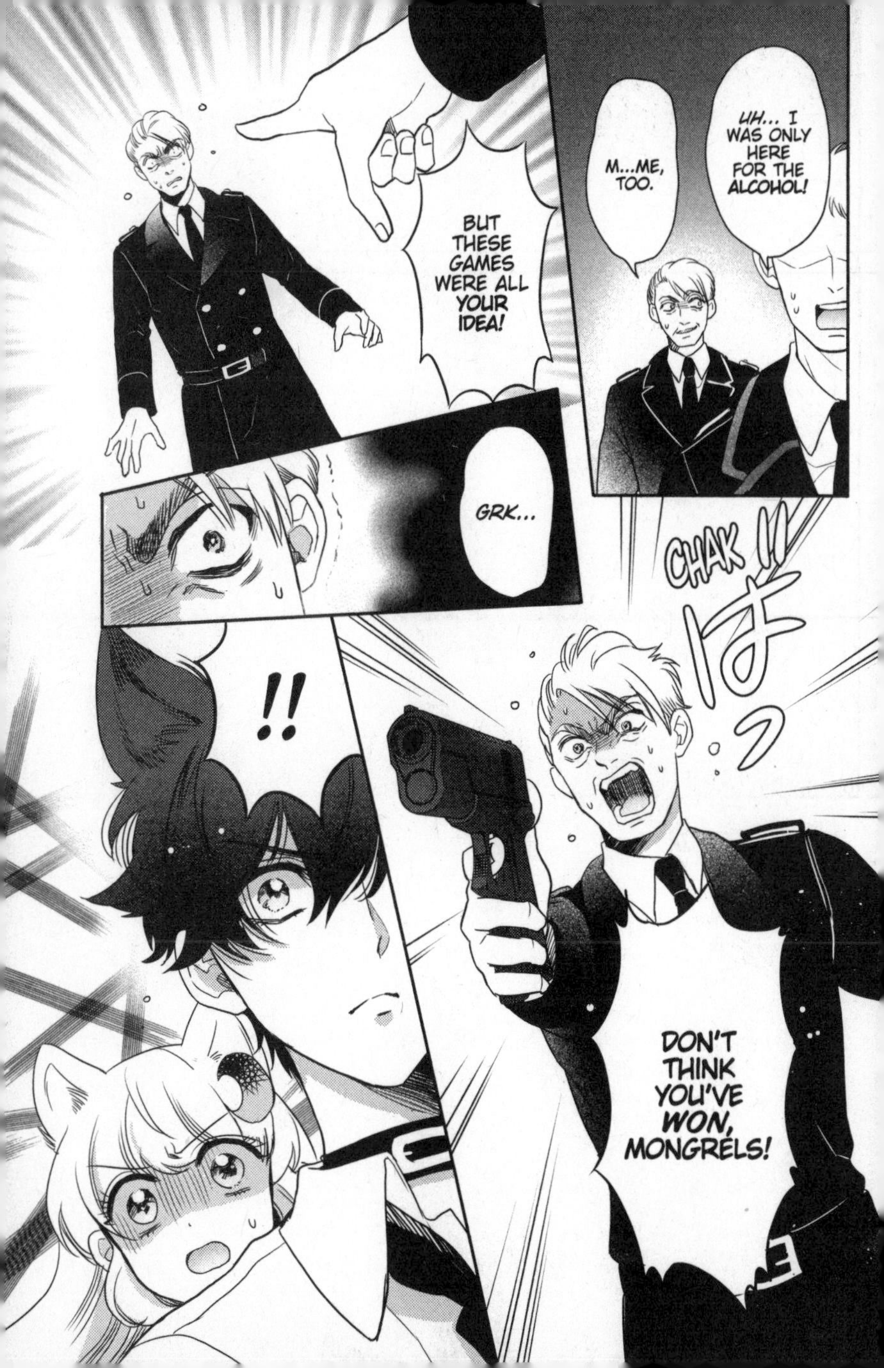
UH... I WAS ONLY HERE FOR THE ALCOHOL!
M...ME, TOO.
BUT THESE GAMES WERE ALL YOUR IDEA!
GRK...
CHAK!!
はっ
DON'T THINK YOU'VE *WON*, MONGRELS!
!!

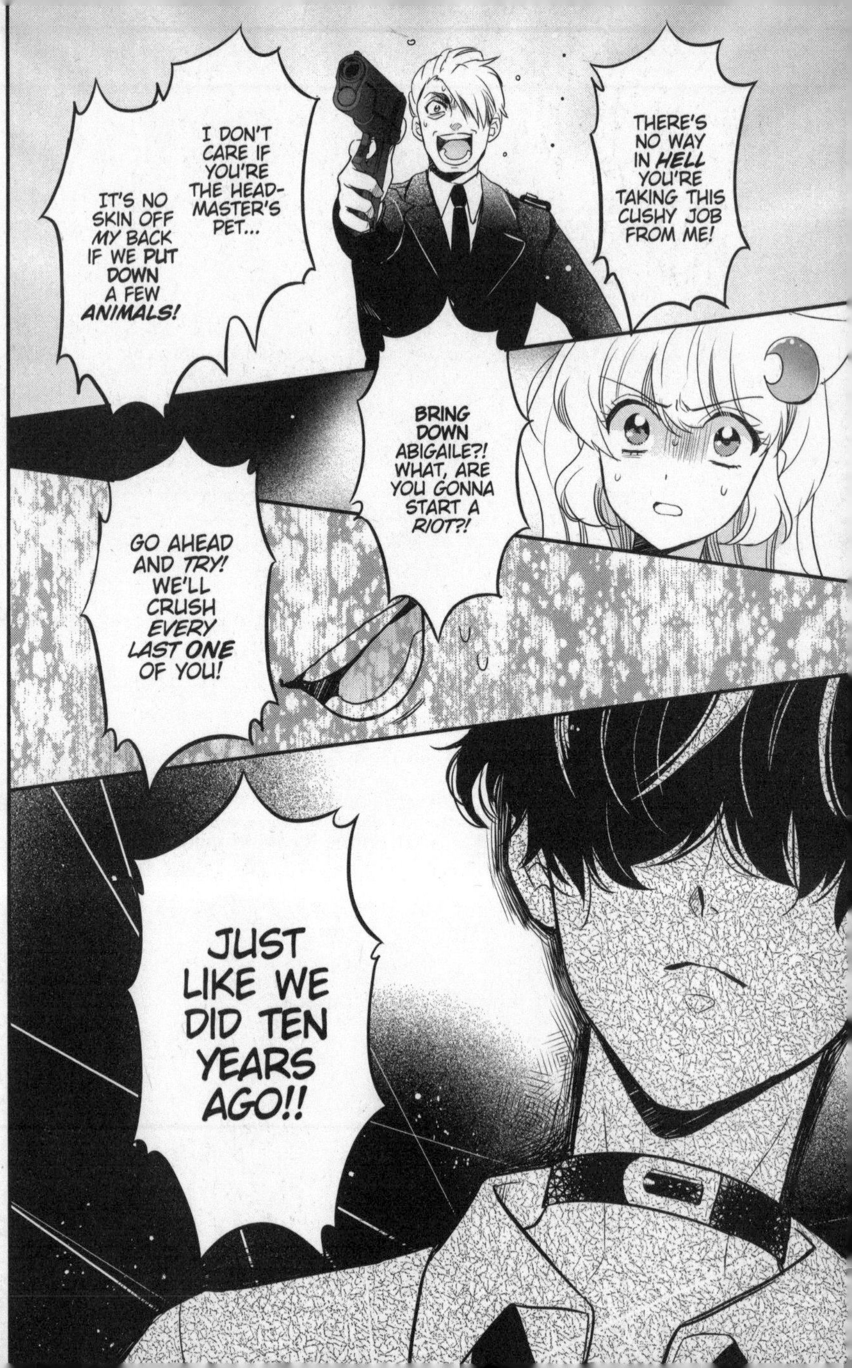
THERE'S NO WAY IN HELL YOU'RE TAKING THIS CUSHY JOB FROM ME!
I DON'T CARE IF YOU'RE THE HEAD-MASTER'S PET...
IT'S NO SKIN OFF MY BACK IF WE PUT DOWN A FEW ANIMALS!
BRING DOWN ABIGAILE?! WHAT, ARE YOU GONNA START A RIOT?!
GO AHEAD AND TRY! WE'LL CRUSH EVERY LAST ONE OF YOU!
JUST LIKE WE DID TEN YEARS AGO!!

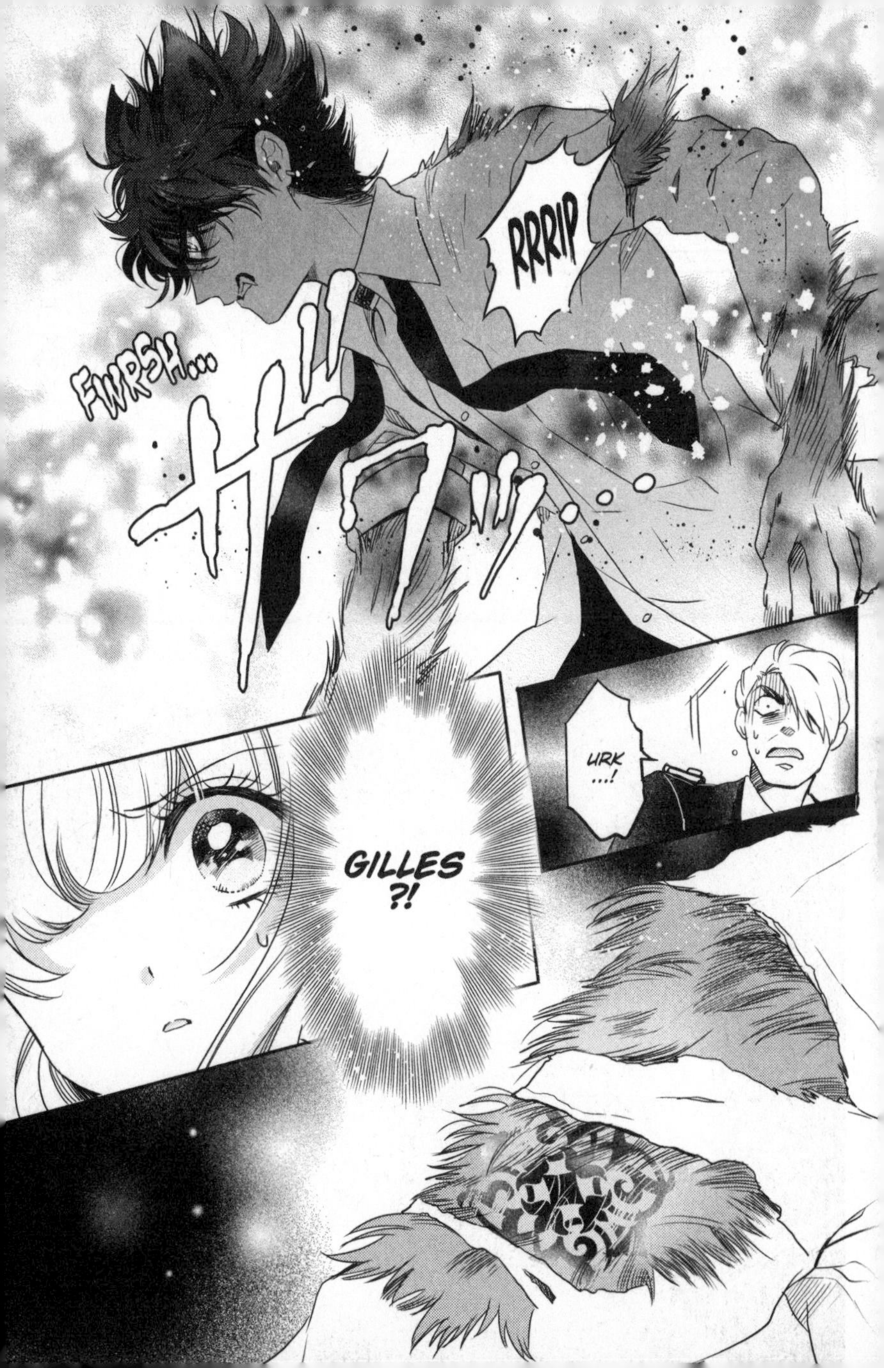
RRRIP
FWRSH...
URK ...!
GILLES ?!

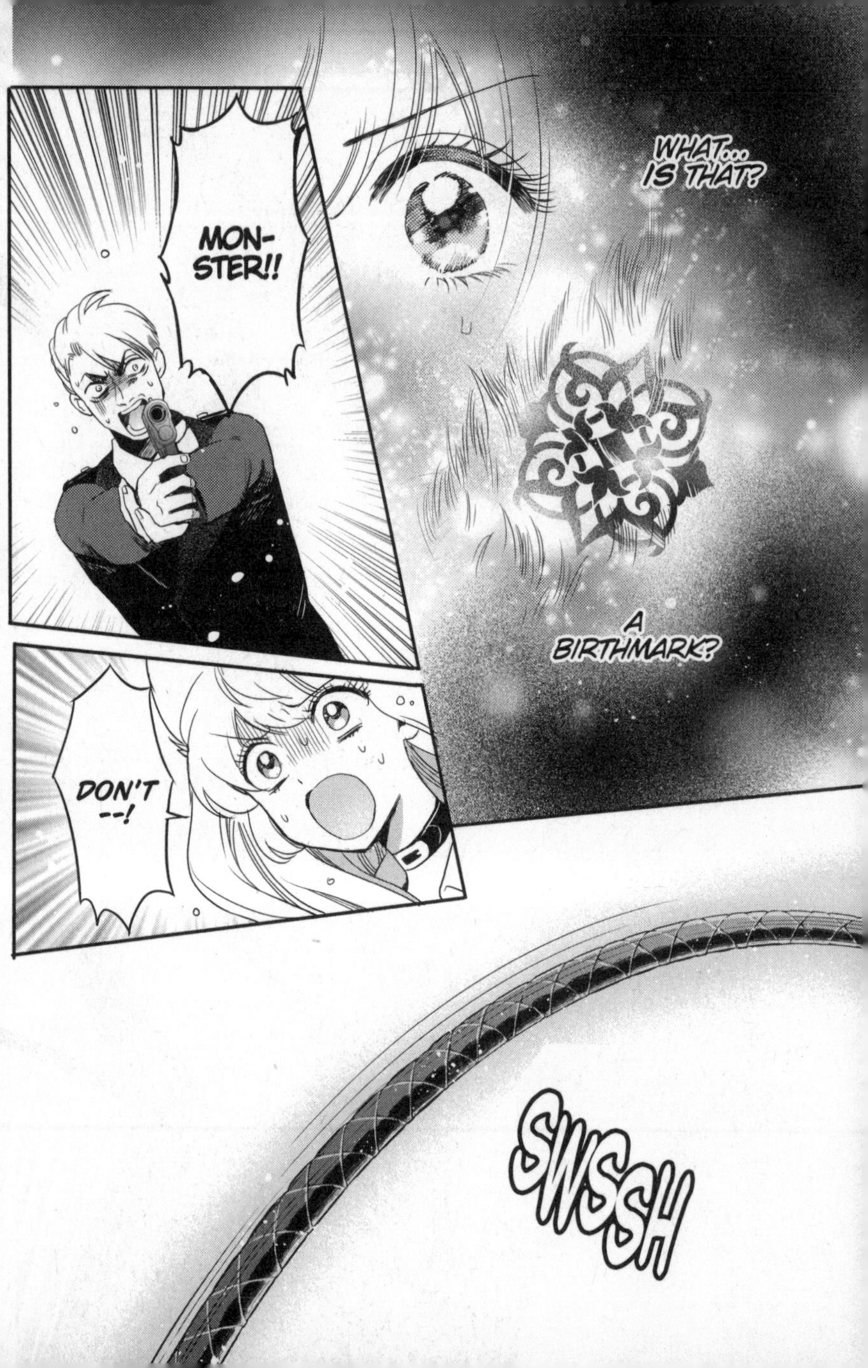
WHAT... IS THAT?
A BIRTHMARK?
MON-STER!!
DON'T --!
SWSSH

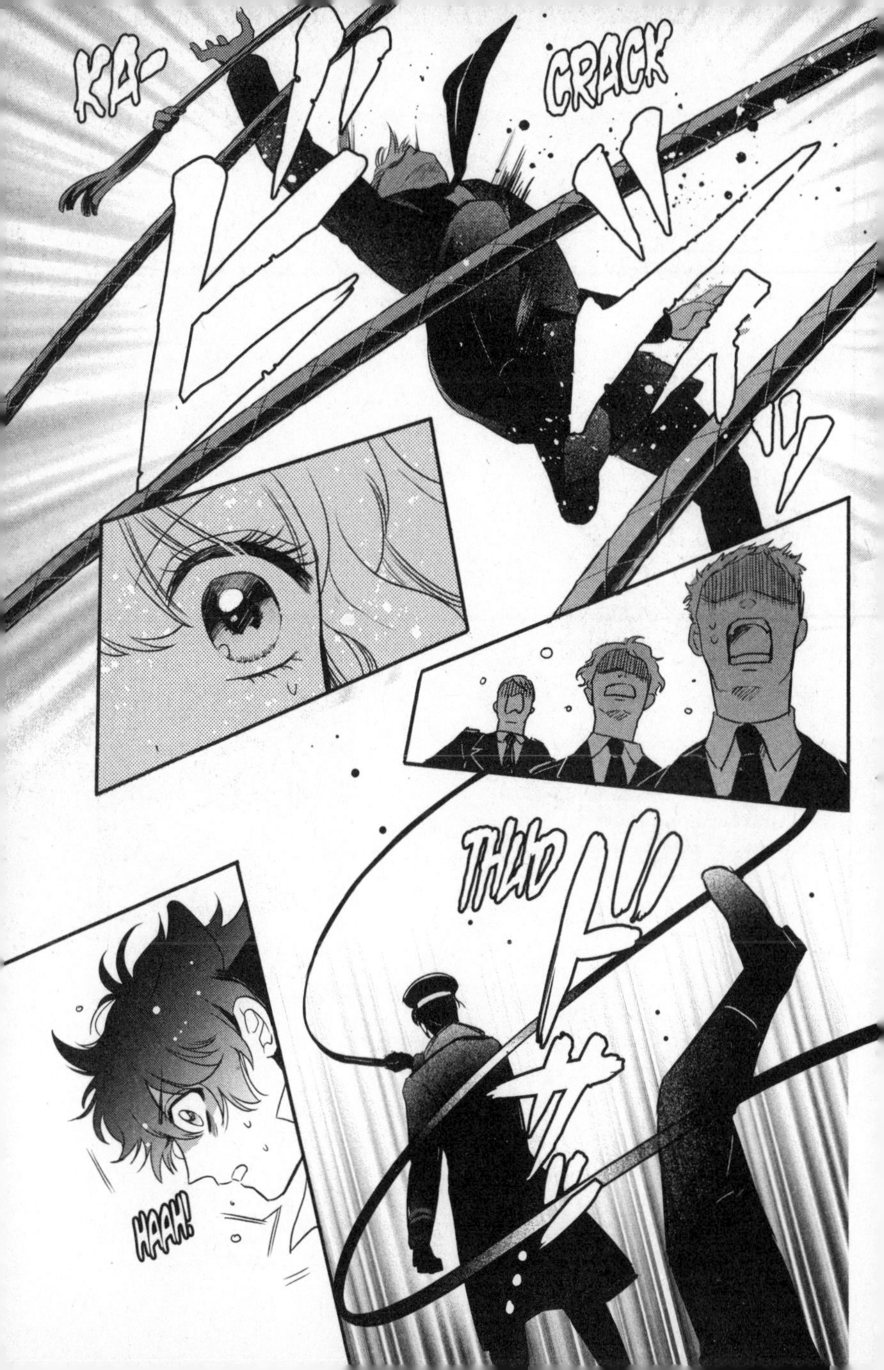
KA-
CRACK
THUD
HAAH!

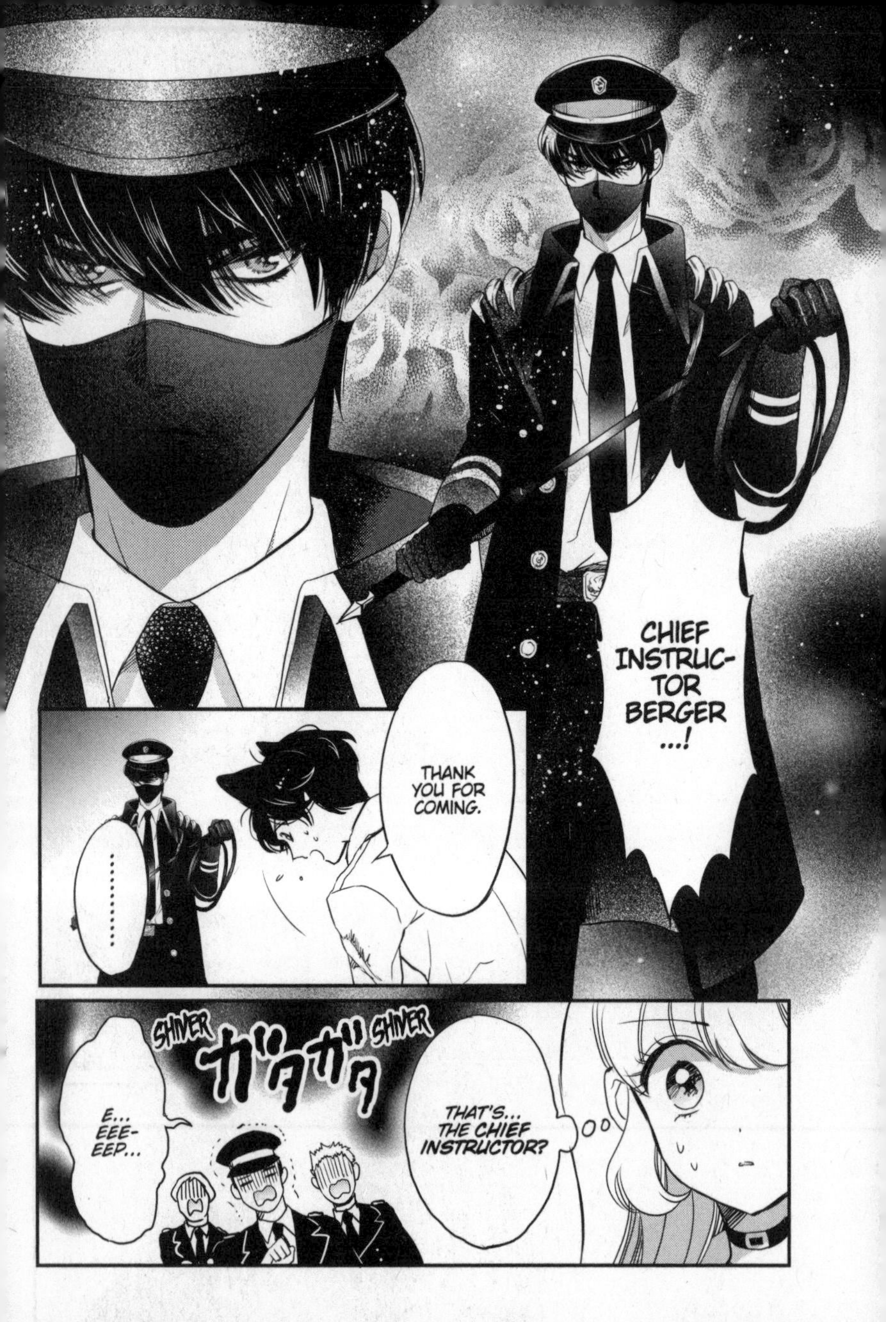
CHIEF INSTRUCTOR BERGER ...!
THANK YOU FOR COMING.
......
THAT'S... THE CHIEF INSTRUCTOR?
SHIVER SHIVER
E... EEE-EEP...

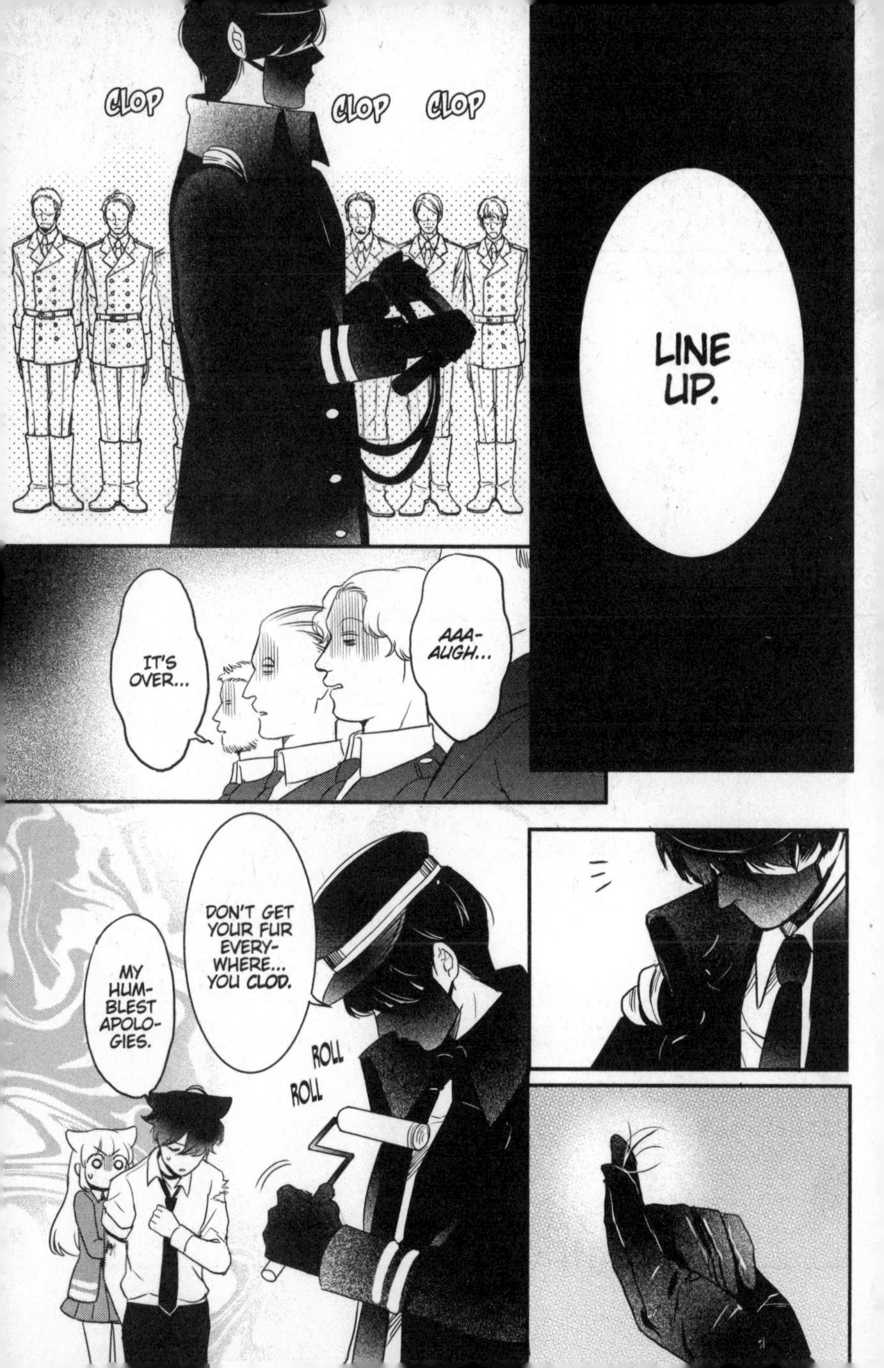
LINE UP.
CLOP CLOP CLOP
AAA-AUGH...
IT'S OVER...
DON'T GET YOUR FUR EVERY-WHERE... YOU CLOD.
ROLL ROLL
MY HUM-BLEST APOLO-GIES.

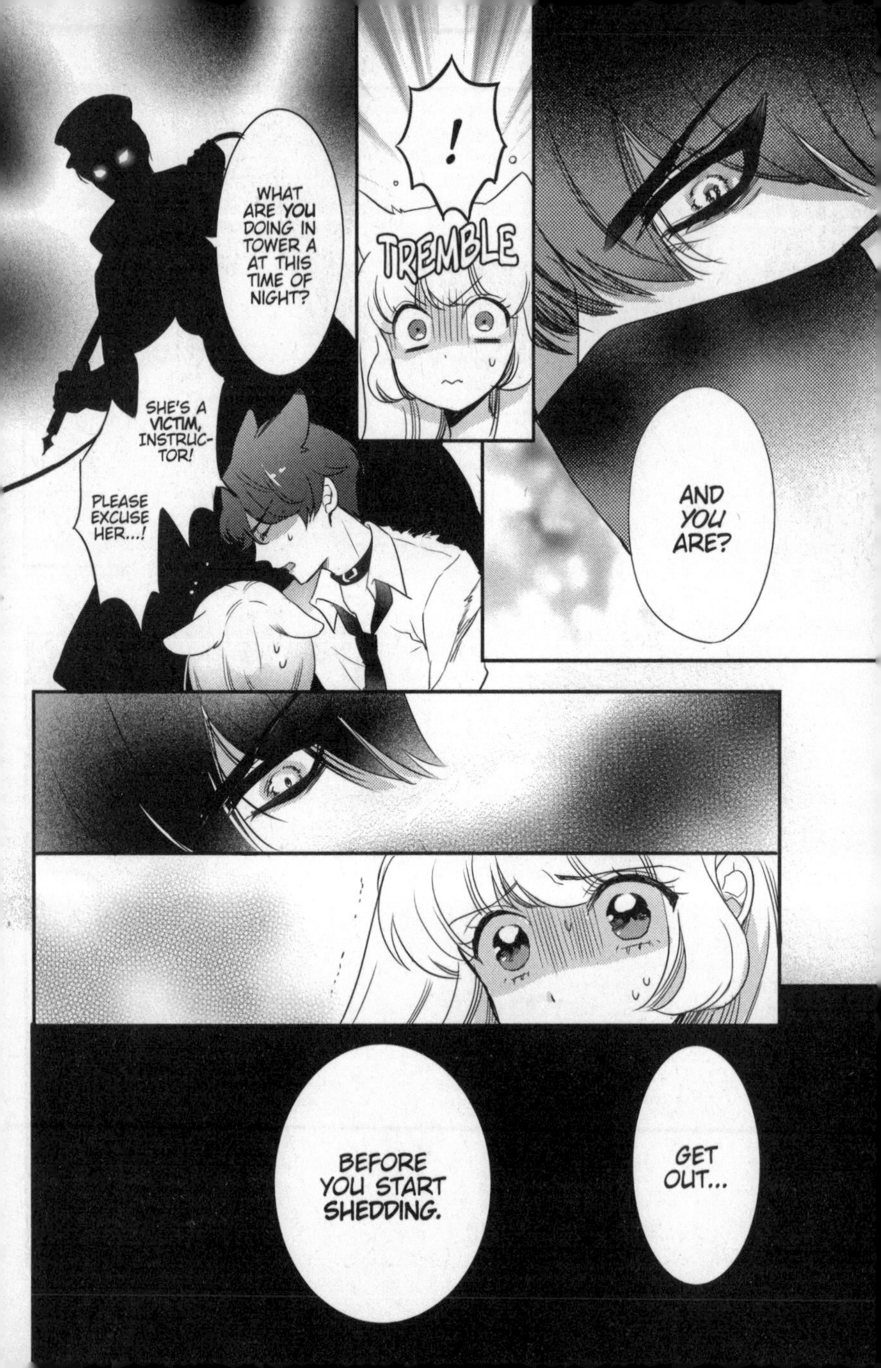
AND YOU ARE?
!
TREMBLE
WHAT ARE YOU DOING IN TOWER A AT THIS TIME OF NIGHT?
SHE'S A VICTIM, INSTRUCTOR!
PLEASE EXCUSE HER...!
GET OUT...
BEFORE YOU START SHEDDING.

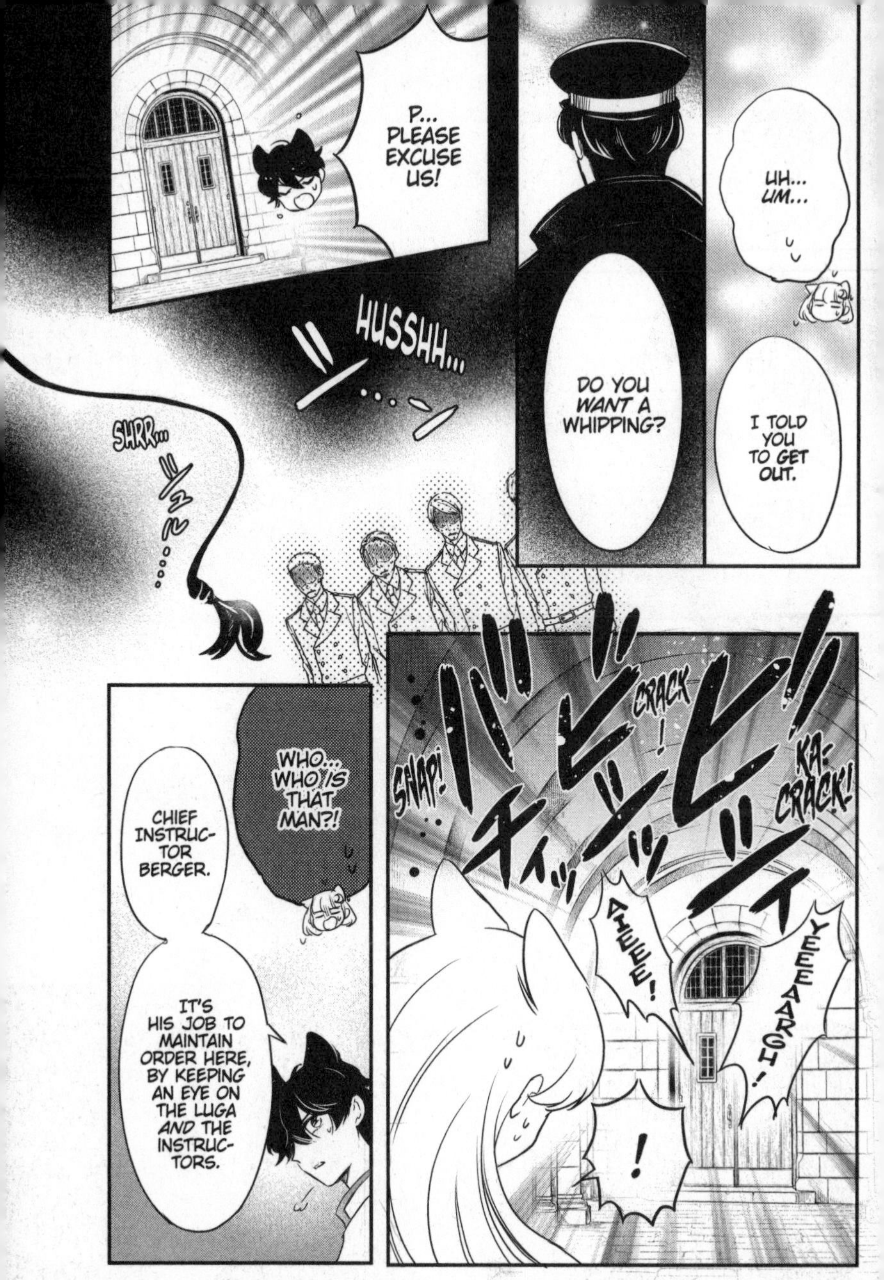
UH... UM...
I TOLD YOU TO GET OUT.
DO YOU WANT A WHIPPING?
P... PLEASE EXCUSE US!
HUSSHH...
SHRR...
KA-CRACK!
CRACK!
SNAP!
YEEEEARGH!
AIEEEE!
!
WHO... WHO IS THAT MAN?!
CHIEF INSTRUCTOR BERGER.
IT'S HIS JOB TO MAINTAIN ORDER HERE, BY KEEPING AN EYE ON THE LUGA AND THE INSTRUCTORS.

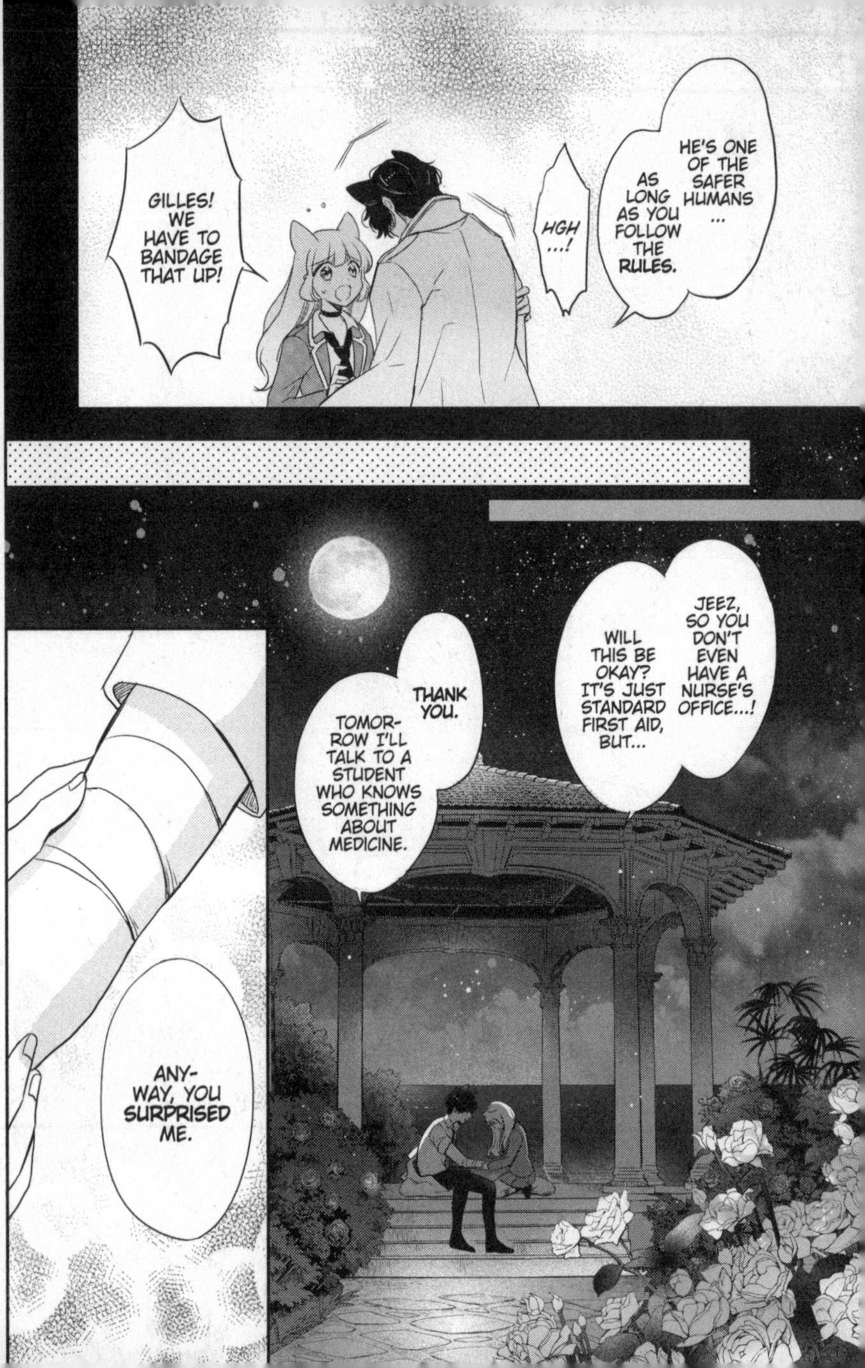
HE'S ONE OF THE SAFER HUMANS...
AS LONG AS YOU FOLLOW THE RULES.
HGH...!
GILLES! WE HAVE TO BANDAGE THAT UP!
JEEZ, SO YOU DON'T EVEN HAVE A NURSE'S OFFICE...!
WILL THIS BE OKAY? IT'S JUST STANDARD FIRST AID, BUT...
THANK YOU.
TOMORROW I'LL TALK TO A STUDENT WHO KNOWS SOMETHING ABOUT MEDICINE.
ANYWAY, YOU SURPRISED ME.

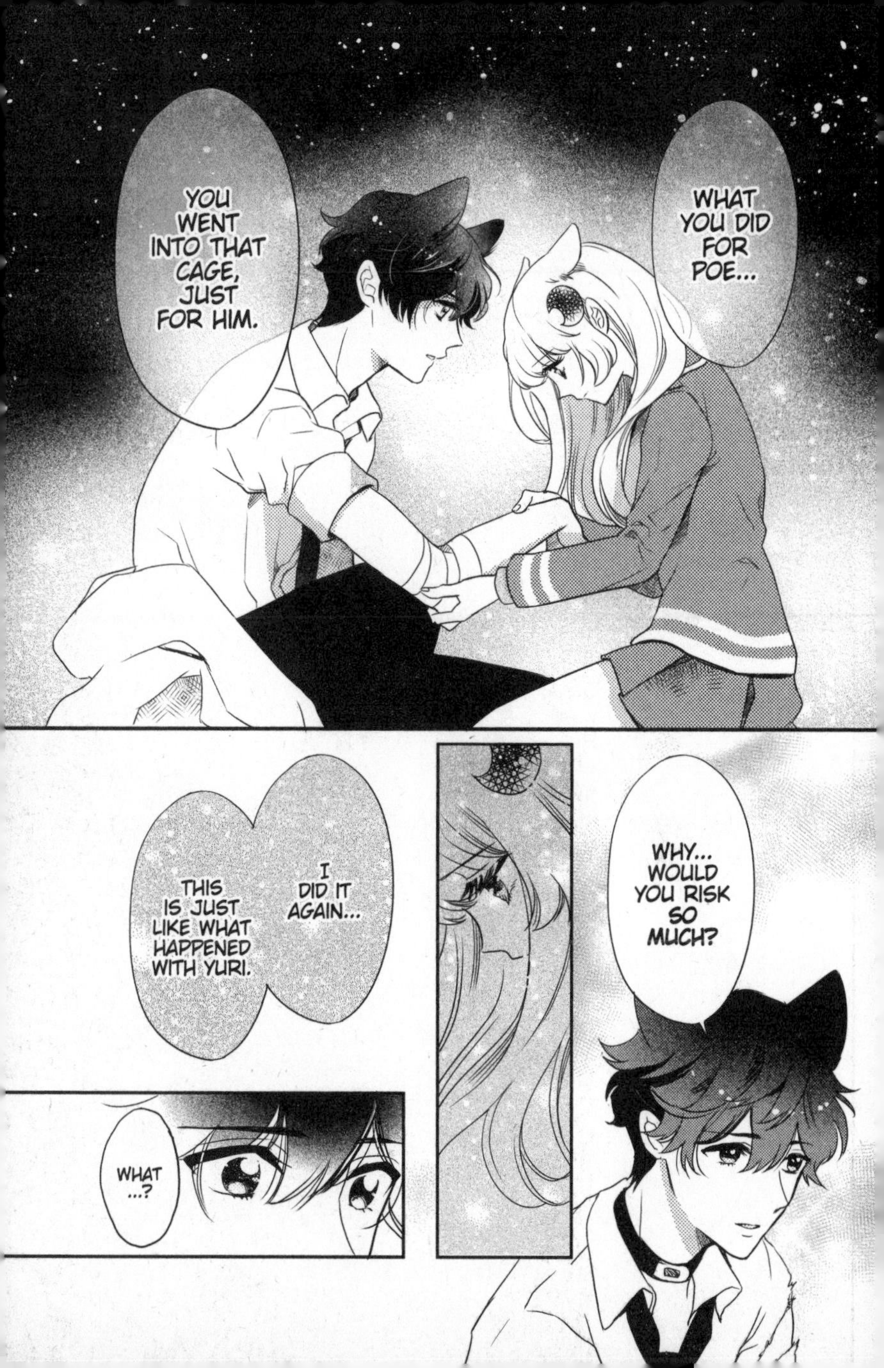
WHAT YOU DID FOR POE...
YOU WENT INTO THAT CAGE, JUST FOR HIM.
WHY... WOULD YOU RISK SO MUCH?
I DID IT AGAIN...
THIS IS JUST LIKE WHAT HAPPENED WITH YURI.
WHAT ...?

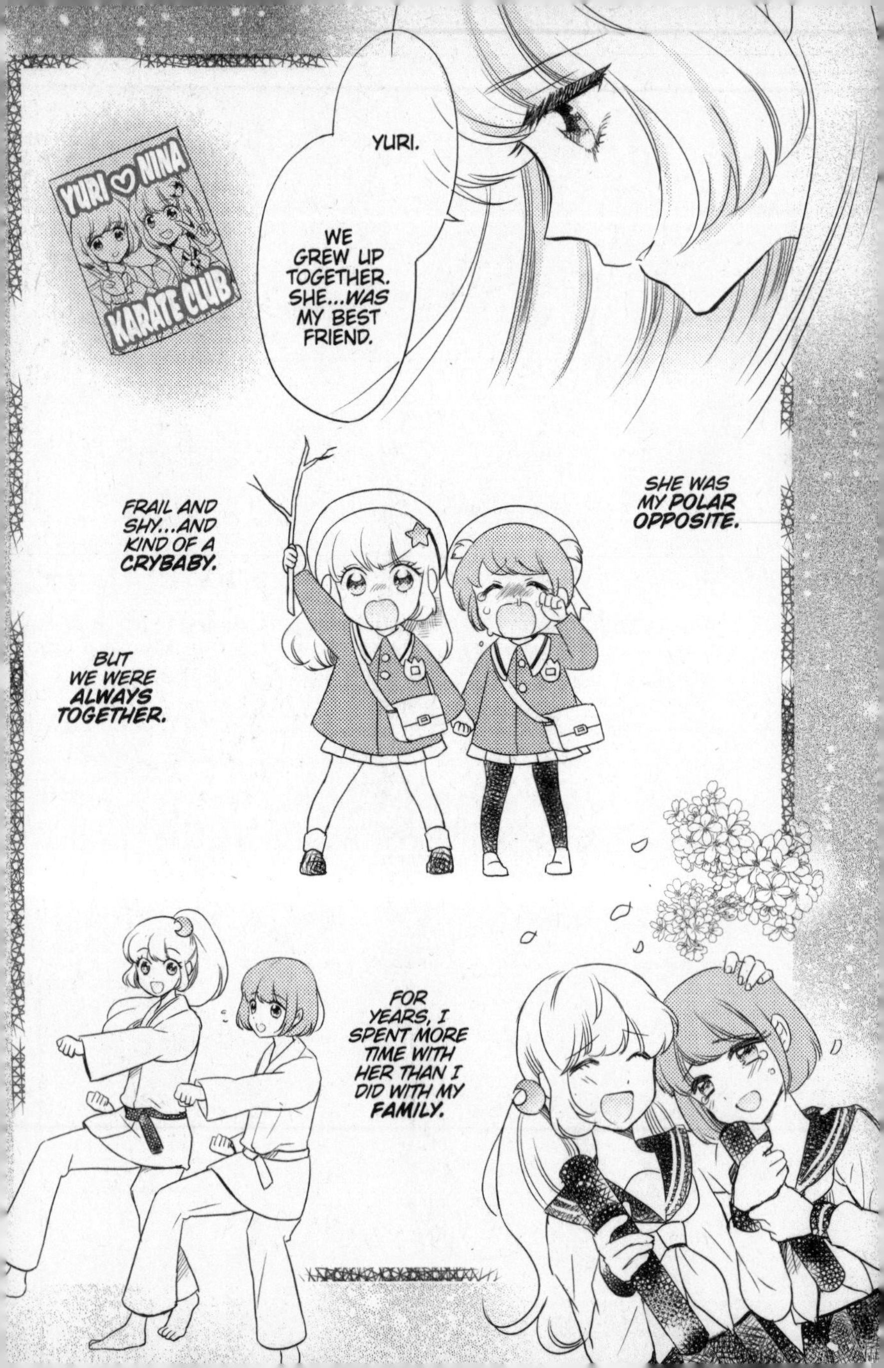
YURI.
WE GREW UP TOGETHER. SHE...WAS MY BEST FRIEND.
YURI ♡ NINA
KARATE CLUB
SHE WAS MY POLAR OPPOSITE.
FRAIL AND SHY...AND KIND OF A CRYBABY.
BUT WE WERE ALWAYS TOGETHER.
FOR YEARS, I SPENT MORE TIME WITH HER THAN I DID WITH MY FAMILY.

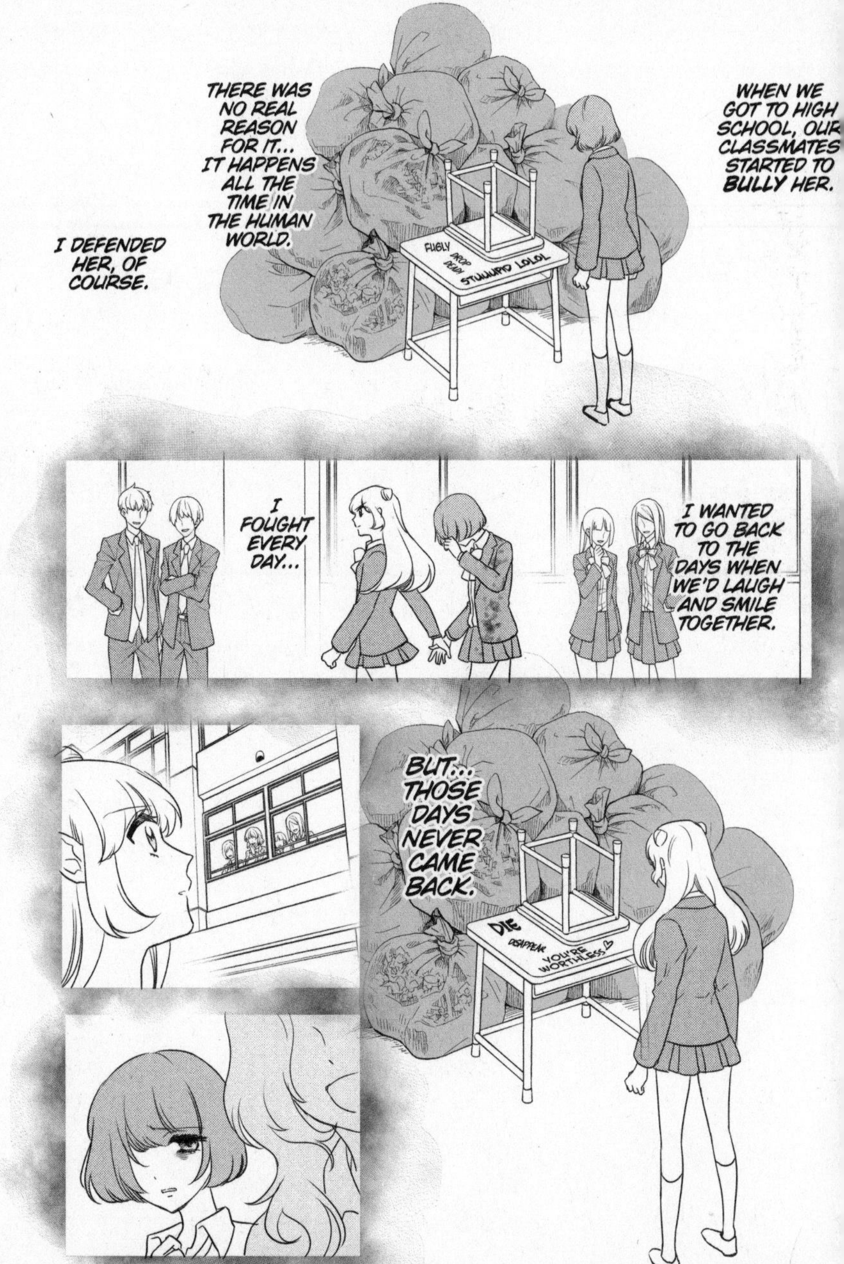
WHEN WE GOT TO HIGH SCHOOL, OUR CLASSMATES STARTED TO BULLY HER.
THERE WAS NO REAL REASON FOR IT... IT HAPPENS ALL THE TIME IN THE HUMAN WORLD.
FUGLY
DROP DEAD!
STUUUPID LOLOL
I DEFENDED HER, OF COURSE.
I WANTED TO GO BACK TO THE DAYS WHEN WE'D LAUGH AND SMILE TOGETHER.
I FOUGHT EVERY DAY...
BUT... THOSE DAYS NEVER CAME BACK.
DIE
DISAPPEAR
YOU'RE WORTHLESS♡

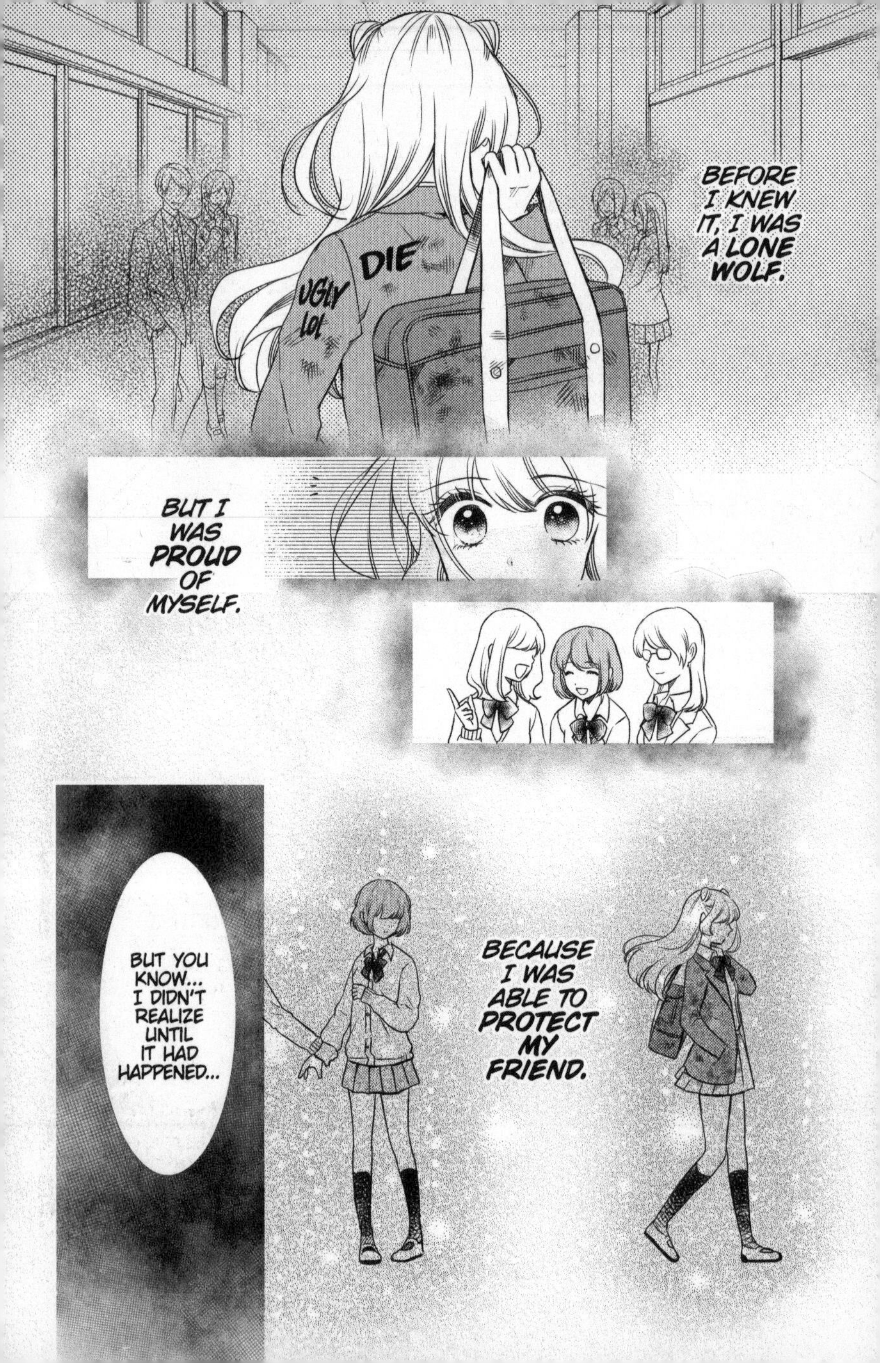
BEFORE I KNEW IT, I WAS A LONE WOLF.
DIE
UGLY LOL
BUT I WAS PROUD OF MYSELF.
BECAUSE I WAS ABLE TO PROTECT MY FRIEND.
BUT YOU KNOW... I DIDN'T REALIZE UNTIL IT HAD HAPPENED...

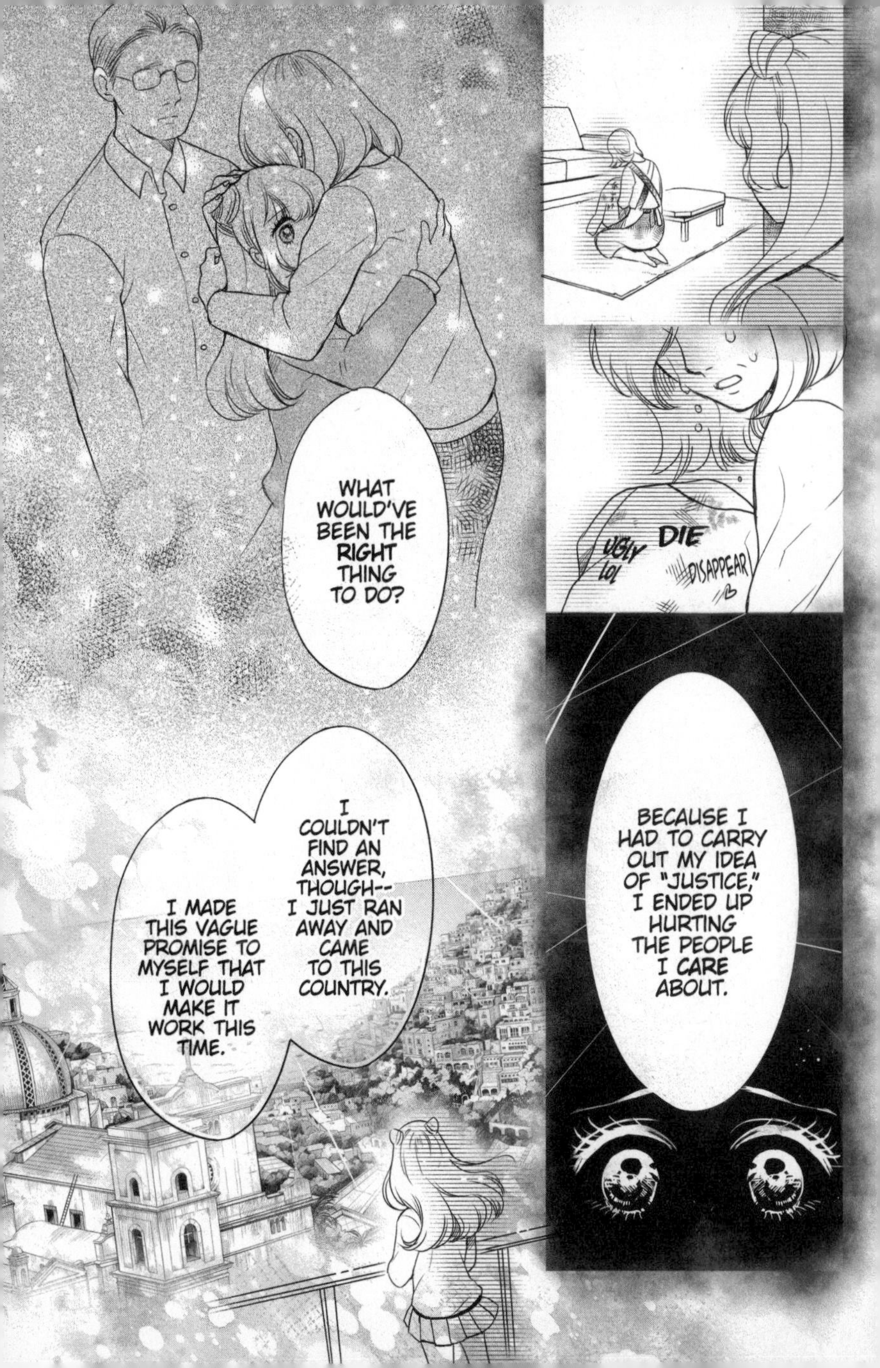
DIE
UGLY LOL
DISAPPEAR
BECAUSE I HAD TO CARRY OUT MY IDEA OF "JUSTICE," I ENDED UP HURTING THE PEOPLE I CARE ABOUT.
WHAT WOULD'VE BEEN THE RIGHT THING TO DO?
I COULDN'T FIND AN ANSWER, THOUGH-- I JUST RAN AWAY AND CAME TO THIS COUNTRY.
I MADE THIS VAGUE PROMISE TO MYSELF THAT I WOULD MAKE IT WORK THIS TIME.

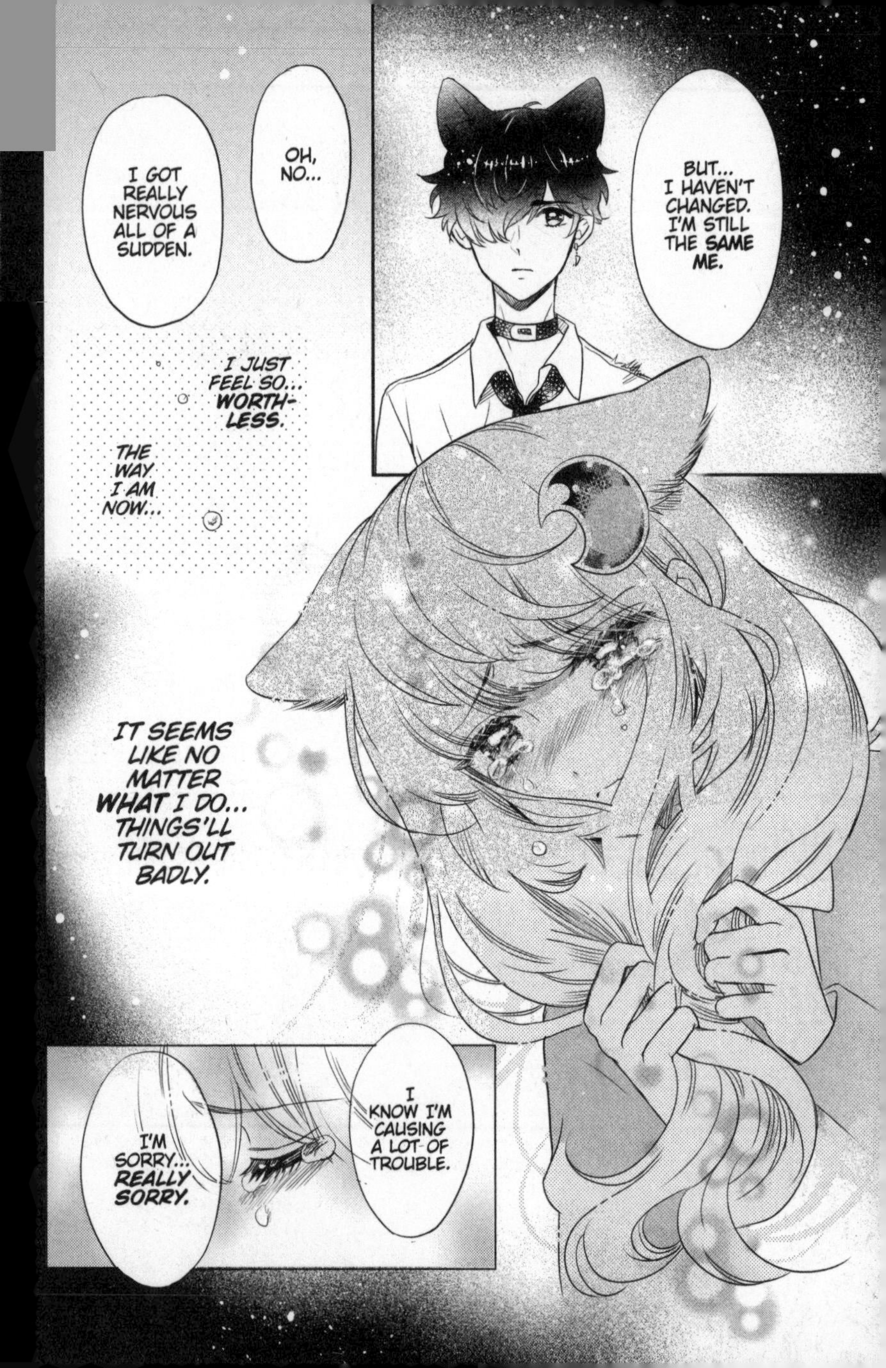
BUT... I HAVEN'T CHANGED. I'M STILL THE SAME ME.
OH, NO...
I GOT REALLY NERVOUS ALL OF A SUDDEN.
I JUST FEEL SO... WORTHLESS.
THE WAY I AM NOW...
IT SEEMS LIKE NO MATTER WHAT I DO... THINGS'LL TURN OUT BADLY.
I KNOW I'M CAUSING A LOT OF TROUBLE.
I'M SORRY... REALLY SORRY.

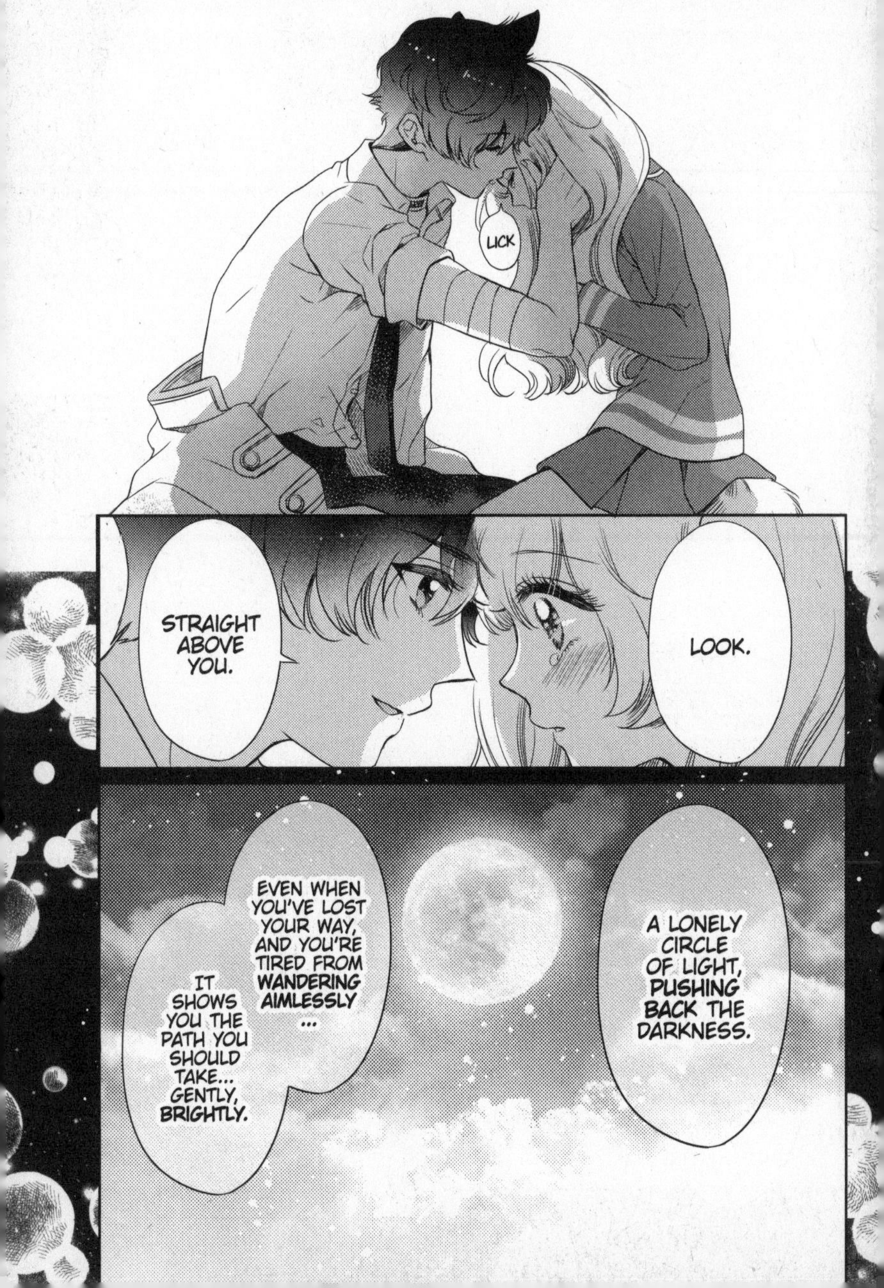
LICK
LOOK.
STRAIGHT ABOVE YOU.
A LONELY CIRCLE OF LIGHT, PUSHING BACK THE DARKNESS.
EVEN WHEN YOU'VE LOST YOUR WAY, AND YOU'RE TIRED FROM WANDERING AIMLESSLY ...
IT SHOWS YOU THE PATH YOU SHOULD TAKE... GENTLY, BRIGHTLY.

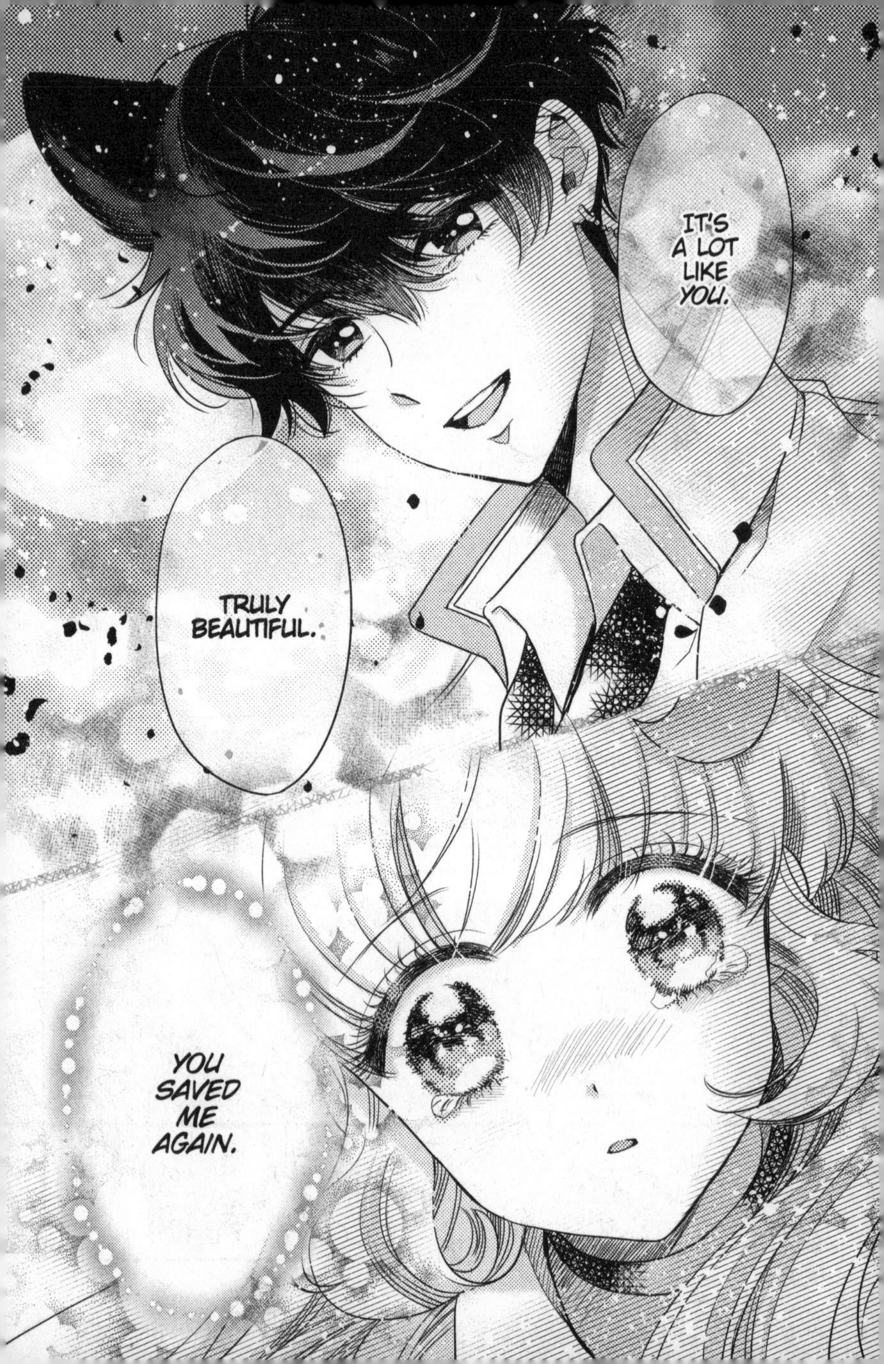
IT'S A LOT LIKE YOU.
TRULY BEAUTIFUL.
YOU SAVED ME AGAIN.

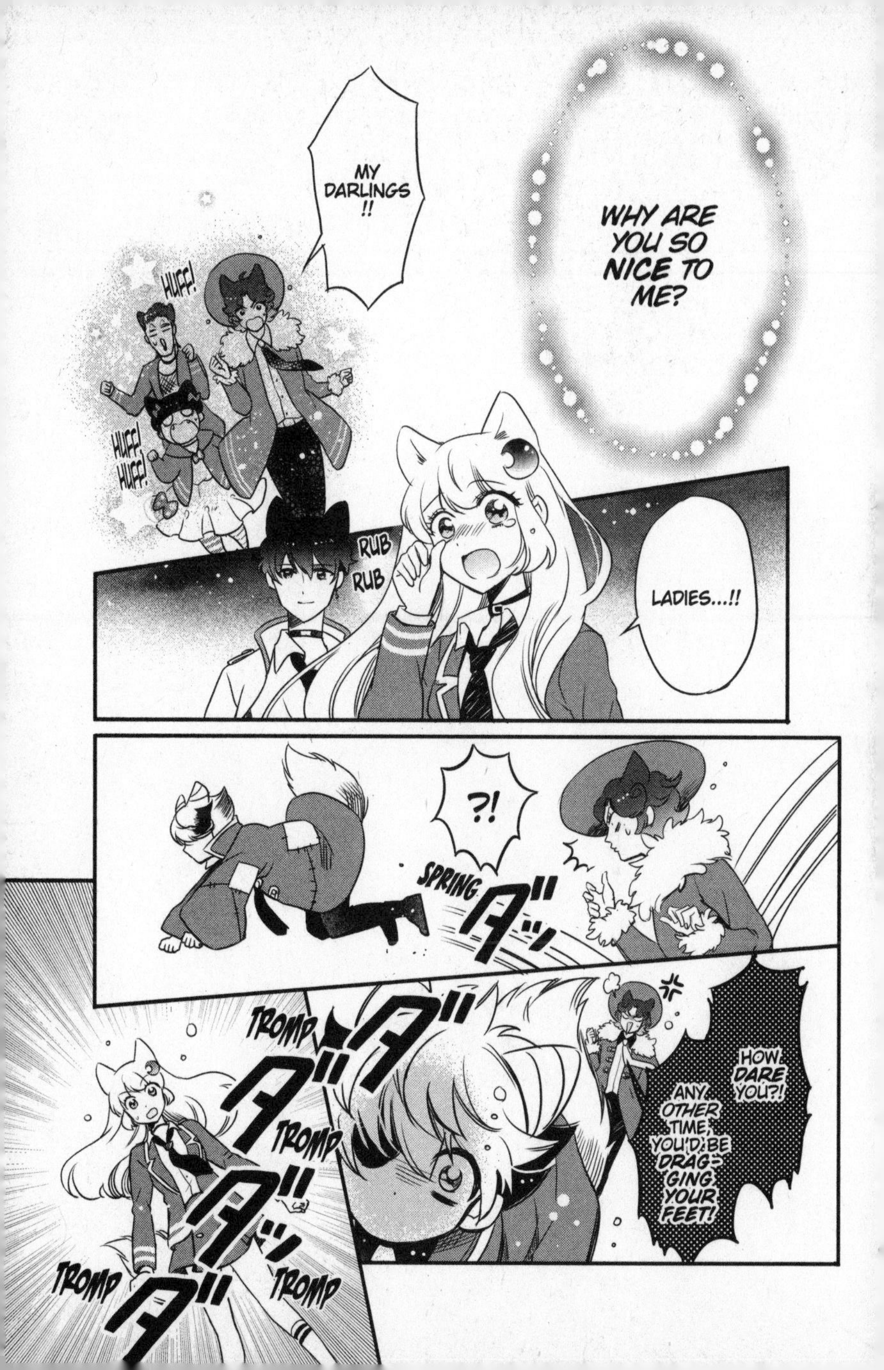
WHY ARE YOU SO NICE TO ME?
MY DARLINGS !!
HUFF!
HUFF! HUFF!
LADIES...!!
RUB RUB
?!
SPRING
ダッ
HOW DARE YOU?!
ANY OTHER TIME, YOU'D BE DRAG-GING YOUR FEET!
TROMP
ダ
TROMP
ダダッ
TROMP
TROMP
ダ

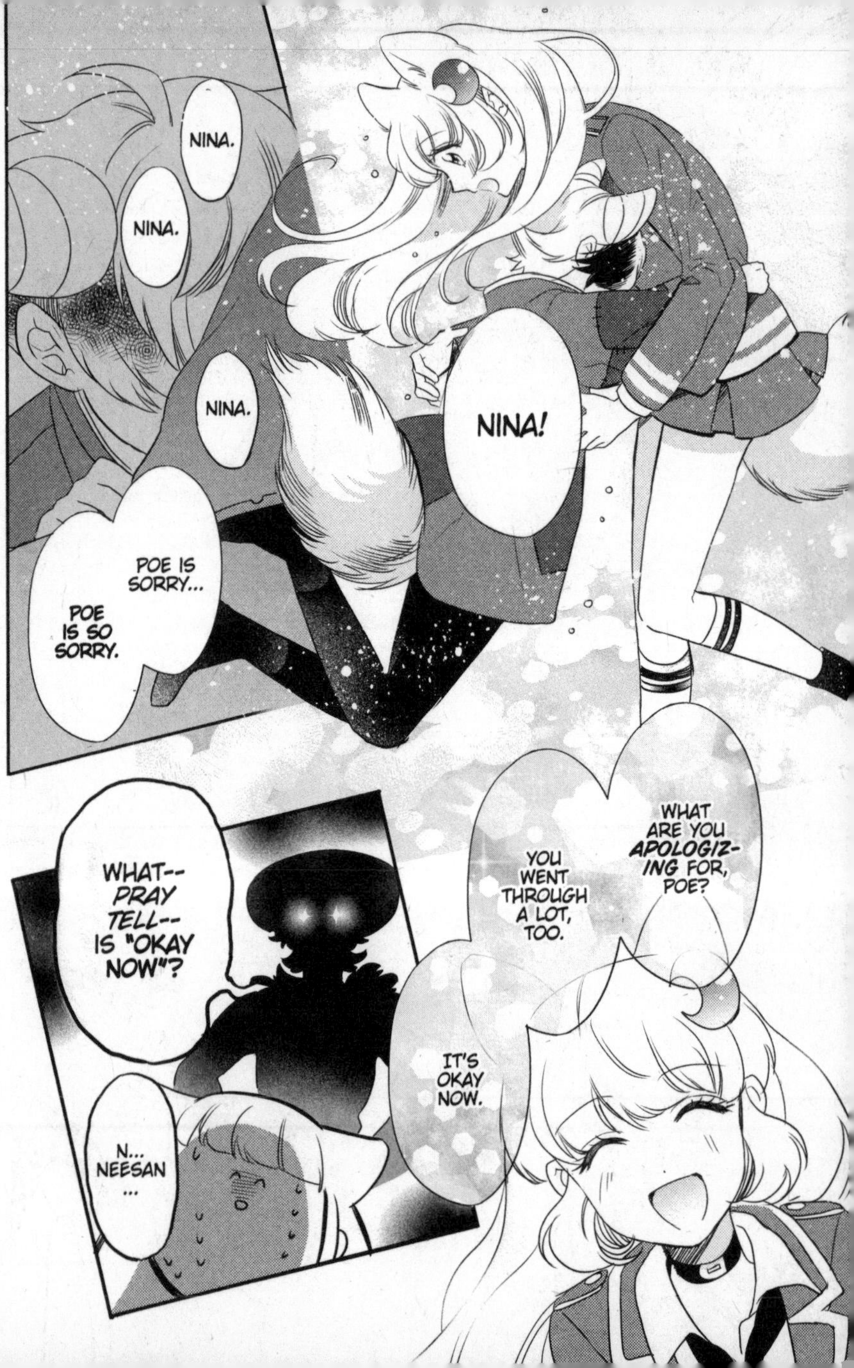
NINA.
NINA.
NINA.
NINA!
POE IS SORRY... POE IS SO SORRY.
WHAT ARE YOU APOLOGIZING FOR, POE?
YOU WENT THROUGH A LOT, TOO.
IT'S OKAY NOW.
WHAT--PRAY TELL--IS "OKAY NOW"?
N... NEESAN ...

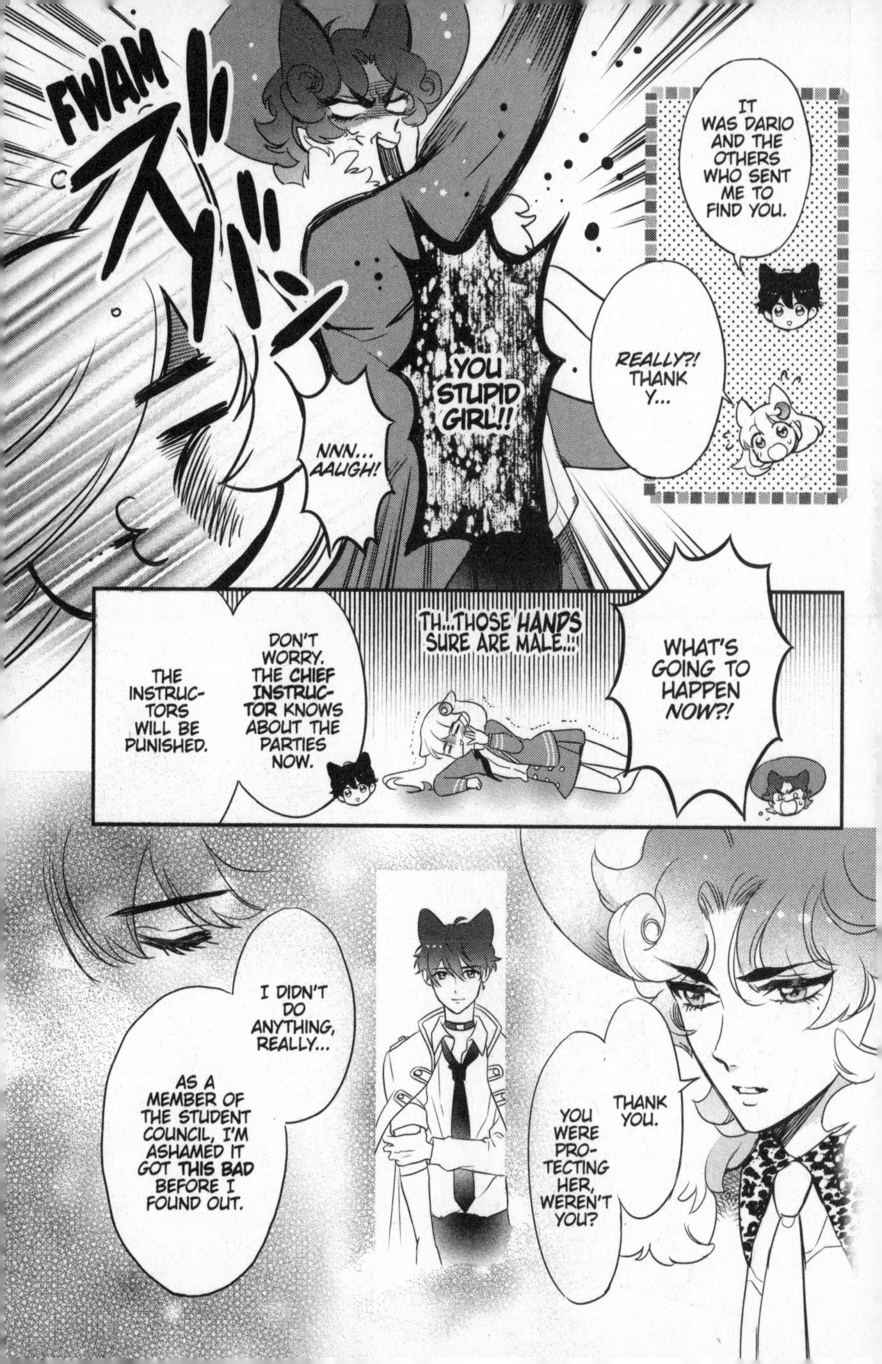
IT WAS DARIO AND THE OTHERS WHO SENT ME TO FIND YOU.
REALLY?! THANK Y...
FWAM
YOU STUPID GIRL!!
NNN... AAUGH!
WHAT'S GOING TO HAPPEN NOW?!
TH...THOSE HANDS SURE ARE MALE...!
DON'T WORRY. THE CHIEF INSTRUCTOR KNOWS ABOUT THE PARTIES NOW.
THE INSTRUCTORS WILL BE PUNISHED.
THANK YOU.
YOU WERE PROTECTING HER, WEREN'T YOU?
I DIDN'T DO ANYTHING, REALLY...
AS A MEMBER OF THE STUDENT COUNCIL, I'M ASHAMED IT GOT THIS BAD BEFORE I FOUND OUT.

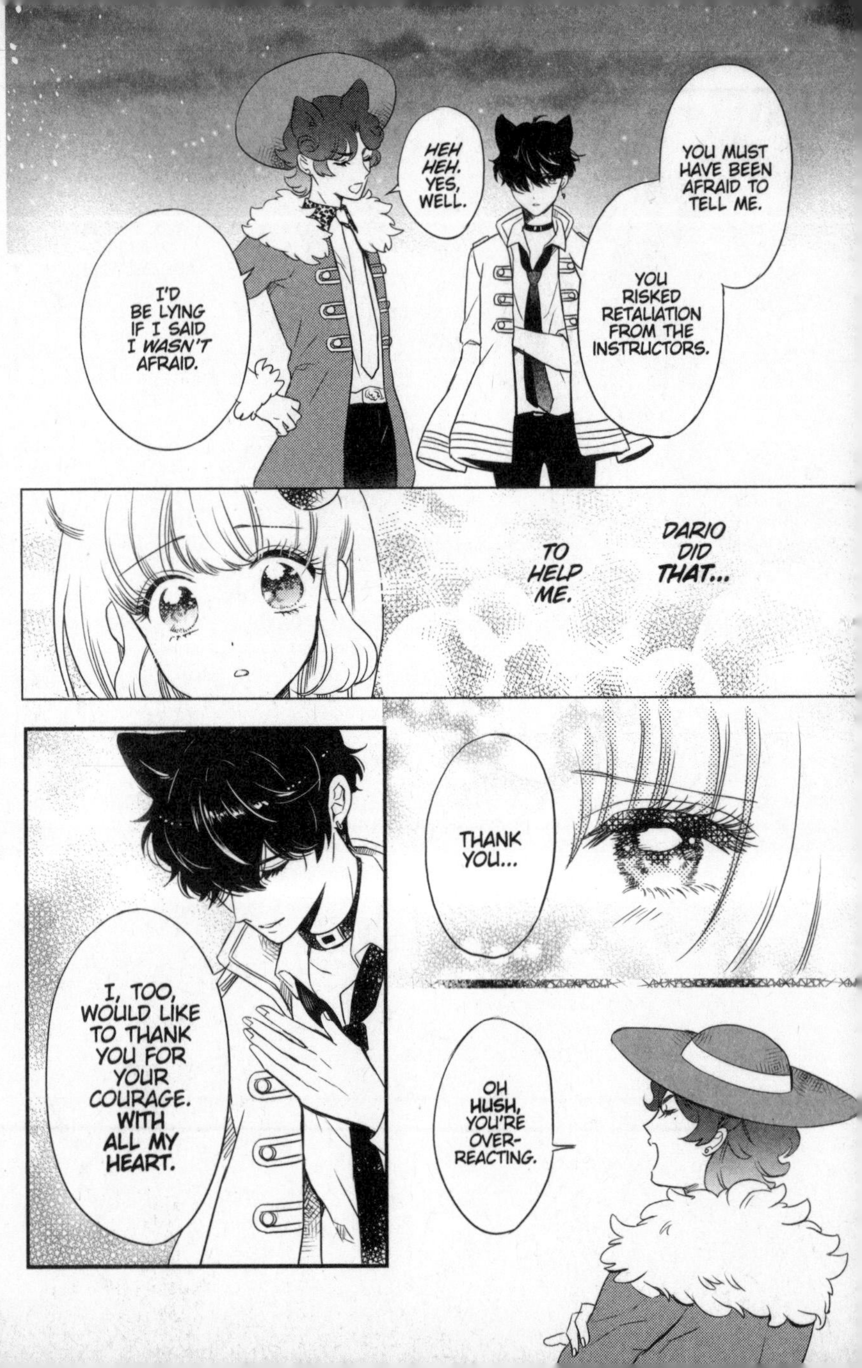
YOU MUST HAVE BEEN AFRAID TO TELL ME.
YOU RISKED RETALIATION FROM THE INSTRUCTORS.
HEH HEH. YES, WELL.
I'D BE LYING IF I SAID I *WASN'T* AFRAID.
DARIO DID THAT...
TO HELP ME.
THANK YOU...
I, TOO, WOULD LIKE TO THANK YOU FOR YOUR COURAGE. WITH ALL MY HEART.
OH HUSH, YOU'RE OVER-REACTING.

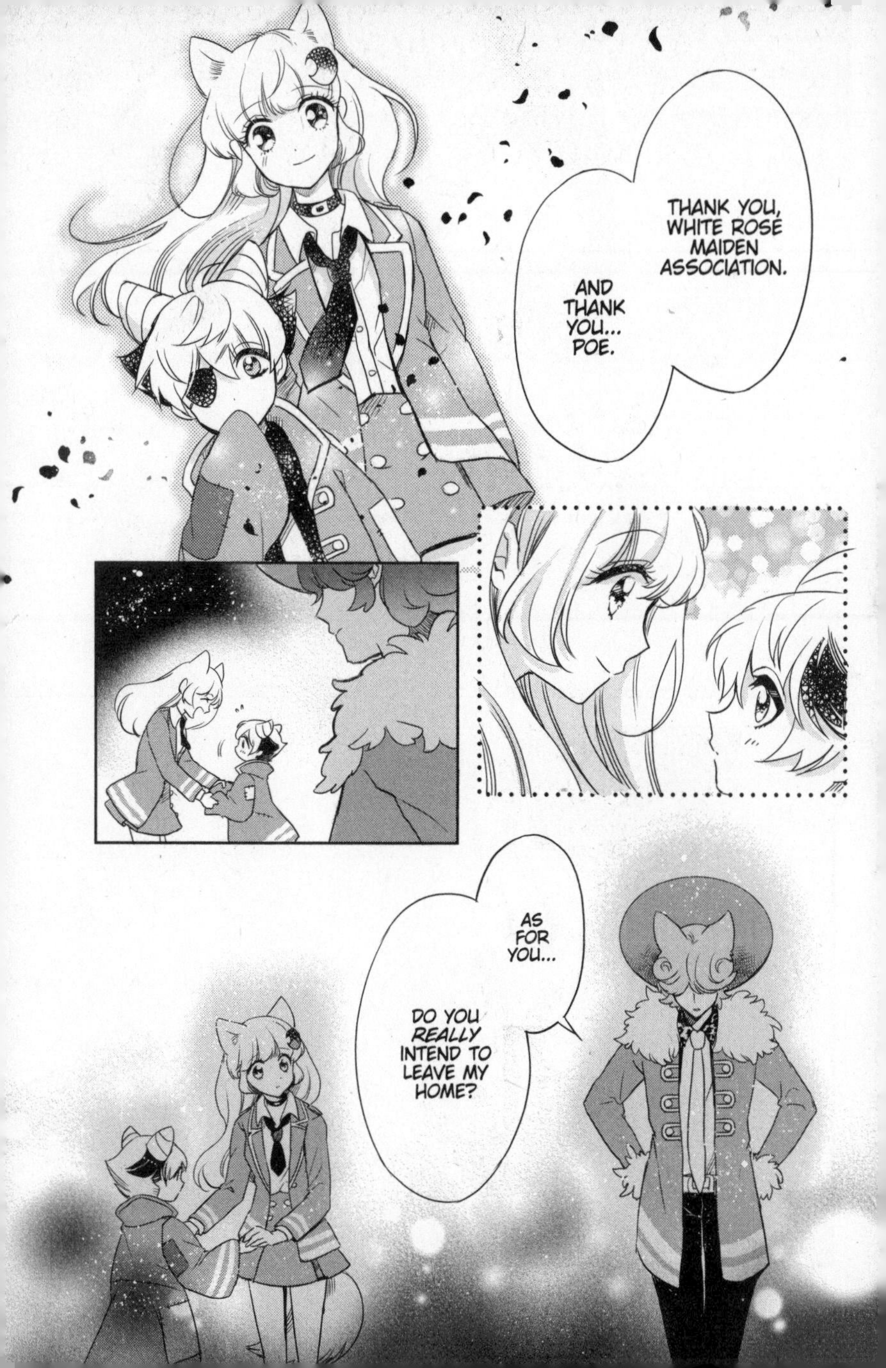
THANK YOU, WHITE ROSE MAIDEN ASSOCIATION.
AND THANK YOU... POE.
AS FOR YOU...
DO YOU *REALLY* INTEND TO LEAVE MY HOME?

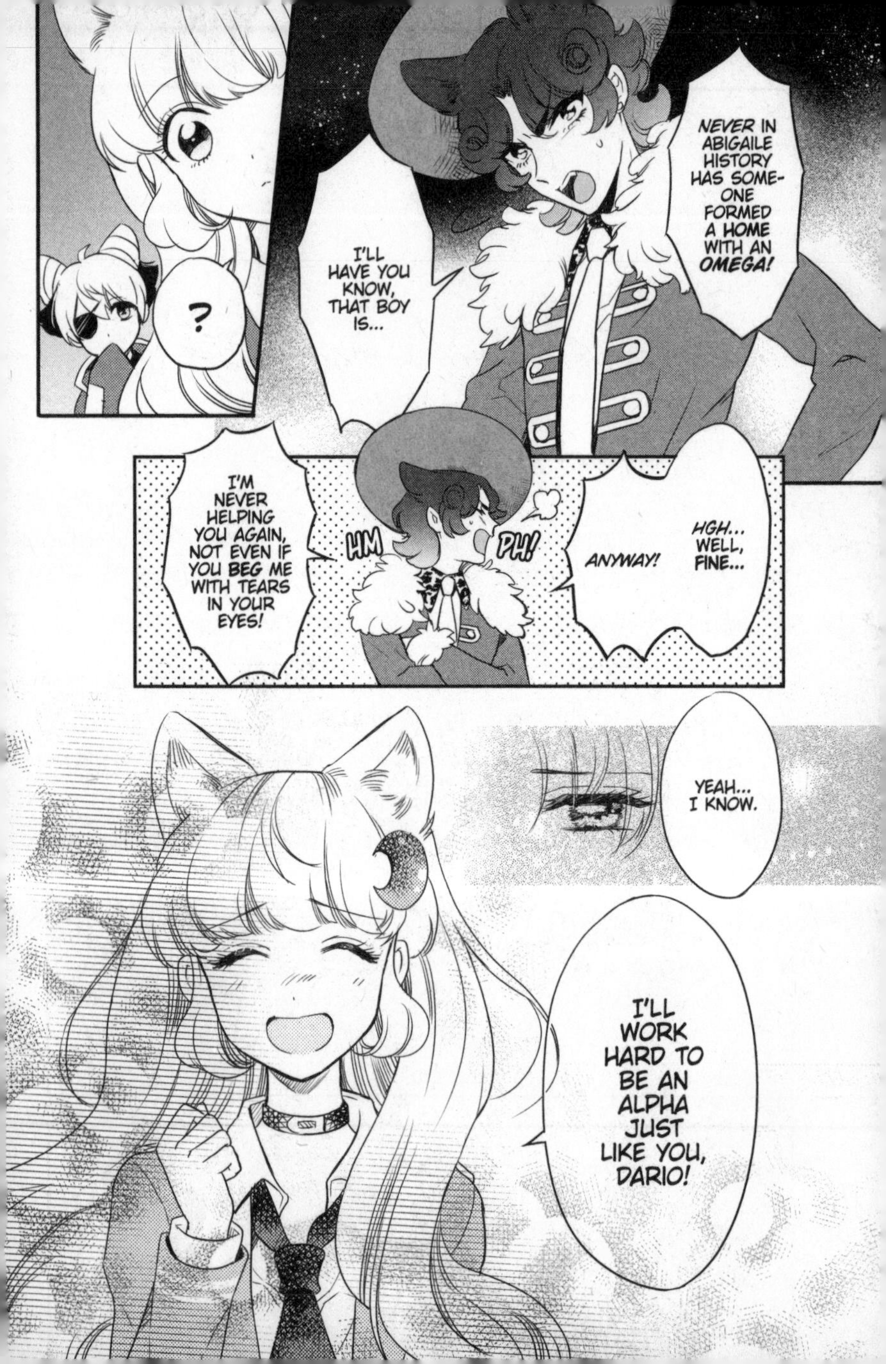
NEVER IN ABIGAILE HISTORY HAS SOME-ONE FORMED A HOME WITH AN OMEGA!
I'LL HAVE YOU KNOW, THAT BOY IS...
?
HGH... WELL, FINE...
ANYWAY!
HMPH!
I'M NEVER HELPING YOU AGAIN, NOT EVEN IF YOU BEG ME WITH TEARS IN YOUR EYES!
YEAH... I KNOW.
I'LL WORK HARD TO BE AN ALPHA JUST LIKE YOU, DARIO!

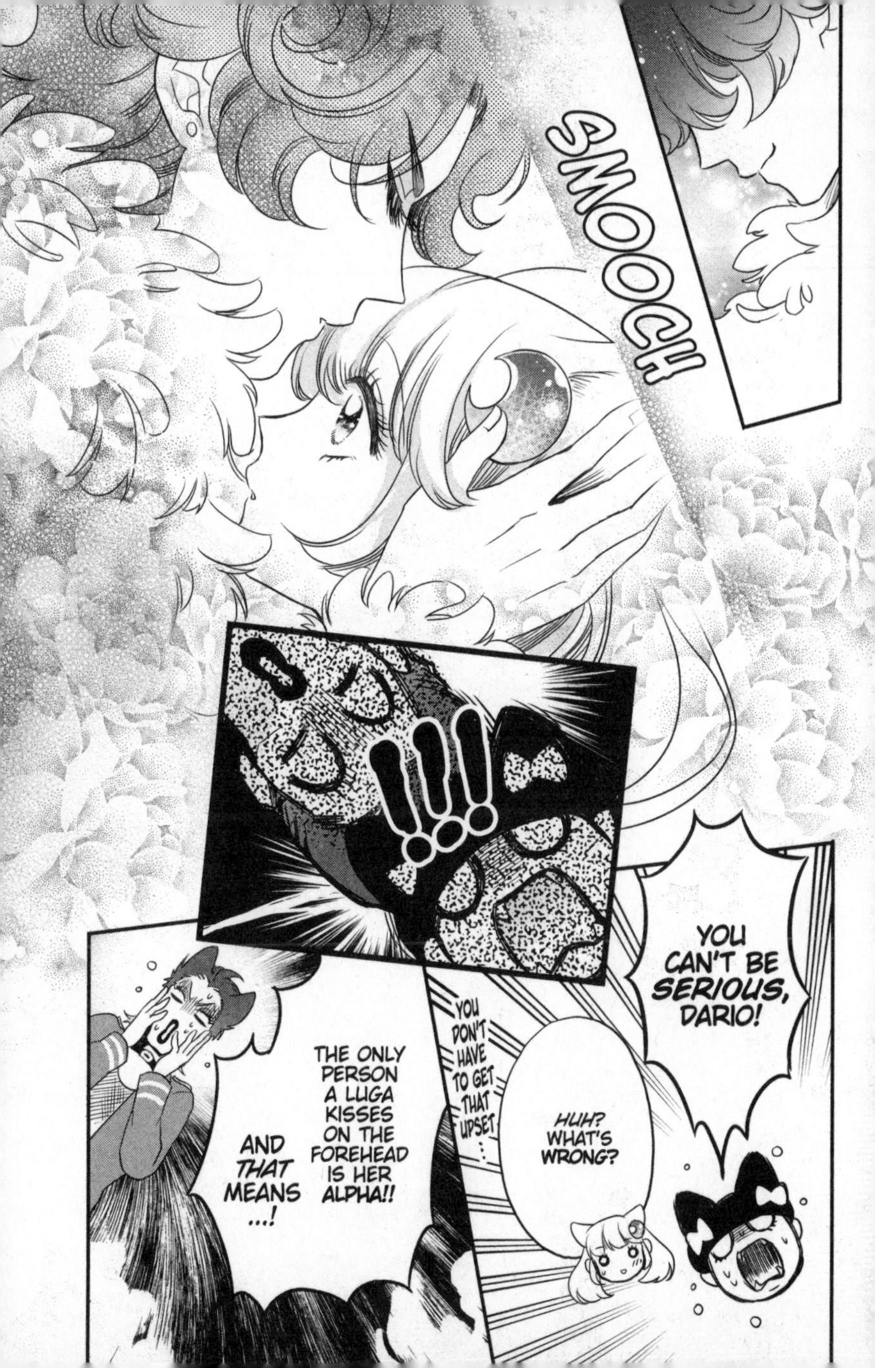
SMOOCH
!!!
YOU CAN'T BE *SERIOUS*, DARIO!
HUH? WHAT'S WRONG?
YOU DON'T HAVE TO GET THAT UPSET...
THE ONLY PERSON A LUGA KISSES ON THE FOREHEAD IS HER ALPHA!!
AND *THAT* MEANS ...!

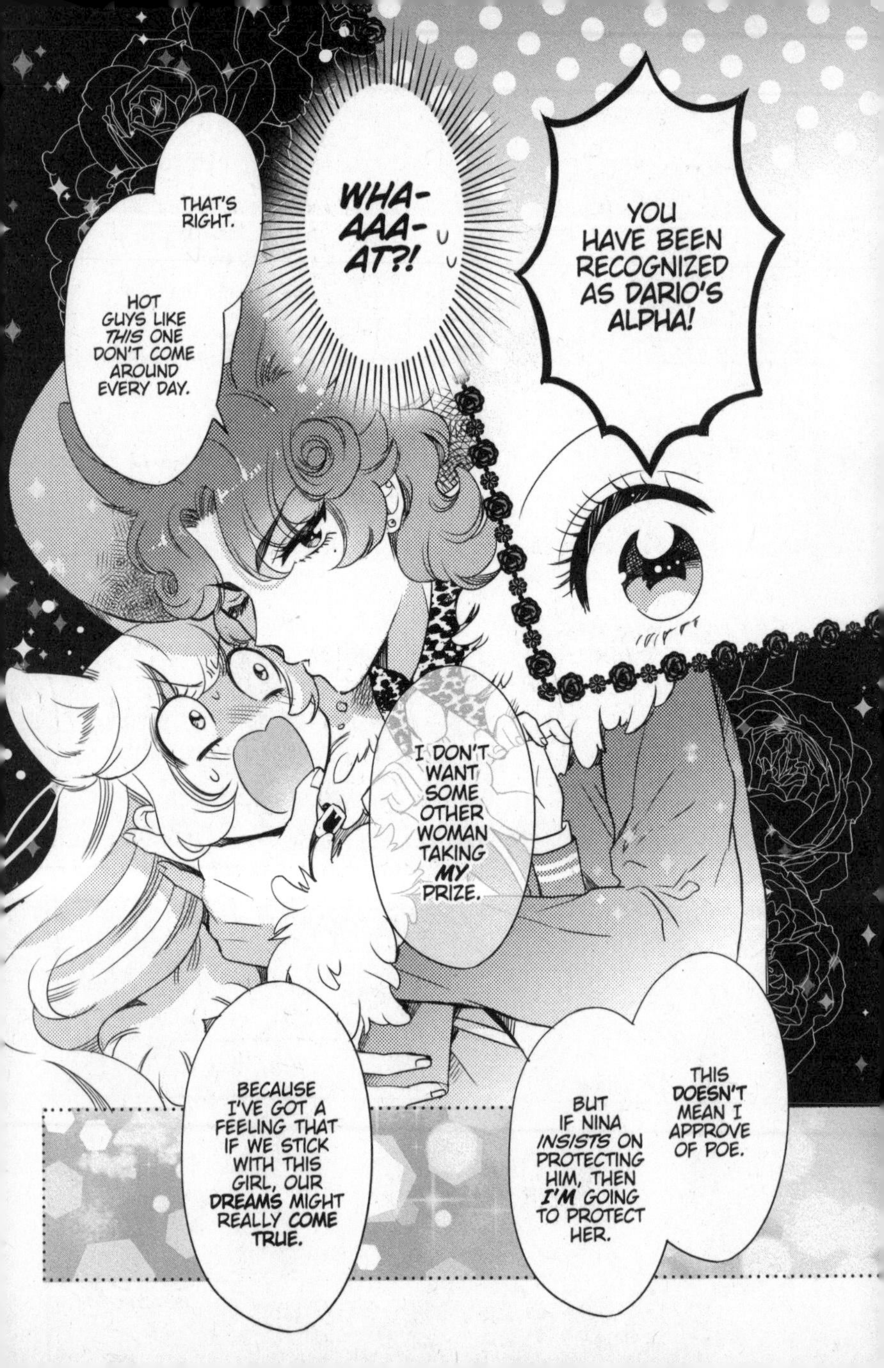
YOU HAVE BEEN RECOGNIZED AS DARIO'S ALPHA!
WHA-AAA-AT?!
THAT'S RIGHT.
HOT GUYS LIKE *THIS* ONE DON'T COME AROUND EVERY DAY.
I DON'T WANT SOME OTHER WOMAN TAKING *MY* PRIZE.
THIS **DOESN'T** MEAN I APPROVE OF POE.
BUT IF NINA *INSISTS* ON PROTECTING HIM, THEN ***I'M*** GOING TO PROTECT HER.
BECAUSE I'VE GOT A FEELING THAT IF WE STICK WITH THIS GIRL, OUR **DREAMS** MIGHT REALLY **COME TRUE.**

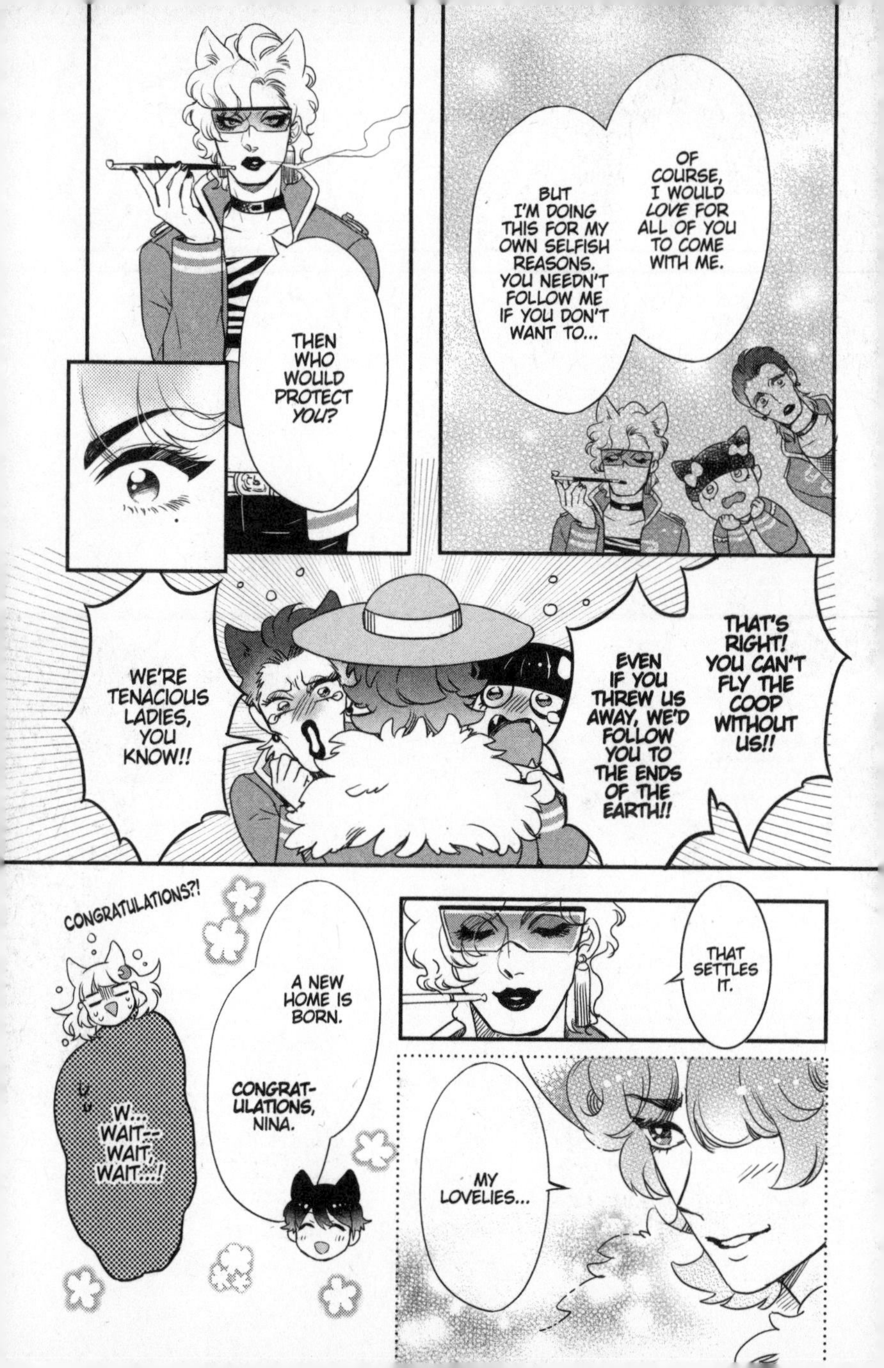
OF COURSE, I WOULD LOVE FOR ALL OF YOU TO COME WITH ME.
BUT I'M DOING THIS FOR MY OWN SELFISH REASONS. YOU NEEDN'T FOLLOW ME IF YOU DON'T WANT TO...
THEN WHO WOULD PROTECT YOU?
THAT'S RIGHT! YOU CAN'T FLY THE COOP WITHOUT US!!
EVEN IF YOU THREW US AWAY, WE'D FOLLOW YOU TO THE ENDS OF THE EARTH!!
WE'RE TENACIOUS LADIES, YOU KNOW!!
THAT SETTLES IT.
MY LOVELIES...
A NEW HOME IS BORN.
CONGRAT-ULATIONS, NINA.
CONGRATULATIONS?!
W... WAIT-- WAIT, WAIT...!

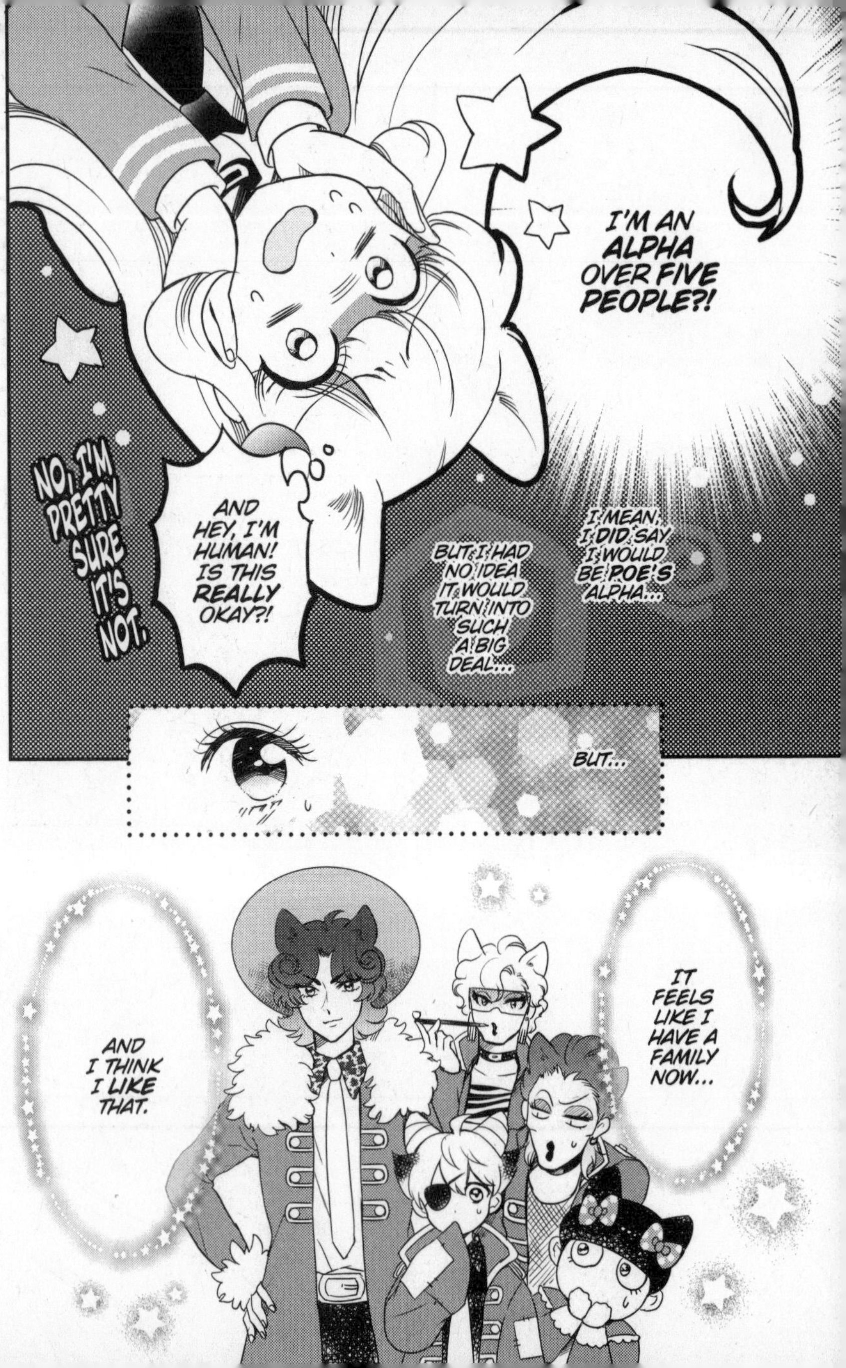
I'M AN ALPHA OVER FIVE PEOPLE?!
I MEAN, I DID SAY I WOULD BE POE'S ALPHA...
BUT I HAD NO IDEA IT WOULD TURN INTO SUCH A BIG DEAL...
AND HEY, I'M HUMAN! IS THIS REALLY OKAY?!
NO, I'M PRETTY SURE IT'S NOT.
BUT...
IT FEELS LIKE I HAVE A FAMILY NOW...
AND I THINK I LIKE THAT.

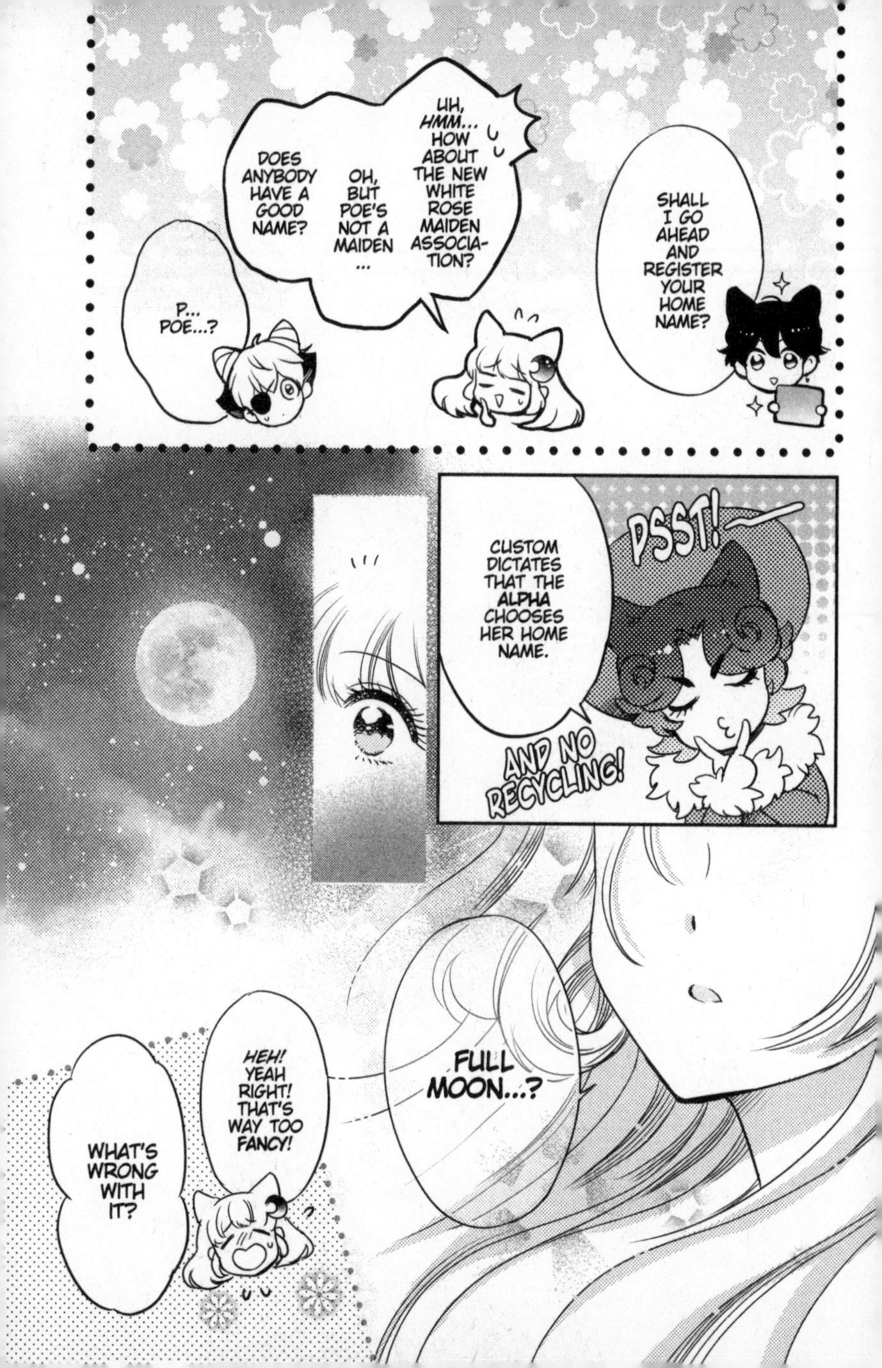
SHALL I GO AHEAD AND REGISTER YOUR HOME NAME?
UH, HMM... HOW ABOUT THE NEW WHITE ROSE MAIDEN ASSOCIATION?
OH, BUT POE'S NOT A MAIDEN ...
DOES ANYBODY HAVE A GOOD NAME?
P... POE...?
PSSST!~
CUSTOM DICTATES THAT THE ALPHA CHOOSES HER HOME NAME.
AND NO RECYCLING!
FULL MOON...?
HEH! YEAH RIGHT! THAT'S WAY TOO FANCY!
WHAT'S WRONG WITH IT?

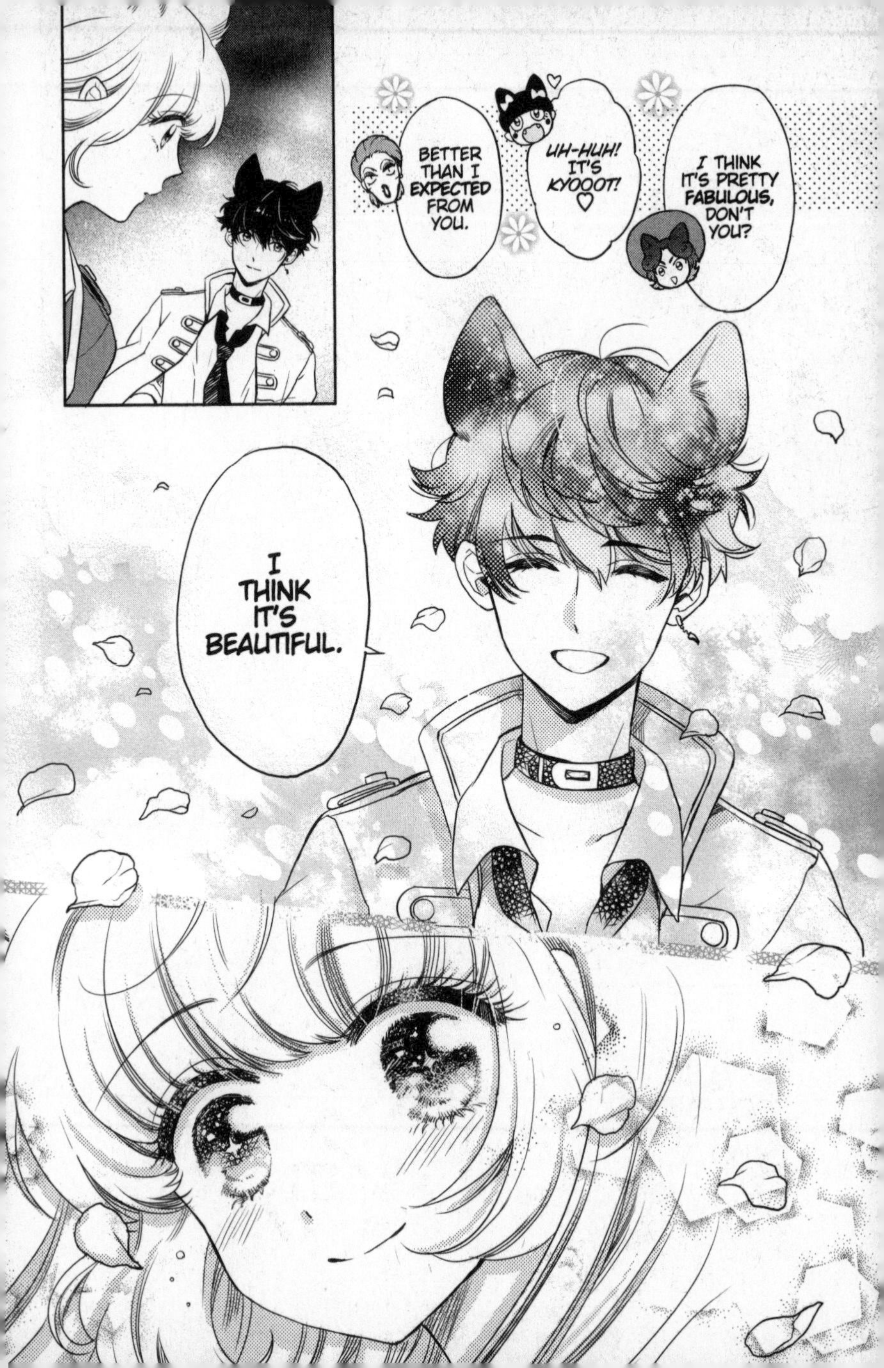
I THINK IT'S PRETTY FABULOUS, DON'T YOU?
UH-HUH! IT'S KYOOOT! ♡
BETTER THAN I EXPECTED FROM YOU.
I THINK IT'S BEAUTIFUL.

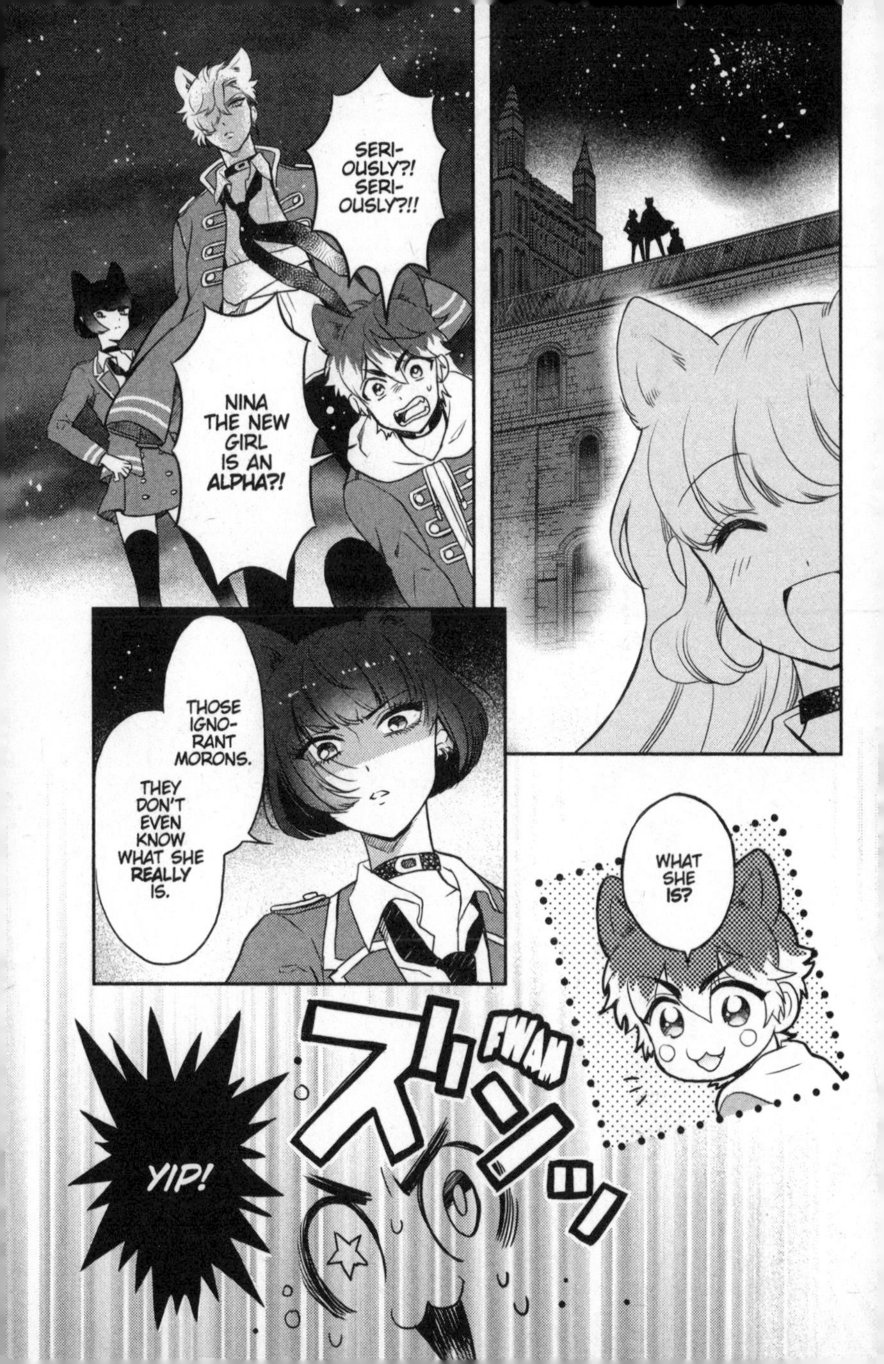
SERI-OUSLY?! SERI-OUSLY?!!
NINA THE NEW GIRL IS AN ALPHA?!
THOSE IGNO-RANT MORONS.
THEY DON'T EVEN KNOW WHAT SHE REALLY IS.
WHAT SHE IS?
FWAM
YIP!

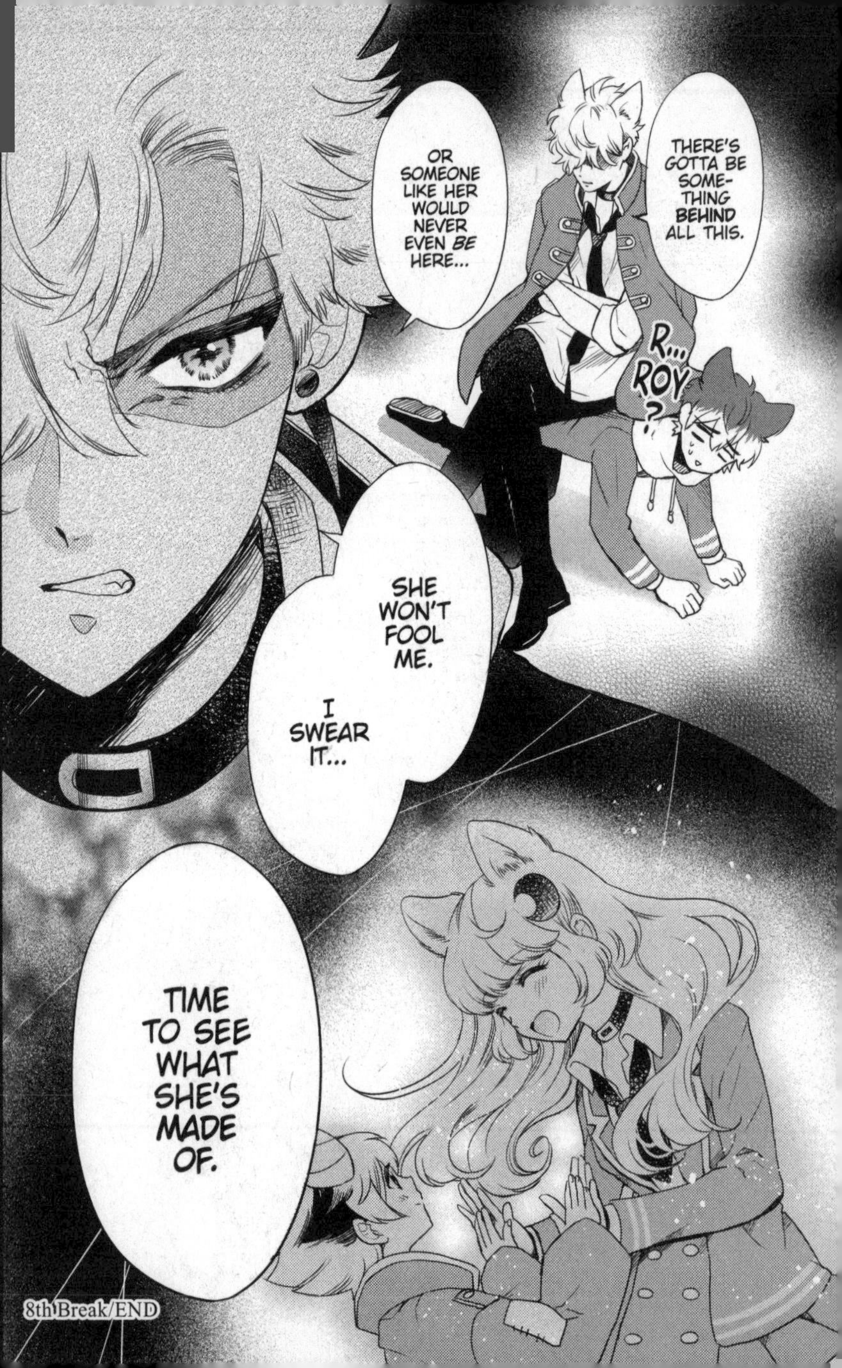
THERE'S GOTTA BE SOME-THING BEHIND ALL THIS.
OR SOMEONE LIKE HER WOULD NEVER EVEN *BE* HERE...
R... ROY?
SHE WON'T FOOL ME.
I SWEAR IT...
TIME TO SEE WHAT SHE'S MADE OF.
8th Break/END

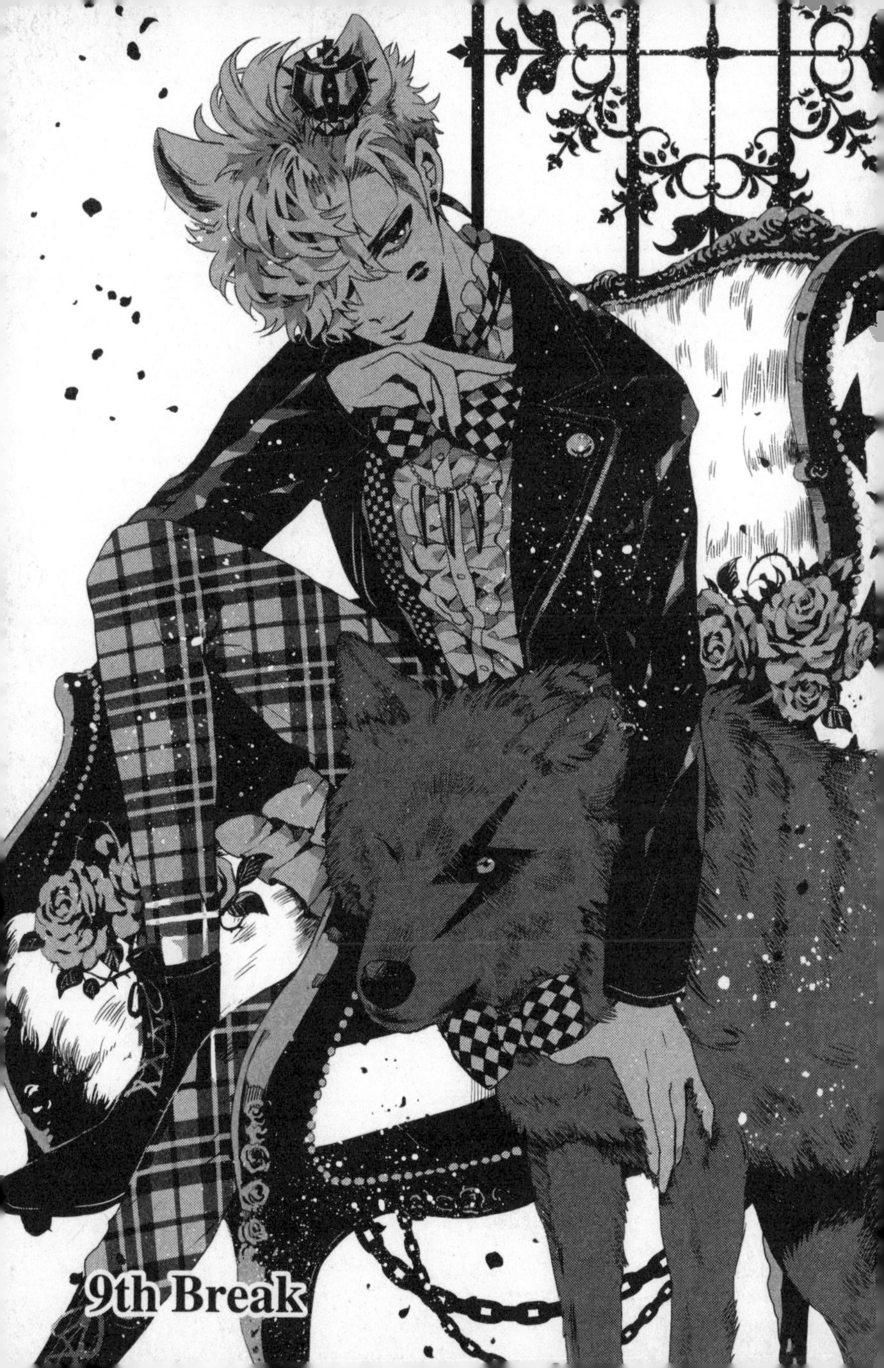
9th Break

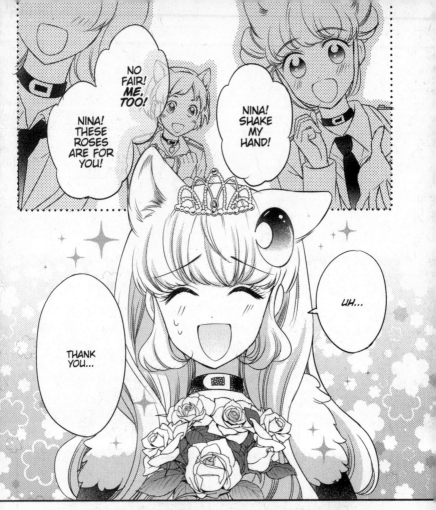

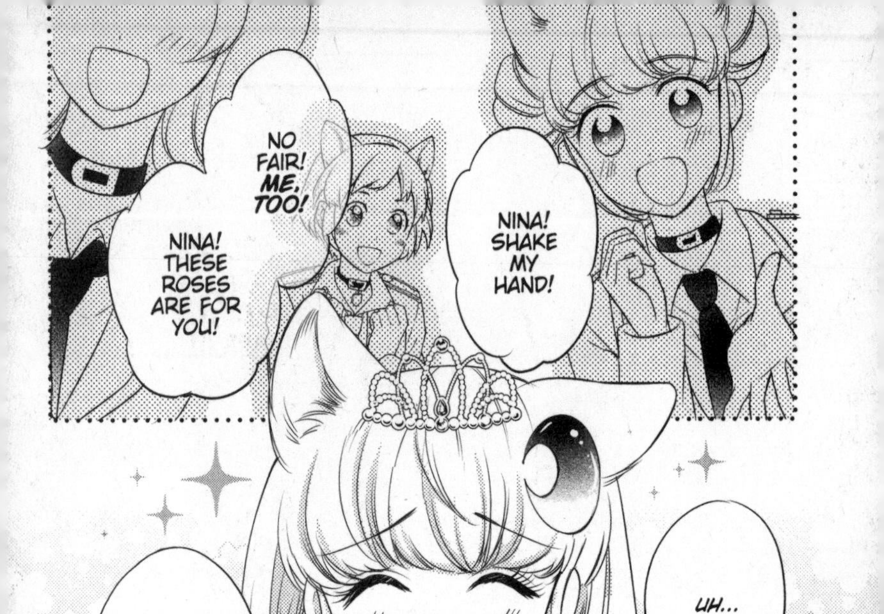
NINA! SHAKE MY HAND!
NO FAIR! ME, TOO!
NINA! THESE ROSES ARE FOR YOU!
UH...
THANK YOU...

Thank you! Editor-san, Designer-san, Assistant-san, Father, Mother, Friends, and all my fans! ♡

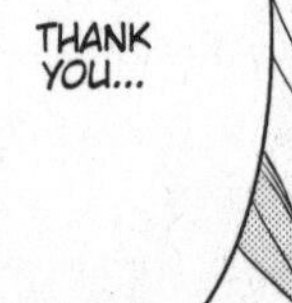

Courtney (18)
I'm going to be a singer-song-writer!!

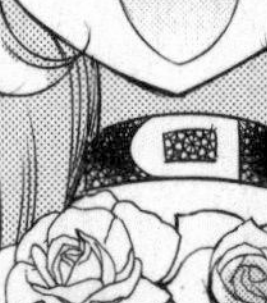

Dorothy (15)
I want to be an idol ♡♡

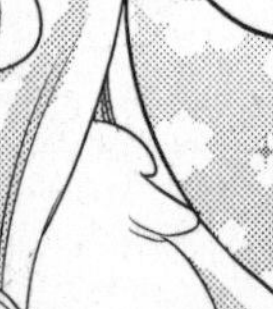

Rebecca (18)
It's my dream to be an actress.

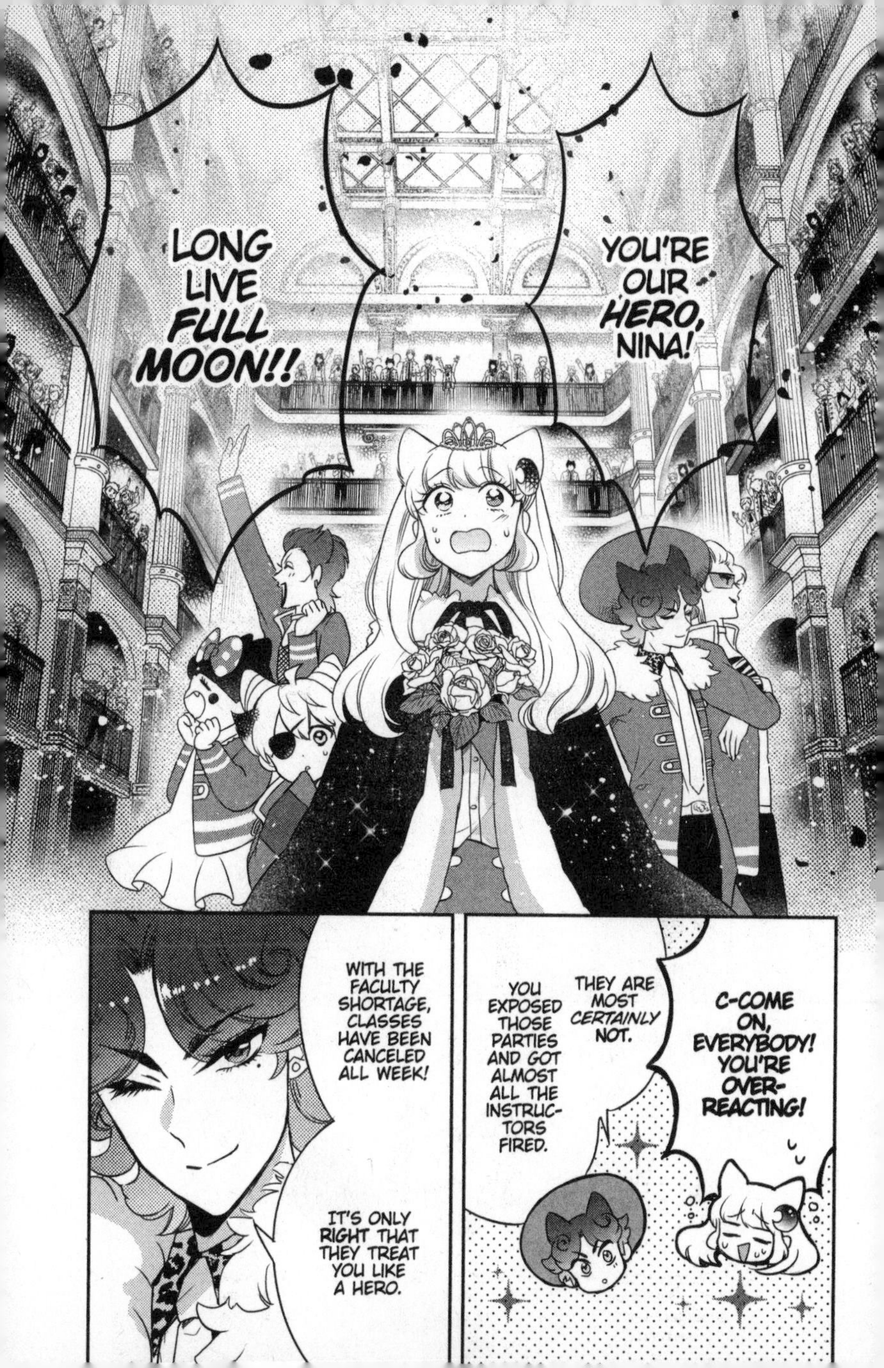
YOU'RE OUR HERO, NINA!
LONG LIVE FULL MOON!!
C-COME ON, EVERYBODY! YOU'RE OVER-REACTING!
THEY ARE MOST CERTAINLY NOT.
YOU EXPOSED THOSE PARTIES AND GOT ALMOST ALL THE INSTRUCTORS FIRED.
WITH THE FACULTY SHORTAGE, CLASSES HAVE BEEN CANCELED ALL WEEK!
IT'S ONLY RIGHT THAT THEY TREAT YOU LIKE A HERO.

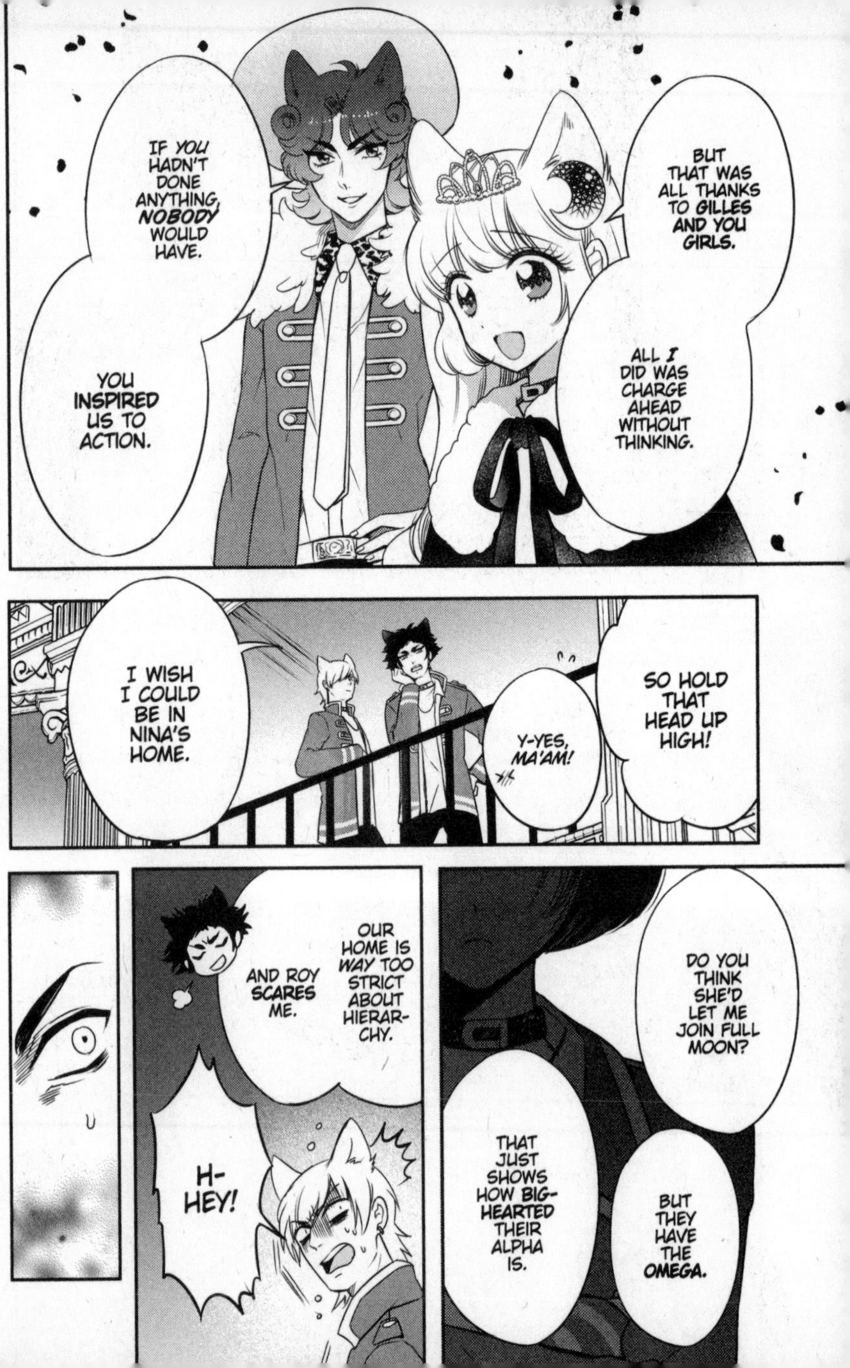
BUT THAT WAS ALL THANKS TO GILLES AND YOU GIRLS.
ALL I DID WAS CHARGE AHEAD WITHOUT THINKING.
IF YOU HADN'T DONE ANYTHING, NOBODY WOULD HAVE.
YOU INSPIRED US TO ACTION.
SO HOLD THAT HEAD UP HIGH!
Y-YES, MA'AM!
I WISH I COULD BE IN NINA'S HOME.
DO YOU THINK SHE'D LET ME JOIN FULL MOON?
BUT THEY HAVE THE OMEGA.
THAT JUST SHOWS HOW BIG-HEARTED THEIR ALPHA IS.
OUR HOME IS WAY TOO STRICT ABOUT HIERAR-CHY.
AND ROY SCARES ME.
H-HEY!

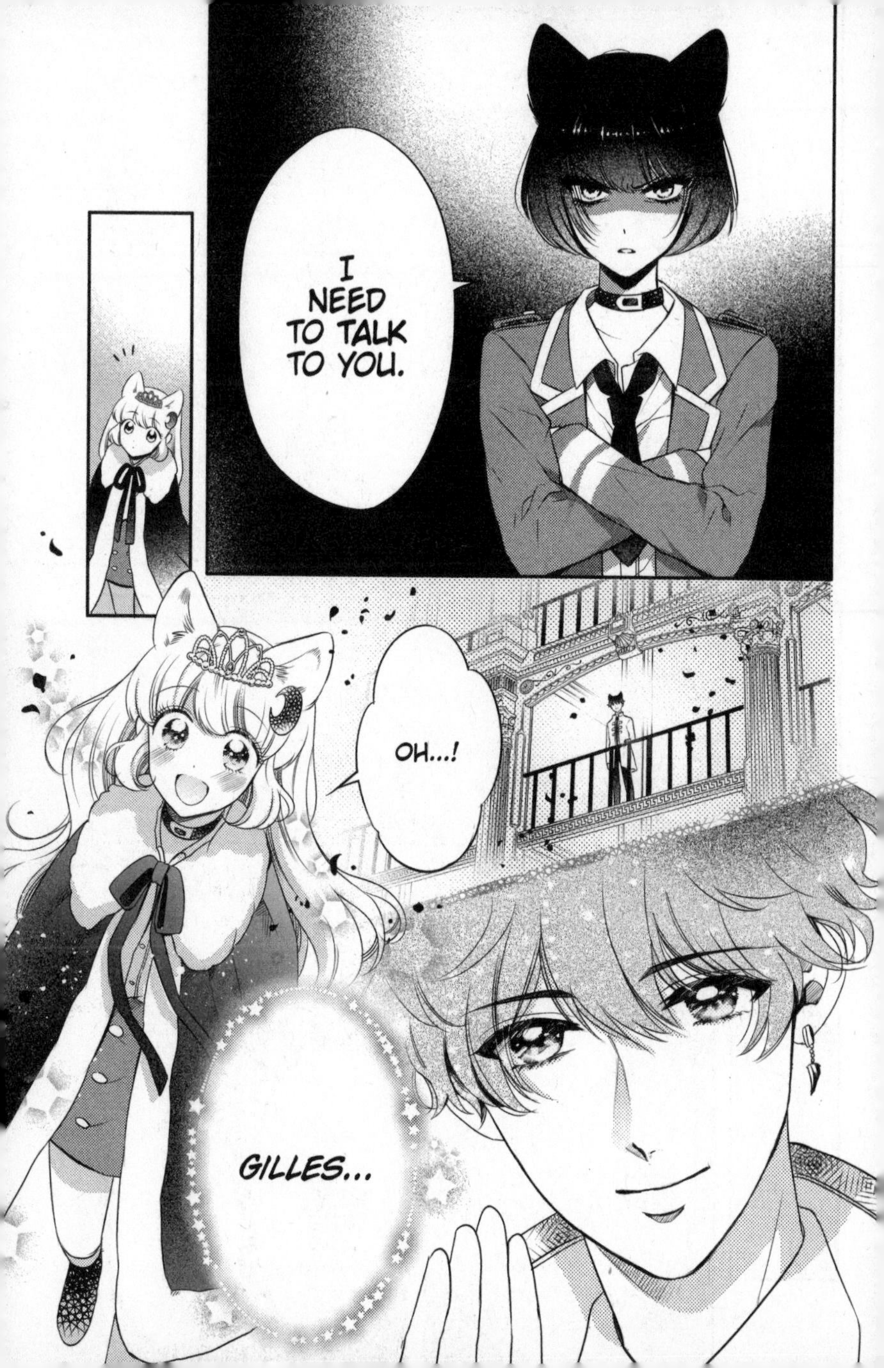
I NEED TO TALK TO YOU.
OH...!
GILLES...

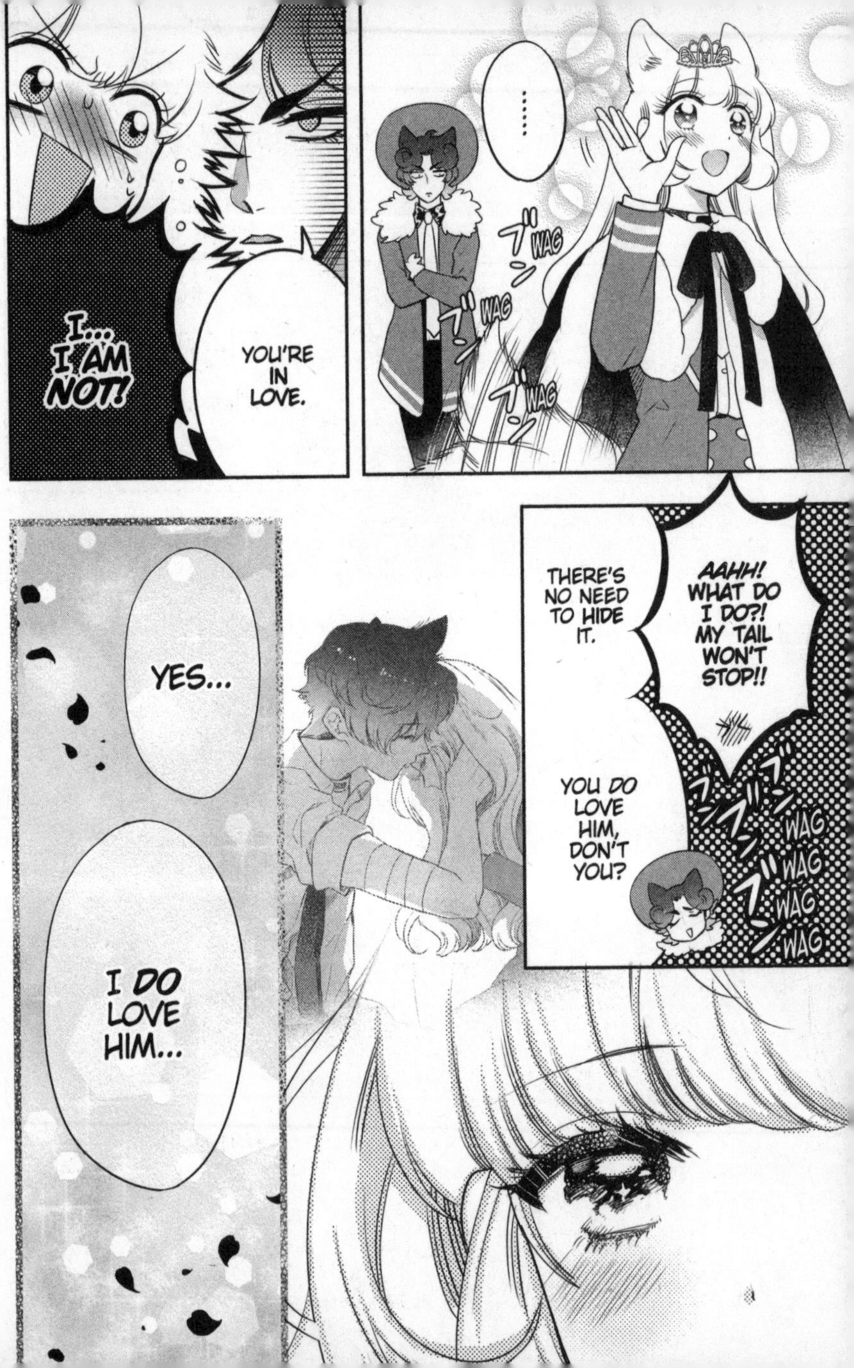
......
WAG
WAG
WAG
YOU'RE IN LOVE.
I... I AM NOT!
AAHH! WHAT DO I DO?! MY TAIL WON'T STOP!!
THERE'S NO NEED TO HIDE IT.
YOU *DO* LOVE HIM, DON'T YOU?
WAG
WAG
WAG
WAG
YES...
I *DO* LOVE HIM...

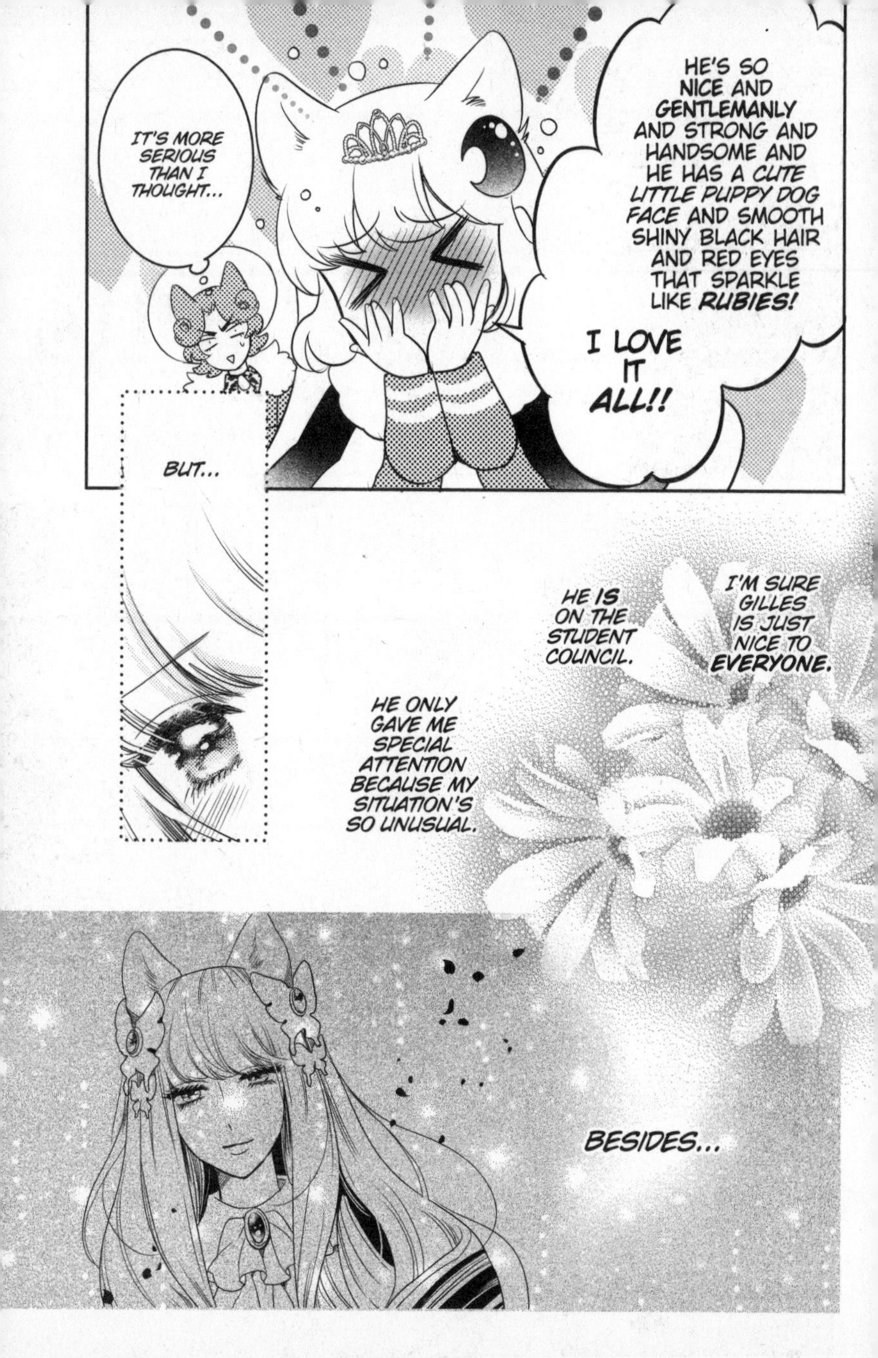
HE'S SO NICE AND GENTLEMANLY AND STRONG AND HANDSOME AND HE HAS A CUTE LITTLE PUPPY DOG FACE AND SMOOTH SHINY BLACK HAIR AND RED EYES THAT SPARKLE LIKE RUBIES!
I LOVE IT ALL!!
IT'S MORE SERIOUS THAN I THOUGHT...
BUT...
I'M SURE GILLES IS JUST NICE TO EVERYONE.
HE IS ON THE STUDENT COUNCIL.
HE ONLY GAVE ME SPECIAL ATTENTION BECAUSE MY SITUATION'S SO UNUSUAL.
BESIDES...

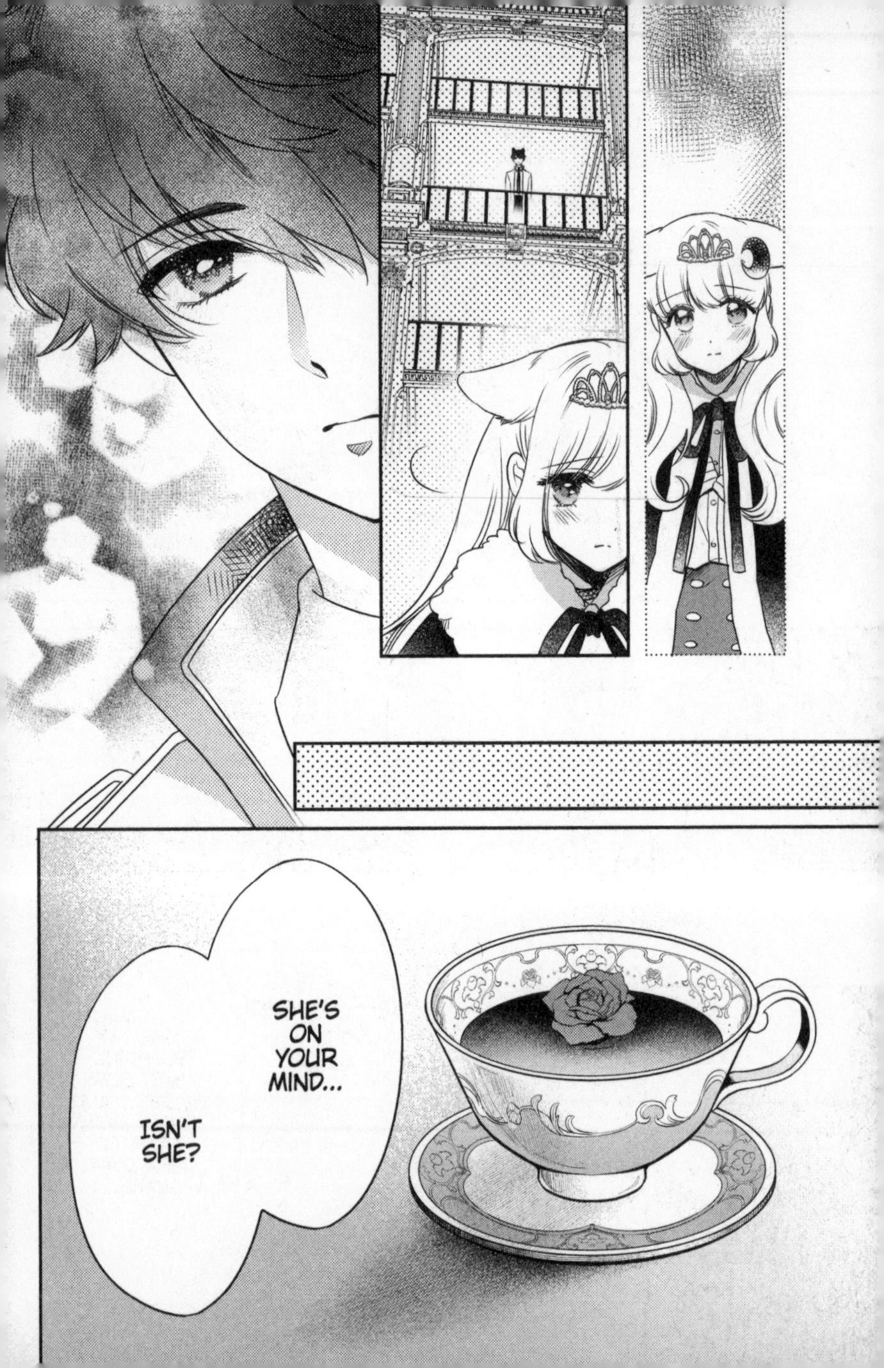
SHE'S ON YOUR MIND...
ISN'T SHE?

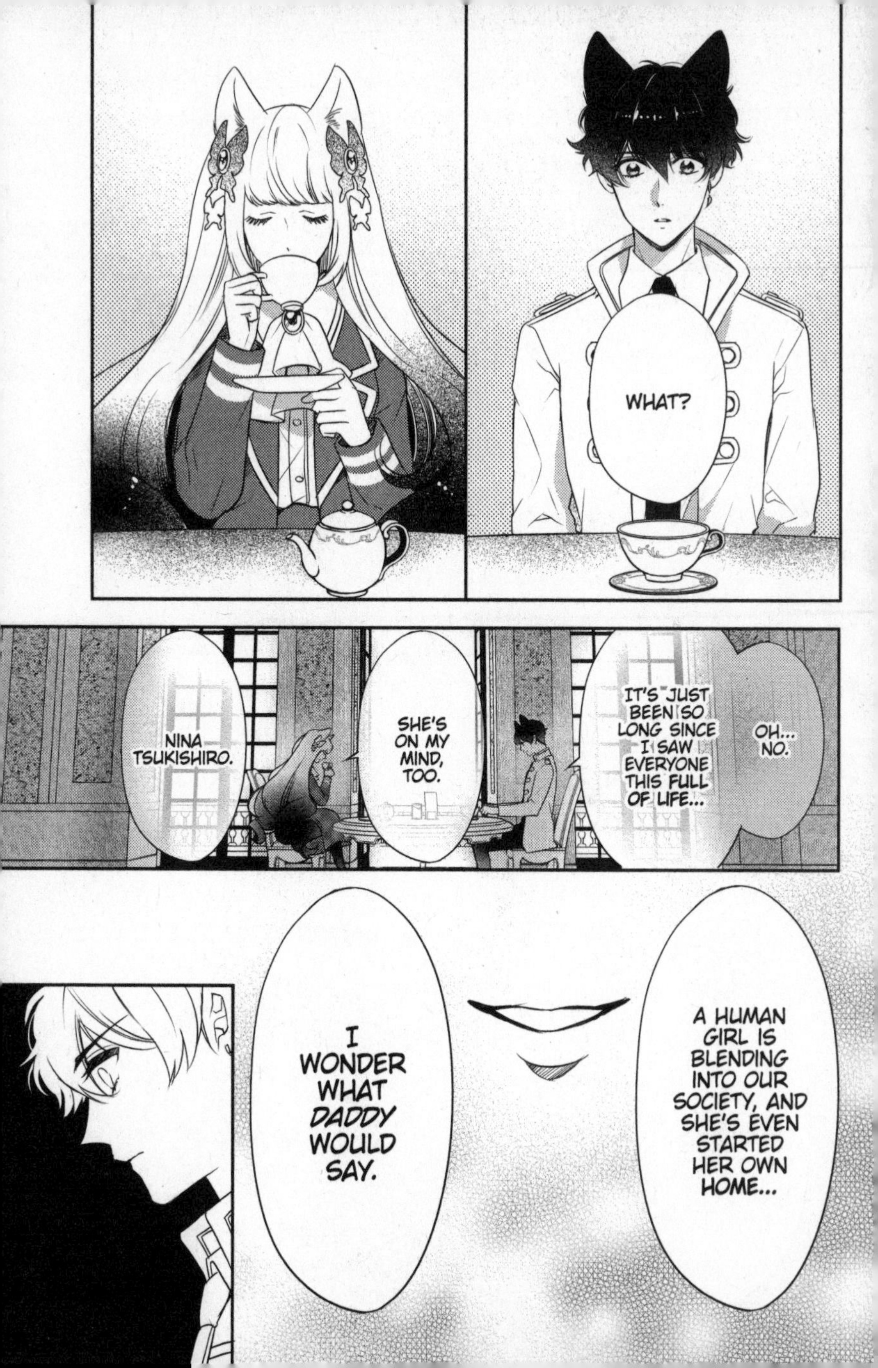
WHAT?
OH... NO.
IT'S JUST BEEN SO LONG SINCE I SAW EVERYONE THIS FULL OF LIFE...
SHE'S ON MY MIND, TOO.
NINA TSUKISHIRO.
A HUMAN GIRL IS BLENDING INTO OUR SOCIETY, AND SHE'S EVEN STARTED HER OWN HOME...
I WONDER WHAT *DADDY* WOULD SAY.

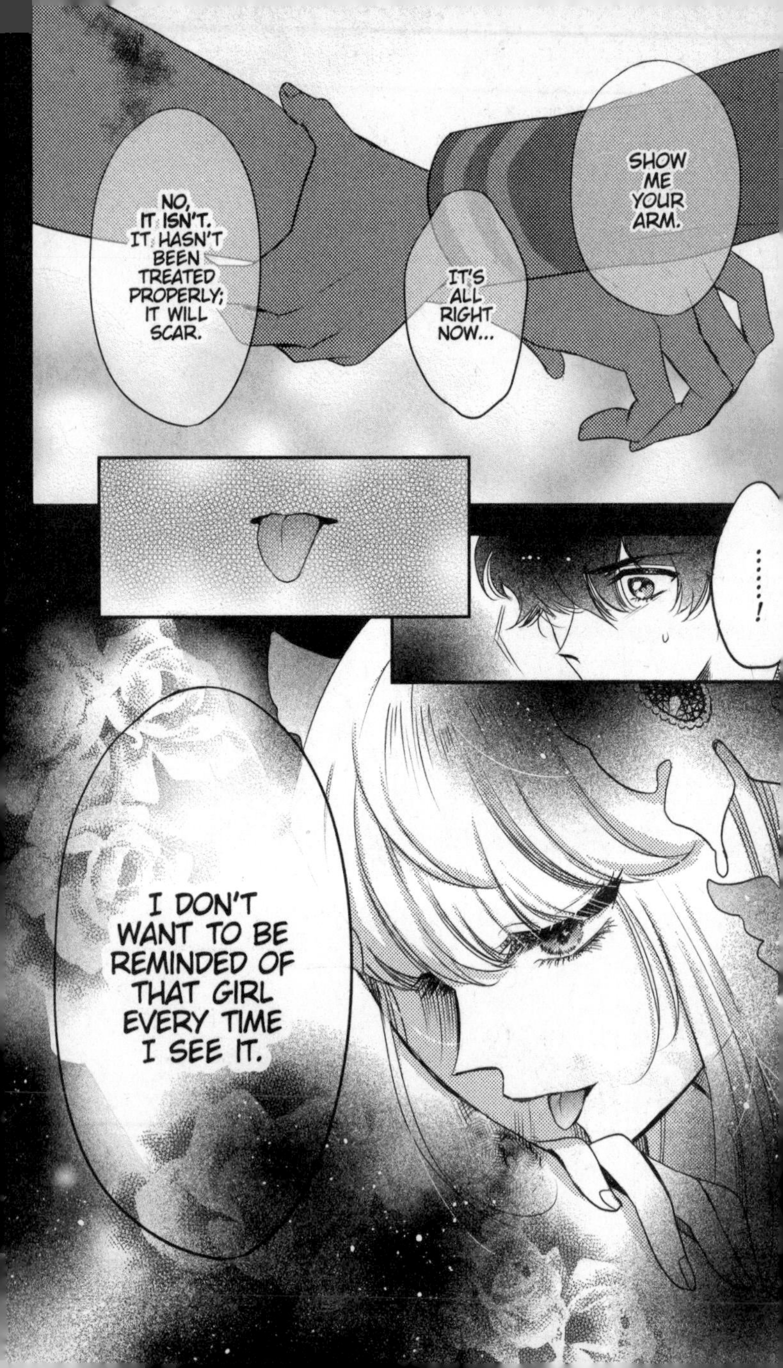
SHOW ME YOUR ARM.
IT'S ALL RIGHT NOW...
NO, IT ISN'T. IT HASN'T BEEN TREATED PROPERLY; IT WILL SCAR.
......!
I DON'T WANT TO BE REMINDED OF THAT GIRL EVERY TIME I SEE IT.

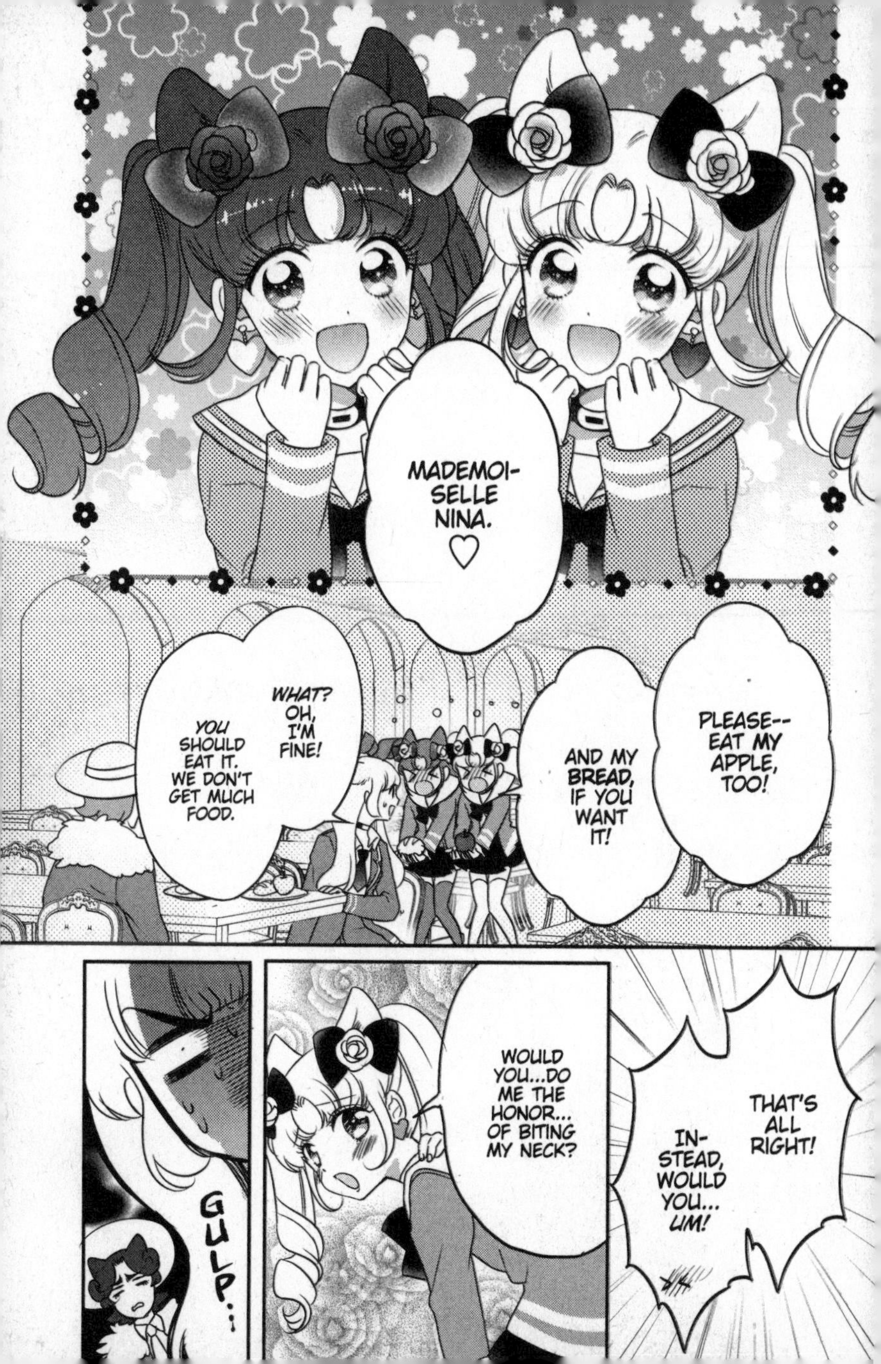
MADEMOI-SELLE NINA. ♡
PLEASE-- EAT MY APPLE, TOO!
AND MY BREAD, IF YOU WANT IT!
WHAT? OH, I'M FINE!
YOU SHOULD EAT IT. WE DON'T GET MUCH FOOD.
THAT'S ALL RIGHT!
IN-STEAD, WOULD YOU... UM!
WOULD YOU...DO ME THE HONOR... OF BITING MY NECK?
GULP...

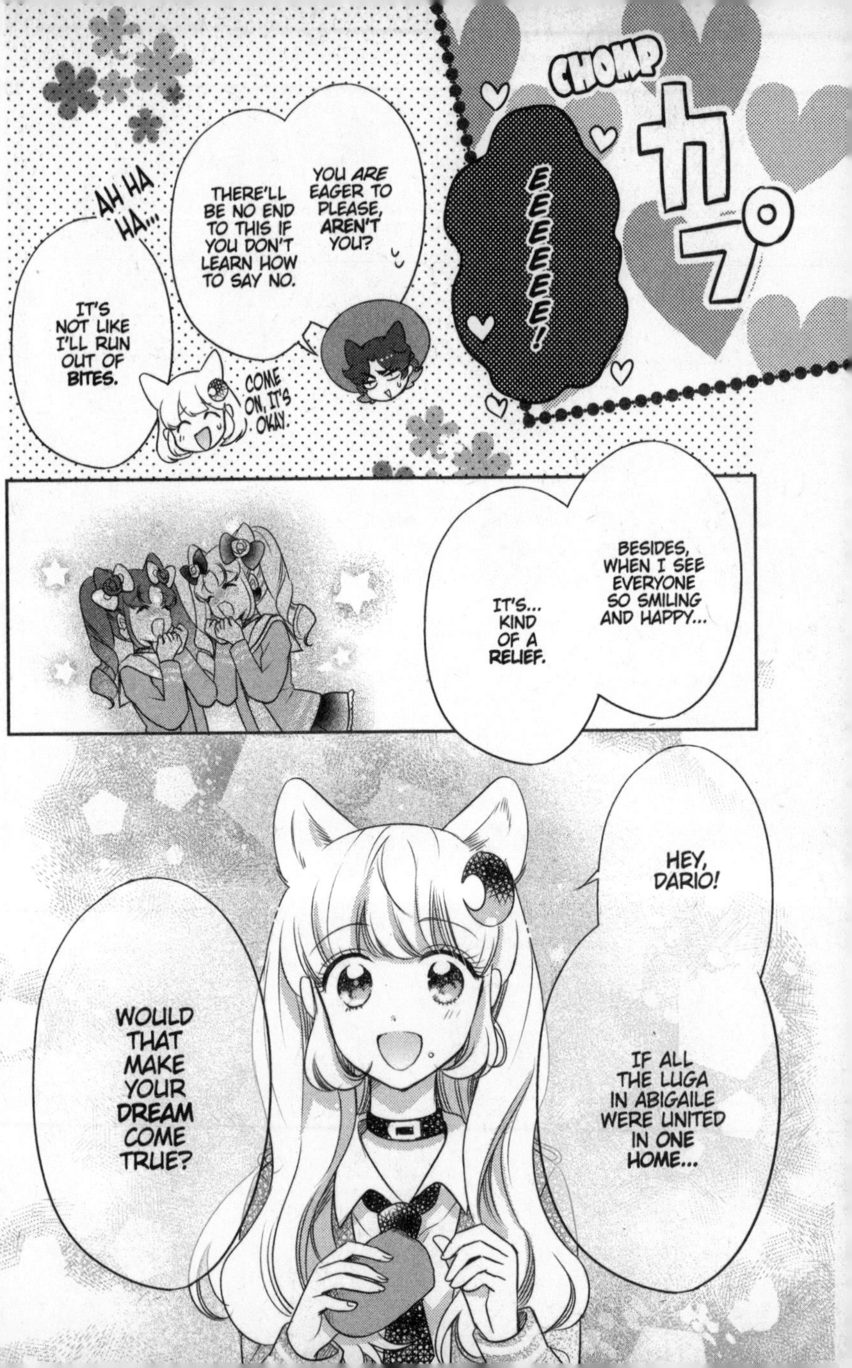
CHOMP
カプ
EEEEEEE!
YOU ARE EAGER TO PLEASE, AREN'T YOU?
THERE'LL BE NO END TO THIS IF YOU DON'T LEARN HOW TO SAY NO.
COME ON, IT'S OKAY.
AH HA HA...
IT'S NOT LIKE I'LL RUN OUT OF BITES.
BESIDES, WHEN I SEE EVERYONE SO SMILING AND HAPPY...
IT'S... KIND OF A RELIEF.
HEY, DARIO!
IF ALL THE LUGA IN ABIGAILE WERE UNITED IN ONE HOME...
WOULD THAT MAKE YOUR DREAM COME TRUE?

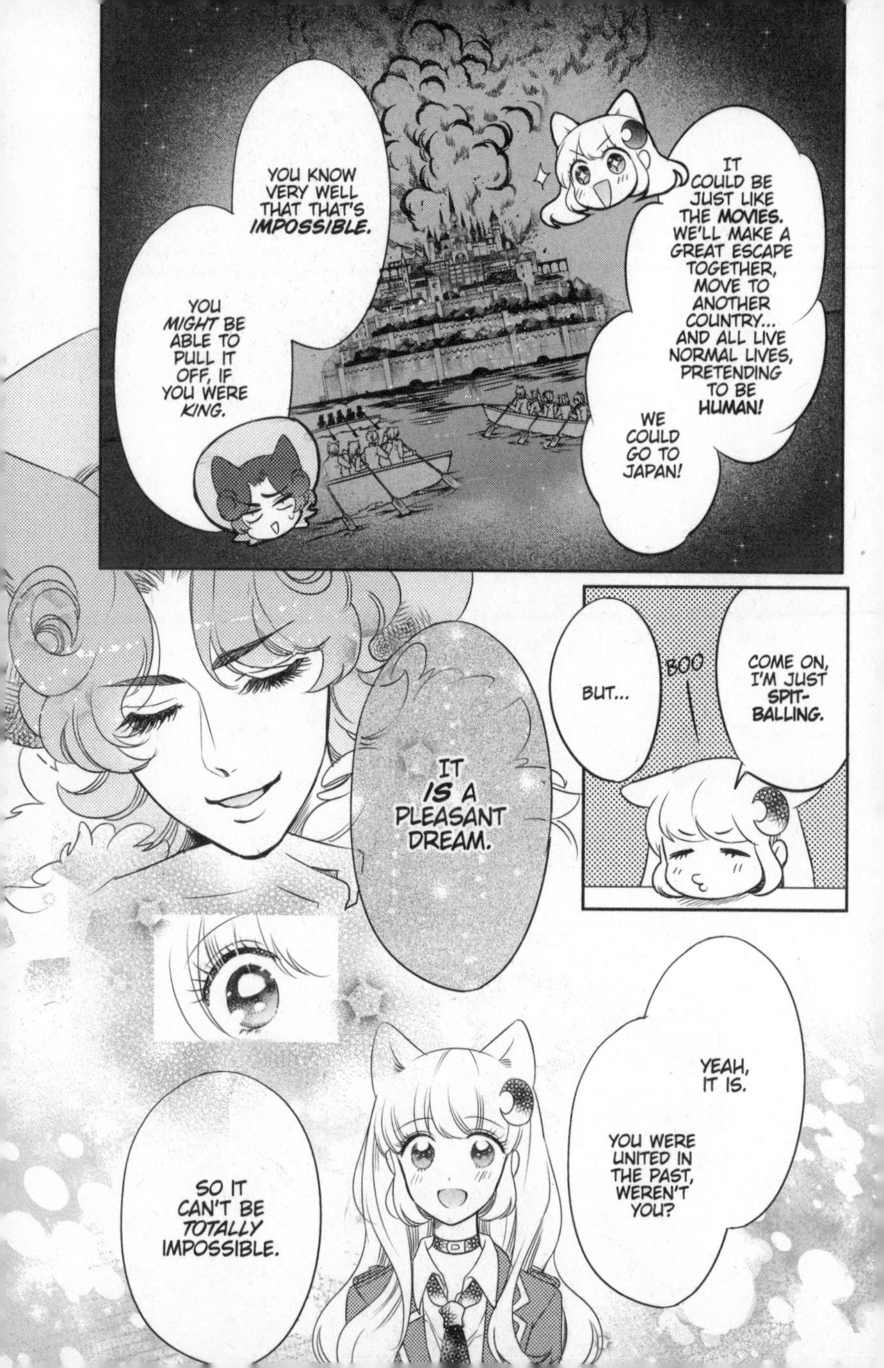
IT COULD BE JUST LIKE THE MOVIES. WE'LL MAKE A GREAT ESCAPE TOGETHER, MOVE TO ANOTHER COUNTRY... AND ALL LIVE NORMAL LIVES, PRETENDING TO BE HUMAN!
WE COULD GO TO JAPAN!
YOU KNOW VERY WELL THAT THAT'S IMPOSSIBLE.
YOU MIGHT BE ABLE TO PULL IT OFF, IF YOU WERE KING.
COME ON, I'M JUST SPIT-BALLING.
BOO
BUT...
IT IS A PLEASANT DREAM.
YEAH, IT IS.
YOU WERE UNITED IN THE PAST, WEREN'T YOU?
SO IT CAN'T BE TOTALLY IMPOSSIBLE.

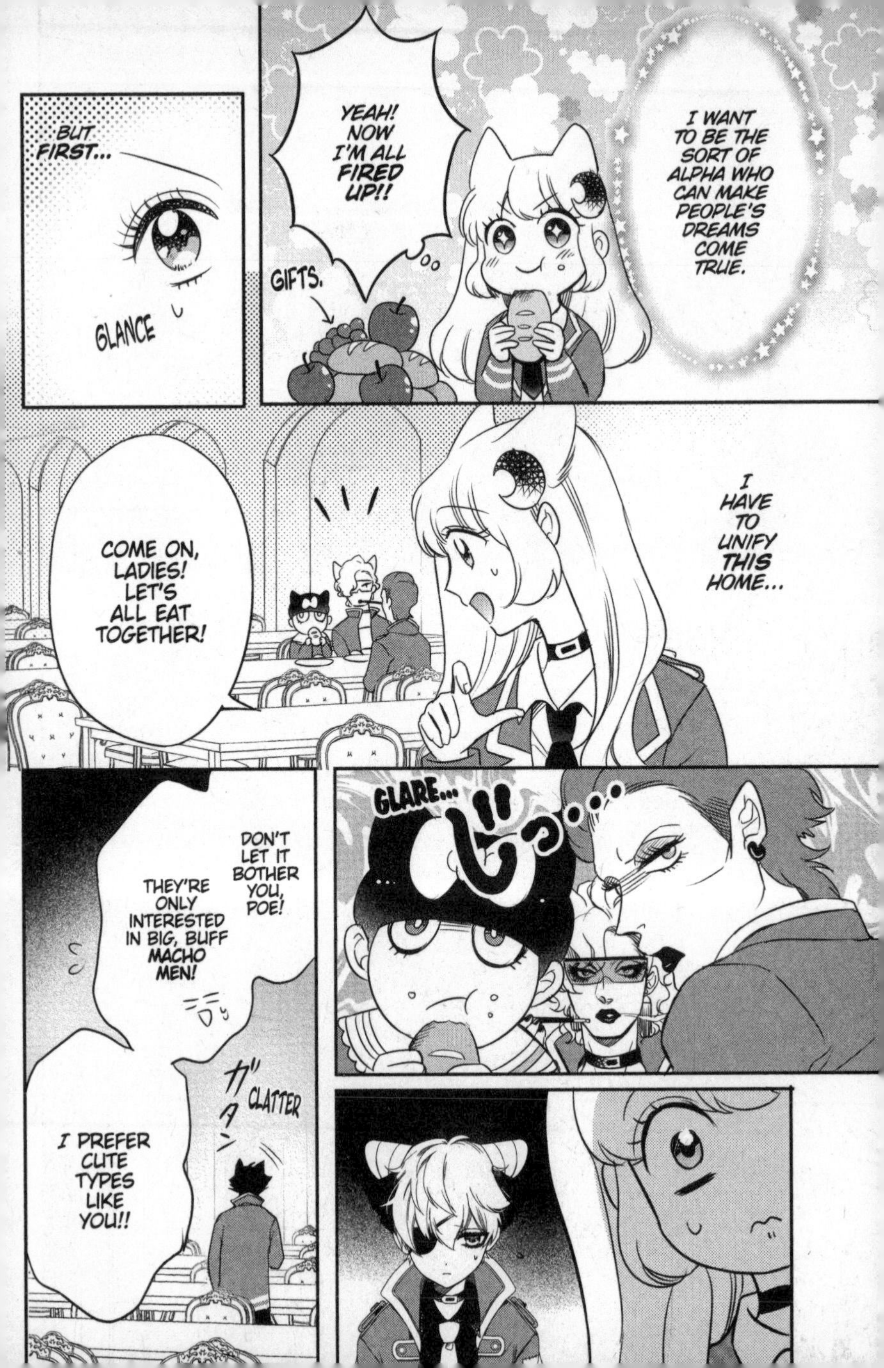
I WANT TO BE THE SORT OF ALPHA WHO CAN MAKE PEOPLE'S DREAMS COME TRUE.
YEAH! NOW I'M ALL FIRED UP!!
GIFTS.
BUT FIRST...
GLANCE
I HAVE TO UNIFY THIS HOME...
COME ON, LADIES! LET'S ALL EAT TOGETHER!
GLARE...
DON'T LET IT BOTHER YOU, POE!
THEY'RE ONLY INTERESTED IN BIG, BUFF MACHO MEN!
ガタン
CLATTER
I PREFER CUTE TYPES LIKE YOU!!

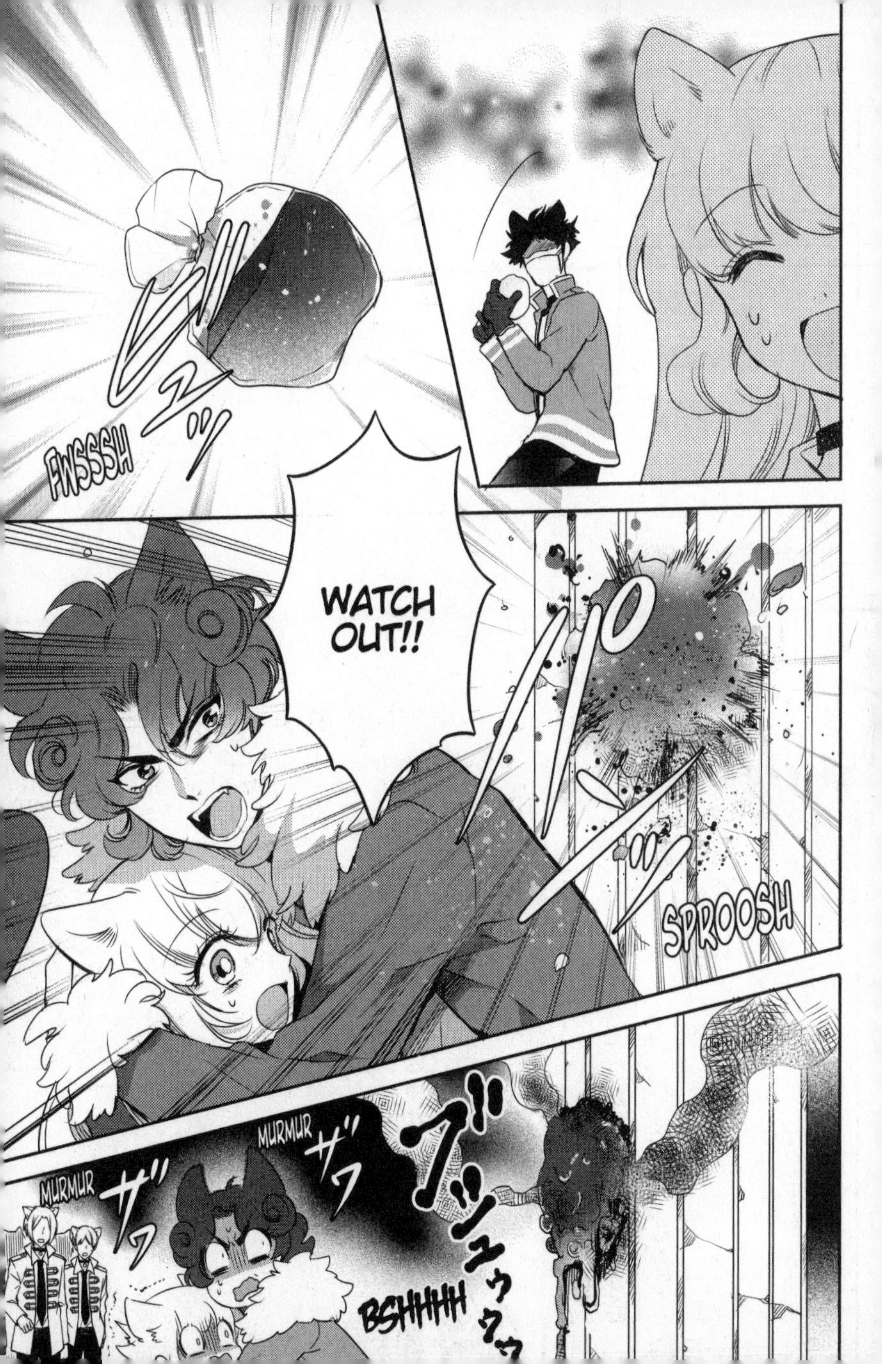
FWSSSH
SPROOSH
WATCH OUT!!
BSHHHH
MURMUR
MURMUR

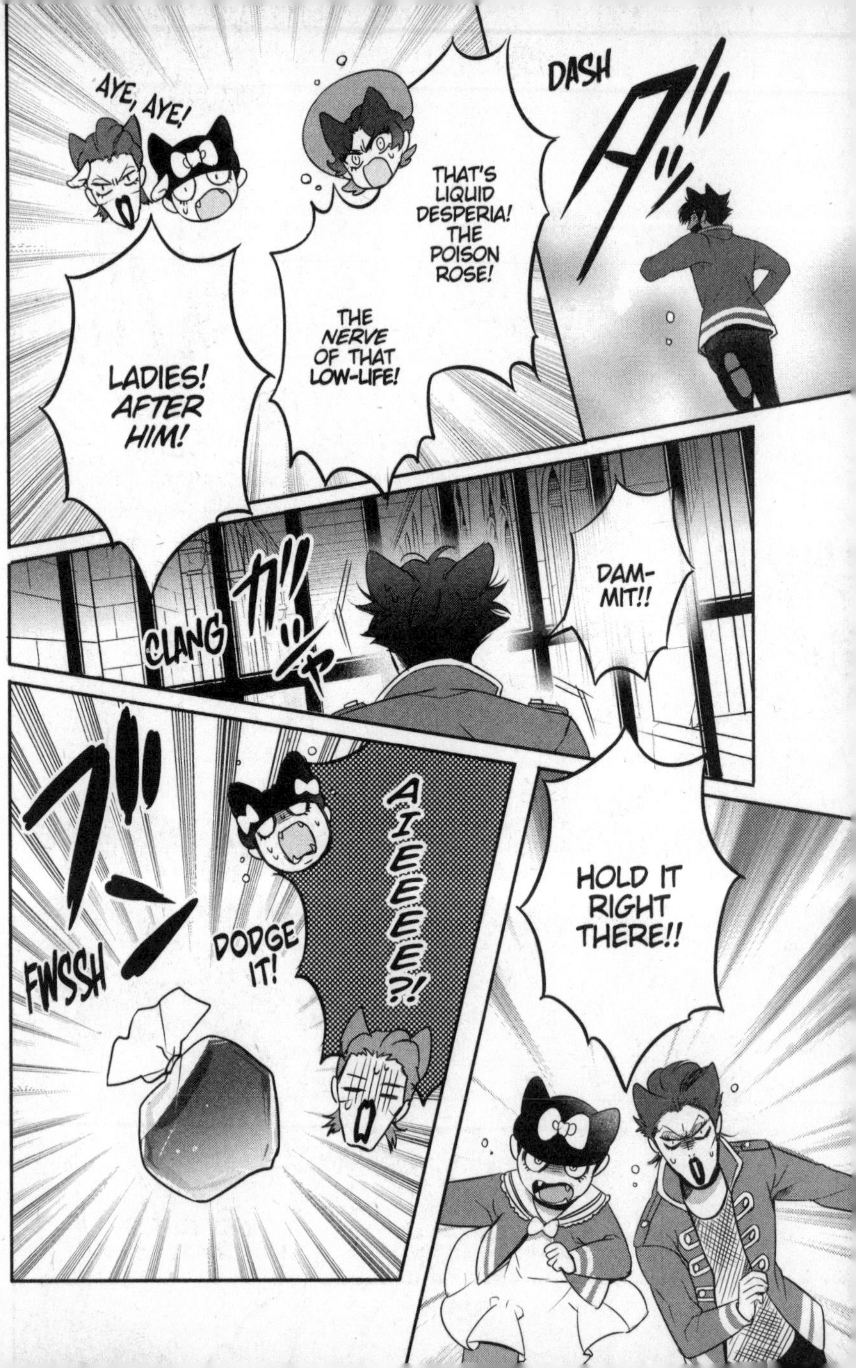
DASH
THAT'S LIQUID DESPERIA! THE POISON ROSE!
THE NERVE OF THAT LOW-LIFE!
LADIES! AFTER HIM!
AYE, AYE!
DAM-MIT!!
CLANG
HOLD IT RIGHT THERE!!
AIEEEEE?!
DODGE IT!
FWSSH

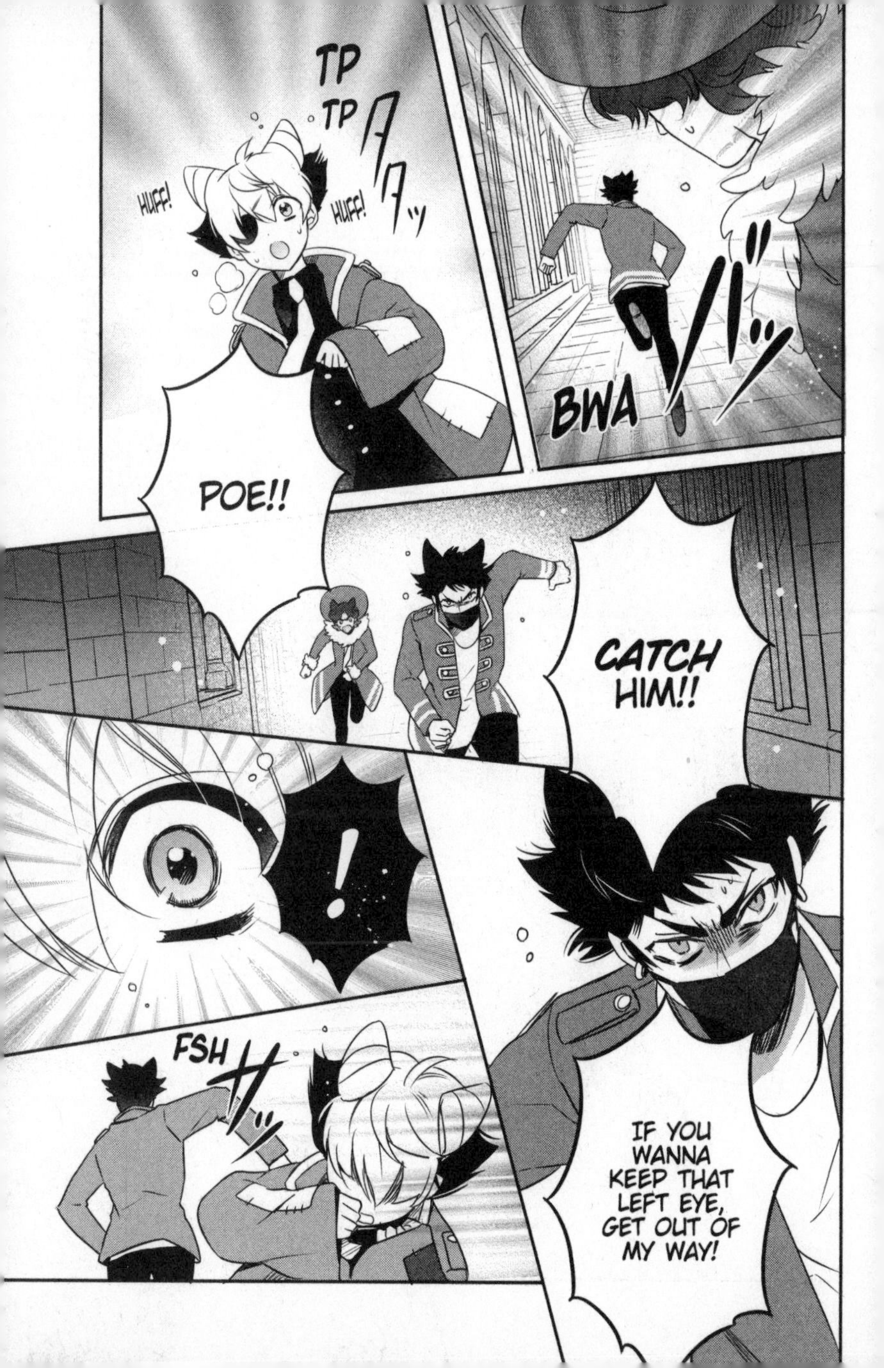
BWA
TP TP
HUFF!
HUFF!
POE!!
CATCH HIM!!
IF YOU WANNA KEEP THAT LEFT EYE, GET OUT OF MY WAY!
!
FSH

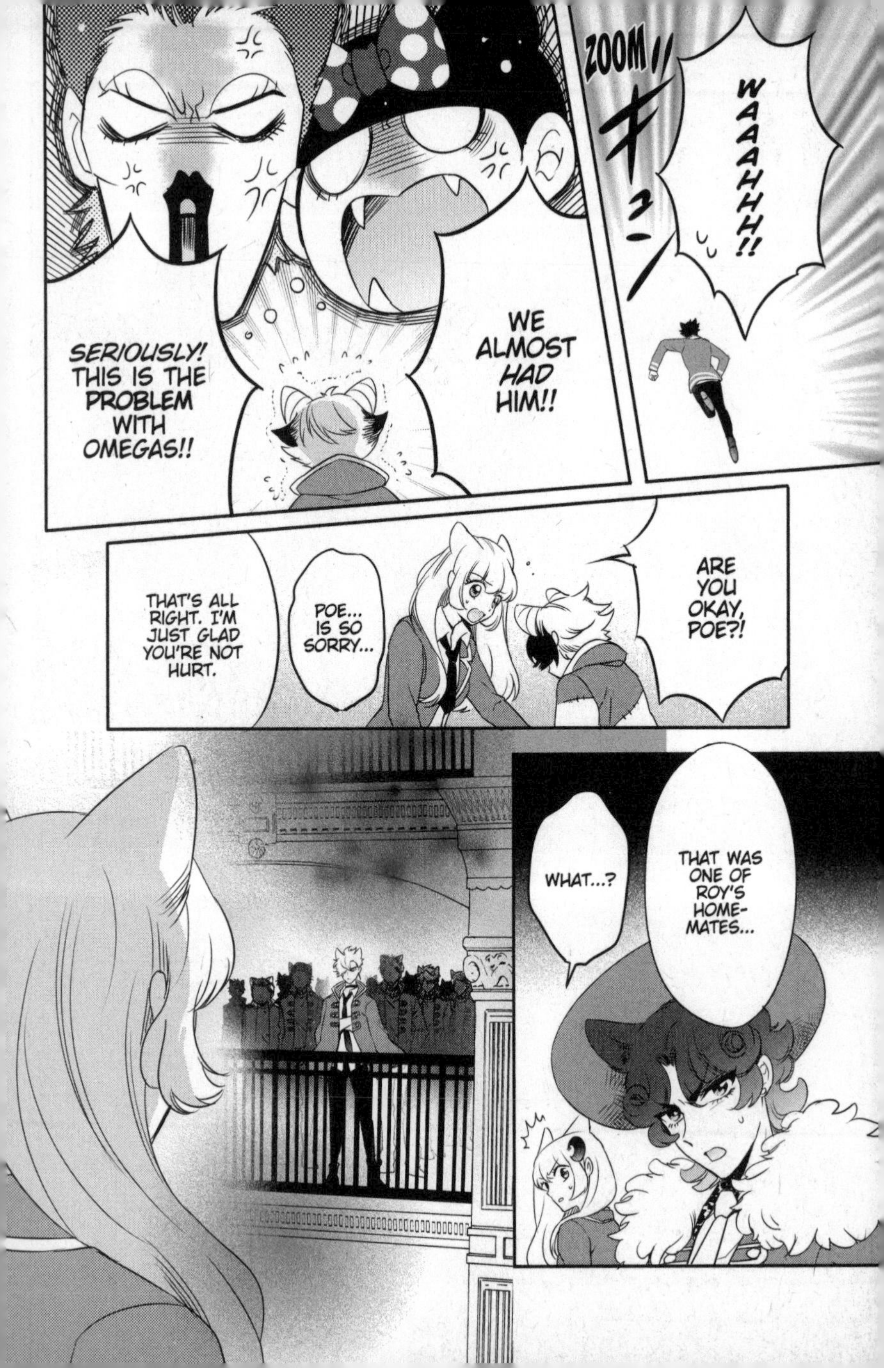
ZOOM!!
WAAAAHHH!!
WE ALMOST HAD HIM!!
SERIOUSLY! THIS IS THE PROBLEM WITH OMEGAS!!
ARE YOU OKAY, POE?!
POE... IS SO SORRY...
THAT'S ALL RIGHT. I'M JUST GLAD YOU'RE NOT HURT.
THAT WAS ONE OF ROY'S HOME-MATES...
WHAT...?

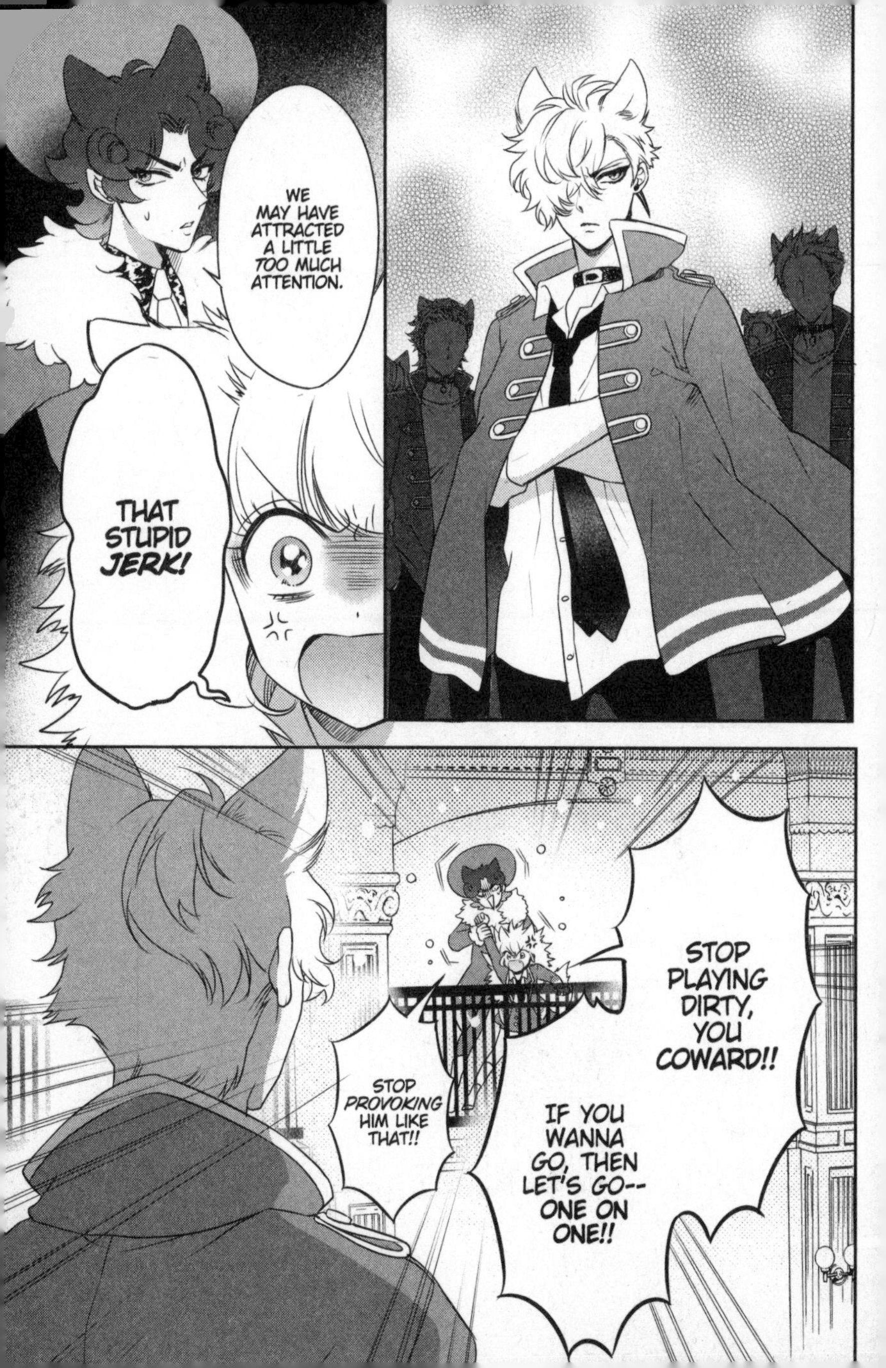

WE MAY HAVE ATTRACTED A LITTLE *TOO* MUCH ATTENTION.
THAT STUPID *JERK!*
STOP PLAYING DIRTY, YOU COWARD!!
IF YOU WANNA GO, THEN LET'S GO-- ONE ON ONE!!
STOP *PROVOKING* HIM LIKE THAT!!

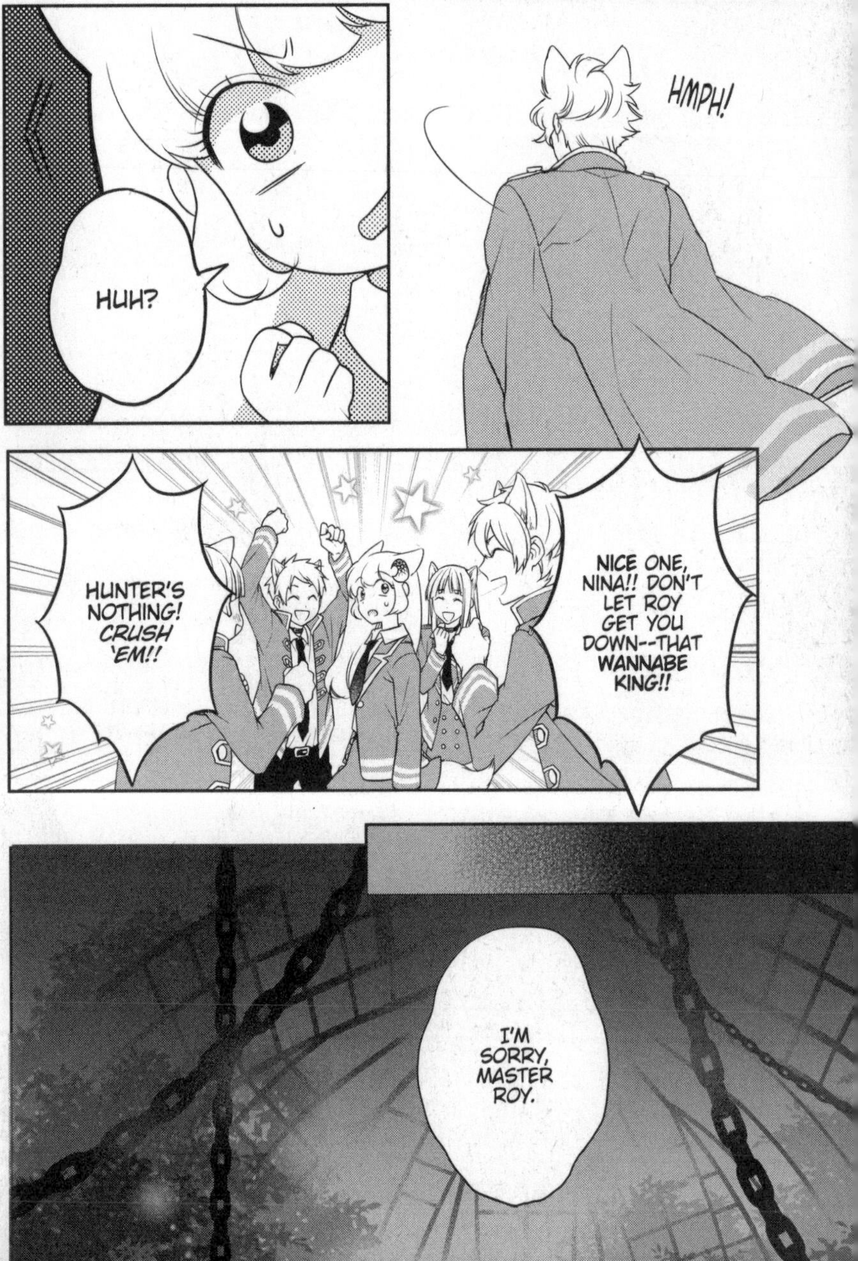
HMPH!
HUH?
NICE ONE, NINA!! DON'T LET ROY GET YOU DOWN--THAT WANNABE KING!!
HUNTER'S NOTHING! CRUSH 'EM!!
I'M SORRY, MASTER ROY.

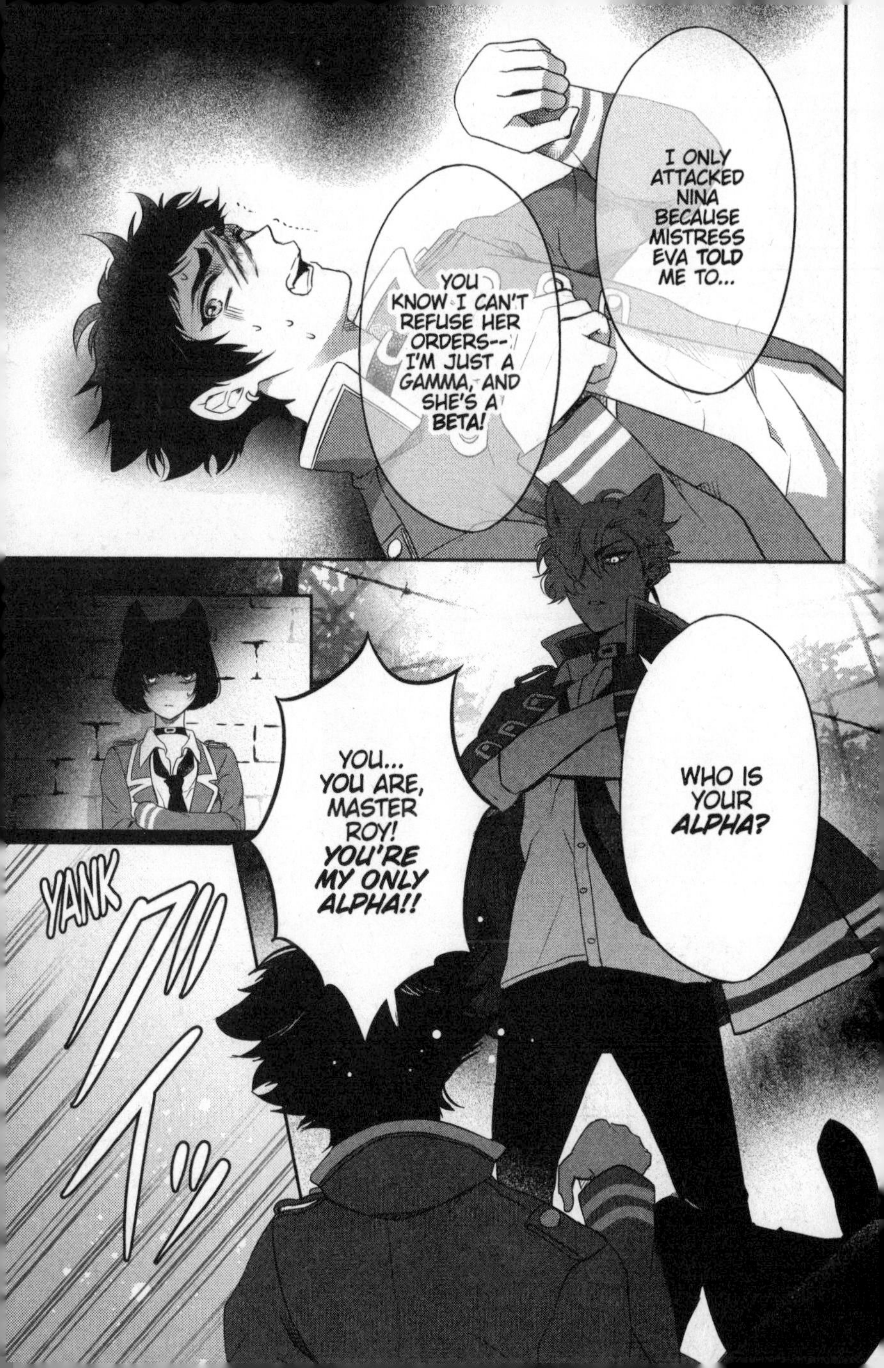
I ONLY ATTACKED NINA BECAUSE MISTRESS EVA TOLD ME TO...
YOU KNOW I CAN'T REFUSE HER ORDERS-- I'M JUST A GAMMA, AND SHE'S A BETA!
WHO IS YOUR ALPHA?
YOU... YOU ARE, MASTER ROY! YOU'RE MY ONLY ALPHA!!
YANK

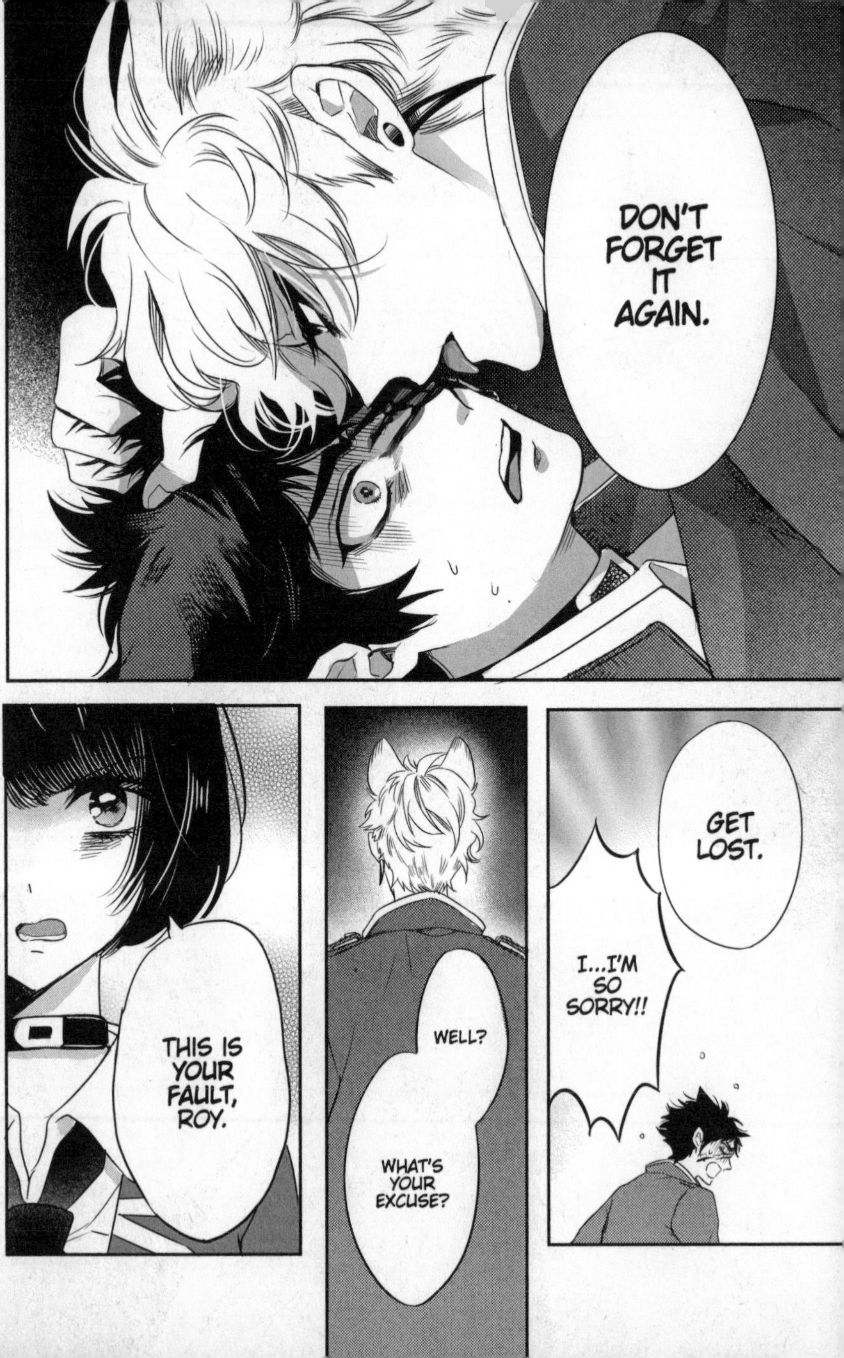
DON'T FORGET IT AGAIN.
GET LOST.
I...I'M SO SORRY!!
WELL?
WHAT'S YOUR EXCUSE?
THIS IS YOUR FAULT, ROY.

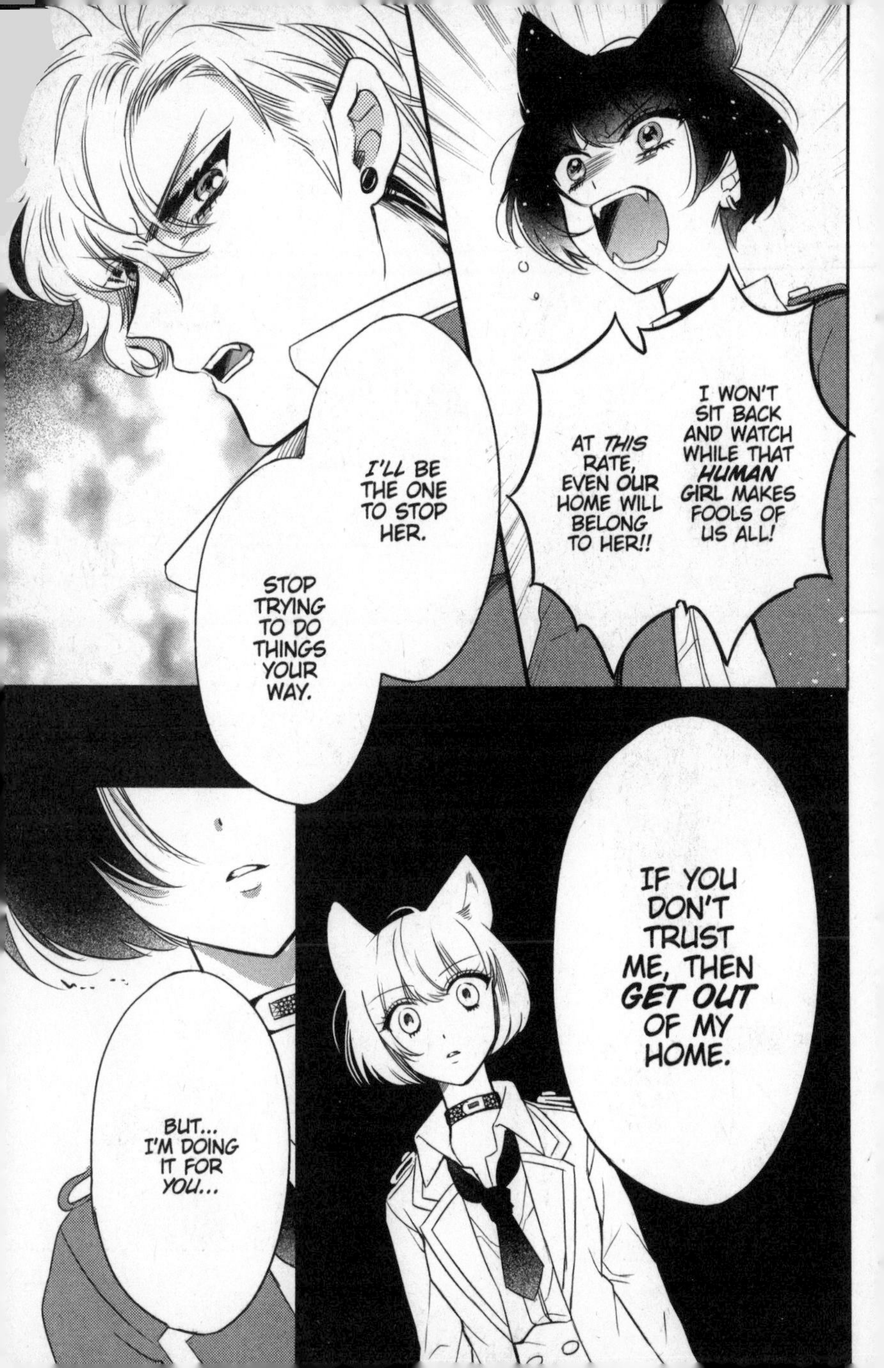
I WON'T SIT BACK AND WATCH WHILE THAT *HUMAN* GIRL MAKES FOOLS OF US ALL!
AT *THIS* RATE, EVEN OUR HOME WILL BELONG TO HER!!
I'LL BE THE ONE TO STOP HER.
STOP TRYING TO DO THINGS YOUR WAY.
IF YOU DON'T TRUST ME, THEN ***GET OUT*** OF MY HOME.
BUT... I'M DOING IT FOR *YOU*...

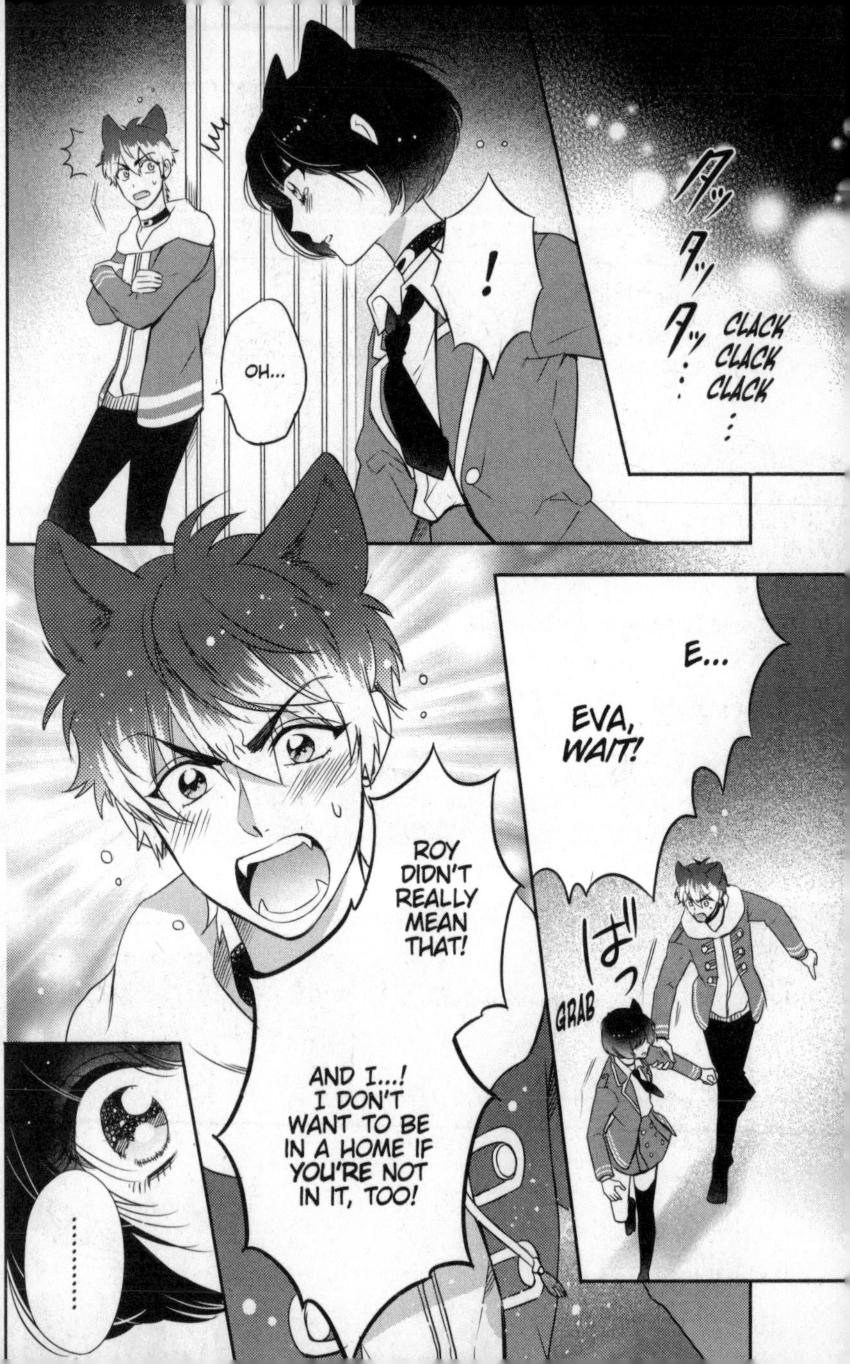
タッタッタッ…
CLACK CLACK CLACK…
!
OH...
E...
EVA, WAIT!
ばっ
GRAB
ROY DIDN'T REALLY MEAN THAT!
AND I...! I DON'T WANT TO BE IN A HOME IF YOU'RE NOT IN IT, TOO!
......

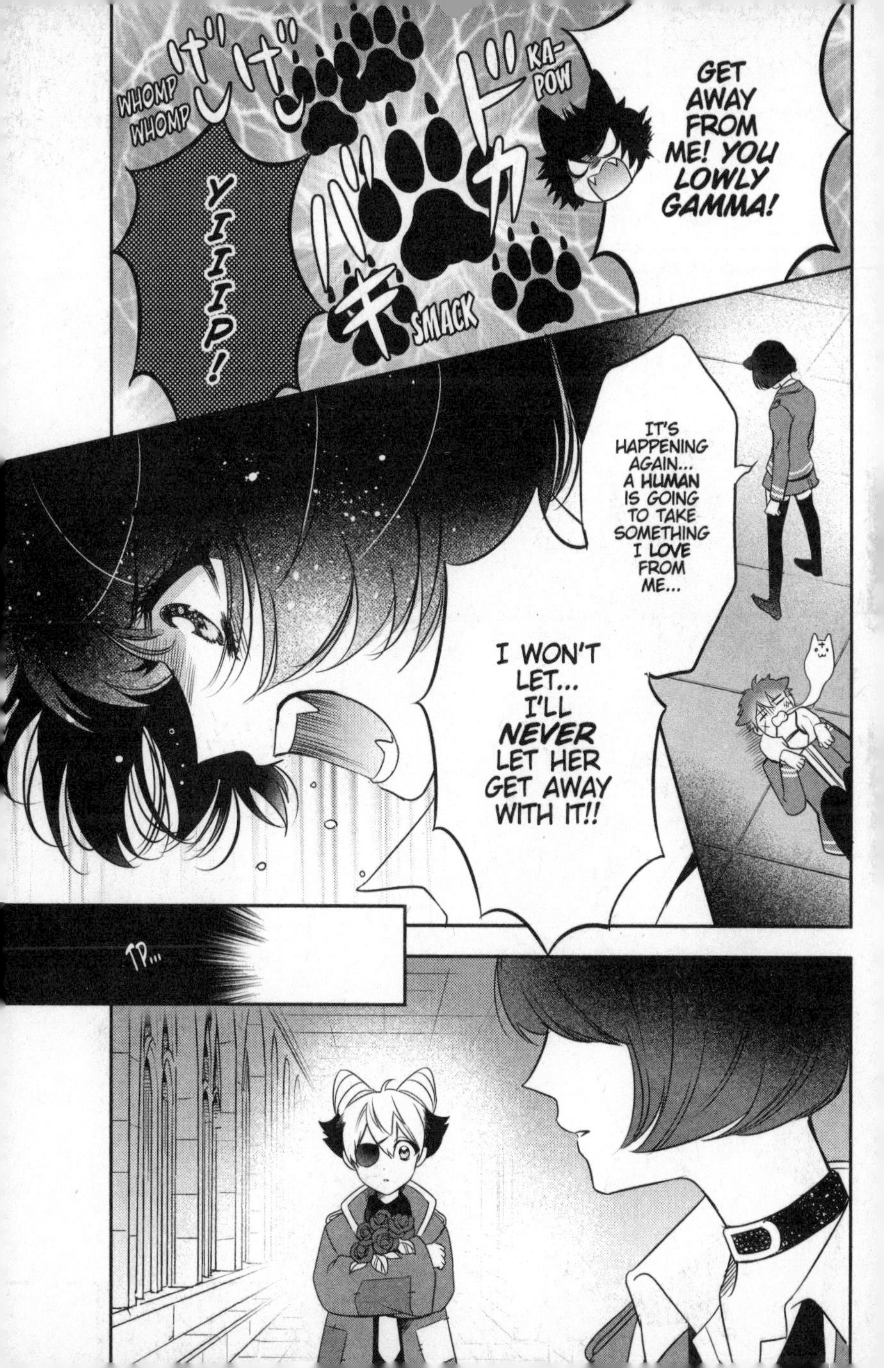
GET AWAY FROM ME! YOU LOWLY GAMMA!
KA-POW
SMACK
WHOMP WHOMP
YIIIIP!
IT'S HAPPENING AGAIN... A HUMAN IS GOING TO TAKE SOMETHING I LOVE FROM ME...
I WON'T LET... I'LL NEVER LET HER GET AWAY WITH IT!!
TP...

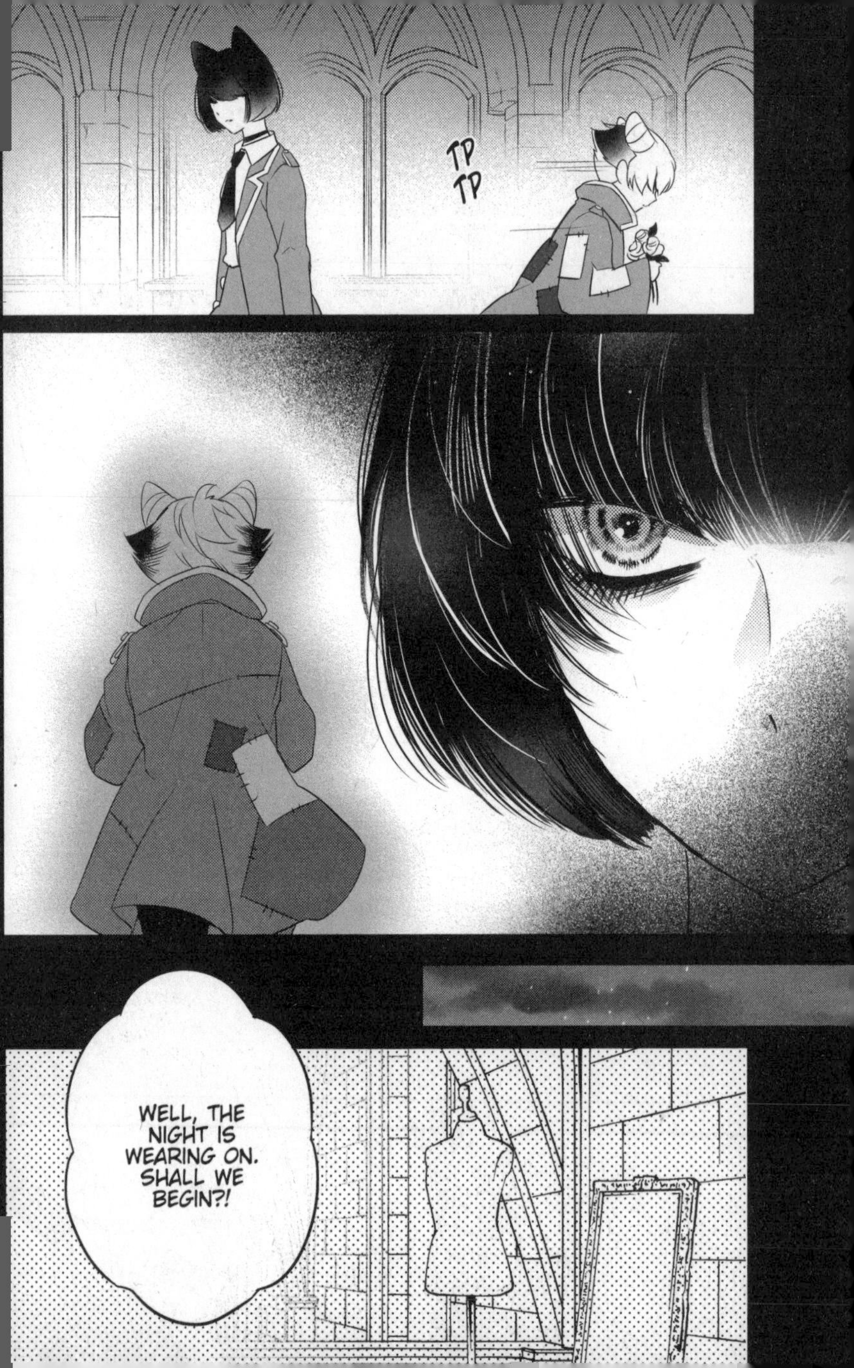
TP
TP
WELL, THE NIGHT IS WEARING ON. SHALL WE BEGIN?!

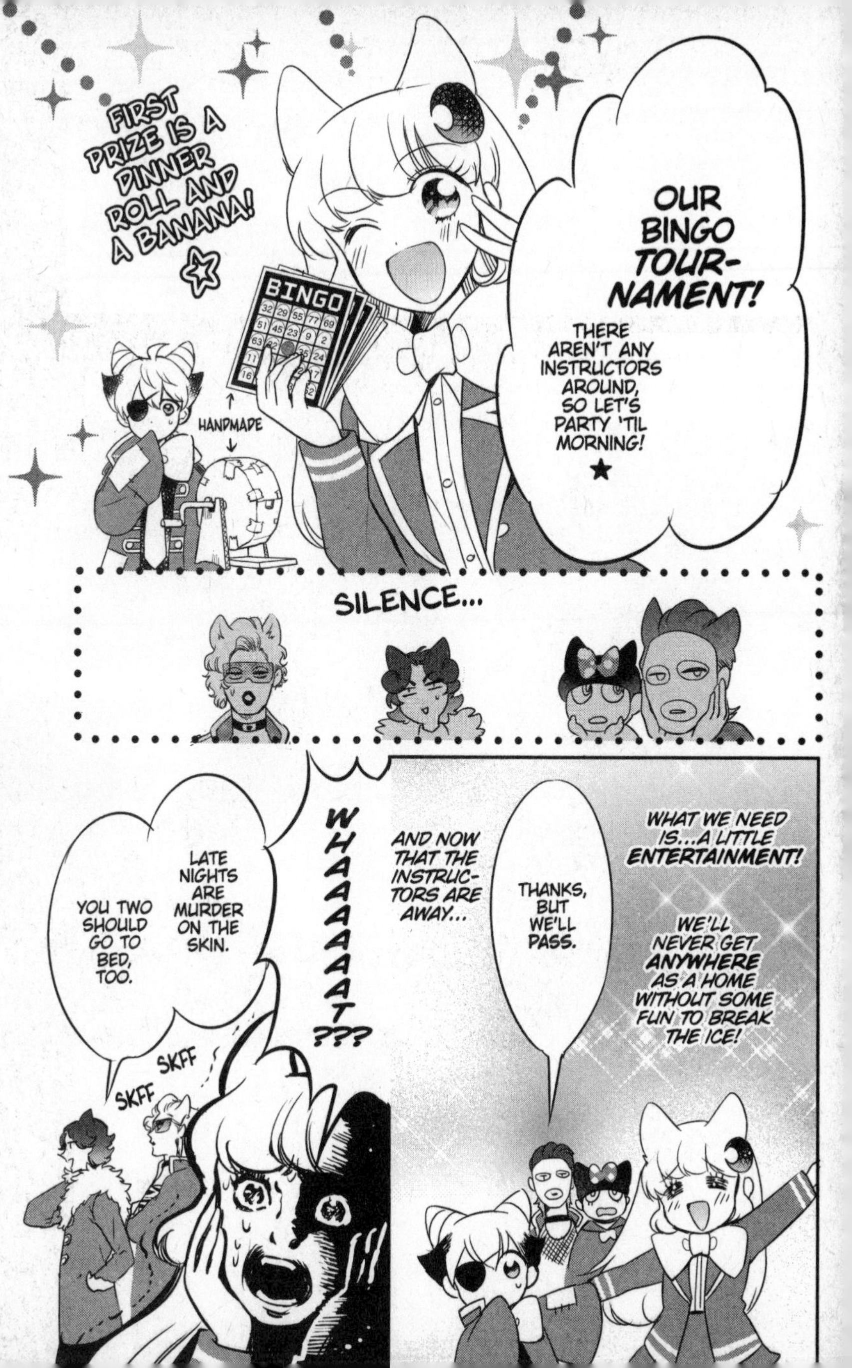
OUR BINGO TOURNAMENT!
THERE AREN'T ANY INSTRUCTORS AROUND, SO LET'S PARTY 'TIL MORNING! ★
FIRST PRIZE IS A DINNER ROLL AND A BANANA! ☆
BINGO
HANDMADE
SILENCE...
WHAT WE NEED IS...A LITTLE ENTERTAINMENT!
WE'LL NEVER GET ANYWHERE AS A HOME WITHOUT SOME FUN TO BREAK THE ICE!
THANKS, BUT WE'LL PASS.
AND NOW THAT THE INSTRUCTORS ARE AWAY...
WHAAAAAAAT???
LATE NIGHTS ARE MURDER ON THE SKIN.
YOU TWO SHOULD GO TO BED, TOO.
SKFF
SKFF

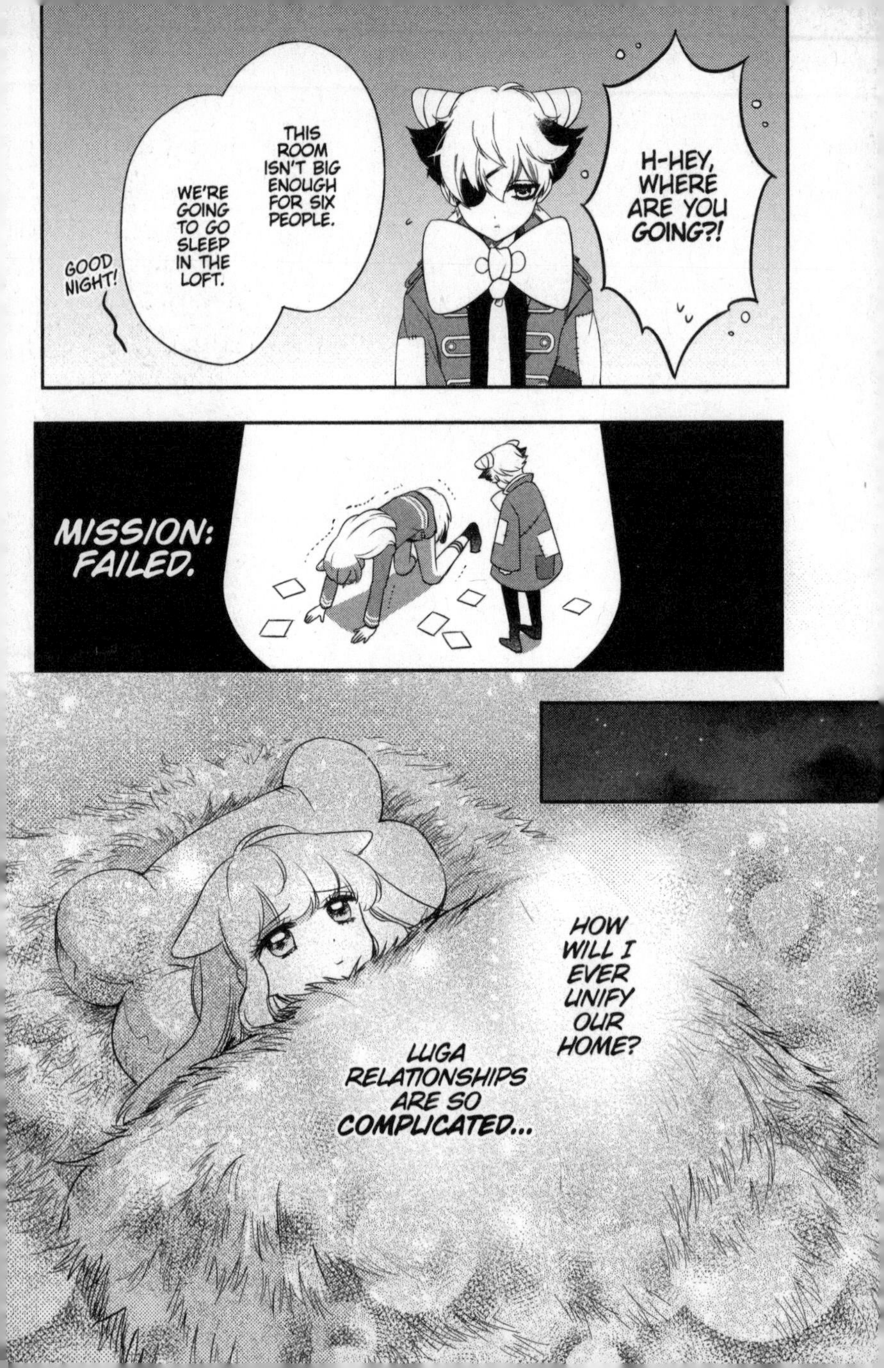
H-HEY, WHERE ARE YOU GOING?!
THIS ROOM ISN'T BIG ENOUGH FOR SIX PEOPLE.
WE'RE GOING TO GO SLEEP IN THE LOFT.
GOOD NIGHT!
MISSION: FAILED.
HOW WILL I EVER UNIFY OUR HOME?
LUGA RELATIONSHIPS ARE SO COMPLICATED...

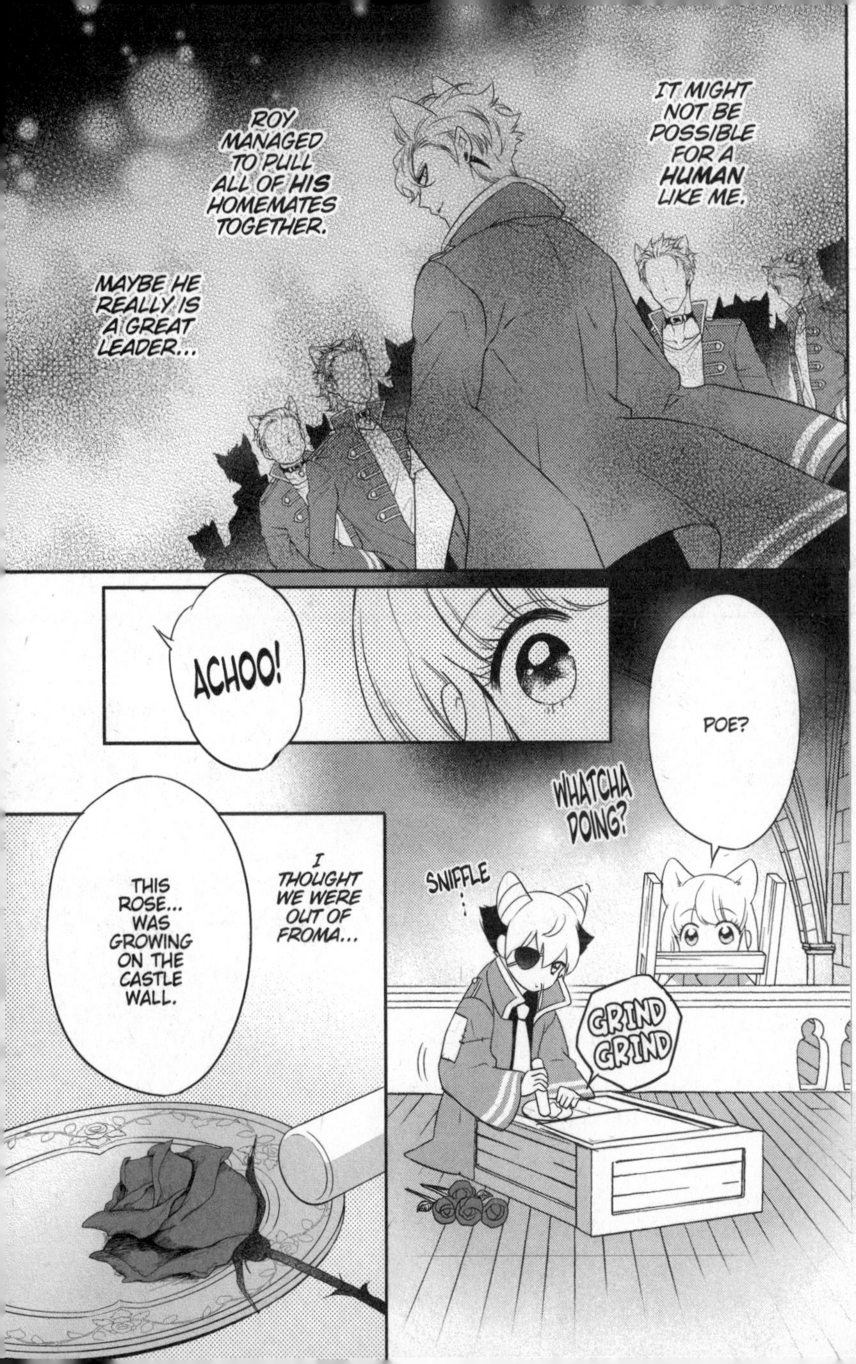
IT MIGHT NOT BE POSSIBLE FOR A HUMAN LIKE ME.
ROY MANAGED TO PULL ALL OF HIS HOMEMATES TOGETHER.
MAYBE HE REALLY IS A GREAT LEADER...
POE?
WHATCHA DOING?
SNIFFLE...
GRIND GRIND
ACHOO!
I THOUGHT WE WERE OUT OF FROMA...
THIS ROSE... WAS GROWING ON THE CASTLE WALL.

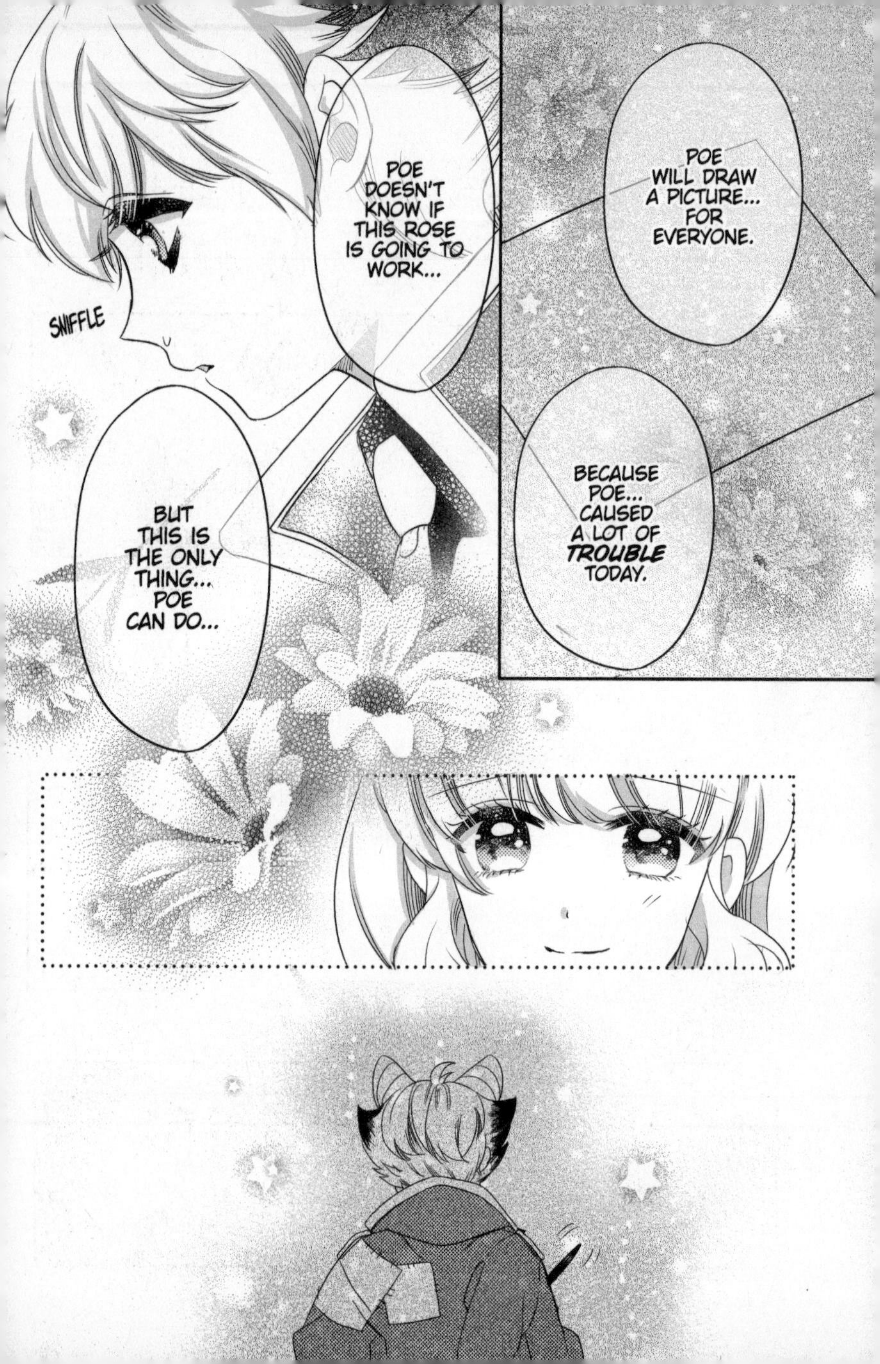
POE WILL DRAW A PICTURE... FOR EVERYONE.
BECAUSE POE... CAUSED A LOT OF TROUBLE TODAY.
POE DOESN'T KNOW IF THIS ROSE IS GOING TO WORK...
SNIFFLE
BUT THIS IS THE ONLY THING... POE CAN DO...

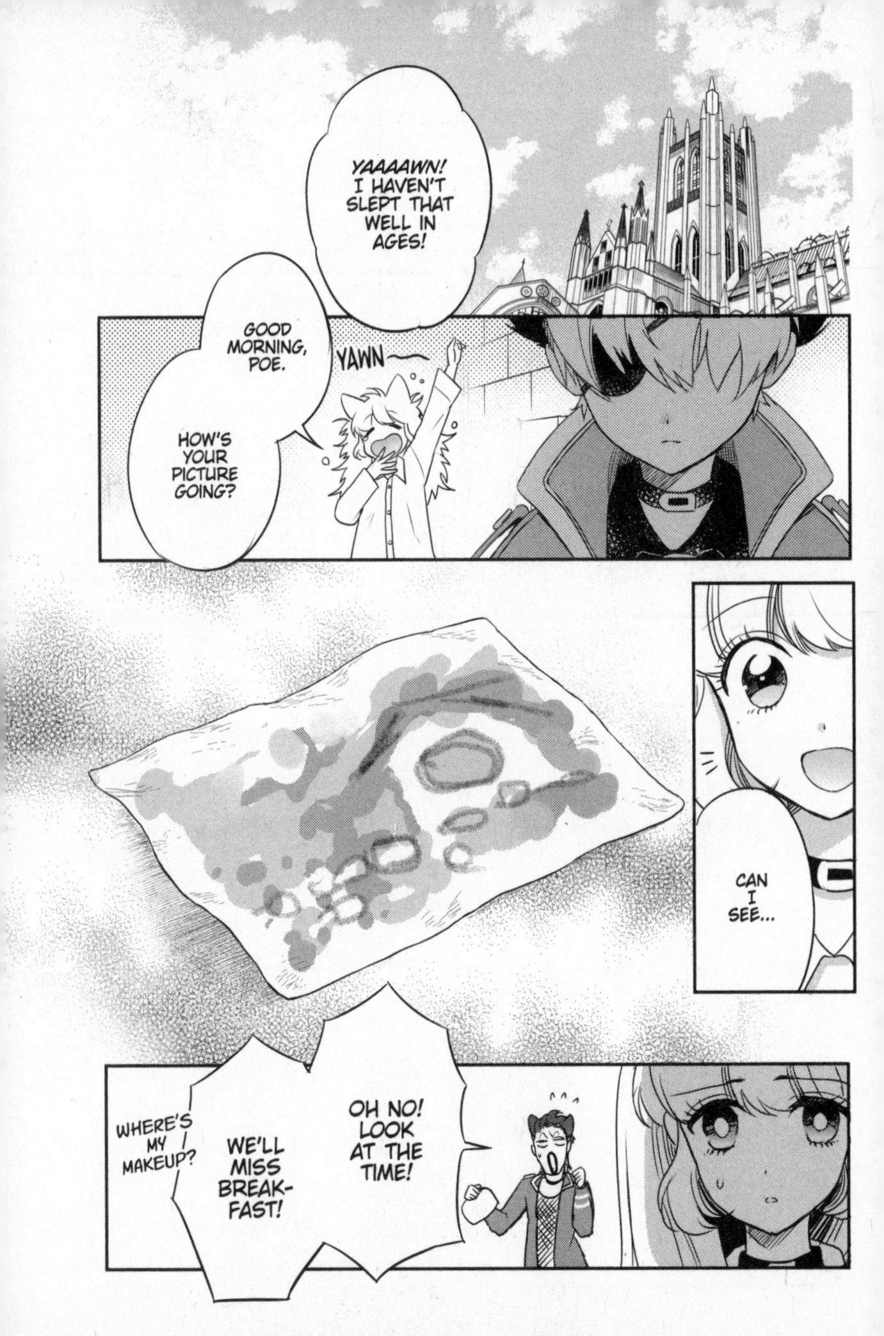
YAAAAWN! I HAVEN'T SLEPT THAT WELL IN AGES!
YAWN
GOOD MORNING, POE.
HOW'S YOUR PICTURE GOING?
CAN I SEE...
OH NO! LOOK AT THE TIME!
WE'LL MISS BREAK-FAST!
WHERE'S MY MAKEUP?

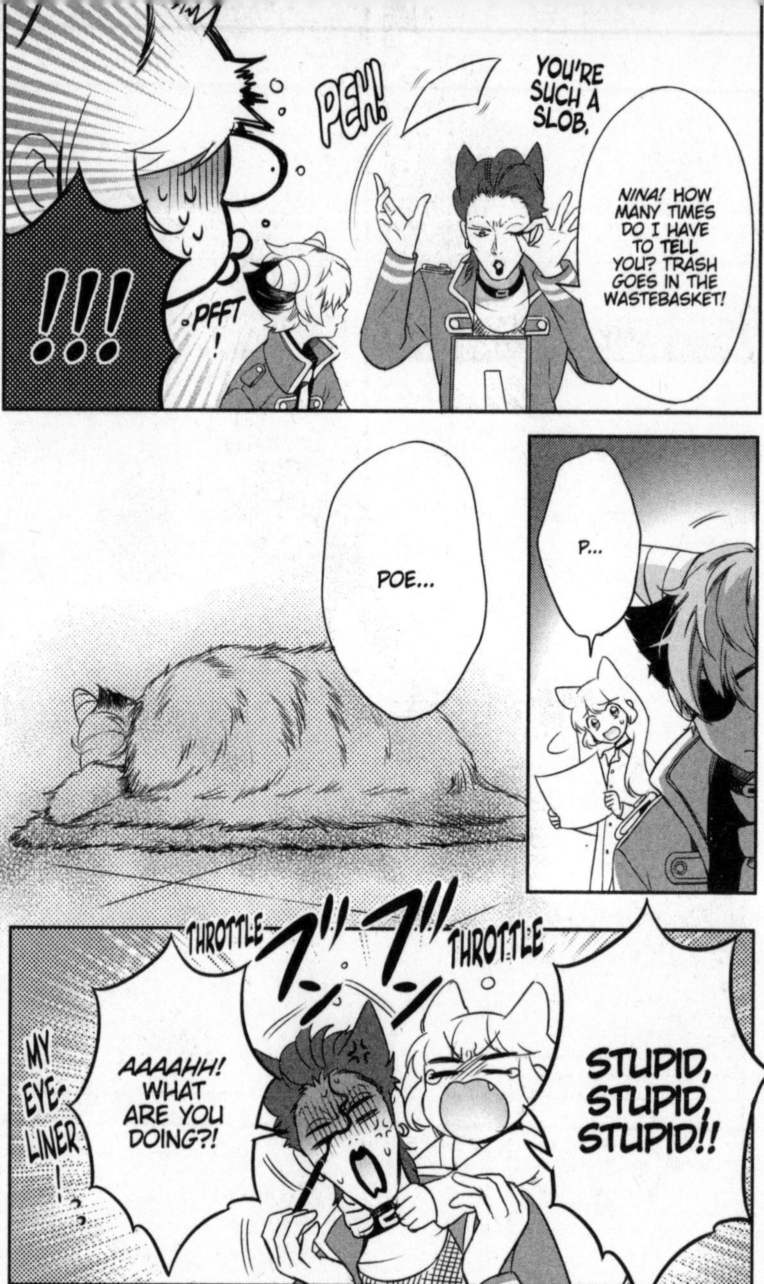
YOU'RE SUCH A SLOB.
NINA! HOW MANY TIMES DO I HAVE TO TELL YOU? TRASH GOES IN THE WASTEBASKET!
PEH!
PFFT!
!!!
P...
POE...
THROTTLE
STUPID, STUPID, STUPID!!
THROTTLE
AAAAHH! WHAT ARE YOU DOING?!
MY EYE-LINER...!

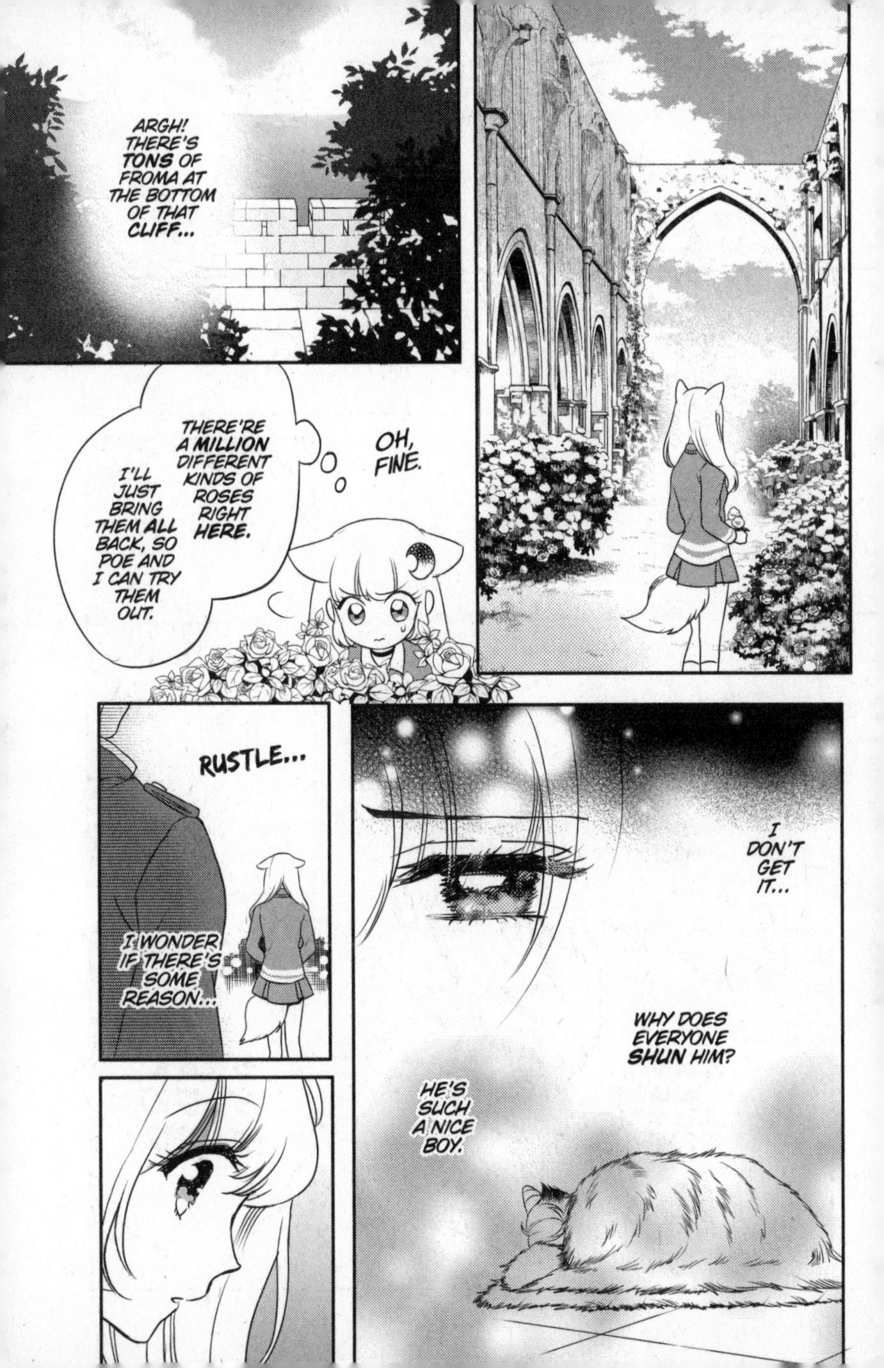
ARGH! THERE'S **TONS** OF FROMA AT THE BOTTOM OF THAT **CLIFF**...
OH, FINE.
THERE'RE A **MILLION** DIFFERENT KINDS OF ROSES RIGHT HERE.
I'LL JUST BRING THEM **ALL** BACK, SO POE AND I CAN TRY THEM OUT.
I DON'T GET IT...
WHY DOES EVERYONE **SHUN** HIM?
HE'S SUCH A NICE BOY.
RUSTLE...
I WONDER IF THERE'S SOME REASON...

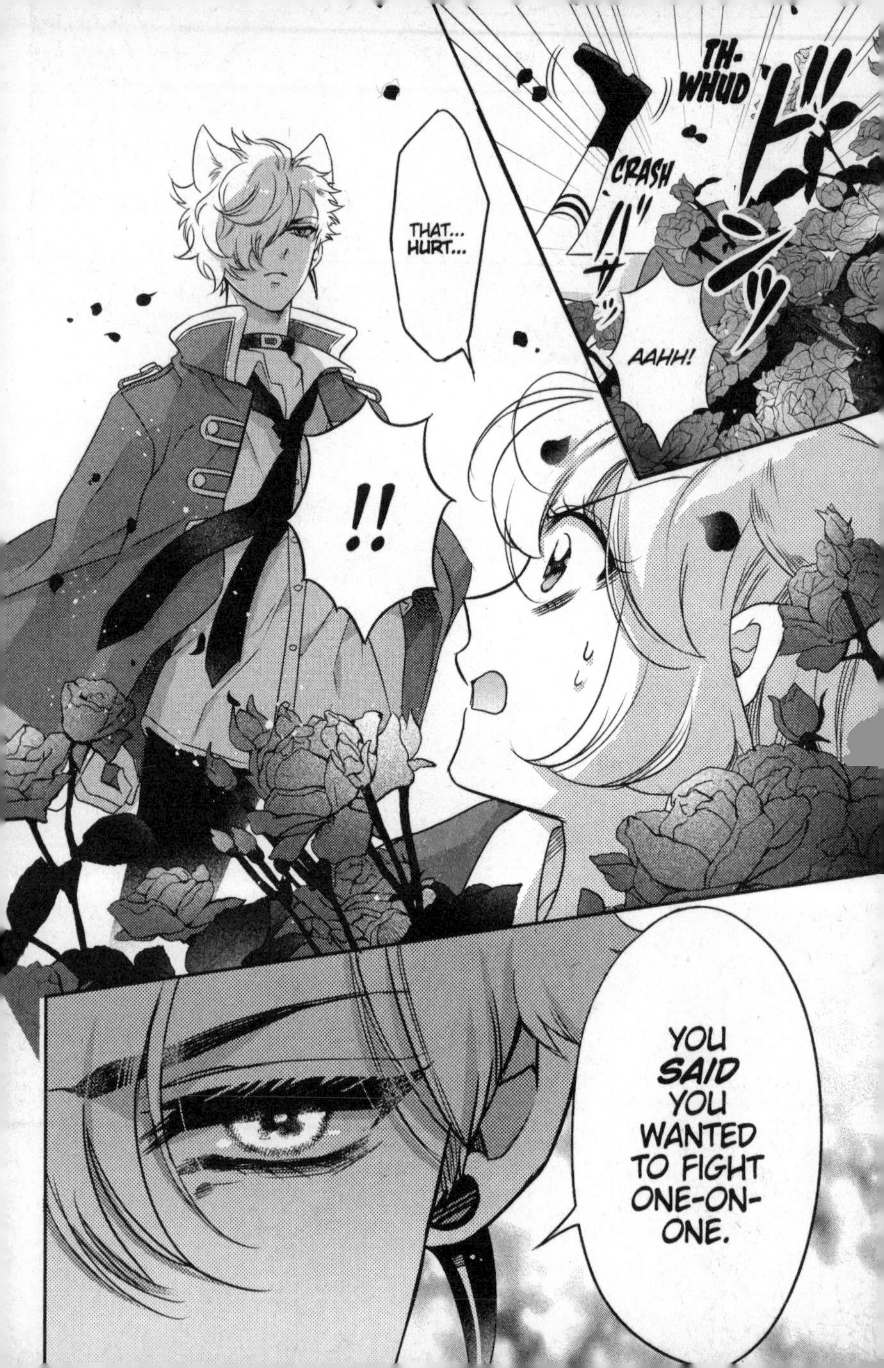
TH-WHUD
CRASH
AAHH!
THAT... HURT...
!!
YOU SAID YOU WANTED TO FIGHT ONE-ON-ONE.

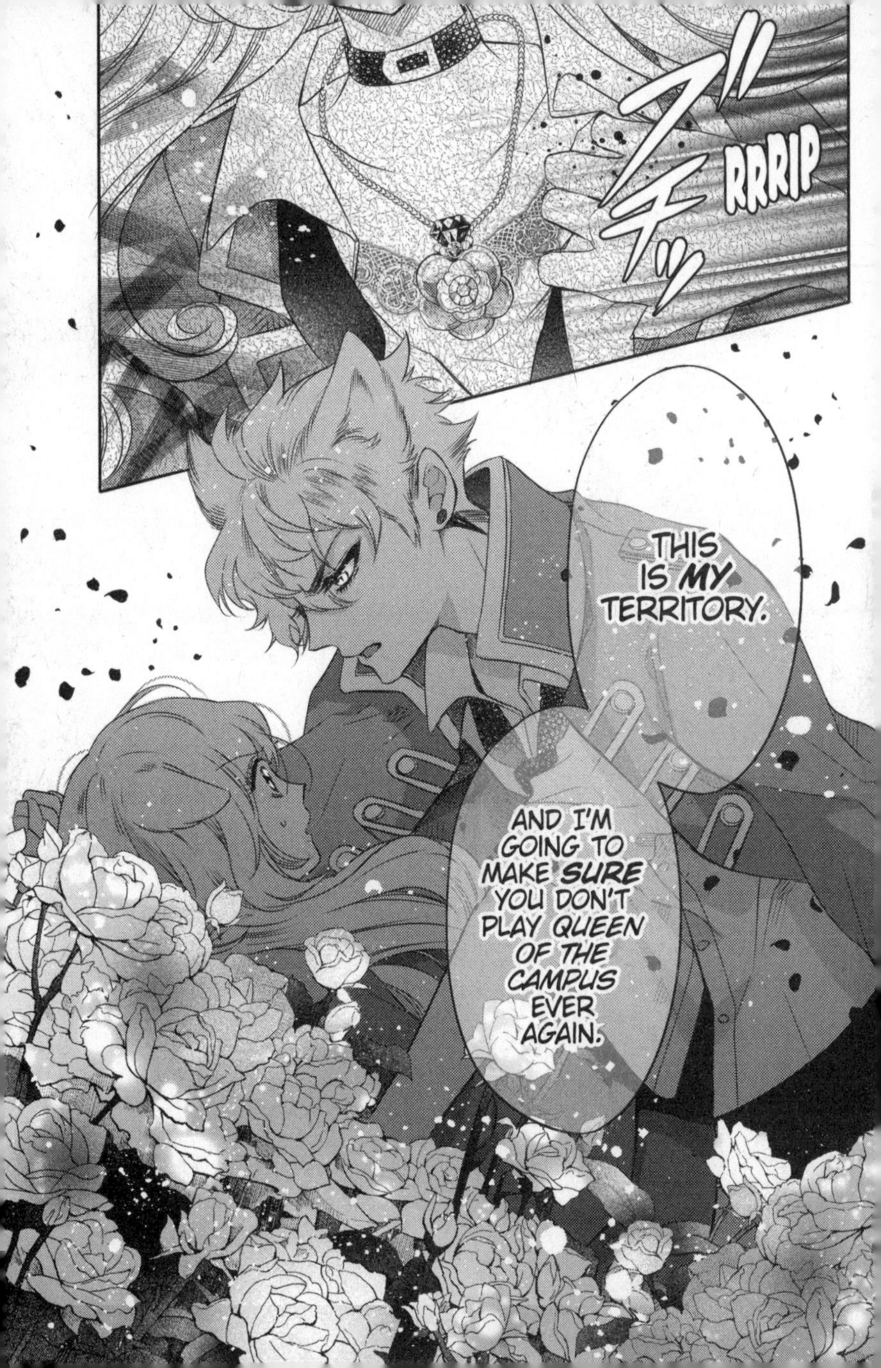
RRRIP
THIS IS MY TERRITORY.
AND I'M GOING TO MAKE SURE YOU DON'T PLAY QUEEN OF THE CAMPUS EVER AGAIN.

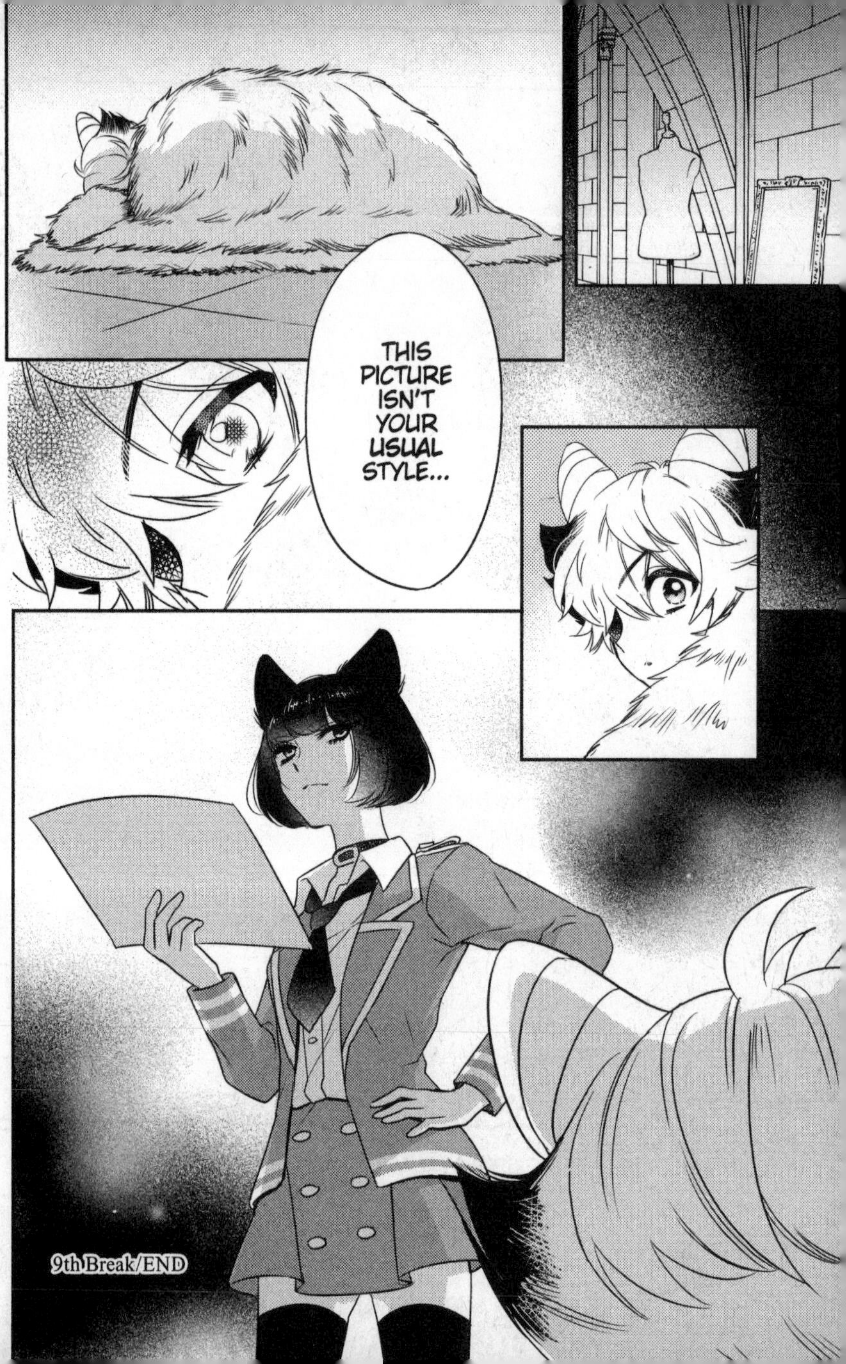
THIS PICTURE ISN'T YOUR USUAL STYLE...
9th Break/END

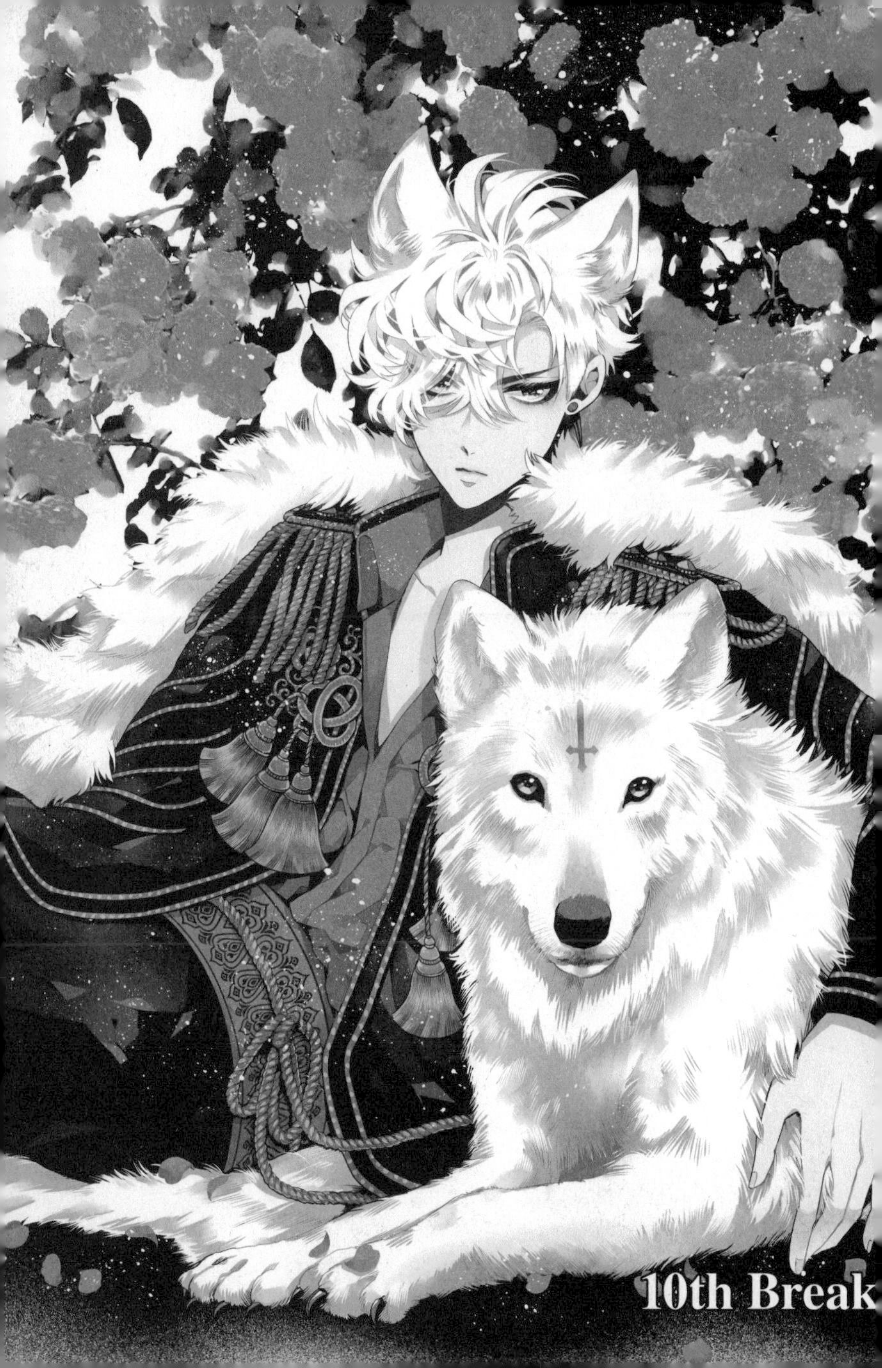
10th Break

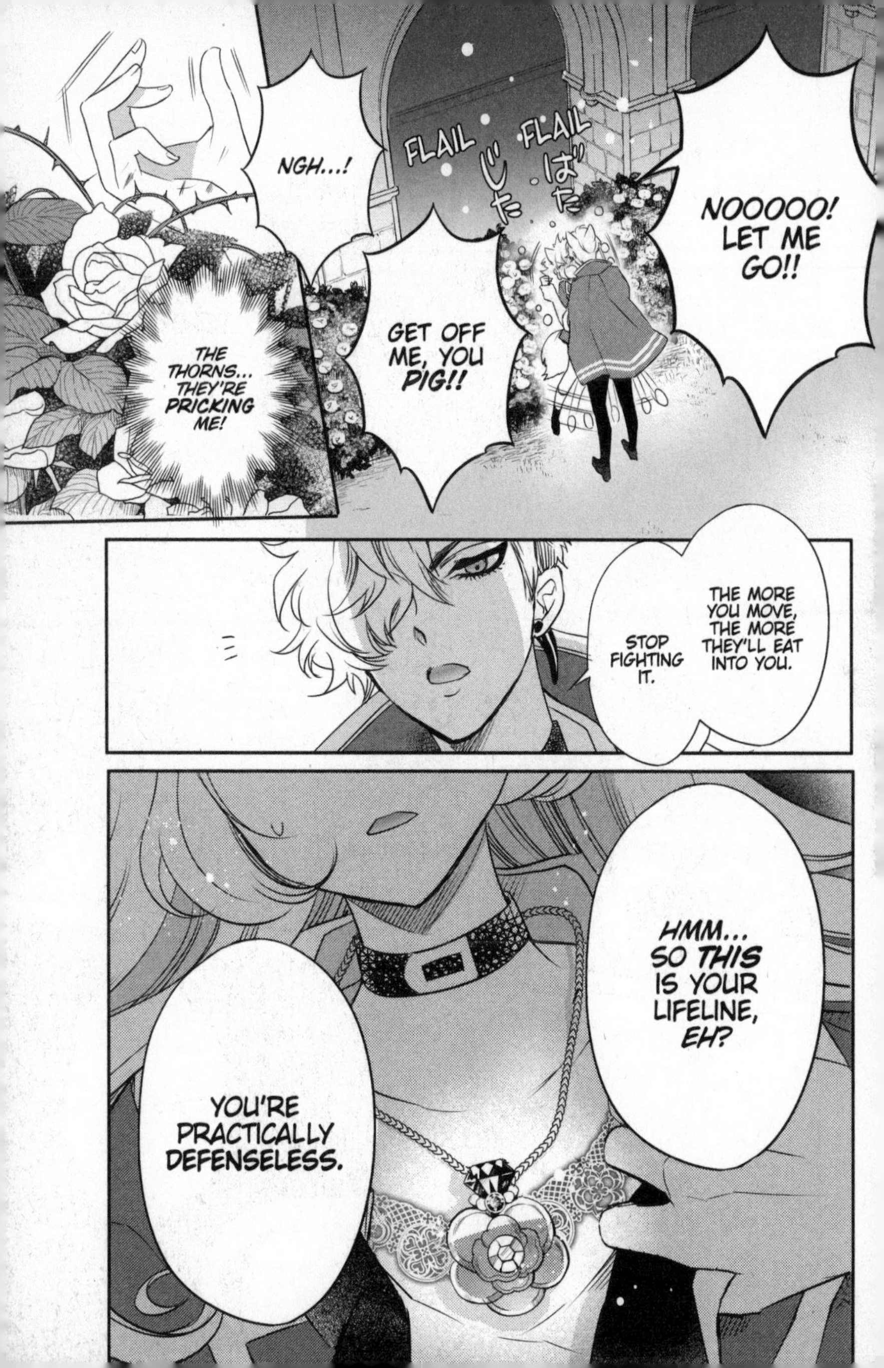
NOOOOO! LET ME GO!!
FLAIL FLAIL
じたばた
GET OFF ME, YOU *PIG!!*
NGH...!
THE THORNS... THEY'RE *PRICKING* ME!
THE MORE YOU MOVE, THE MORE THEY'LL EAT INTO YOU.
STOP FIGHTING IT.
HMM... SO *THIS* IS YOUR LIFELINE, *EH?*
YOU'RE PRACTICALLY DEFENSELESS.

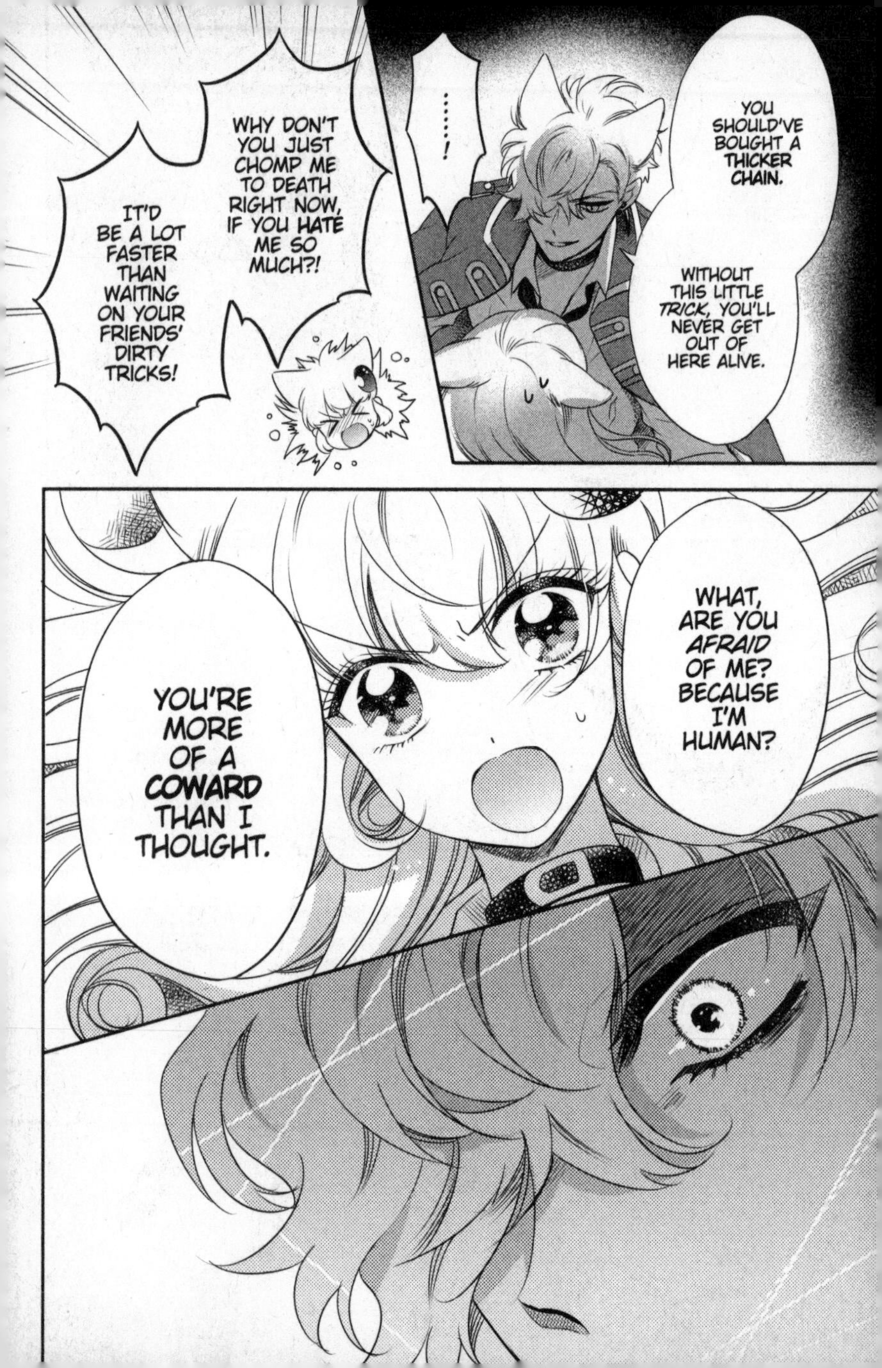
YOU SHOULD'VE BOUGHT A THICKER CHAIN.
WITHOUT THIS LITTLE *TRICK*, YOU'LL NEVER GET OUT OF HERE ALIVE.
……!
WHY DON'T YOU JUST CHOMP ME TO DEATH RIGHT NOW, IF YOU HATE ME SO MUCH?!
IT'D BE A LOT FASTER THAN WAITING ON YOUR FRIENDS' DIRTY TRICKS!
WHAT, ARE YOU *AFRAID* OF ME? BECAUSE I'M HUMAN?
YOU'RE MORE OF A **COWARD** THAN I THOUGHT.

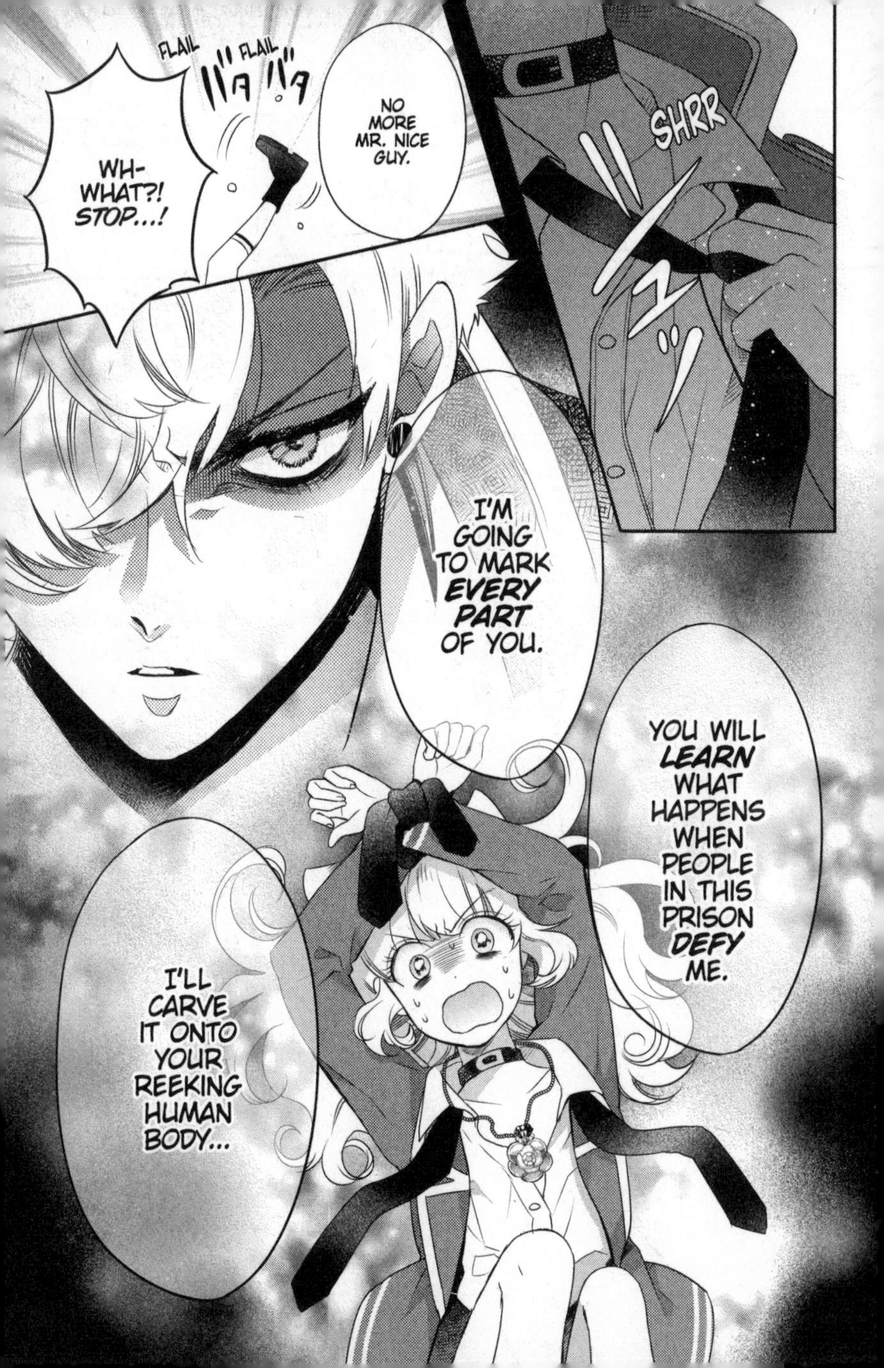
SHRR
NO MORE MR. NICE GUY.
FLAIL
FLAIL
WH-WHAT?! STOP...!
I'M GOING TO MARK EVERY PART OF YOU.
YOU WILL LEARN WHAT HAPPENS WHEN PEOPLE IN THIS PRISON DEFY ME.
I'LL CARVE IT ONTO YOUR REEKING HUMAN BODY...

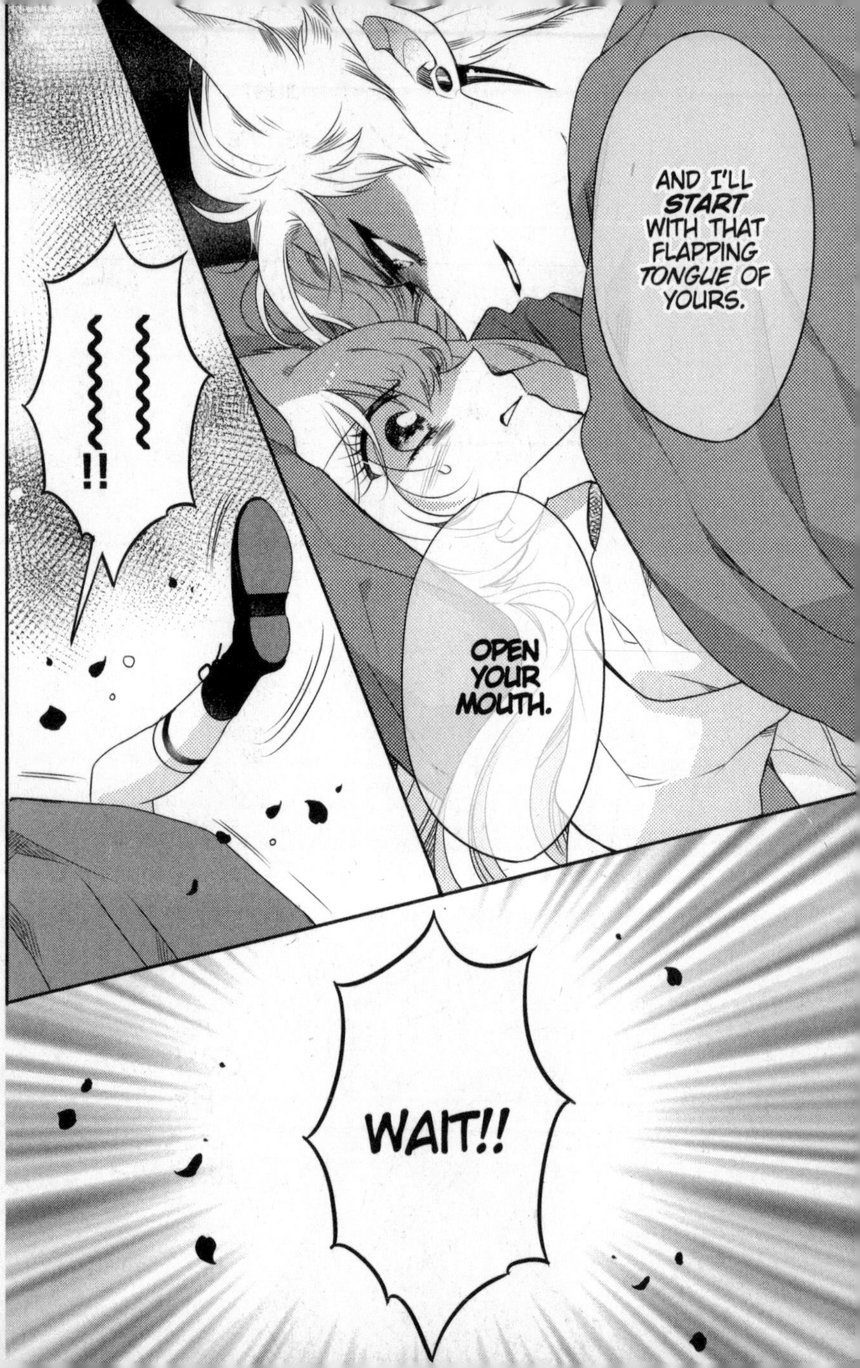
AND I'LL *START* WITH THAT FLAPPING *TONGUE* OF YOURS.
OPEN YOUR MOUTH.
!!
WAIT!!

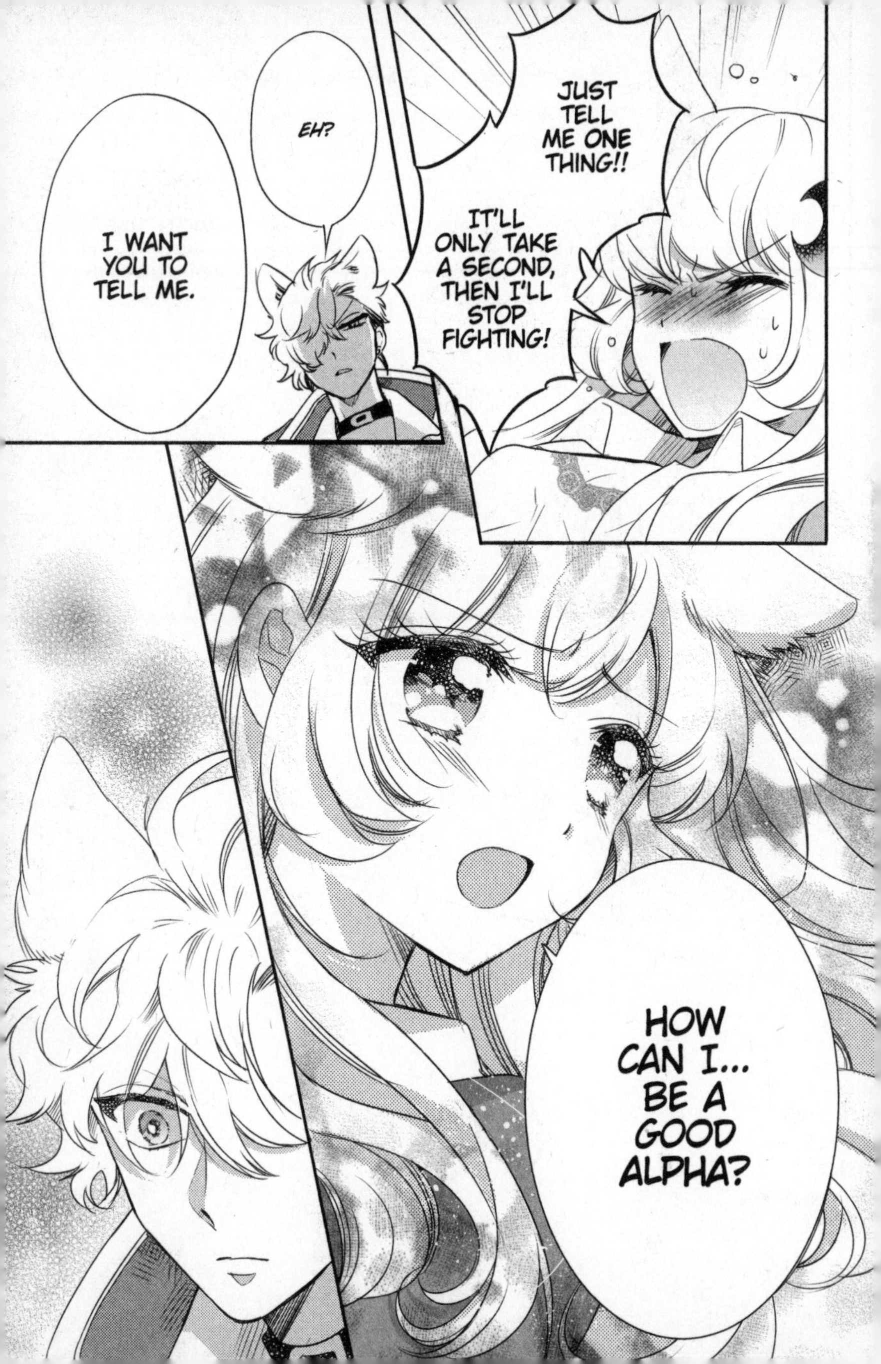
JUST TELL ME ONE THING!!
IT'LL ONLY TAKE A SECOND, THEN I'LL STOP FIGHTING!
EH?
I WANT YOU TO TELL ME.
HOW CAN I... BE A GOOD ALPHA?

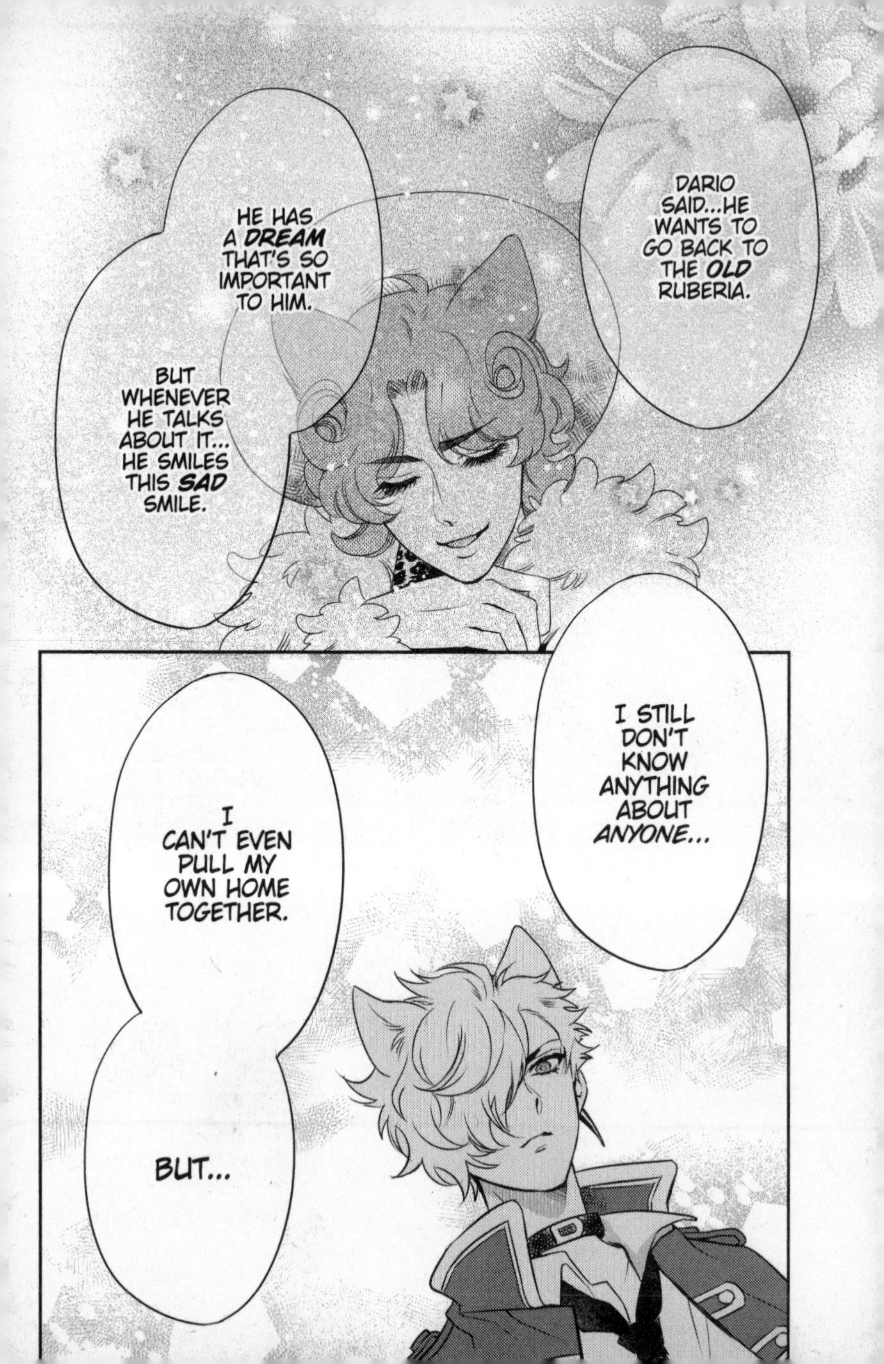
DARIO SAID...HE WANTS TO GO BACK TO THE OLD RUBERIA.
HE HAS A DREAM THAT'S SO IMPORTANT TO HIM.
BUT WHENEVER HE TALKS ABOUT IT... HE SMILES THIS SAD SMILE.
I STILL DON'T KNOW ANYTHING ABOUT ANYONE...
I CAN'T EVEN PULL MY OWN HOME TOGETHER.
BUT...

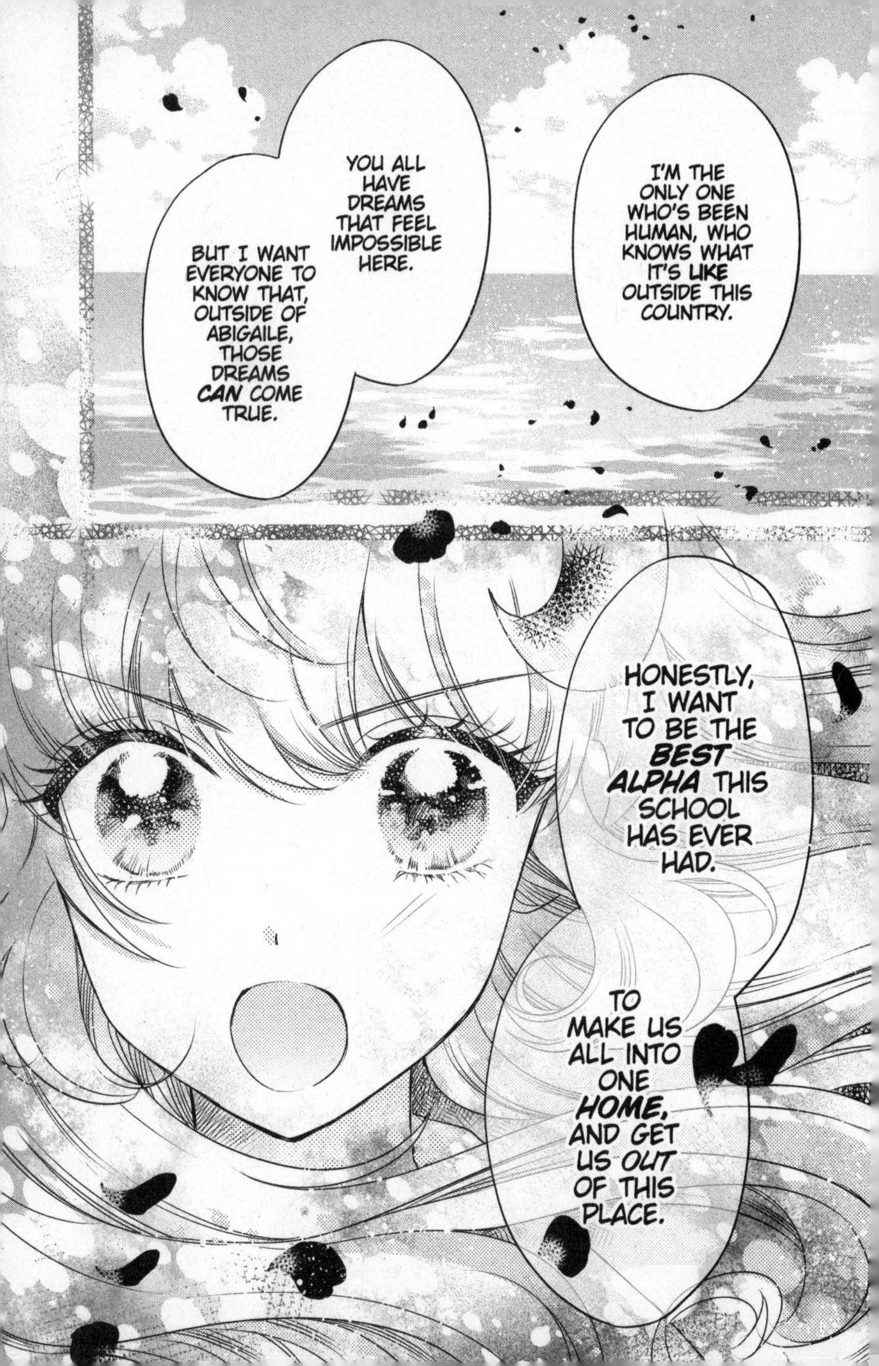
I'M THE ONLY ONE WHO'S BEEN HUMAN, WHO KNOWS WHAT IT'S LIKE OUTSIDE THIS COUNTRY.
YOU ALL HAVE DREAMS THAT FEEL IMPOSSIBLE HERE.
BUT I WANT EVERYONE TO KNOW THAT, OUTSIDE OF ABIGAILE, THOSE DREAMS *CAN* COME TRUE.
HONESTLY, I WANT TO BE THE ***BEST ALPHA*** THIS SCHOOL HAS EVER HAD.
TO MAKE US ALL INTO ONE ***HOME,*** AND GET US *OUT* OF THIS PLACE.

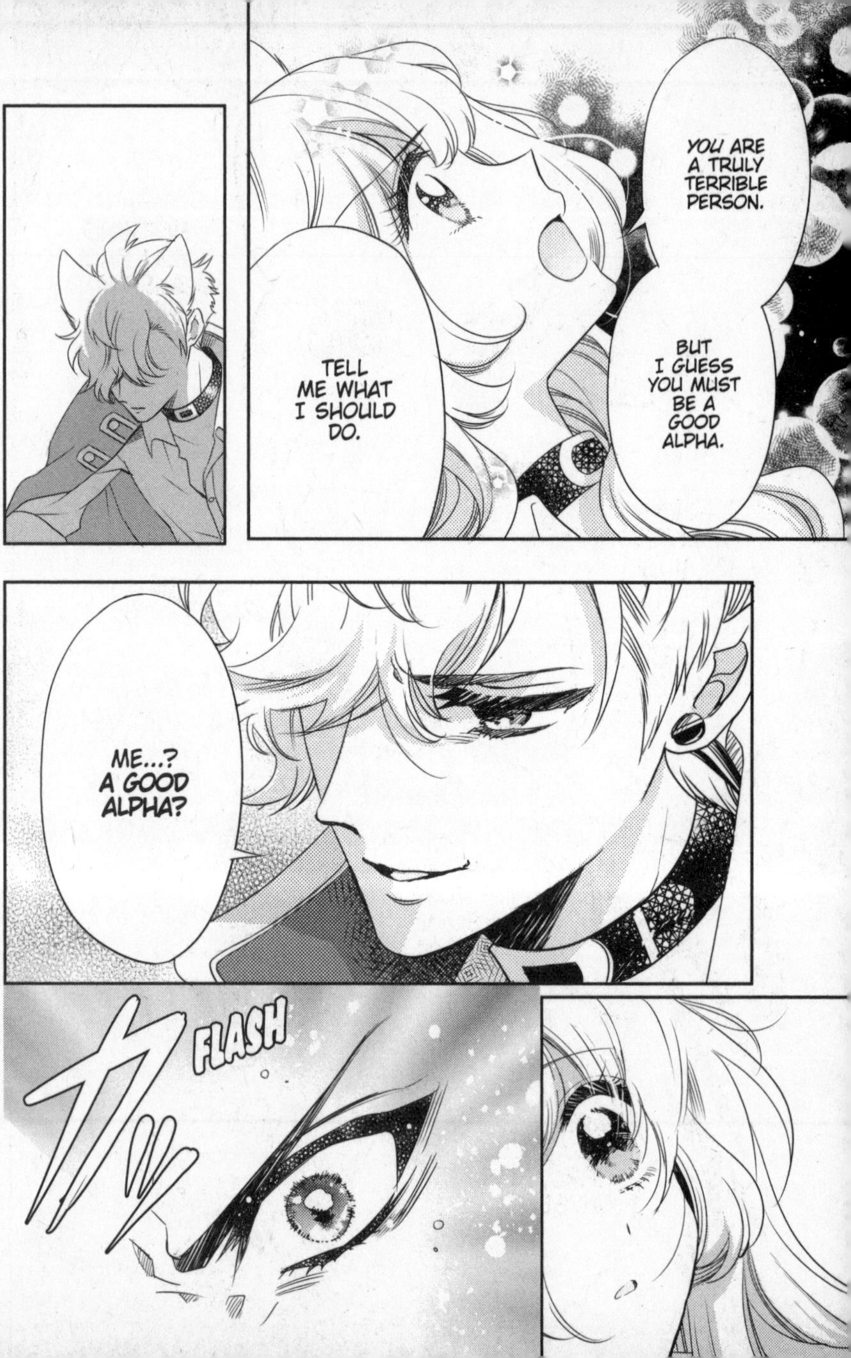
YOU ARE A TRULY TERRIBLE PERSON.
BUT I GUESS YOU MUST BE A GOOD ALPHA.
TELL ME WHAT I SHOULD DO.
ME...? A GOOD ALPHA?
FLASH

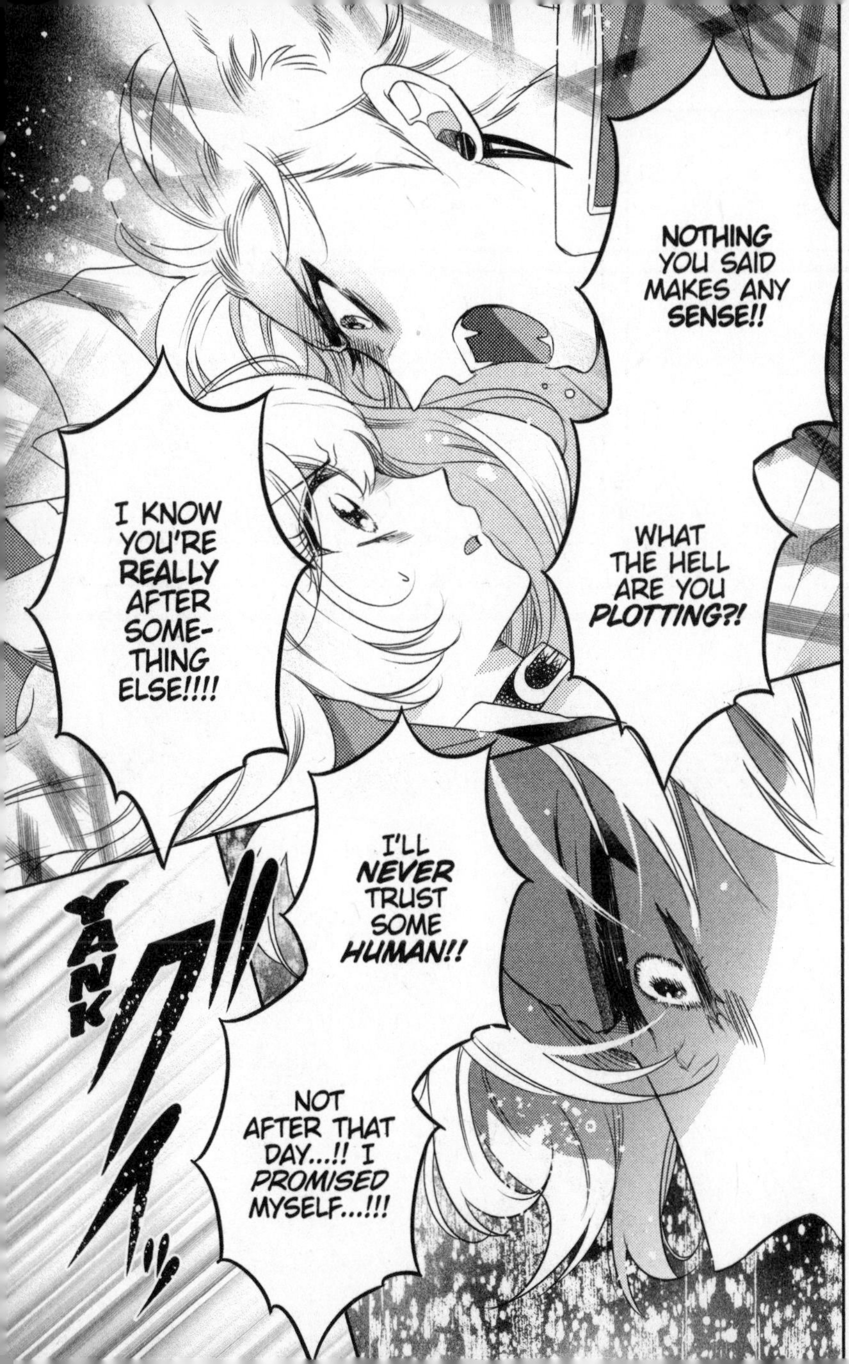
NOTHING YOU SAID MAKES ANY SENSE!!
WHAT THE HELL ARE YOU *PLOTTING*?!
I KNOW YOU'RE REALLY AFTER SOME-THING ELSE!!!!
I'LL *NEVER* TRUST SOME *HUMAN*!!
NOT AFTER THAT DAY...!! I *PROMISED* MYSELF...!!!
YANK

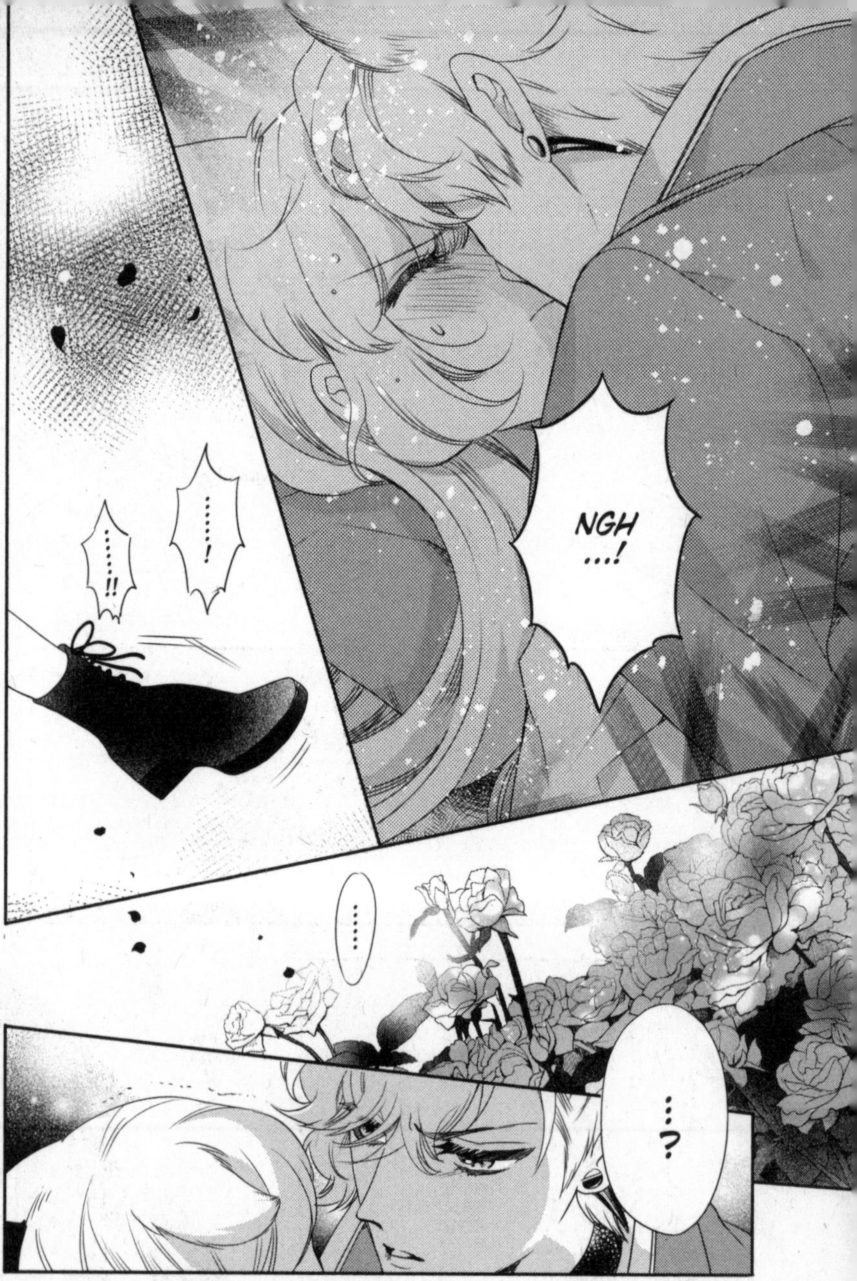
NGH ...!
......!
......!!
......
...?

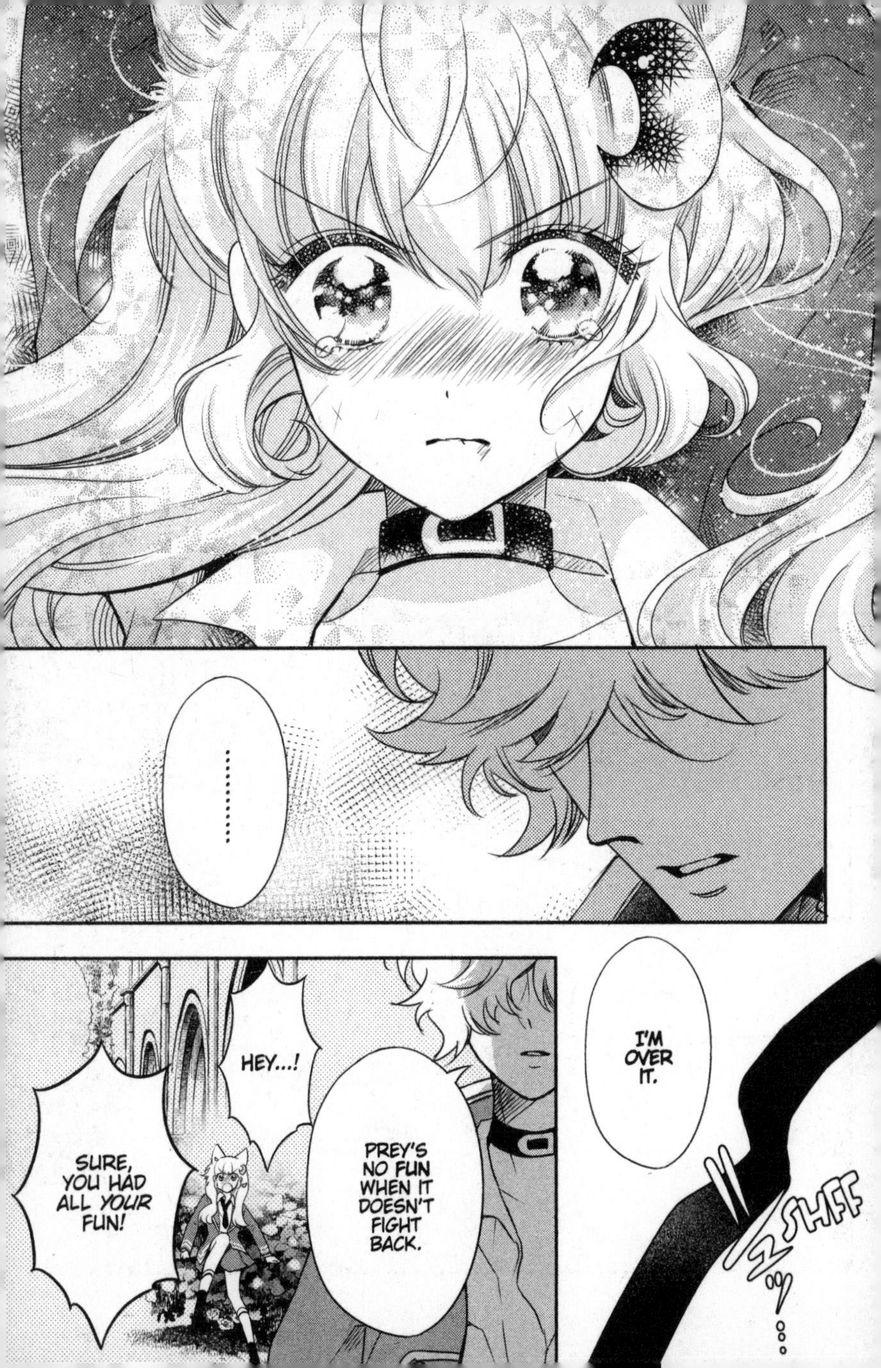
......
I'M OVER IT.
SHFF
PREY'S NO FUN WHEN IT DOESN'T FIGHT BACK.
HEY...!
SURE, YOU HAD ALL YOUR FUN!

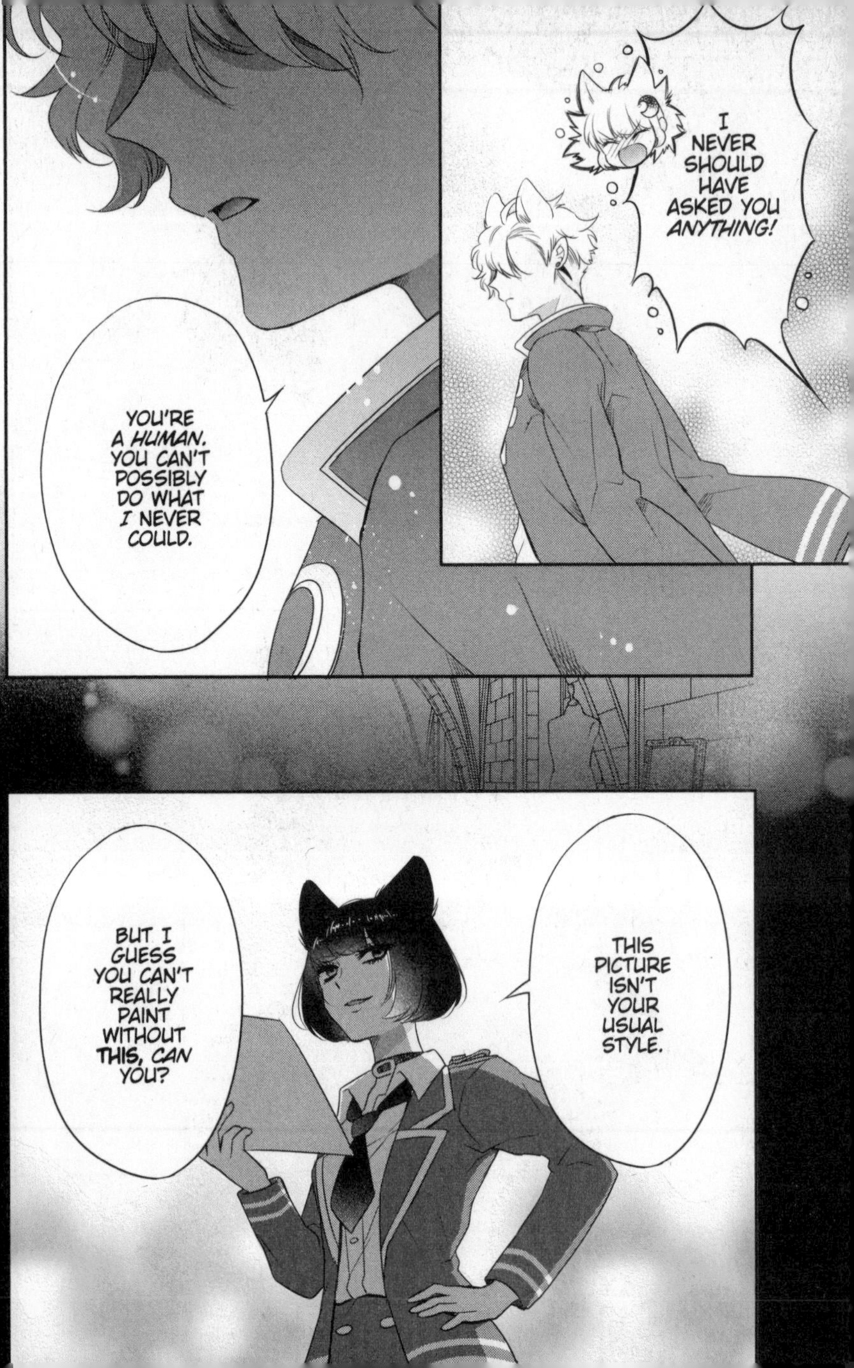
I NEVER SHOULD HAVE ASKED YOU ANYTHING!
YOU'RE A HUMAN. YOU CAN'T POSSIBLY DO WHAT I NEVER COULD.
THIS PICTURE ISN'T YOUR USUAL STYLE.
BUT I GUESS YOU CAN'T REALLY PAINT WITHOUT THIS, CAN YOU?

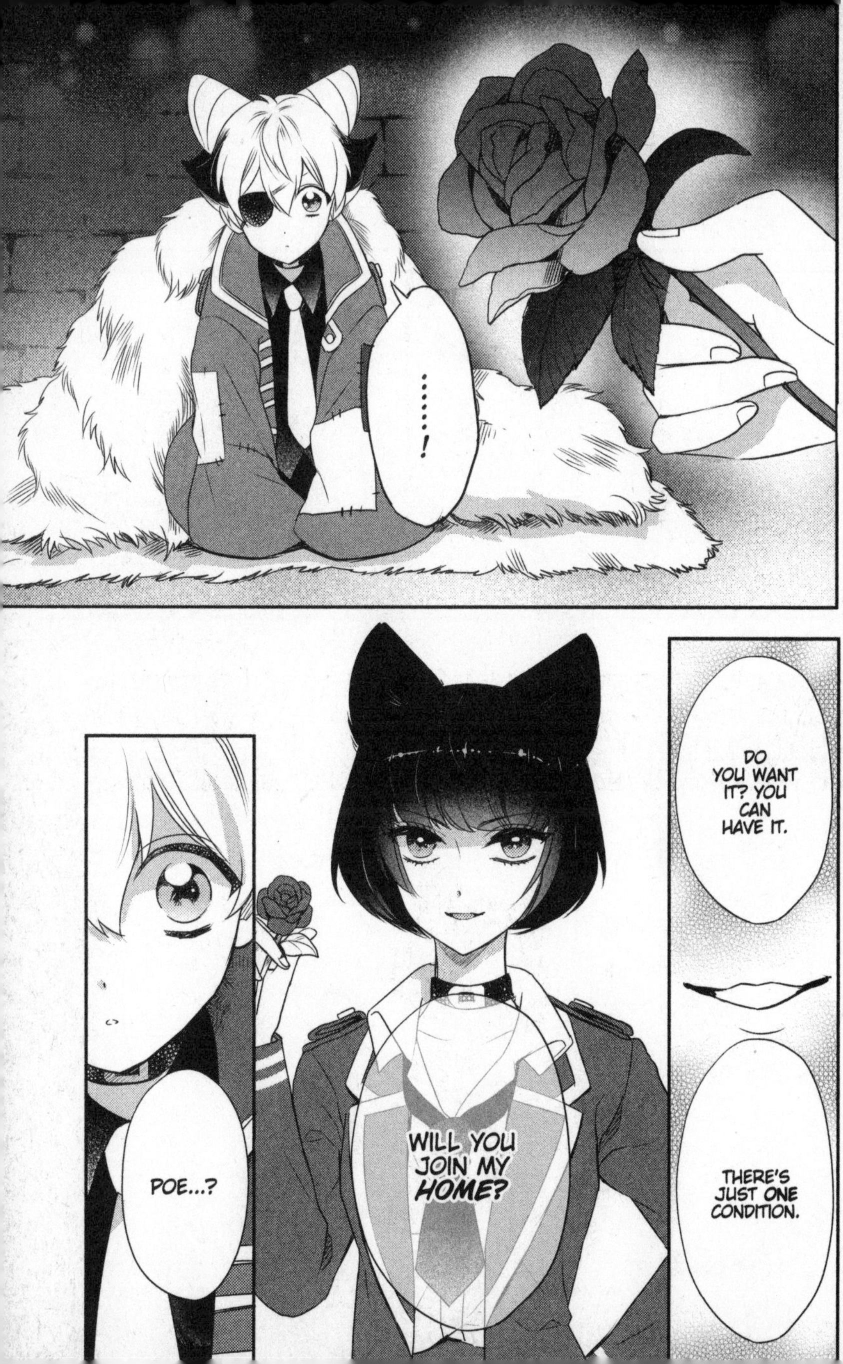
......!
DO YOU WANT IT? YOU CAN HAVE IT.
THERE'S JUST ONE CONDITION.
WILL YOU JOIN MY *HOME*?
POE...?

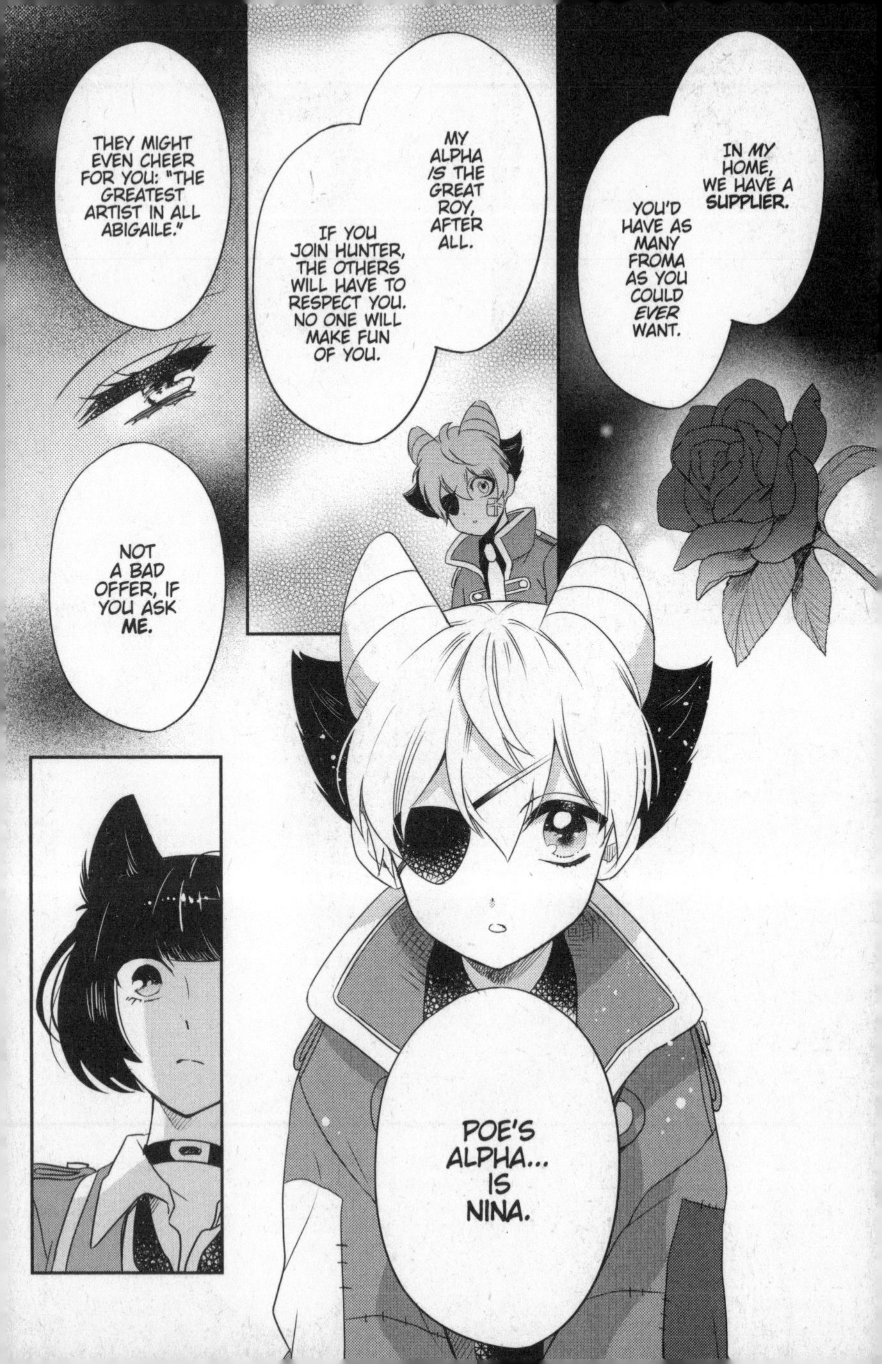
IN MY HOME, WE HAVE A SUPPLIER.
YOU'D HAVE AS MANY FROMA AS YOU COULD EVER WANT.
MY ALPHA IS THE GREAT ROY, AFTER ALL.
IF YOU JOIN HUNTER, THE OTHERS WILL HAVE TO RESPECT YOU. NO ONE WILL MAKE FUN OF YOU.
THEY MIGHT EVEN CHEER FOR YOU: "THE GREATEST ARTIST IN ALL ABIGAILE."
NOT A BAD OFFER, IF YOU ASK ME.
POE'S ALPHA... IS NINA.

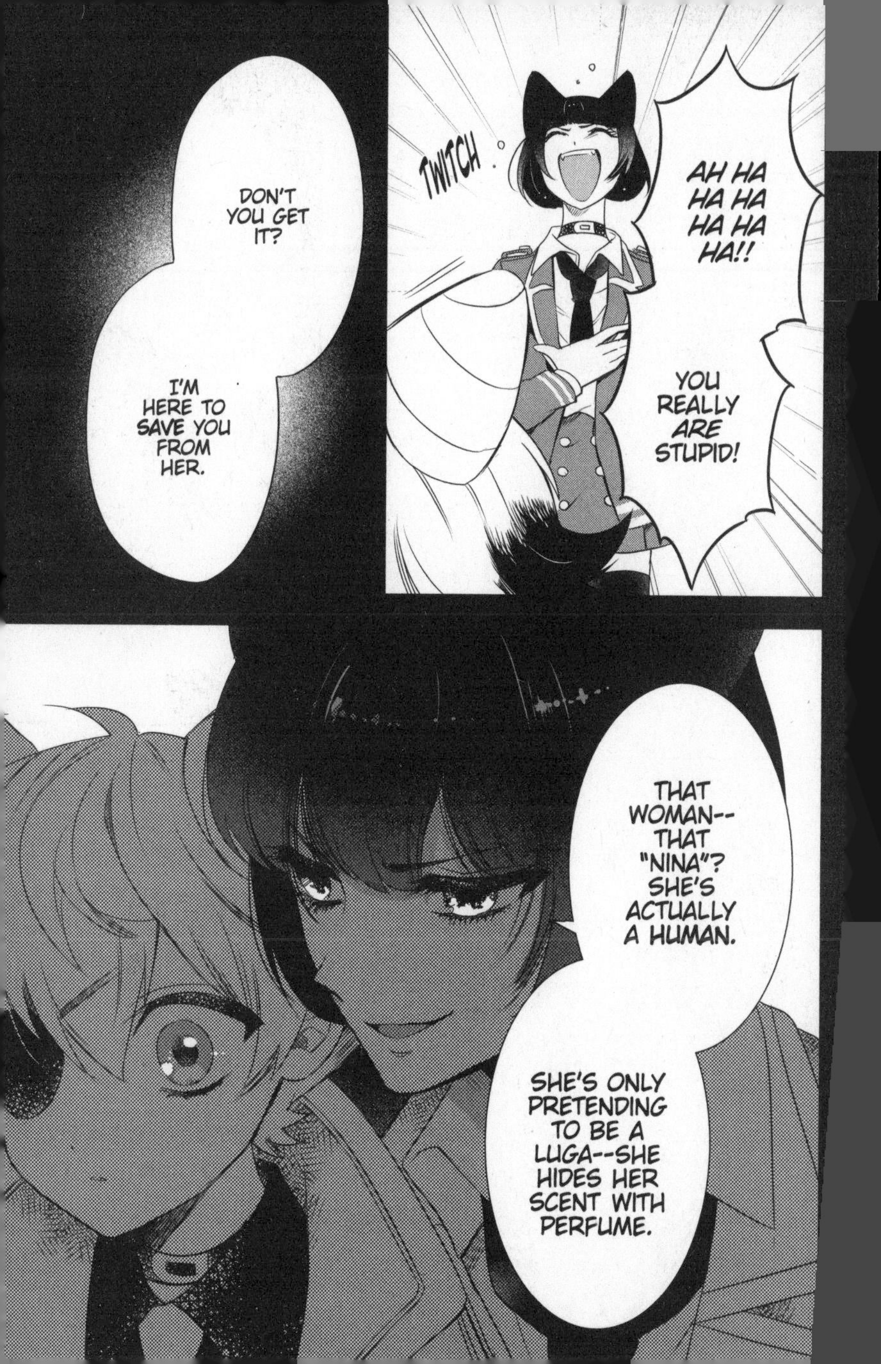
AH HA HA HA HA HA HA!!
YOU REALLY ARE STUPID!
TWITCH
DON'T YOU GET IT?
I'M HERE TO SAVE YOU FROM HER.
THAT WOMAN--THAT "NINA"? SHE'S ACTUALLY A HUMAN.
SHE'S ONLY PRETENDING TO BE A LUGA--SHE HIDES HER SCENT WITH PERFUME.

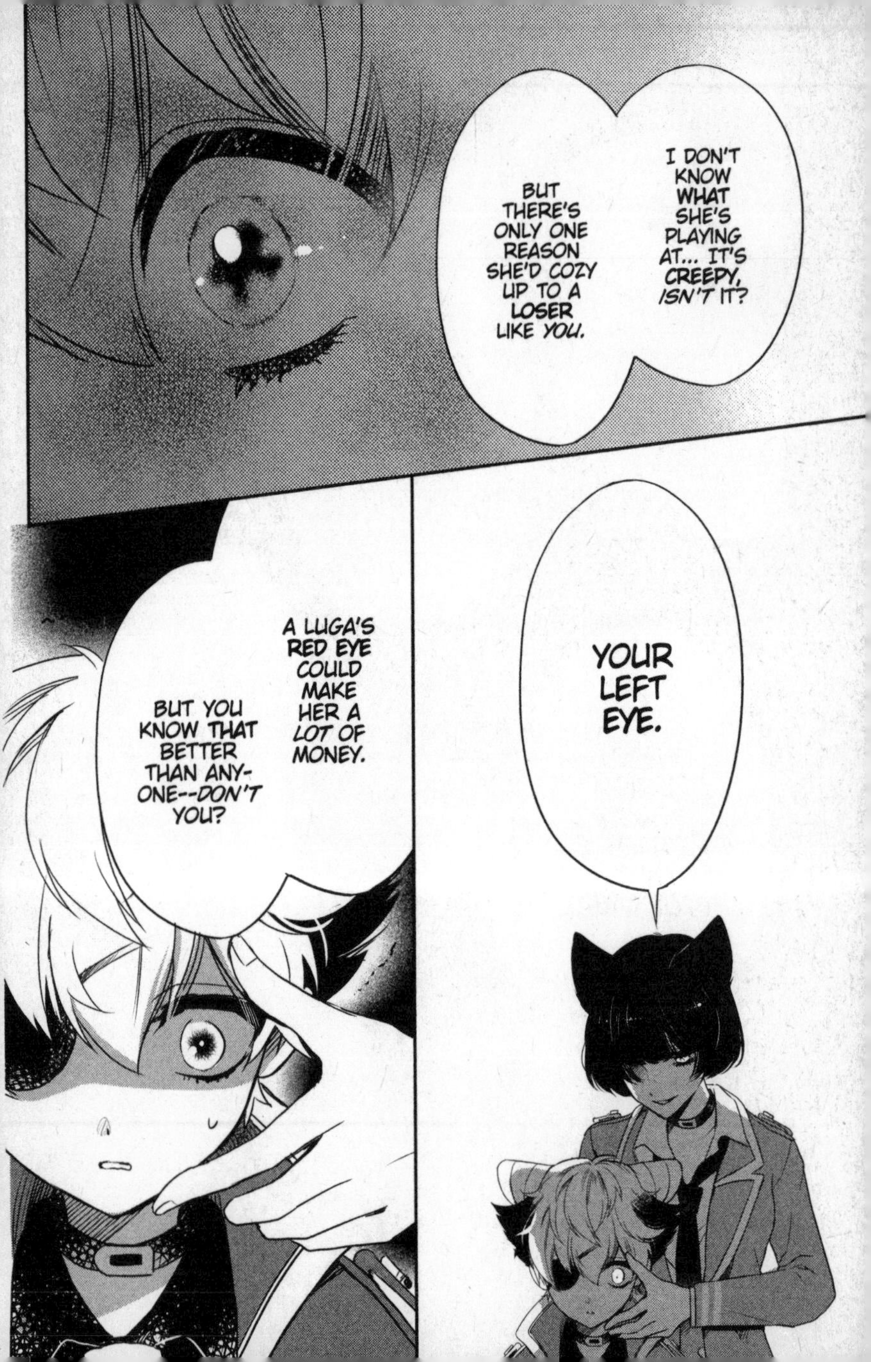
I DON'T KNOW WHAT SHE'S PLAYING AT... IT'S CREEPY, *ISN'T* IT?
BUT THERE'S ONLY ONE REASON SHE'D COZY UP TO A LOSER LIKE *YOU*.
YOUR LEFT EYE.
A LUGA'S RED EYE COULD MAKE HER A *LOT* OF MONEY.
BUT YOU KNOW THAT BETTER THAN ANY-ONE--*DON'T* YOU?

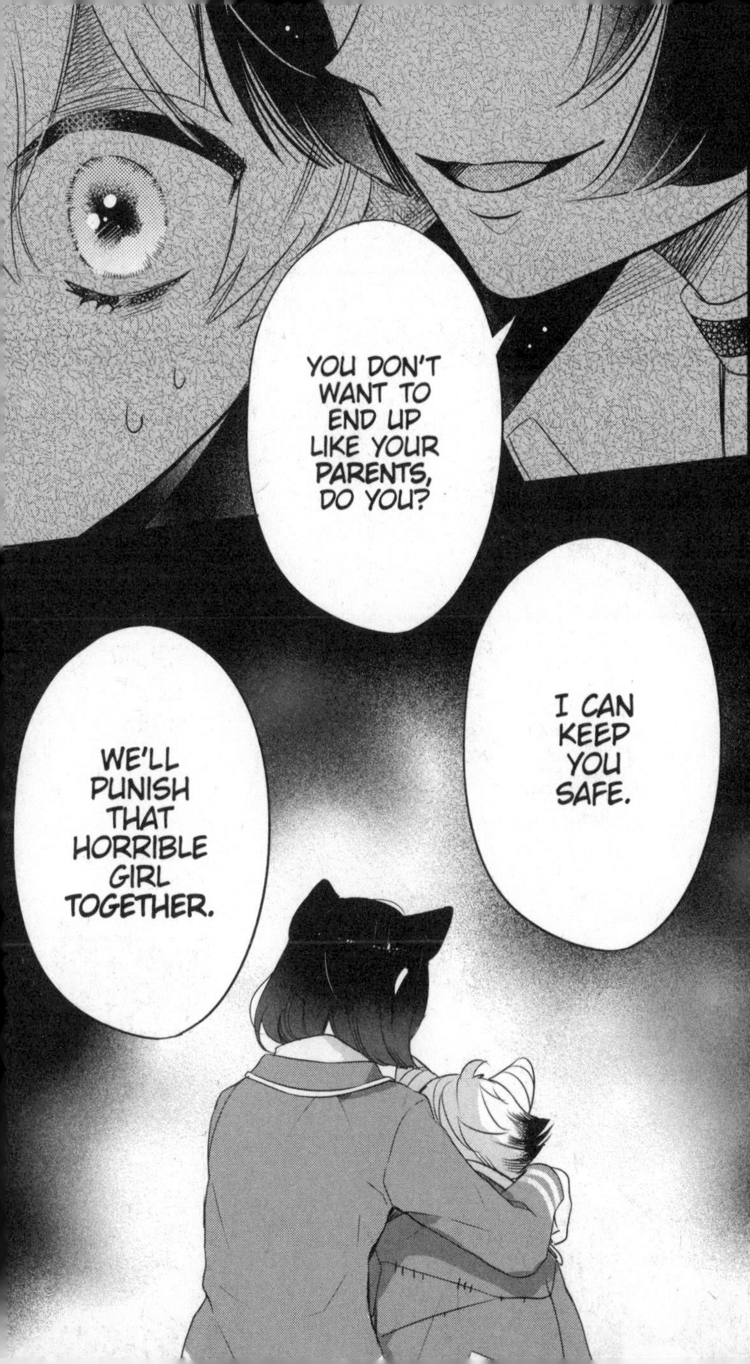
YOU DON'T WANT TO END UP LIKE YOUR PARENTS, DO YOU?
I CAN KEEP YOU SAFE.
WE'LL PUNISH THAT HORRIBLE GIRL TOGETHER.

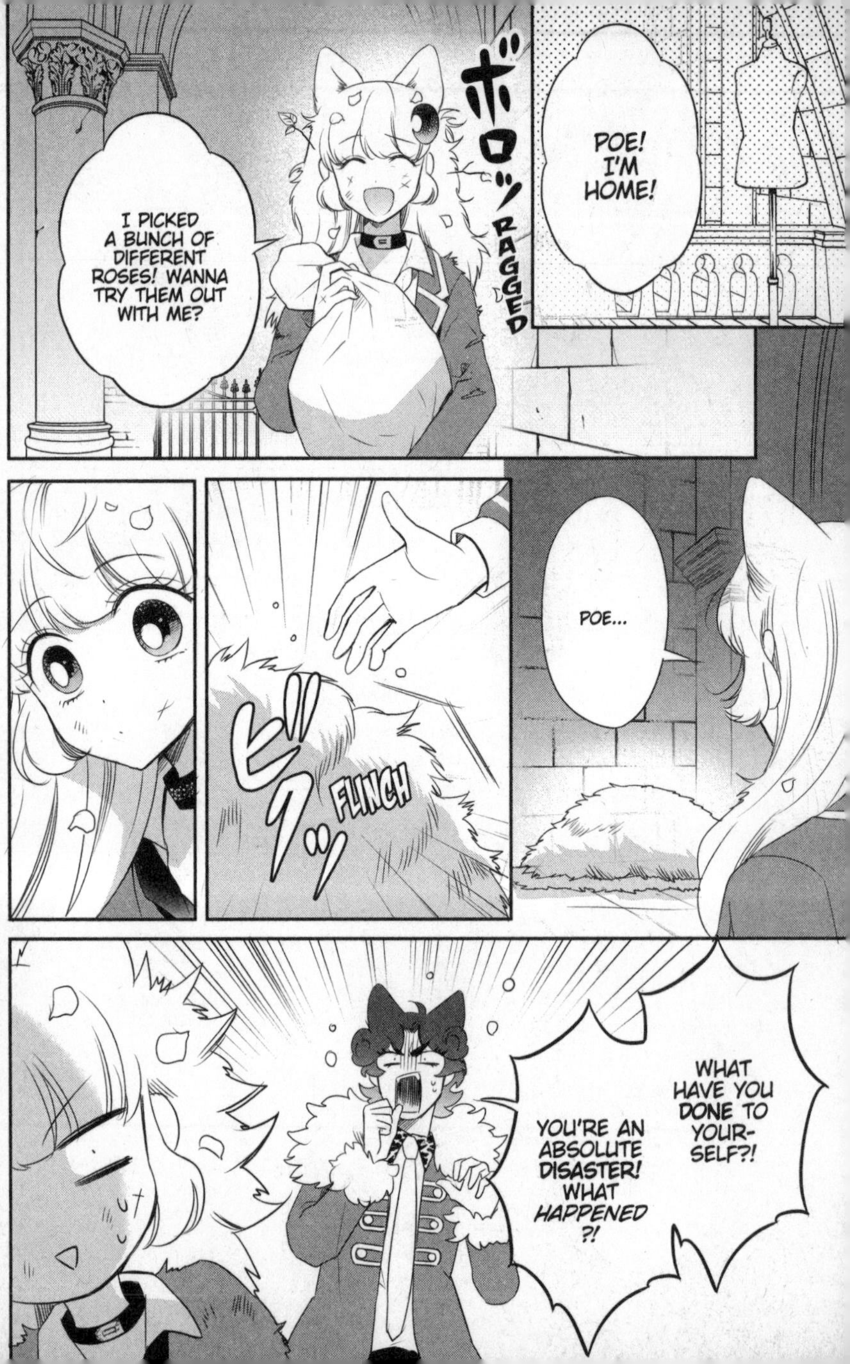
POE! I'M HOME!
ボロッ
RAGGED
I PICKED A BUNCH OF DIFFERENT ROSES! WANNA TRY THEM OUT WITH ME?
POE...
ビクッ
FLINCH
WHAT HAVE YOU DONE TO YOURSELF?!
YOU'RE AN ABSOLUTE DISASTER! WHAT HAPPENED?!

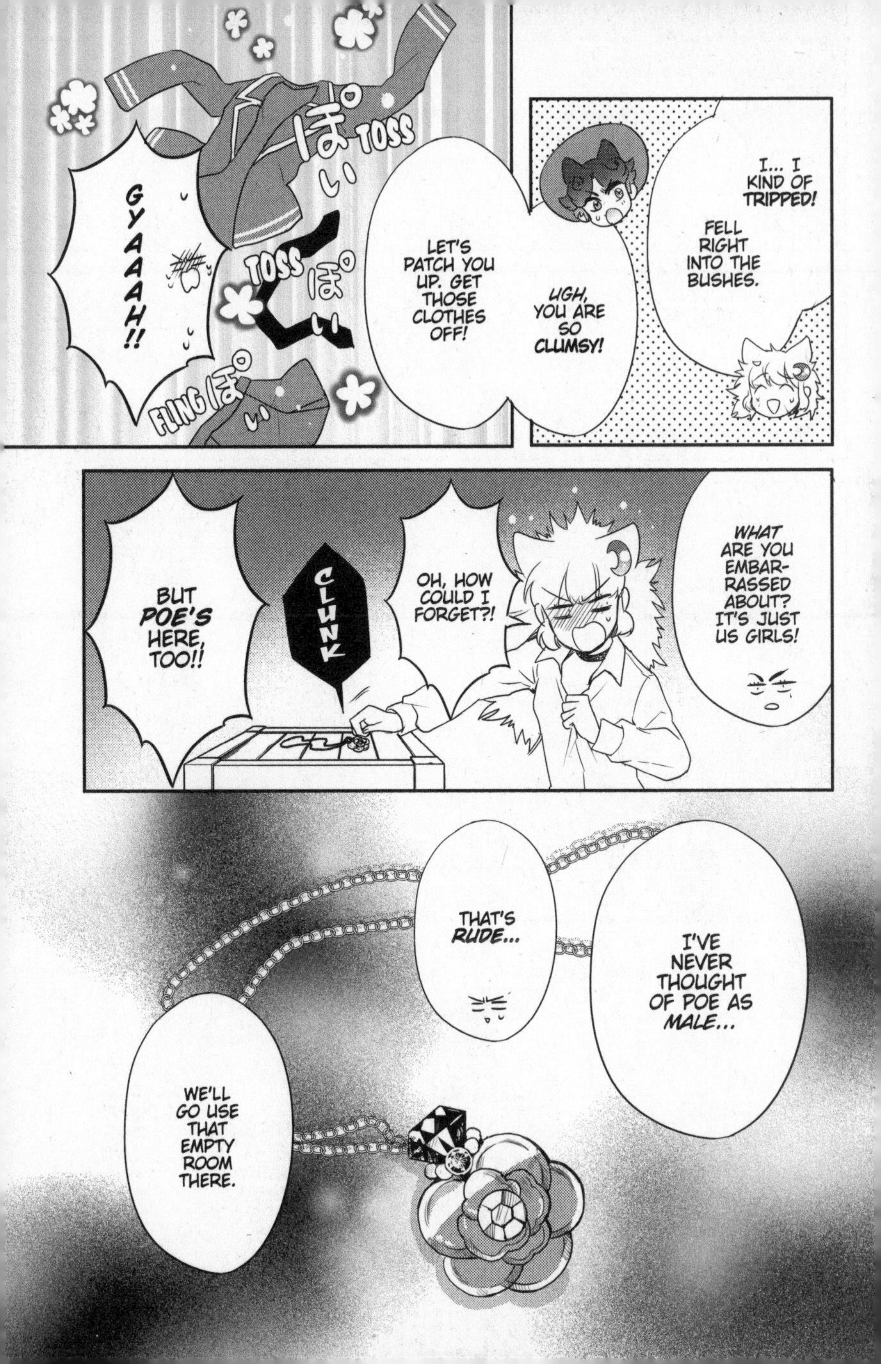
I... I KIND OF TRIPPED!
FELL RIGHT INTO THE BUSHES.
UGH, YOU ARE SO CLUMSY!
LET'S PATCH YOU UP. GET THOSE CLOTHES OFF!
TOSS ぽい
TOSS ぽい
FLING ぽい
GYAAAAH!!
WHAT ARE YOU EMBAR-RASSED ABOUT? IT'S JUST US GIRLS!
OH, HOW COULD I FORGET?!
CLUNK
BUT POE'S HERE, TOO!!
I'VE NEVER THOUGHT OF POE AS MALE...
THAT'S RUDE...
WE'LL GO USE THAT EMPTY ROOM THERE.

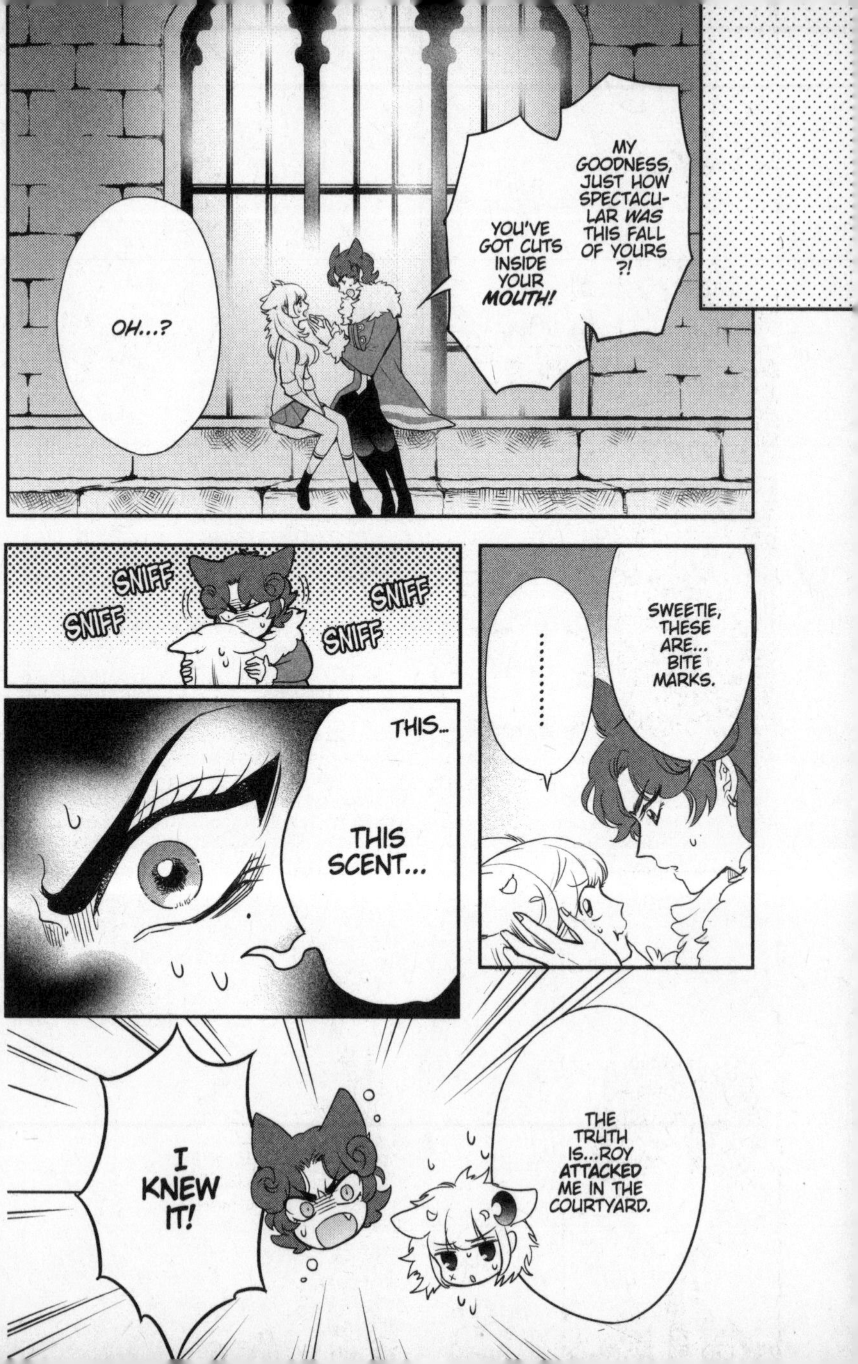
MY GOODNESS, JUST HOW SPECTACULAR WAS THIS FALL OF YOURS?!
YOU'VE GOT CUTS INSIDE YOUR MOUTH!
OH...?
SWEETIE, THESE ARE... BITE MARKS.
......
SNIFF
SNIFF
SNIFF
SNIFF
THIS...
THIS SCENT...
THE TRUTH IS...ROY ATTACKED ME IN THE COURTYARD.
I KNEW IT!

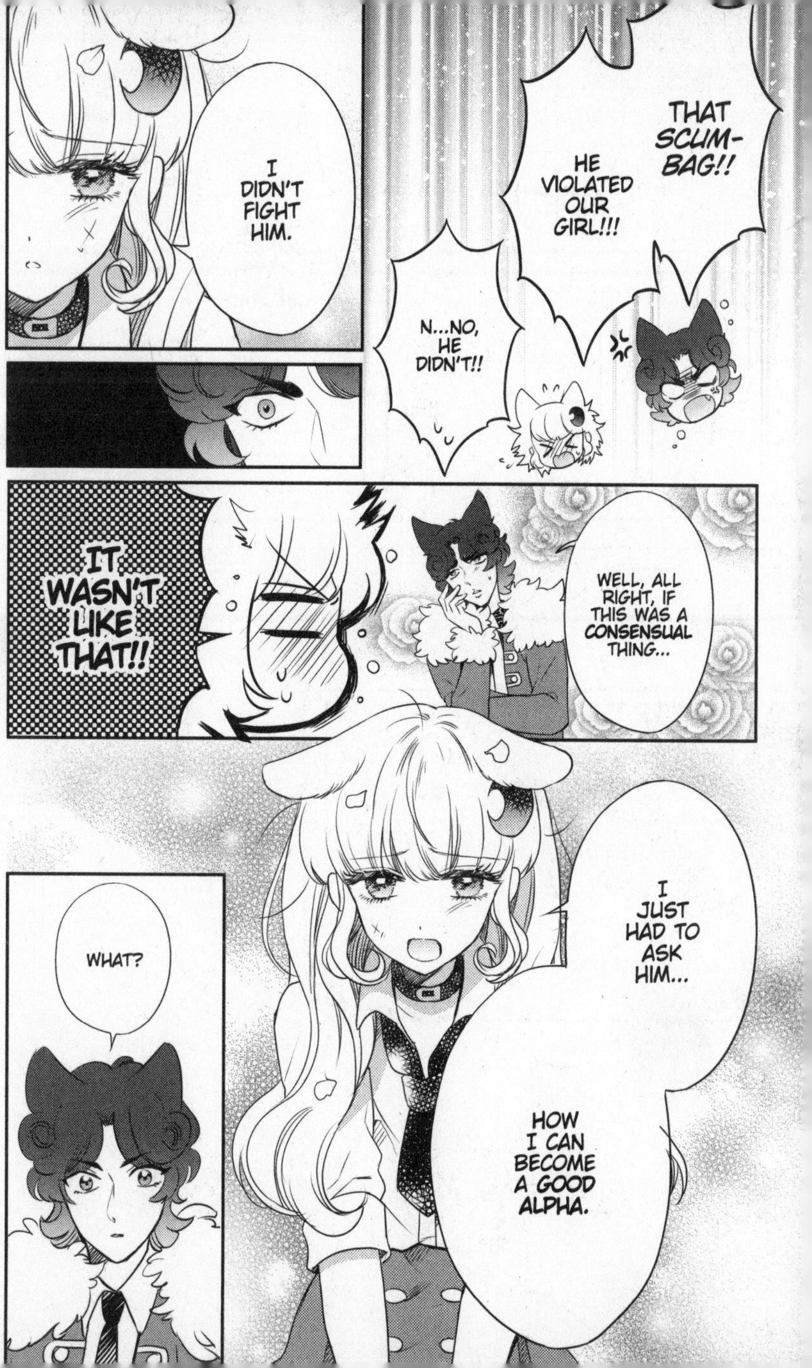
THAT SCUMBAG!!
HE VIOLATED OUR GIRL!!!
N...NO, HE DIDN'T!!
I DIDN'T FIGHT HIM.
WELL, ALL RIGHT, IF THIS WAS A CONSENSUAL THING...
IT WASN'T LIKE THAT!!
I JUST HAD TO ASK HIM...
HOW I CAN BECOME A GOOD ALPHA.
WHAT?

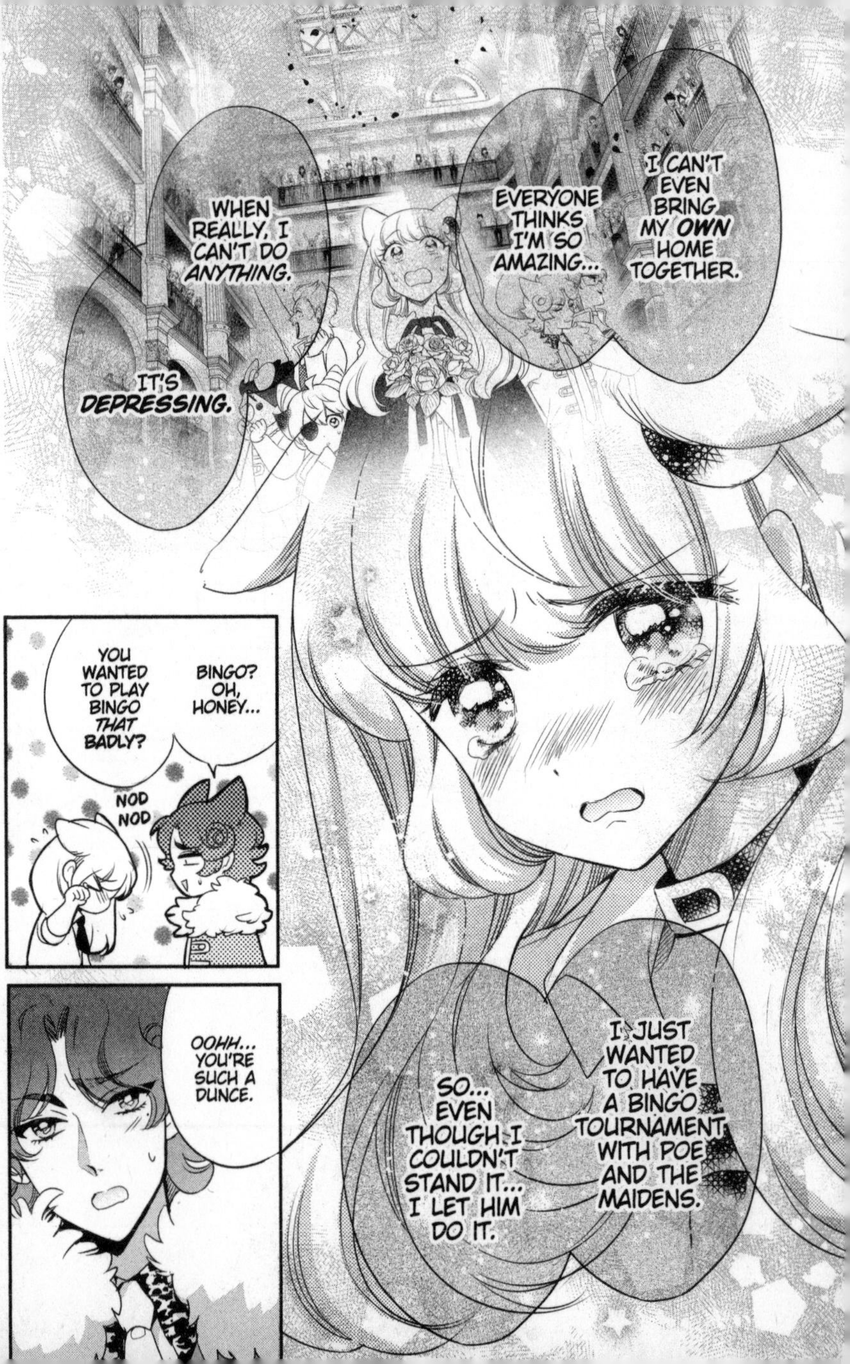

I CAN'T EVEN BRING MY OWN HOME TOGETHER.
EVERYONE THINKS I'M SO AMAZING...
WHEN REALLY, I CAN'T DO ANYTHING.
IT'S DEPRESSING.
I JUST WANTED TO HAVE A BINGO TOURNAMENT WITH POE AND THE MAIDENS.
SO... EVEN THOUGH I COULDN'T STAND IT... I LET HIM DO IT.
BINGO? OH, HONEY...
YOU WANTED TO PLAY BINGO THAT BADLY?
NOD NOD
OOHH... YOU'RE SUCH A DUNCE.

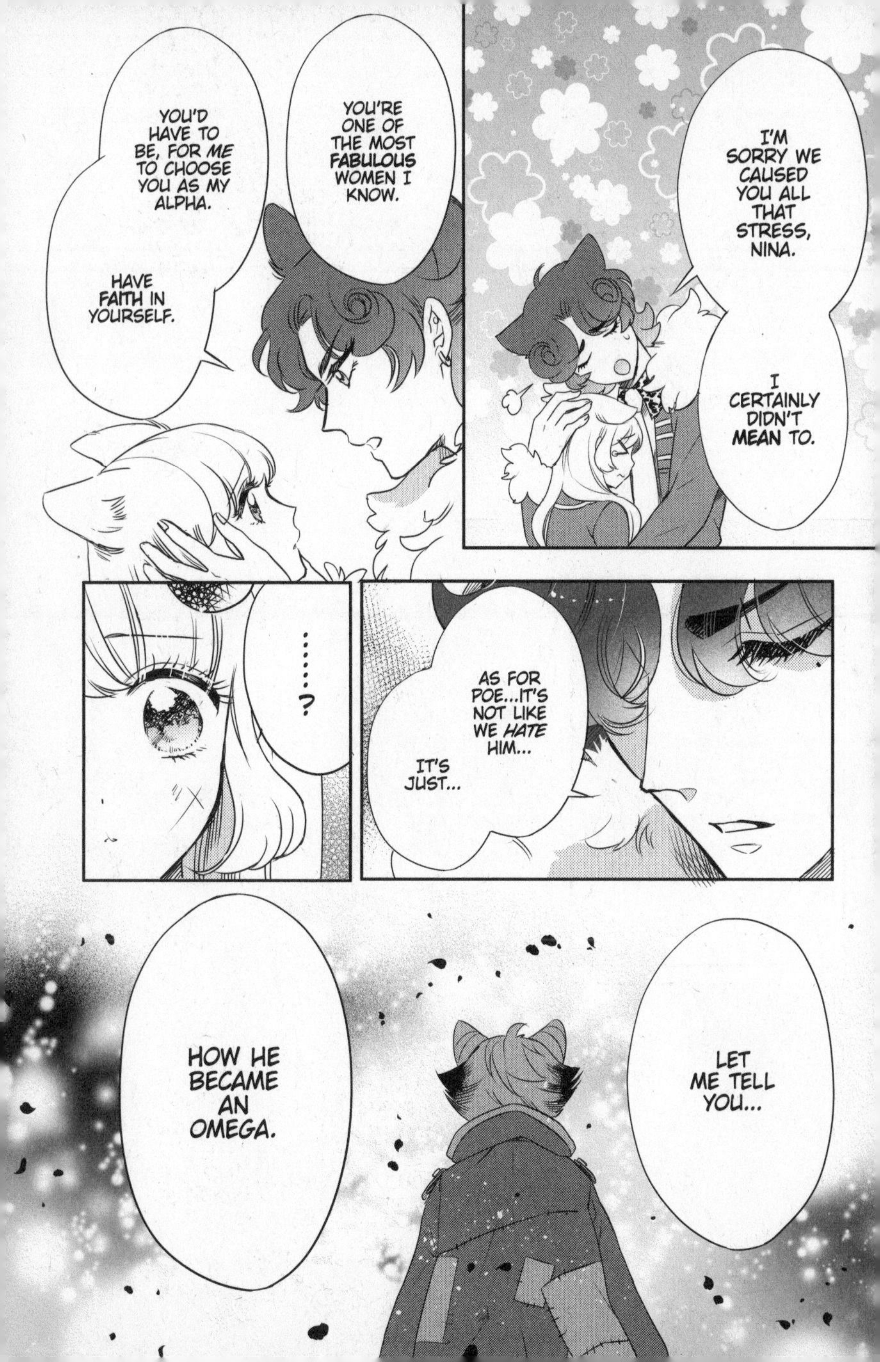
I'M SORRY WE CAUSED YOU ALL THAT STRESS, NINA.
I CERTAINLY DIDN'T MEAN TO.
YOU'RE ONE OF THE MOST FABULOUS WOMEN I KNOW.
YOU'D HAVE TO BE, FOR *ME* TO CHOOSE YOU AS MY ALPHA.
HAVE FAITH IN YOURSELF.
AS FOR POE...IT'S NOT LIKE WE *HATE* HIM...
IT'S JUST...
......?
LET ME TELL YOU...
HOW HE BECAME AN OMEGA.

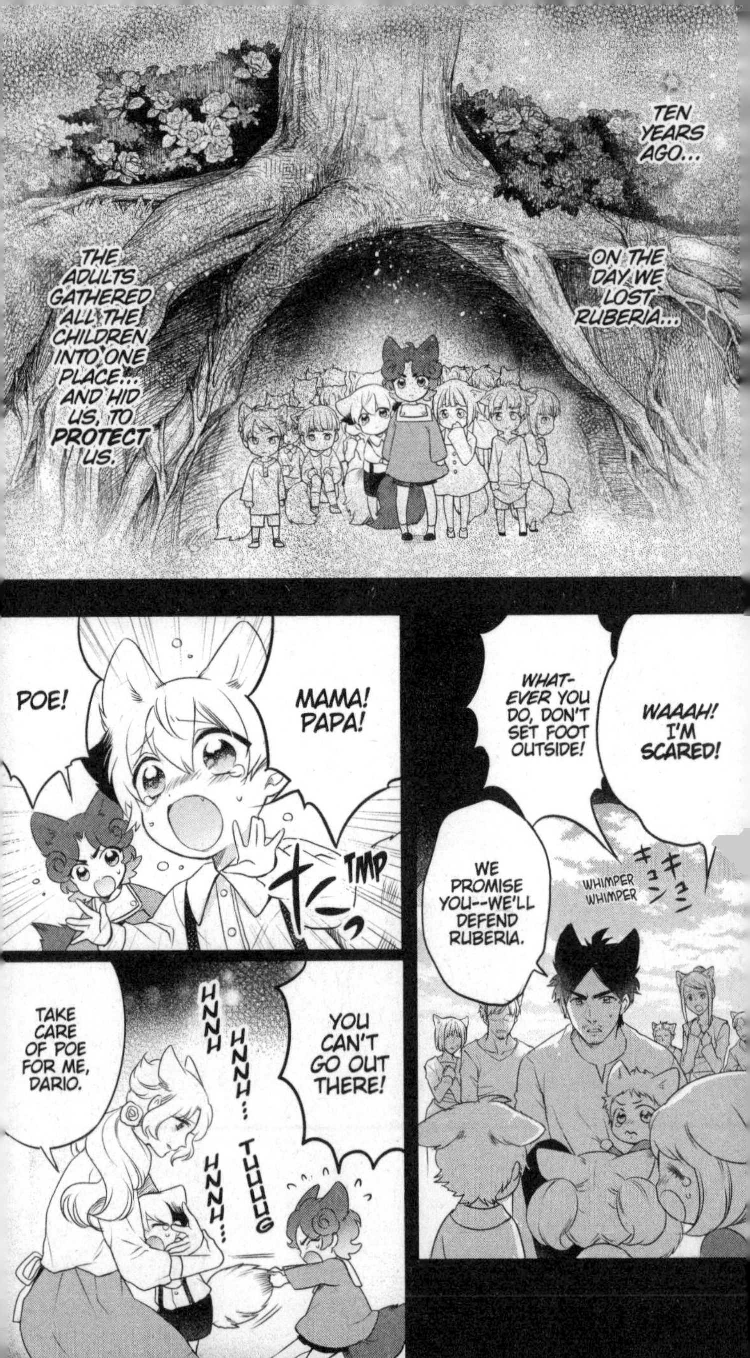
TEN YEARS AGO...
ON THE DAY WE LOST RUBERIA...
THE ADULTS GATHERED ALL THE CHILDREN INTO ONE PLACE... AND HID US, TO PROTECT US.
WAAAH! I'M SCARED!
WHAT-EVER YOU DO, DON'T SET FOOT OUTSIDE!
キュンキュン
WHIMPER WHIMPER
WE PROMISE YOU--WE'LL DEFEND RUBERIA.
MAMA! PAPA!
POE!
TMP
YOU CAN'T GO OUT THERE!
HNNH HNNH... HNNH...
TAKE CARE OF POE FOR ME, DARIO.
TUUUUG

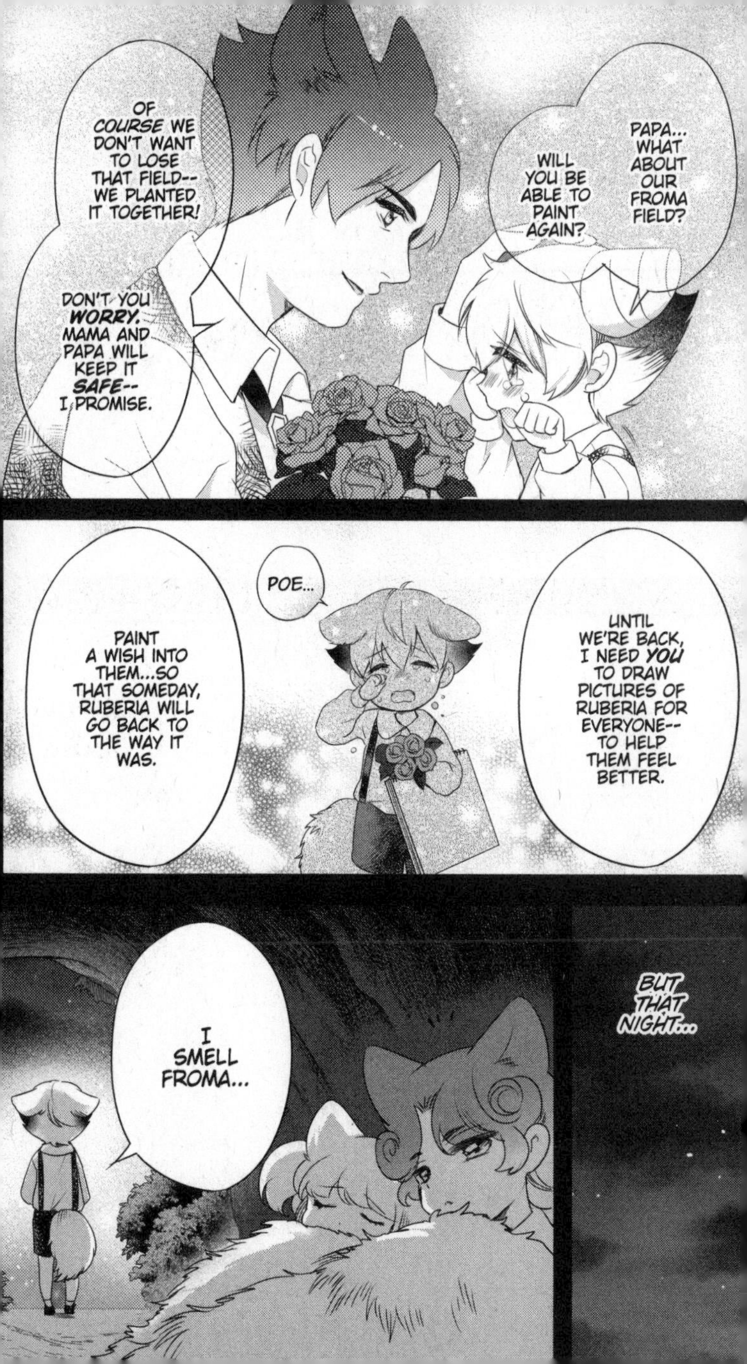
PAPA... WHAT ABOUT OUR FROMA FIELD?
WILL YOU BE ABLE TO PAINT AGAIN?
OF COURSE WE DON'T WANT TO LOSE THAT FIELD-- WE PLANTED IT TOGETHER!
DON'T YOU WORRY. MAMA AND PAPA WILL KEEP IT SAFE-- I PROMISE.
UNTIL WE'RE BACK, I NEED YOU TO DRAW PICTURES OF RUBERIA FOR EVERYONE-- TO HELP THEM FEEL BETTER.
POE...
PAINT A WISH INTO THEM...SO THAT SOMEDAY, RUBERIA WILL GO BACK TO THE WAY IT WAS.
BUT THAT NIGHT...
I SMELL FROMA...

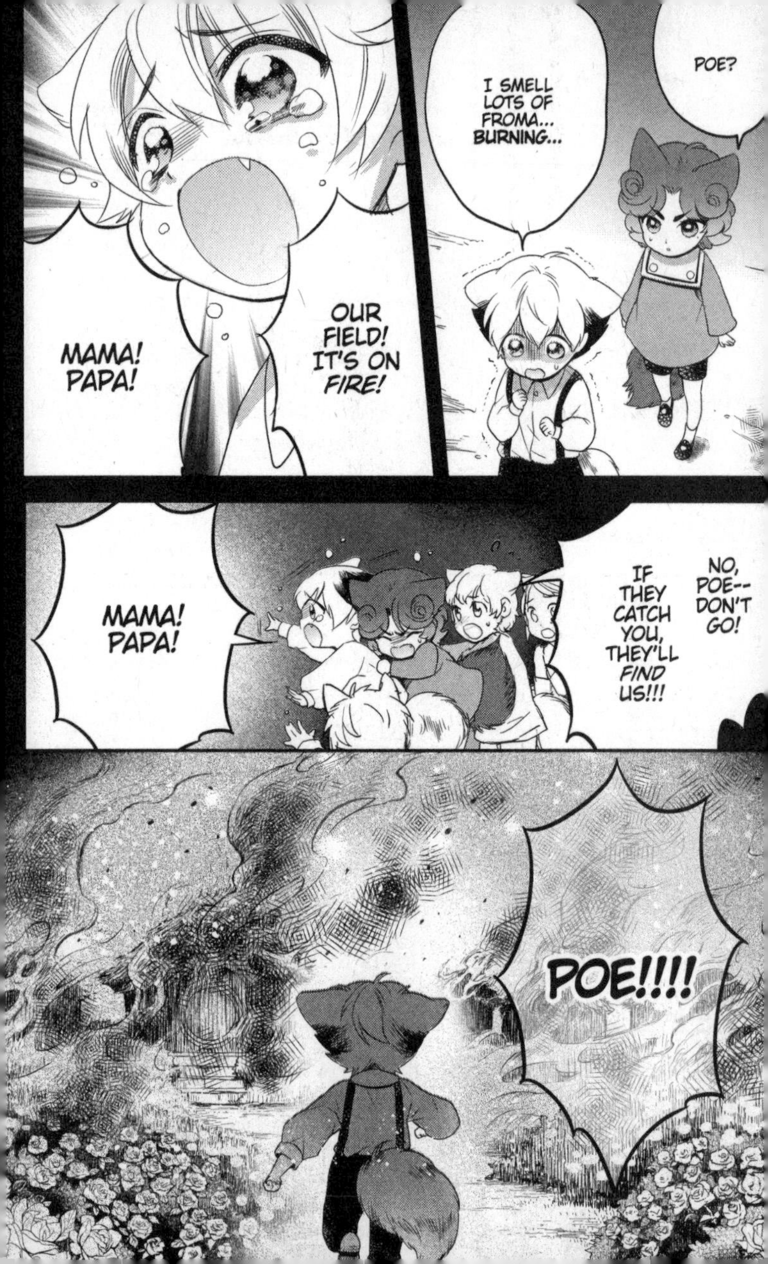
POE?
I SMELL LOTS OF FROMA... BURNING...
OUR FIELD! IT'S ON FIRE!
MAMA! PAPA!
NO, POE-- DON'T GO!
IF THEY CATCH YOU, THEY'LL FIND US!!!
MAMA! PAPA!
POE!!!!

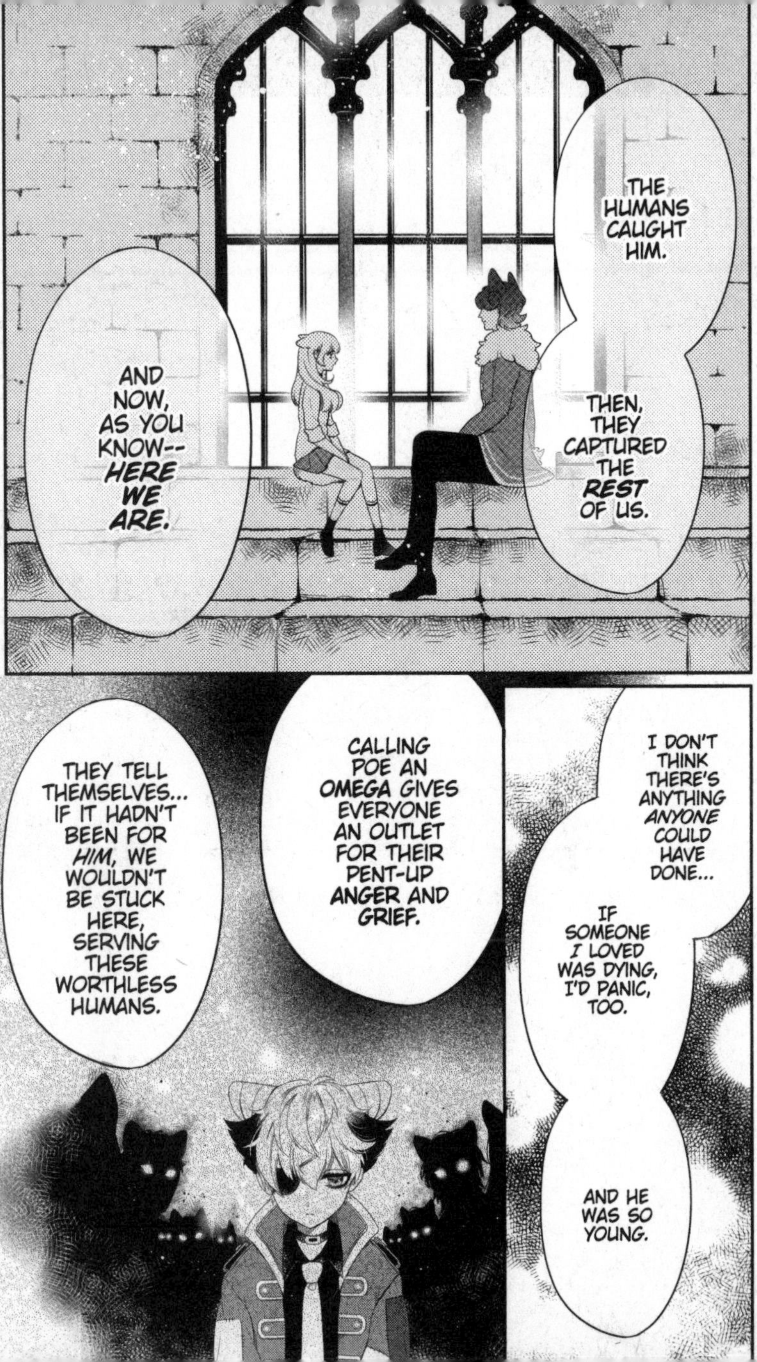
THE HUMANS CAUGHT HIM.
THEN, THEY CAPTURED THE REST OF US.
AND NOW, AS YOU KNOW-- HERE WE ARE.
I DON'T THINK THERE'S ANYTHING ANYONE COULD HAVE DONE...
IF SOMEONE I LOVED WAS DYING, I'D PANIC, TOO.
AND HE WAS SO YOUNG.
CALLING POE AN OMEGA GIVES EVERYONE AN OUTLET FOR THEIR PENT-UP ANGER AND GRIEF.
THEY TELL THEMSELVES... IF IT HADN'T BEEN FOR HIM, WE WOULDN'T BE STUCK HERE, SERVING THESE WORTHLESS HUMANS.

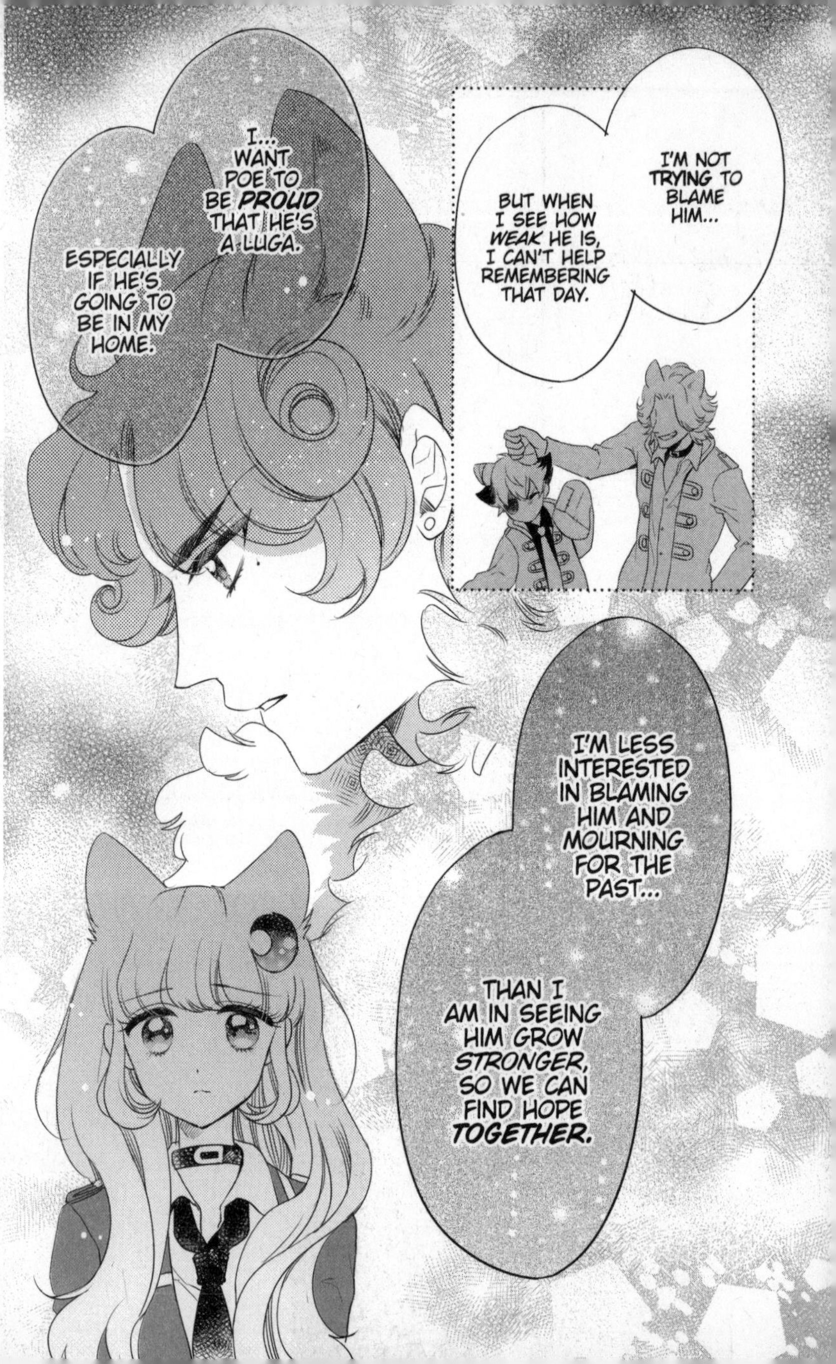
I'M NOT TRYING TO BLAME HIM...
BUT WHEN I SEE HOW WEAK HE IS, I CAN'T HELP REMEMBERING THAT DAY.
I... WANT POE TO BE PROUD THAT HE'S A LUGA.
ESPECIALLY IF HE'S GOING TO BE IN MY HOME.
I'M LESS INTERESTED IN BLAMING HIM AND MOURNING FOR THE PAST...
THAN I AM IN SEEING HIM GROW STRONGER, SO WE CAN FIND HOPE TOGETHER.

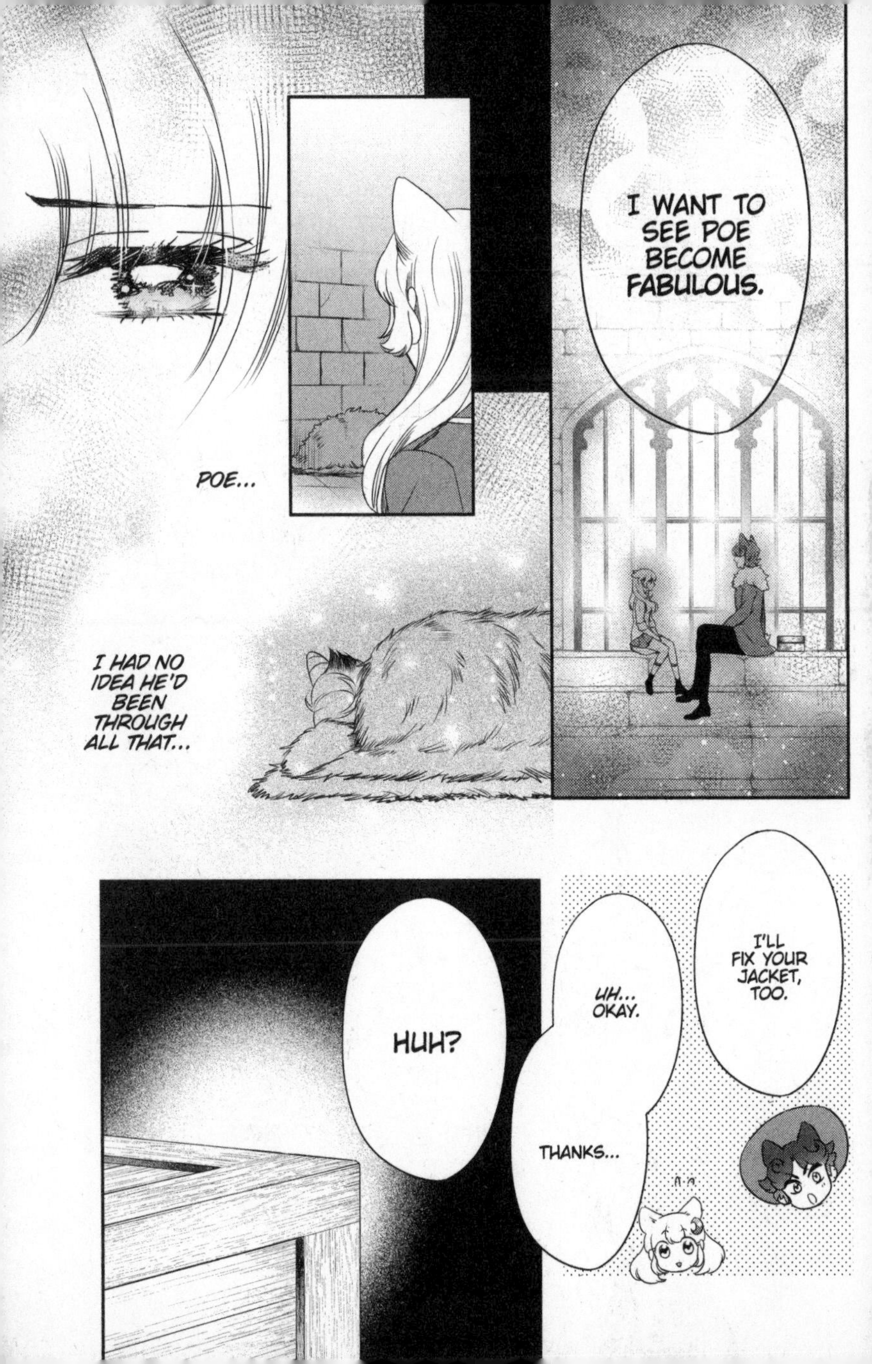
I WANT TO SEE POE BECOME FABULOUS.
POE...
I HAD NO IDEA HE'D BEEN THROUGH ALL THAT...
I'LL FIX YOUR JACKET, TOO.
UH... OKAY.
THANKS...
HUH?

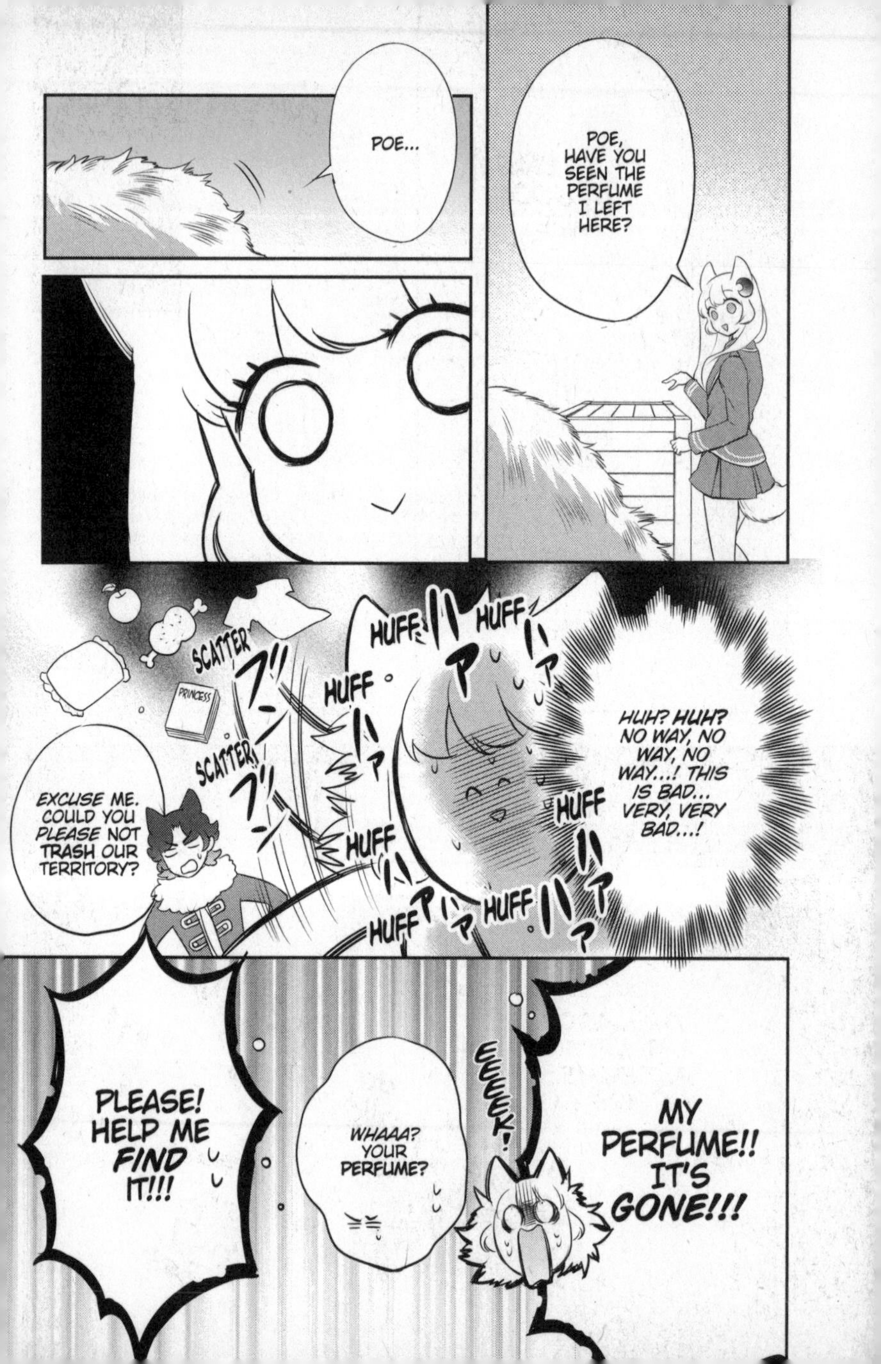
POE, HAVE YOU SEEN THE PERFUME I LEFT HERE?
POE...
HUH? HUH? NO WAY, NO WAY, NO WAY...! THIS IS BAD... VERY, VERY BAD...!
HUFF HUFF
HUFF
HUFF
HUFF
HUFF HUFF
SCATTER
SCATTER
PRINCESS
EXCUSE ME. COULD YOU PLEASE NOT TRASH OUR TERRITORY?
MY PERFUME!! IT'S GONE!!!
EEEEK!
WHAAA? YOUR PERFUME?
PLEASE! HELP ME FIND IT!!!

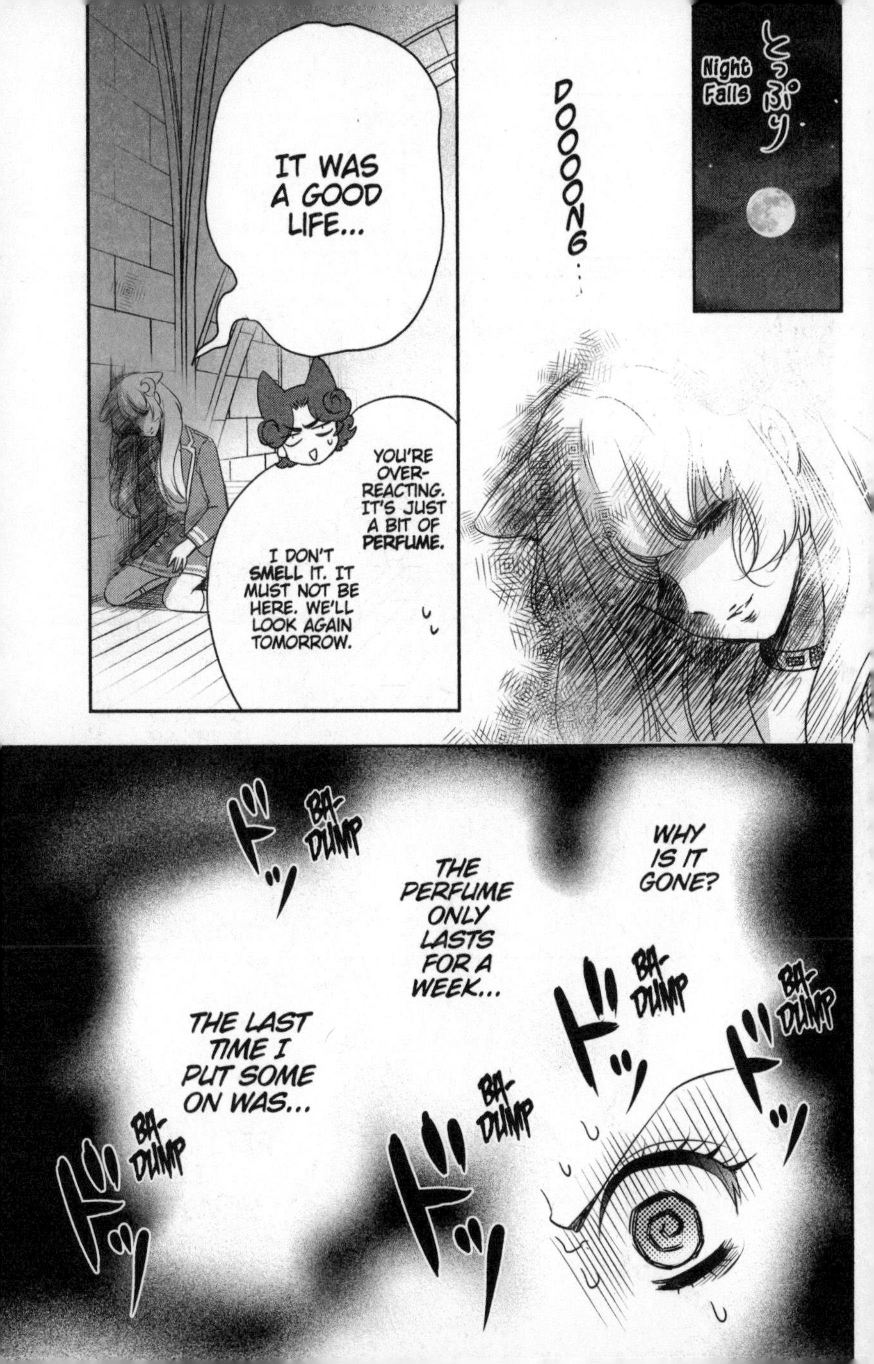
とっぷり
Night Falls
DOOOOONG...
IT WAS A GOOD LIFE...
YOU'RE OVER-REACTING. IT'S JUST A BIT OF PERFUME.
I DON'T SMELL IT. IT MUST NOT BE HERE. WE'LL LOOK AGAIN TOMORROW.
WHY IS IT GONE?
ドッ
BA-DUMP
ドッ
BA-DUMP
THE PERFUME ONLY LASTS FOR A WEEK...
ドッ
BA-DUMP
ドッ
BA-DUMP
THE LAST TIME I PUT SOME ON WAS...
ドッ
BA-DUMP

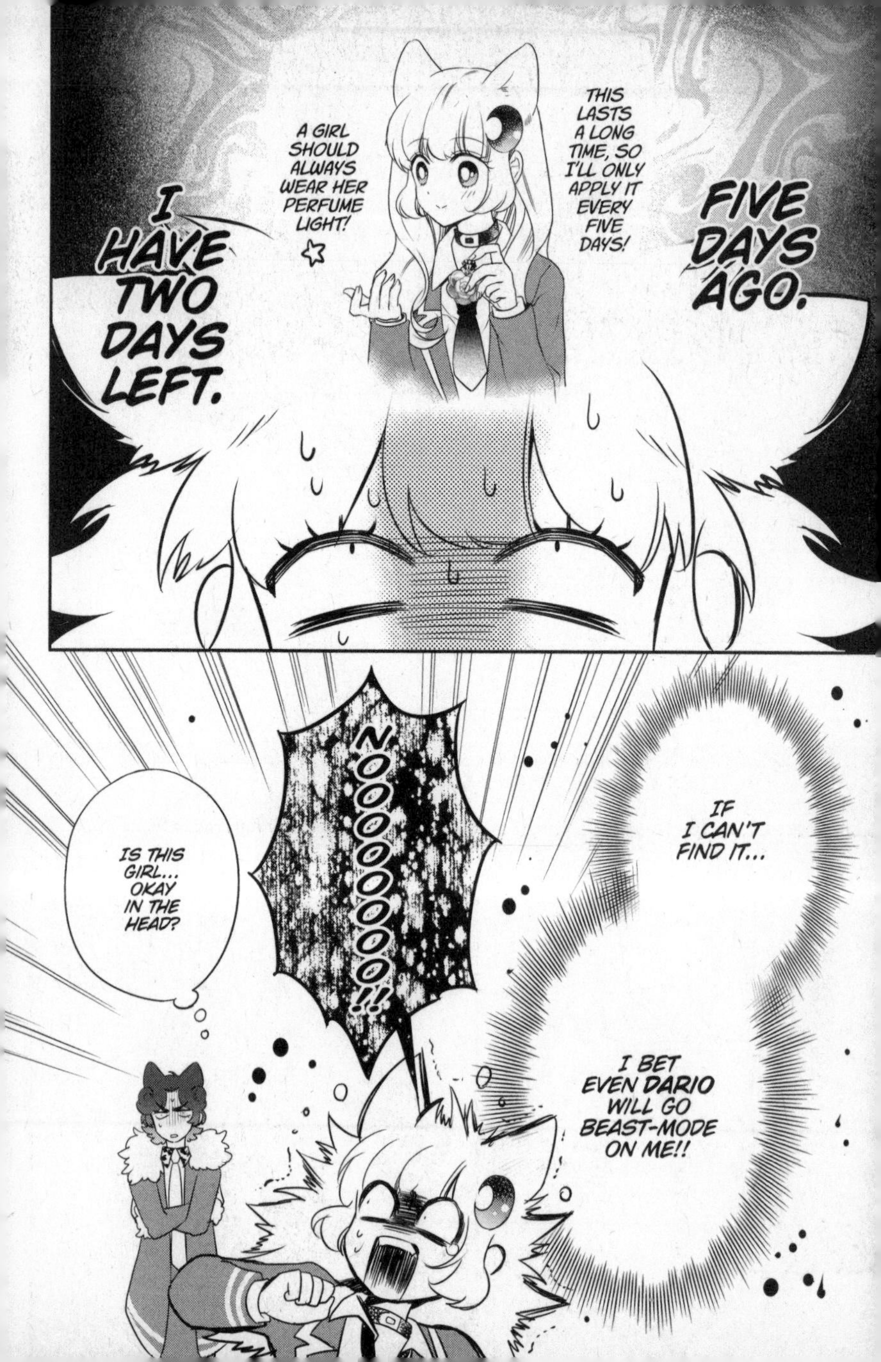
FIVE DAYS AGO.
THIS LASTS A LONG TIME, SO I'LL ONLY APPLY IT EVERY FIVE DAYS!
A GIRL SHOULD ALWAYS WEAR HER PERFUME LIGHT!
I HAVE TWO DAYS LEFT.
IF I CAN'T FIND IT...
I BET EVEN DARIO WILL GO BEAST-MODE ON ME!!
NOOOOOOOOOOOO!!
IS THIS GIRL... OKAY IN THE HEAD?

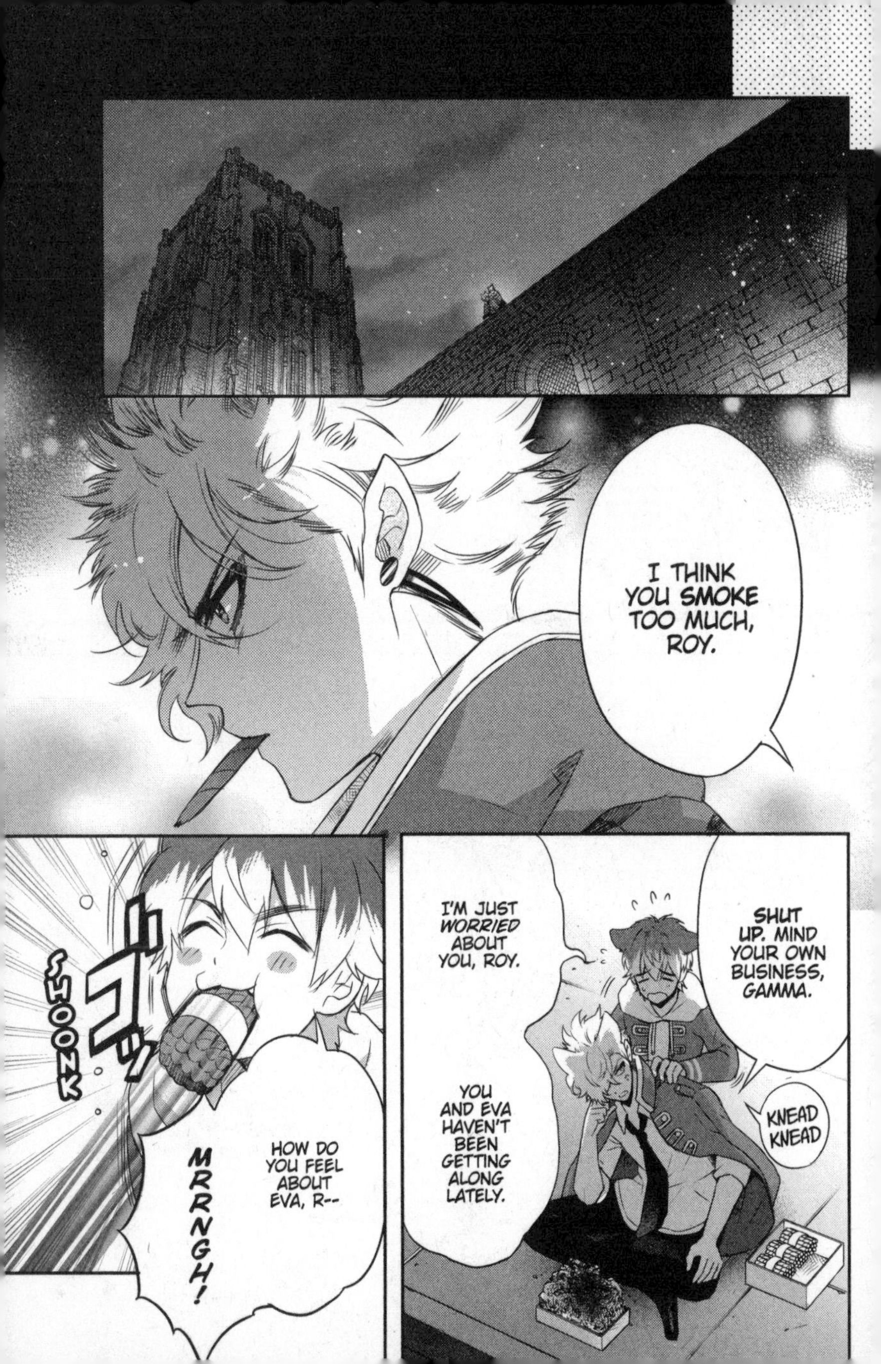
I THINK YOU SMOKE TOO MUCH, ROY.
SHUT UP. MIND YOUR OWN BUSINESS, GAMMA.
I'M JUST WORRIED ABOUT YOU, ROY.
KNEAD KNEAD
YOU AND EVA HAVEN'T BEEN GETTING ALONG LATELY.
HOW DO YOU FEEL ABOUT EVA, R--
SHOONK
MRRNGH!

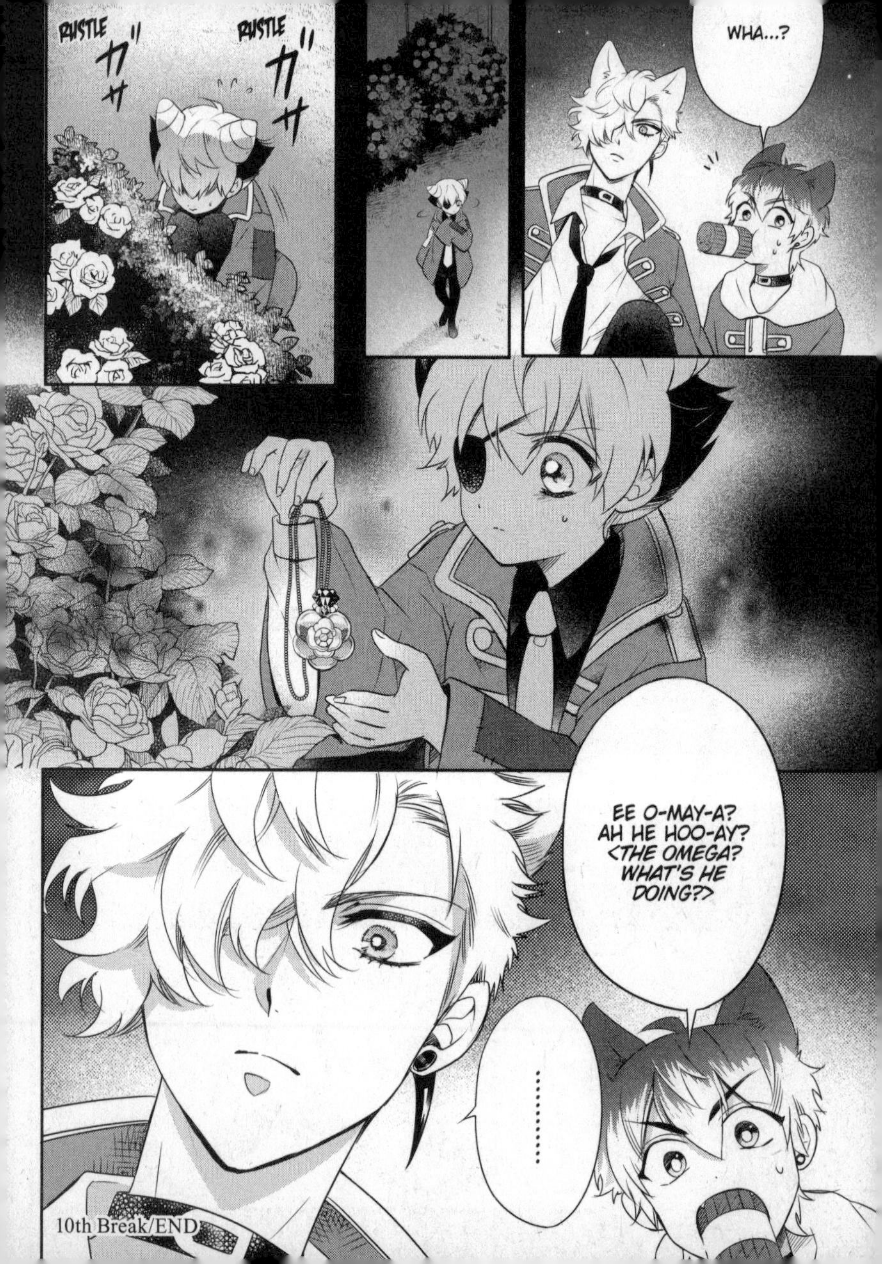
WHA...?
RUSTLE
ガサ
RUSTLE
ガサ
EE O-MAY-A? AH HE HOO-AY? <THE OMEGA? WHAT'S HE DOING?>
......

10th Break/END

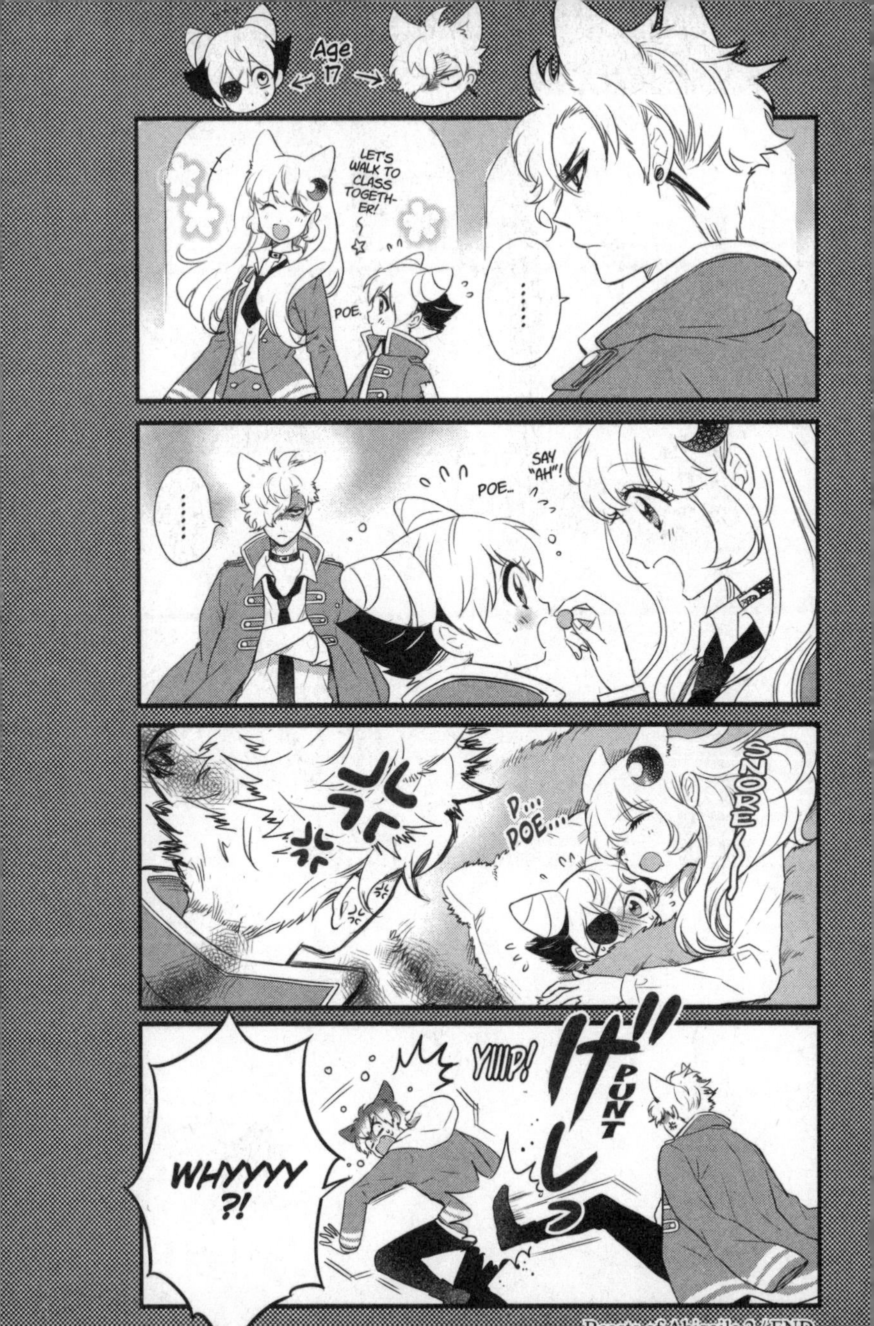
Age 17
LET'S WALK TO CLASS TOGETHER!
POE.
......
SAY "AH"!
POE..
......
SNORE
P... POE....
YIIIP!
げし
PUNT
WHYYYY?!

Beasts of Abigaile 2 / END

Beasts of
Abigaile

Hatsune Miku
Bad End Night
1
Miss Kobayashi's
Dragon Maid
3
STORY AND ART BY
coolkyousinnjya
Kase-san and
Bento
Hiromi
Kentaro Sato
2
Magical Girl Site
夢みる太陽
Dreamin' Sun
1
Ichigo Takano
#1 New York Times bestselling creator of orange
2
Captive Hearts of Oz
Bloom into You
story & art
Nakatani Nio
2
The Girl from the Other Side
2
1
The High School Life of a Fudanshi

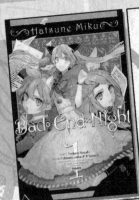

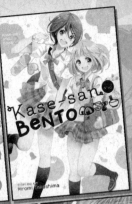

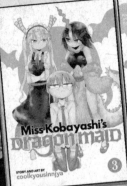

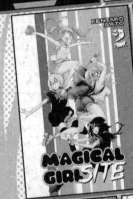

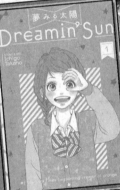

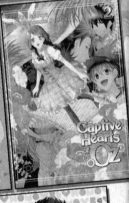

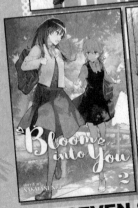

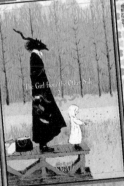

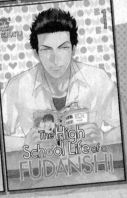

SEVEN SEAS ENTERTAINMENT PRESENTS

Beasts of Abigaile

story and art by SPICA AOKI

VOLUME 2

TRANSLATION
Alethea and Athena Nibley

ADAPTATION
Marykate Jasper

LETTERING AND RETOUCH
Rina Mapa

COVER DESIGN
Nicky Lim

PROOFREADER
Janet Houck

ASSISTANT EDITOR
Jenn Grunigen

PRODUCTION ASSISTANT
CK Russell

PRODUCTION MANAGER
Lissa Pattillo

EDITOR-IN-CHIEF
Adam Arnold

PUBLISHER
Jason DeAngelis

ABIGAIL NO KEMONO TACHI VOL. 2
© SPICA AOKI 2016
Originally published in Japan in 2016 by Akita Publishing Co., Ltd..
English translation rights arranged with Akita Publishing Co., Ltd. through
TOHAN CORPORATION, Tokyo.

Seven Seas books may be purchased in bulk for educational, business, or pro-
motional use. For information on bulk purchases, please contact Macmillan Cor-
porate & Premium Sales Department at 1-800-221-7945 (ext 5442)
or write specialmarkets@macmillan.com.

Seven Seas and the Seven Seas logo are trademarks of
Seven Seas Entertainment, LLC. All rights reserved.

ISBN: 978-1-626925-67-0

Printed in Canada

First Printing: October 2017

10 9 8 7 6 5 4 3 2 1

FOLLOW US ONLINE: *www.gomanga.com*

READING DIRECTIONS

This book reads from *right to left*, Japanese style.
If this is your first time reading manga, you start
reading from the top right panel on each page and
take it from there. If you get lost, just follow the
numbered diagram here. It may seem backwards at
first, but you'll get the hang of it! Have fun!!

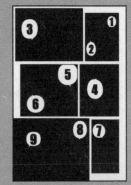